Boeing's Cold War Warrior

B-52
STRATOFORTRESS

D1610973

Boeing's Cold War Warrior

B-52
STRATOFORTRESS

ROBERT F DORR
&
LINDSAY PEACOCK

OSPREY
AVIATION

First published in Great Britain in 1995 by Osprey Publishing
Elms Court, Chapel Way, Botley, Oxford OX2 9LP
E-mail: info@ospreypublishing.com

This edition published 2000

ISBN 1 84176 097 8

00 01 02 03 04   10 9 8 7 6 5 4 3 2 1

Edited by Tony Holmes
Page design by TT Designs
© Line and cutaway drawings by Mike Badrocke
Printed through Bookbuilders, Hong Kong

CONTENTS

INTRODUCTION

I SAW MY FIRST EXAMPLE of Boeing's most enduring military creation way back in September 1960. It was at RAF Biggin Hill, of all places, when a solitary B-52G made an unexpected appearance in one of the 'Battle of Britain' flying displays that were staged annually at this famous wartime airfield to commemorate the epic exploits of the celebrated 'Few'. To be honest, the 'Buff' didn't leave much of an impression, but that's probably not too surprising since I was still fairly ignorant when it came to the subject of military aircraft, and I certainly didn't appreciate what I was seeing.

Within five years, however, I had realised my error. In the intervening half-decade I had become a hardened military enthusiast, and was much more familiar with the mighty 'Buff', for I was one of the 'faithful' that made regular visits to the clutch of SAC bases around Oxford and Newbury. Some of those visits provided opportunities to gawp at a machine that, even in repose, was always imposing. In the early 1960s, of course, the Stratofortress was undeniably at its most handsome, by virtue of featuring a basically natural metal finish that was adorned with SAC's star-spangled sash and a fascinating collection of command and unit insignia. It was the sight of those aircraft, and its much neglected predecessor, the B-47 Stratojet, that laid the foundations for my abiding interest in SAC and its history, and it is a matter of profound regret that this command, which was for many years both the 'shield' and the 'sword' of the USA, no longer survives.

Happily, that same state of affairs isn't true of the 'Buff' itself. Three decades on, it is still going strong, and it is astonishing to contemplate the fact that the B-52 is still with us and still very much a key element in the USAF inventory, for most of the other aircraft that were so commonplace then have long since faded from the scene. That it has proved so durable says much for the soundness of the original design, but that is just part of the saga, for it has also demonstrated remarkable adaptability, particularly with regard to weaponry – and, when all is said and done, any bomber is only ever intended to be a vehicle for the carriage and delivery of weapons.

Whether they be 'smart' or 'dumb' bombs, precision attack missiles or thermonuclear devices, they all seem to come alike to the B-52. It is to be hoped that this account of the history of Boeing's illustrious product does justice to those who were responsible for its creation in the first instance, as well as to the thousands of individuals who have flown, armed and serviced it in times of peace and war for more than 40 years.

Responsibility for any errors rests solely with the authors, but credit is due to those whose contributions have immeasurably improved the quality of the finished article. Space does not permit a comprehensive listing, but mention should be made of the assistance provided by Aerospace Publishing, Bob Archer, Joe Bruch, Jeremy Flack, Chris Pocock and Mark Pressland, and it would be gravely remiss to ignore the work of Graham Luxton and Dave Wilton in helping to ensure that the many appendices were as complete as humanly possible. Thanks guys!

Lindsay Peacock

EVOLUTION OF THE STRATOFORTRESS

GO TO ANY AIRPORT IN THE WORLD and ask any member of the travelling public to name an aircraft manufacturer and the chances are you'll get just one answer - Boeing. It's a famous name. It's a name that is inextricably linked with mass air transportation on a truly global scale. It's a name that has even achieved the rare distinction of lending itself to a successful stage show, an accolade no other aircraft manufacturer can claim. And yet, while Boeing's reputation and wealth is now firmly based on huge success in the commercial aircraft marketplace, readers might care to reflect upon the fact that it wasn't always thus.

Indeed, little more than three decades ago, the company was indisputably acknowledged first and foremost as a manufacturer of military hardware. In fact, it is fair to remark that the foundations of corporate wealth were laid through the construction of weapons of mass destruction, Boeing having earlier produced a string of bomber aircraft that were every bit as successful as the B.707, B.727, B.737, etc, etc, etc, even if they weren't anything like as well known. That process began in the mid-1930s with the Model 299, which evolved in response to a US Army Air Corps need for a multi-engined bomber.

As it transpired, the Model 299 was to provide Boeing with mixed fortunes and mixed emotions. In the first instance, the loss of the prototype just three months after its maiden flight brought the company to the brink of financial ruin, even though the cause of the accident was quickly identified as pilot error. Subsequently, the imperatives of war allowed the Model 299 to atone by providing the basis for the hugely successful B-17 series. Well over 12,000 examples of the Flying Fortress were eventually completed by Boeing and two of its competitors, specifically Lockheed and Douglas. That's an impressive production run by any standard, but the B-17 was far from being the most numerous US-built bomber.

That distinction was claimed by Consolidated (later part of the Convair group) which churned out over 18,000 B-24 Liberators, and it is worth noting that the respective fortunes of the builders of the B-17 and B-24 ebbed and flowed during the next decade, as first one and then the other secured major production contracts for even larger bomber aircraft. Ultimately, as will be seen, Boeing emerged pre-eminent, while Convair's star shone ever less brightly until it was swallowed up by the General Dynamics conglomerate.

Even though the B-17 was an outstanding product, it takes more than one success to build a dynasty and Boeing's talent as a designer and maker of bombers was still far from proven. With the B-29 Superfortress, however, the Seattle-based manufacturer took a gamble that paid off handsomely, utilising radical design and construction practices to produce a bomber that was far in advance of anything that had gone before. Development was by no means trouble-free, with the Wright R-3350 engine being a particular source of concern, but close to 4000 examples were built, with plans to complete another 5000 being cancelled in the immediate aftermath of the cessation of hostilities with Japan.

The war actually had little more than a year left to run when the first B-29 combat mission took place in early June 1944. Involving roughly 100 aircraft, the target was a railway centre at Bangkok, Thailand and the attack took place in daylight. It was, in fact, a fairly insignificant operation when compared with some of the later raids, although it is doubtful if any of those in the vicinity of the target saw it in quite the same way.

Two weeks later, on 15 June, the Japanese mainland was attacked for the first time, with a force of about 70 Superfortresses being despatched to the steel works at Yawata. By all accounts, those early missions were relatively ineffective, but it didn't take long to turn things around and within a year, almost all of

Japan's major centres of population and industry had been devastated by a mixture of bombs and incendiary devices. However, despite the fact that these raids took a fearsome toll of life, the Japanese stubbornly refused to surrender and the Allies became increasingly resigned to the unenviable prospect of having to mount an invasion in order to bring the Pacific war to a conclusion.

Two further attacks, undertaken in early August 1945, did away with that unwelcome possibility – and changed the face of warfare forever, for these were the atom bomb missions. In each case, a single weapon was dropped, with the 'Little Boy' device that was used against Hiroshima on 6 August killing more than 70,000 people and flattening almost five square miles of the city, while the 'Fat Man' weapon dropped on Nagasaki on 9 August achieved comparable degrees of death and destruction. Five days after Nagasaki was virtually razed to the ground, Japan agreed to surrender unconditionally, an action that brought the war to an end save for a few isolated pockets of resistance in the Pacific.

Eight months later, on 21 March 1946, an organisation known as Strategic Air Command (SAC) was established under the leadership of Gen George C Kenney. At this time, part of the mission specified for the new command by Gen Carl Spaatz, Commanding General of the Army Air Forces, was the provision of 'combat units capable of intense and sustained combat operations employing the latest and most advanced weapons'.

This clearly alluded to nuclear weaponry similar to that employed in the raids on Hiroshima and Nagasaki, but it was still a tall order. For starters, demobilisation was proceeding apace and this inevitably meant that the task of trying to create an

BELOW Boeing got into the bomber business early. The manufacturer's B-9 bomber of the 1930s was the biggest and fastest thing on wings. The B-17 Flying Fortress was designed and developed before the United States' entry into World War 2 and eventually flew some of the most dangerous missions of all time. 12,731 Flying Fortresses carried the fight to the Axis

ABOVE B-29 Superfortress (42-93844) in flight near Seattle before delivery to an operational squadron. This particular 'ship' was later flown in combat against Japanese targets by Capt George Wale. The B-29 was in many ways Boeing's masterpiece: the Superfortress firebombed Tokyo, razed Hiroshima and Nagasaki and carried the war across the 38th Parallel during the Korean conflict. In service long after the B-50, B-47 and B-52 were being developed, the 'Superfort' was clearly a symbol of its builder's unmatched experience at manufacturing heavy bombers *(USAF)*

efficient force was being accomplished against a background of rapidly diminishing resources in terms of personnel and equipment. In fact, at the time of its creation, SAC possessed just one unit that was considered capable of operating with nuclear weapons. This was the 509th Composite Group, which had been responsible for the attacks on Japan – and which was tasked with dropping a third weapon in the Operation *Crossroads* nuclear tests that took place at Bikini Atoll little more than three months after SAC came into being.

Of greater significance was the fact that the USA could hardly claim to be suffering an embarrassment of riches when it came to stocks of the new-fangled bombs. In 1946, for example, the stockpile consisted of nine devices – a year later, it had risen to just 13. Admittedly, that was 13 more than anybody else had, but it is clear that even such an elite unit as the 509th would have found it difficult to maintain 'intense and sustained combat operations' in the event of being called upon to deliver any or all of these weapons.

At around this time, it was also becoming evident

that the Soviet Union was bent on playing a leading role in world affairs. Although it was not yet in a position to resort to force of arms in challenging the USA for supremacy (the latter nation's possession of the 'bomb' saw to that), those in power and authority in the USA recognised that it would be wise to be prepared for trouble from the eastern bloc.

Advocates of air power, bolstered by the B-29's success in bringing the Pacific war to an abrupt end, argued that bomber aircraft possessing intercontinental range could have a part to play in countering the threat from the east – and that SAC was a logical organisation to operate any such aircraft. By a stroke of good fortune, such an aircraft already existed in the form of Convair's mighty B-36.

In reality, the USA could count itself lucky that this project was still up and running, for it had come close to cancellation on several occasions. The reasons for that were many and varied. There's no doubt that development problems figured among them, as did post-war cuts in defence spending and a belief that the B-36 would be inferior in several respects to Boeing's B-50. The latter type was itself far from a major advance, since it was fundamentally just an improved B-29. In addition, an inordinately long gestation period also conspired against the Convair heavyweight, which continued to rely on piston engines, whereas the rapid development of propulsion systems held out the prospect of acquiring much faster jet-powered bombers.

Two factors were instrumental in the survival of the B-36. The first had its origins in the 1941 requirement that it possess a combat radius of 4000 miles with a 10,000-lb bombload. That basically translated into the capability of flying from the eastern seaboard of the USA to bomb targets in Europe and returning to the original point of departure. At the time of its creation, SAC had no warplane with anything like that capability and no other immediate prospect of obtaining such capability. In simple terms, the B-36 was the 'only game in town', but even that was not enough to guarantee its survival.

The second vital factor was an accident of history and came about as a direct result of the Soviet decision to blockade Berlin in June 1948. In the weeks leading up to that event, the B-36 project had again been under fire and its future was far from assured, with those arguing for cancellation including SAC's commander-in-chief, Gen Kenney. On 25 June, just one week after the blockade began, all thoughts of cancellation were shelved, with Secretary of the Air Force (as the Army Air Corps had become in September 1947) W Stuart Symington and other key officials (including Kenney) unanimously choosing to press on with procurement of Convair's bomber.

On the very next day, the first five B-36As entered service with the 7th Bomb Group at Carswell AFB, Texas. This event did not, in fact, materially improve SAC's combat posture, for the five aircraft – and 17 more B-36As delivered in 1948-49 – were unarmed and were mostly employed on training tasks until early 1950 when they were adapted for reconnaissance as RB-36Es.

Despite further debate and a re-emergence of the spectre of cancellation in 1949, the B-36 survived. Indeed, it would be fair to say that it prospered in the early part of Gen Curtis E LeMay's period of tenure as CinC SAC (October 1948-June 1957), for he wasted no time in throwing his not inconsiderable weight behind the B-36. Eventually, SAC accepted delivery of well over 300 aircraft between 1948 and 1954 and did not withdraw its final examples of the 'Aluminium Overcast' until shortly before the end of the 1950s.

In contemplating bomber resources, the B-36 was the only type to offer any real challenge to Boeing's domination of SAC's line-up between 1946 and 1960. During this period, the command made the transition from being an all-propeller force to an all jet one, an objective it finally achieved when the last B-36 droned its way into retirement in February 1959. As it transpired, that event was overshadowed by deployment of the first Convair Atlas Intercontinental Ballistic Missiles (ICBMs) and their assumption of limited alert status in October of that year, an occurrence that signalled the beginning of the end of the manned bomber's primacy as a nuclear weapon delivery system.

Some 13 years earlier, no such alternative existed and the nuclear-armed bomber was the supreme weapon. On its formation, SAC was wholly dependent upon the B-29 and this veteran of combat in World War 2 constituted the backbone of the command until the dawn of the 1950s. At peak strength, attained in 1948, the number of pure bomber B-29s in the SAC inventory numbered almost 500, while other specialised versions were utilised for reconnaissance and in-flight refuelling tasks.

As already mentioned, 1948 was noteworthy in witnessing the arrival of the first B-36s. However, that was by no means the only new bomber to make its debut

RIGHT Together with the unbuilt XB-54, the B-50 Superfortress was in most respects an improved B-29 rather than a new bomber. Ironically, more capable B-50s were serving with stateside SAC units while older B-29s were fighting in Korea: throughout the Korean conflict, the Cold War enjoyed priority *(USAF)*

in that year, for the delivery of the first 'Peacemaker' was predated in February by acceptance of the initial B-50 at Davis-Monthan AFB, Arizona. This aircraft was immediately assigned to the 43rd Bomb Wing.

The B-50 was the first SAC bomber to be specifically earmarked for the nuclear mission and routine training would undoubtedly have reflected that tasking, even though the number of weapons available at the start of 1948 could almost have been counted on the fingers of both hands. Despite being intended to carry and deliver the most powerful weapon yet conceived, the B-50 was still a throwback to an earlier generation. It had begun life as the B-29D, with the redesignation exercise being intended mainly to forestall the possibility of cancellation. In that, it was successful, but the improved Superfortress was only ever perceived as a stop-gap system and was effectively obsolete in 1951, when some examples were little more than a few months old.

Unfortunately for SAC, classification of the B-50 as obsolete didn't automatically permit it to be immediately retired from service. That event was dependent upon delivery of a more modern replacement and for various reasons this just wasn't available in the quantities required in the period in question. As a result, the piston-powered B-50 did not start leaving the inventory until 1953 and it was destined to remain in frontline use in ever-decreasing quantities until as late as 1955, when the replacement was well established in service.

That replacement was yet another Boeing product and one which merits recognition as being the third great bomber aircraft to originate from the Seattle-based manufacturer. Somewhat confusingly, in view of the fact that it did not enter service until long after the B-50, it was given the designation B-47 and the name Stratojet. Flying for the first time in December 1947, production of the six-engined Stratojet eventually came to an end almost exactly a decade later, after more than 2000 examples had been completed at three manufacturing centres.

Despite that – and despite being SAC's first truly effective jet bomber – the Stratojet failed to win anything like the recognition it deserved and is now largely forgotten. Even though it has been ill-served by those who document aviation history, it would not be an exaggeration to claim that the first XB-47 ranks up there alongside the Wright Flyer, for it was a hugely significant aircraft as well as a quite revolutionary one.

While the 707 and the 747 and the B-52 may have claimed all the kudos that were going, they, like other Boeing products, betray clear evidence of having their roots in the design philosophy that found its first expression in the XB-47. In view of that, more than any other post-war aircraft, the first Stratojet can fairly be said to have set Boeing on the path to pre-eminence while at the same time influencing the design teams of a host of other manufacturers in the USA and around the world.

Development of the B-47 turned out to be a fairly protracted process and production-configured examples did not begin reaching SAC until October 1951, when the 306th Bomb Wing at MacDill AFB, Florida accepted the first of its eventual complement of 45 aircraft. Even then, it was to take quite some time before this unit attained operational capability and was considered ready to deploy overseas. That milestone was actually passed during early June 1953, when the three bomber squadrons of the 306th BW were ferried on successive days to RAF Fairford, England for a 90-day rotational training mission.

At the end of that tour of duty, MacDill's second B-47 outfit (the 305th BW) was ready to go overseas and several more units were well advanced with the business of transitioning from pistons to jets. After that, progress surged ahead at a remarkable pace to the extent that within less than four years, SAC's re-equipment programme was completed and the command had attained its planned Stratojet force of 28 operational Bomb Wings and five Strategic Reconnaissance Wings.

By then, Boeing had further consolidated its position as the premier supplier of equipment to SAC and was busy churning out production-configured examples of an even more impressive bomber in the guise of the B-52 Stratofortress, the evolution of which had begun some months before SAC itself came into being. Many would also say that this was Boeing's greatest bomber and there is plenty of evidence to support such claims on its behalf.

Considering just one of those aspects, with regard to the matter of longevity, there's certainly no other US bomber that even comes close to emulating the B-52. Had the Cold War not ended when it did, there is every reason to believe that the Stratofortress would have still been around in respectable numbers when the time came to celebrate the 50th anniversary of its introduction to service. Even though there now appears little likelihood that it will surpass the half-century, the B-52 does seem certain to complete 40 years of front-line duty. That is, without doubt, a truly remarkable achievement and is put in better perspective by observing that had the B-17 enjoyed a career of similar duration, the last Flying Fortresses would not have left the Air Force inventory until as recently as 1977.

On 29 June 1955, of course, those who gathered at Castle AFB in California to witness the delivery of the first Stratofortress would have been far more concerned with operational matters, for the latest acquisition posed formidable problems. A training syllabus had to be drawn up, so as to ensure a steady flow of qualified personnel to fly and maintain the new machine; existing bases had to be virtually rebuilt, as well as new ones created; weapons had to be obtained; and operating methods had to be radically modified, since the advent of the B-52 more or less coincided with the implementation of new concepts designed to give SAC a force that was both survivable and capable.

Any one of those problems would in isolation have been daunting. In concert, however, they would take time to resolve and would tax SAC's planning staff to

BELOW The first true heavyweight bomber to enter service with elements of Strategic Air Command was the Convair B-36 'Peacemaker'. Heavily armed, the stately passage of the 'Aluminium Overcast' was always audible, by virtue of a propulsion system that consisted of no less than six pusher piston engines and four pod-mounted auxiliary turbojets (*via USAF*)

the limit, since nobody had yet determined the exact scale of the Stratofortress production programme. In essence, then, the delivery of the first of the eight-engined monsters to Castle merely marked the end of the beginning . . .

BOEING'S NEW BOMBER

Few military aircraft that emerged in the immediate post-World War 2 era endured such a protracted or convoluted gestation as the B-52, for an interlude of almost seven years elapsed between circulation of the initial US Army Air Force document stipulating the military characteristics sought in a new bomber and the maiden flight of the aircraft that ultimately resulted. A number of factors were responsible for the long interval, not least of which was that the USAAF (and the US Air Force which succeeded it in September 1947) seemed quite unable to make up its collective mind on the nature of just what it wanted.

As a direct consequence of this vacillation, the focus and thrust of the project changed frequently in the early years – and the job of recounting that focus is made all the more difficult by the fact that changes on one side of the fence were not always matched by changes on the other. Indeed, at times, it appears that those who should have been working in harness were actually ploughing their own independent furrows.

Evidence of that is provided by the fact that the original military characteristics of November 1945 were subjected to a far-reaching reappraisal in 1946; were superseded in June 1947; again in December 1947 and at least twice during the course of 1948. The

upshot of all this was that by December 1948 the military characteristics specified an aircraft weighing somewhere in the region of 280,000 lbs and with the ability to carry a 10,000 lb bomb load some 6909 miles at a maximum speed of 513 mph at 35,000 ft. That clearly sounds quite imposing, but actually bears little relationship to the finished article, for other events were beginning to generate their own impetus and these would have far-reaching consequences for the Stratofortress saga.

In attempting to trace the development path that ultimately culminated in the B-52, it will probably be easiest to consider the various Boeing projects that evolved as the company sought to stay abreast of changing military requirements, demands and stipulations. This process was actually launched on 13 February 1946 when the US aviation industry was invited to respond to a formal request for proposals based on the military characteristics laid down in November 1945. In their original form, the key criteria anticipated an aircraft with a combat radius of 5000 miles, a top speed of 450mph; an average speed of 300 mph at 34,000 ft and the ability to deliver a 10,000 lb bomb load. What was being sought was fundamentally a second-generation intercontinental bomber to replace the mighty Consolidated-Vultee B-36 which itself had still to make its maiden flight.

It was a tall order, but Boeing was not alone in refusing to view it as an insurmountable one, for the Glenn L Martin Company and the Consolidated-Vultee Aircraft Corporation also responded with cost estimates and preliminary design submissions. Boeing's contender was the Model 462, which was selected as the victorious entry on 5 June 1946 and assigned the service designation XB-52 just a couple of weeks later, as a prelude to being awarded an initial contract on 28 June. As far as fiscal aspects were concerned, this contract (W-33-03A-ac-15065) was actually very restricted, with Boeing not allowed to exceed expenditure of $1.7 million on work that included the construction of a full-scale mock-up and engineering development in key areas such as powerplant, defensive weapons and structural testing.

Perhaps surprisingly, the USAAF chose to overlook a serious deficiency in as much as the Model 462's estimated combat radius of 3110 miles fell a long way short of that specified. In physical appearance, the Boeing submission bore a strong family resemblance to the B-50, albeit on a much larger scale. It was of conventional straight-winged design, with an estimated span of 221 ft, a length of just over 161 ft and a gross weight of around 360,000 lbs. Perhaps the most distinctive feature was the powerplant arrangement, for the Model 462 featured no fewer than half-a-dozen Wright XT35 Typhoon turboprop engines. Each was rated at 5500 shp and the fairings of the four inboard units also doubled as housings for the main undercarriage units, bestowing a distinctly odd appearance when viewed from dead ahead.

All in all, it was a pretty impressive piece of hardware and one that in most respects did satisfy the requirement. As far as the range deficiency was concerned, development might well have led to a marked improvment but in-flight refuelling also seemed to offer a way out of this dilemma. However, the USAAF very quickly began to back away from this proposal, expressing grave disquiet over the sheer size of the aircraft. Within a very short time, that disquiet led to the Model 462's demise, for it was effectively killed off in October when the Assistant Chief of Air Staff for Operations, Maj Gen Earle E Partridge, observed bluntly that it just didn't meet the requirement.

Undaunted, Boeing went back to the drawing board and came up with the Model 464, thereafter running through a succession of sub-models as the design slowly evolved into a form essentially recognisable as the B-52 we know today. This, however, didn't happen overnight and the first Model 464 proposals continued to rely on turboprop engines as a means of propulsion, although the number fell from six to four. Wright's T35 was still the preferred engine and at 230,000 lbs, there's no doubt that the first submission was certainly much lighter than the Model 462.

As it turned out, an individual who was to play a crucial role in the development of SAC now also exerted influence on development of the B-52. This was Gen Curtis E LeMay, then Deputy Chief of Air Staff for Research and Development. In November 1946, he argued that the future B-52 must possess a faster cruise speed and extra range and in the following month the USAAF requested studies for a four-engined, general purpose bomber with a range of 12,000 miles, a tactical speed of 400 mph and the ability to carry and drop the atomic bomb.

Possibly feeling that it was experiencing the aeronautical design equivalent of being trapped between the proverbial 'rock and a hard place', Boeing responded with a 'belt and braces' approach and came

back with two proposals, specifically the Model 464-16 and the Model 464-17. The former was optimised for so called 'special missions' (i.e. as a delivery system for nuclear weapons) and could carry only a 10,000-lb bomb load, but over great range. The latter was optimised for conventional bombing tasks and could take up to a 90,000-lb bomb load, but was range restricted. Apart from that and the fact that they only had four engines instead of six, they were similar to the Model 462.

Neither option was really satisfactory and there was certainly no way that the USAAF could afford to fund both, so the Model 464-17 emerged as the favoured candidate, even though its range was inadequate. As it turned out, the military characteristics that had been prepared in November 1945 were revised in June 1947 to take account of desired performance improvements. At this time, assuming that improvements promised for the Wright T35 were delivered, the 464-17 seemed to fit the bill apart from in respect of range. But, with in-flight refuelling on the brink of becoming an operational reality, that would be less critical.

A few weeks later, the 464-17 had manifestly passed its 'sell-by date', a victim of criticisms levelled by LeMay himself. In this case, the main objection was again related to size, with a secondary concern that excessive cost might well reduce the number of bombers that could be afforded to barely 100. Another authoritative 'anti' was Maj Gen Laurence C Craigie of the USAAF's Engineering Division who felt that in the form envisaged, the XB-52 was scarcely an improvement over the B-36 and that it might well be obsolescent before it could enter service.

At this stage, consideration was even given to abandoning the project entirely and it was now that LeMay came to the rescue by recommending a cautious approach. As was so often the case, LeMay got his way – and secured a six-month stay of execution for the

ABOVE SAC B-47E Stratojet (51-7025) with its underside painted high-gloss white to reflect the heat of an atomic blast. The B-47 equipped the mightiest armada the world has ever seen – nearly 2000 operational bombers – all capable of hauling atomic bombs (the term nuclear weapons came into use later) at the height of the Cold War. Though it resembles a mini-B-52, the Stratojet flew more like a fighter, lighter on the touch, more responsive, less stable and far more difficult to operate in the airfield pattern. Experience with the B-47 was invaluable in helping shape the B-52 programme (USAF)

XB-52 project while those involved examined and explored other options. For Boeing, this effectively meant the end of the Model 464-17 but the company continued to investigate ways and means whereby it might improve the product and come up with a bomber that was better suited for service with SAC.

It duly ran through a succession of design configurations including the Models 464-23, 464-25 and 464-27 during the first few months of 1947, before settling on the 464-29 which for a time was the definitive XB-52. A number of noteworthy new features were introduced during this phase, including the incorporation of some 20 degrees of sweep-back to the wing; addition of an extended dorsal fin and adoption of a drastically revamped landing gear which henceforth consisted of four twin wheel units that retracted into fuselage cut-outs plus smaller outriggers which were suspended from and retracted into the outer engine fairings.

Dimensionally, the 464-29 spanned some 205 ft and was expected to tip the scales at about 400,000 lbs, with a maximum speed of approximately 455 mph and an operating radius of 5000 miles. It was better - but it still wasn't right, especially in view of developments that occurred in the latter half of 1947.

Throughout that interval, the Air Materiel Command had been directed to examine other ways and

ABOVE RB-52B (52-8711) low over the runway at about the time this model was delivered to the 93rd Bomb Wing at Castle AFB, California. The 27 RB-52Bs were capable of carrying a two-man pressurised capsule in the bomb bay, and were able to carry cameras for photographic reconnaissance or electronic gear for detection and countermeasures. The Stratofortress handled well in the airfield pattern and was relatively easy to land and take-off *(USAF)*

means of ensuring that nuclear weapons would reach their targets. Some of the ideas that were eventually considered had potential but some were just plain daft, and few ever progressed far beyond the concept stage. Nevertheless, they all competed for money at a time when the purse strings were being drawn ever more tightly, as least as far as spending on defence was concerned.

At the same time, the newly constituted United States Air Force (USAF) was also eager to assert its standing as an independent organisation and had therefore convened the Heavy Bombardment Committee (HBC). As its main brief, the HBC was tasked with conducting 'a fresh evaluation of the long-range bomber program', particularly with regard to the development of systems able to fly from bases within the contiguous USA. It didn't need too strenuous an effort of thought to recognise that speed and altitude were key qualities in the survival of the manned bomber at a time when the primary means of defence against air attack was the anti-aircraft gun. The Committee concluded by appending a set of preliminary military characteristics which anticipated a requirement for a special-purpose (ie, nuclear) bomber capable of delivering an atomic device across a range of 8,000 miles at a minimum cruising speed of 550mph.

In the face of that conclusion, Boeing's Model 464-29 was pretty well dead in the water and the entire XB-52 project came within a whisker of being cancelled in the winter of 1947-48, when the USAF gave serious thought to the idea of starting again from scratch with a new competition. In the end, it seemed as if that would indeed happen, for on 11 December 1947 the Air Materiel Command was actually directed to terminate the Boeing contract. Not surprisingly, Boeing's chairman William M Allen protested vociferously to Stuart Symington (the Secretary of the Air Force) on learning the news and his eleventh-hour intervention brought a stay of execution.

In fact, it wasn't much of a reprieve, for Symington's January 1948 response to Boeing basically informed the company that its existing proposal was not suitable but that no final decision would be taken until such time as other possibilities (including the Northrop B-49 'Flying Wing') had been examined in detail. That examination doesn't seem to have taken too long to complete, for in March 1948 Symington told Boeing that the contract would be modified in order to allow development of a bomber that satisfied the revamped military characteristics of December 1947.

Against this uncertain background, Boeing had continued to refine its design and next came up with the Model 464-35. This version was evidently first drawn to the attention of the USAF in January 1948 and was then submitted in April as the core of a bid for Phase II design, development, manufacture and flight testing of two XB-52 aircraft. The design now featured a more sharply swept wing but still relied on the use of four Wright turboprop engines, although these now drove contra-rotating propellers. Dimensions were down on previous proposals, with the newest offering being some 131 ft 4 ins long and having a span of 185 ft. Considerable attention had also been devoted to weight reduction throughout the airframe, and it now had a gross weight of 280,000 lbs. As far as performance was concerned, maximum speed was anticipated to be around the 500-mph mark at an altitude of 41,000 ft.

This was certainly closer to the 550 mph figure which had been mooted in late 1947, but which now appeared to have been forgotten in view of Boeing's July 1948 success in securing authority from the USAF to proceed with Phase II objectives. Just how much of that success stemmed from Boeing having the right product is questionable, for it should not be forgotten that the Cold War confrontation between east and west flared up in late June when Russian forces began the blockade of Berlin.

SAC was at the forefront of the US response to this action and there is little doubt that the crisis in Germany also focussed the minds of those responsible for overseeing procurement policy on behalf of the US armed forces. So, while the XB-52 may not have been the perfect answer, as far as upcoming bombers were concerned, it was pretty much the only game in town – and in view of that, it's hardly surprising that the money was found to press on with the next stage of the development process.

It was at this time that the Boeing project began to absorb serious amounts of money, for this stage of development was expected to cost somewhere in the region of $30 million. Previous expenditure totalled barely a third of that but the sums of money that were to be swallowed up by the B-52 in later years make the Phase II investment seem like pretty small beer – as an inkling of just how much the cost was to the American taxpayer, it is worth noting that procurement of the 744 aircraft set the country back to the tune of $4500 million. And that doesn't take into account operating costs, post-production modification costs or even the cost of manufacturing the stockpiles of conventional and nuclear weapons built for carriage by the B-52 in its 40 years of service.

If you could determine accurately what those figures were and then added them on to the original price tag, there's no doubt that the USA has spent a vast amount of money on the Boeing bomber over the years. As to whether or not that money has been well-spent, that's a matter for debate and personal opinion, but it seems likely that most of those who support the

military would agree that it was – and that SAC and its successor, Air Combat Command, have had a more than fair return on investment.

In 1948, of course, nobody could have anticipated that and the main item on the agenda would have been the urgent need to get things moving with the turboprop-powered Model 464-35. Work on a full-scale mock-up forged ahead, but this was destined to be curtailed in the autumn of that year, following the latest twist in an already complex saga. It was this development that culminated in the XB-52 taking on a more familiar form and it arose over the course of a quite hectic weekend at the Van Cleve Hotel in Dayton, Ohio, during October 1948. At the end of that weekend, the Boeing contender had undergone a remarkable transformation as well as one that assured its eventual success, acquiring jet in place of turboprop propulsion.

In fact, some consideration had already been given to the idea of using turbojet power during the previous few years, only to be discarded on the grounds of high specific fuel consumption. By the early part of 1948, however, technological progress meant that later developments in the field of turbojet engines offered the promise of sufficient thrust with satisfactory economy. It was that promise which prompted the USAF to enquire in May 1948 if Boeing thought it feasible to switch to jets on the XB-52. Boeing did – and came back with the Model 464-40, submitting a preliminary study in late July. It was based on the use of eight Westinghouse XJ40-WE-12 engines in podded pairs as per the XB-47 which had flown for the first time just a few months earlier.

The 464-40 was broadly similar to the Dash 35 proposal in general appearance as well as dimensions and weights, although performance was marginally superior in terms of speed and much better in terms of altitude. Despite that promise, it was destined to die stillborn, a victim of antipathy on the part of the Deputy Chief of Staff for Materiel, Gen Howard A Craig, the same individual who had earlier directed the Air Materiel Command to cancel the XB-52 project. Paradoxically, in explaining his reasoning during October 1948, Craig argued that while future bombers would be powered by turbojets, he felt that the jet hadn't yet progressed sufficiently far to permit elimination of the intermediate turboprop stage. Within days, he was to be proved wrong in quite dramatic style.

SUBMISSIONS AND ADOPTION

IT'S THE SORT OF TALE that sounds apocryphal, although in this case there's no doubt that the events about to be recounted actually happened. Had they not, there's good reason to believe that the B-52 may not have appeared at all, let alone in the form in which it was to become so well known, so much loved and also so much feared.

Mention was made in the closing stages of the previous chapter of Dayton's Van Cleve Hotel – and it was to that hotel that a number of Boeing engineers repaired after a surprise had been sprung on them by Col Henry 'Pete' Warden of the Air Materiel Command's Wright Air Development Center. In essence, Warden was one of the main points of contact between the Air Force and Boeing in connection with the XB-52 project – and it was to meet him on 21 October 1948 that Edward C Wells, George S Schairer, Vaughn Blumenthal, Harold 'Bob' Withington, Art Carlsen and Maynard Pennell had gone to Wright-Patterson AFB.

With them, they had a wealth of documentation relating to the Model 464-35 submission and they must have been rather taken aback when Warden paid scant attention to that material, but instead requested them to come up with a proposal based on the use of turbojet engines. This was a complete reversal of the position taken by Gen Craig such a short time before and the Boeing team could well have been forgiven had they chosen to adopt a dismissive attitude in the face of such a complete about turn. To their credit and to the company's eternal good fortune, they didn't.

By coincidence, and unbeknown to the Boeing team, Warden had already been pushing Pratt & Whitney to press on with development of the JT3 turbojet engine, a project that was in fact well outside his terms of reference. In addition, he had also recently been on the receiving end of a passionate bit of advocacy of the potential advantages of the jet over the tur-boprop by a German aeronautical engineer named Voigt. It seems that between them these two factors tipped the scales in favour of jet power and persuaded Warden to take a calculated risk and see what kind of response was forthcoming from the Boeing designers. They didn't let him down.

Today, of course, it is doubtful if such a situation could arise in the first place, since even the most trivial decision now has to be taken by committee. In the late 1940s, though, things were different, perhaps as a legacy of the 'can-do' attitude of the war years which undoubtedly still lingered in certain areas. The aerospace industry was one of those areas and, after giving the idea due consideration during the afternoon and evening of 21 October, the Boeing team called Warden the very next morning and informed him that they would have a fresh proposal ready for presentation by the following Monday.

The best part of 72 hours of frantic work ensued as the team capitalised on experience gained with the XB-47 Stratojet. Using a recently completed in-house medium bomber study as a baseline on which to build, the Boeing engineers basically just doubled everything, made a few adjustments here and there, fine-tuned the resulting data in the light of thrust gains and fuel consumption reductions and, lo and behold, they had the Model 464-49.

In truth, it probably wasn't quite that simple, but the end result was an eight-engined jet, using podded pairs of the Pratt & Whitney J57, as the military equivalent of the JT3 was soon to be designated. In the format prepared at Dayton, a certain amount of growth had occurred and the latest proposal was now expected to weigh approximately 330,000 lbs. As for performance, the anticipated top speed was around 490 kts and the 464-49 theoretically had the potential to deliver a 10,000-lb weapons load over a distance of 2660 nautical miles and then return to base. In addition to having picked up two more engines of a completely different type, the new proposal also featured a radically redesigned wing. Span remained constant at 185 ft but the increased chord and a greater angle of sweep (35 degrees) resulted in wing area rising by over 50 per cent, from 2600 sq ft to 4000 sq ft.

Preparation of drawings to support the proposal was done on a humble hotel table, while the mass of statistical data and other information accruing from the hurried preparation was dictated to a stenographer for typing up and binding in the form of a 33-page study. One of the team even went as far as building a scale model of the proposal using materials purchased nearby.

The work done in that Dayton hotel room over the weekend of 23-24 October 1948 was sufficient to con-

BELOW American taxpayers might be forgiven for wondering why their dollars went into the Convair YB-60, an ill-advised attempt to compete with the B-52 which never had a chance but attained a new level of ugliness. Scarcely more than a B-36 fuselage mated to swept wing and tail (and designated B-36G while still on the drawing board), the YB-60 would probably have not warranted a production contract even if the B-52 design had turned out to be a catastrophic disaster. The first of two prototypes (49-2676) is seen near Fort Worth, Texas, in this pictorial evidence that it doesn't have to look aerodynamic in order to fly *(USAF)*

BELOW This near-perfect plan view of the B-47 Stratojet shows the slender wing and podded engine layout that was adopted so successfully by the ensuing B-52 Stratofortress, and other Boeing products *(Boeing)*

vince Warden that the XB-52 should henceforth proceed as a jet-powered design. Not that he needed much convincing since it was evident that the latest version possessed rather more potential and also that any delay arising from the changes would be slight.

Nevertheless, it was to take some time before the USAF officially accepted that jet-propulsion was the way to go, with formal endorsement not occurring until January 1949 in the wake of a final detailed study by members of the USAF Board of Senior Officers. Boeing finally got word on 26 January when the company was advised that development would continue under the terms of an amendment to the existing contractual arrangement.

Further refinement of the basic design followed, but one of the more notable milestones was the mock-up inspection which took place at Seattle during 26-29 April 1949. Even though the project had been under way for a number of years and even though Boeing had invested a considerable amount of energy in the construction of mock-ups, the constant changes and revisions that had bedevilled the project meant that until the beginning of 1948, none had progressed as far as the hurdle of examination by Air Force personnel. Even then, such inspections as did occur were limited to the nose sections and were of questionable value.

So, the Seattle presentation of late April was clearly a good omen and so was the news that no significant criticisms could be levelled at the arrangement as it then stood. What was less satisfactory was that the examining board commented that a J40-powered XB-52 would be unable to achieve a combat radius of 4000 nautical miles although it went on to add that an improved version of the J57 might allow it to reach this figure, but not until 1954 at the earliest.

The resultant report was formally approved by the Air Staff at the beginning of October. However, that approval was far from being a whole-hearted endorsement, and certainly didn't give Boeing carte blanche to forge ahead with the XB-52 in its present form. In fact, there were still many doubts and no certainty that it would reach fruition. Most of those doubts centered around the inadequate range – which was not likely to surpass 2700 nautical miles. And that just wasn't anything like enough!

Nevertheless, the programme survived through the

BELOW The second Stratofortress to be built becomes the first to fly as the Boeing YB-52 (49-0231) lifts off at Seattle on 15 April 1952. When this photo was first released, the 'quadricycle' crosswind landing gear (shown here) was touched out because the USAF considered it a secret. The bomber's four twin-wheel trucks were steerable and could be slewed in unison to allow crosswind landings with the wings level and the aircraft crabbing diagonally toward the runway. Test pilots Tex Johnston and Lt Col Guy M Townsend were not made immediately available to the press because publicity for the new bomber was neither sought nor desired (Boeing)

ABOVE This early in-flight study of the YB-52 Stratofortress (49-0231) displays to advantage the huge plank-like wing structure, as well as the original tandem-seating cockpit arrangement adopted as standard by both of the prototypes. Following strenuous objections by Curtis E LeMay, this layout was replaced by side-by-side seating in production aircraft *(Boeing)*

remainder of 1949, although Maj Gen Orville R Cook of the Air Materiel Command advocated yet another revision of the military characteristics and argued for a review of the project. Gen LeMay, on the other hand, felt that continued development of the engine would resolve the range question but did recommend that key agencies involved in the B-52 ought to convene a conference to study developments.

In the meantime, Boeing's designers continued beavering away as they explored alternative ways and means of addressing the worrying range deficiency before eventually coming up with a somewhat heavier proposal in November 1949. This was the Model 464-67, which weighed in at 390,000 lbs. According to the company, production-configured examples would possess a combat radius of 3785 nautical miles in 1953, rising to 4185 nautical miles in 1957. This was far better than the 464-49 and was looked upon fairly favourably by SAC personnel including LeMay, who had taken over from Gen George Kenney in October 1948.

Eventually, in late January 1950, LeMay finally got his conference, although it had a much wider ranging agenda than that envisaged by SAC's commander, and was actually called to consider not only the B-52 but also several possible alternatives. One which superficially appeared to pose the biggest threat to the XB-52 was the swept-wing, jet-powered Convair B-36G (later redesignated YB-60) – others included contenders from Douglas, Fairchild and Republic, while there were even a couple of variations on the B-47 theme. No firm decision was reached but LeMay made his position crystal clear by consistently supporting the XB-52 as best able to fulfil the strategic bombing mission.

Further Air Staff study of the proposals put forward at the January meeting followed during February, while LeMay's support for the revised Model 464-67 culminated in him urging the Board of Senior Officers to authorise a switch from the 464-49 which was still the officially-endorsed contender, but which, as we have seen, just didn't have anything like long enough 'legs'. This they duly did on 24 March 1950, although even then there was still no guarantee that production of the bomber would go ahead, nor that it would ever attain operational status.

This unsatisfactory state of affairs was allowed to persist throughout the remainder of the year and it wasn't until 1951 that the decision was finally taken to commit the Boeing machine to production. Even then, the interval had seen some supporters of the B-36G/YB-60 and long-range B-47Z pushing those projects hard. SAC remained unconvinced of their merits, basing its continued support for the B-52 on the belief

ABOVE Characteristic wing flexing is apparent in this starboard side view of the YB-52 at altitude during the course of the development programme in the north-eastern USA *(Boeing)*

that it would be faster than both of these alternatives, as well as possessing greater potential for growth in regard to electronic countermeasures equipment when compared with the B-47Z.

By the autumn of 1950, the matter was still unresolved and the Air Staff showed little inclination to dispel the uncertainty that surrounded bomber development. It was at this point, possibly exasperated by the hiatus, that LeMay again showed his hand. This time, he was aided by the Korean War which had begun in the summer and which was largely responsible for worsening relations between the superpowers. In the light of that unhappy state of affairs, LeMay argued powerfully and persuasively for modernisation of the SAC force with the B-52. His support finally tipped the balance and on 9 January 1951, the USAF Chief of Staff, Gen Hoyt S Vandenberg, approved a proposal that the B-52 be obtained in quantity as a replacement for the B-36.

Just over two weeks later, on 24 January, Secretary of the Air Force Thomas K Finletter endorsed that recommendation and little time was wasted in preparing letter contract AF33(038)-21096 to authorise a move from the purely developmental to the production phase. Signature of the contract by representatives of Boeing and the USAF occurred on 14 February 1951, and there is no doubt that this was a crucial moment in the Stratofortress saga, since it cleared the way for procurement of long lead time items, as well as the manufacture of an initial batch of

13 B-52As (USAF serial numbers 52-0001 to 52-0013). Delivery of the first example was slated for April 1953, a target date that proved optimistic.

Thus far, it had taken almost exactly five years to settle upon a suitable design for the new bomber, which was obviously a far cry from the 'hard-charging' approach that had so epitomised the USA during the period of the war years. What perhaps made things even more frustrating was that still more controversy ensued when argument broke out among the more elevated levels of the USAF hierarchy as to whether or not the Model 464-67 should be used as a bomber or if it might be better employed as a reconnaissance tool. This took time to sort out and inevitably led to energy that could have been more usefully channelled elsewhere being wasted in debating the exact nature of the mission to be undertaken by the Boeing machine.

SAC, for example, wanted a dual-capable aircraft, which could use pod-mounted reconnaissance sensors and be easily reconfigured as a straightforward bomber with the ability to carry nuclear or conventional weapons. USAF Headquarters, on the other hand, wanted it to concentrate on reconnaissance to the exclusion of all else. At first glance, it might appear that the latter won the day, for the Air Staff issued a directive in October 1951 to the effect that all aircraft would be to RB-52 configuration, which implied that they would indeed be specialised. What is more, the directive categorically stated 'there is no requirement for a B-52'. This, not surprisingly, was in contravention of the rationale that had been responsible for the advent of the Model 464-67 in the first instance.

However, this was actually an instance of confusing terminology, for the RB-52 did make use of reconnaissance pods carried in the bomb bay area – these could easily be removed and replaced by racks to carry weapons. In this way, while SAC may have lost the battle (and, perhaps, some face), it undoubtedly had the satisfaction of knowing it had won the war. Of course, this sorry episode was just another in the seemingly endless string of affairs and events that conspired to delay the day when SAC could expect to get its hands on the new warplane.

PRODUCTION BEGINS

Once the decision to commit the B-52 to production had been taken, things at last began to move along much more rapidly, with construction of the first two aircraft getting under way in earnest at Boeing's Plant 2 in Seattle. These were, in fact, destined to be the only examples of the Stratofortress for which Boeing bore the lion's share of the fabrication process and they were also unrepresentative of the production article in a number of other ways. Not least of these was the

BELOW Progenitors of more than 700 production examples, both B-52 prototypes pose for the cameras early in the test programme. After participating in the flight trials, both jets were eventually broken up at Wright-Patterson AFB, Ohio, in the mid-1960s. Sadly, the YB-52 had actually been donated to the USAF Museum for preservation in 1958, but a government clean-up drive eventually saw it scrapped (Boeing)

cockpit layout, with both the XB-52 and YB-52 utilising tandem seating for pilot and co-pilot, rather than the side-by-side arrangement which was adopted as standard from the B-52A onwards.

With quantity production virtually assured before the first of the prototype aircraft emerged from its birthplace in Seattle, Boeing was confronted with the task of planning and organising what eventually became the largest manufacturing effort ever undertaken in the USA up to that time. Fortunately, earlier work on the B-29 and B-47 had provided Boeing with considerable expertise in overseeing major production programmes, but the company was still to need every last vestige of that experience when it came to transforming the Stratofortress from the status of a promising project into that of an operational weapon system.

Things weren't made any easier by the fact that increasing urgency prompted the establishment of a second-source production centre at Wichita, Kansas, with an announcement to this effect being made public a few days before the end of September 1953. Approval of a second centre had previously been given as early as the summer of 1951, only to be shelved a few weeks later, but this time the decision was not rescinded and Boeing's Wichita factory was eventually to be responsible for turning out well over half the number built, even though it didn't roll out its first 'Buff' until June 1956.

ABOVE Washington state's imposing Mount Rainier provides an impressive backdrop to this fine study of the XB-52 and YB-52 prototypes in the mid-1950s when testing forged ahead at a rapid rate *(Boeing)*

Long before that, in the spring of 1951, Boeing had selected those sub-contractors who were to play a major part in the ultimate success of the programme. Their initial combined contribution was slightly in excess of a third, measured solely by weight, but it built to a peak of just under 57 per cent during the course of the B-52D production run. Thereafter, it remained more or less constant at that level, with Boeing responsible only for the front fuselage, inner wing structure and inner leading edge section, while other major components and sub-assemblies poured from a number of locations in the USA into the final assembly halls at Seattle and Wichita.

Key companies involved in the production effort came from all over the USA, with over 5000 firms making a contribution of greater or lesser significance at some stage in the programme. Despite the disparate locations of origin, it appears that no major difficulties were encountered in the assembly and mating process. Amongst the major sub-contractors were Goodyear, which had responsibility for the fuselage fuel cells and side panel assemblies, fuel decks and panels, wing stub structure and, in concert with Firestone, the wing fuel cells; Aeronca, which contributed bomb bay doors and panels, wheel well doors, rudder, elevators, ailerons and spoilers; Fairchild, which weighed in with the outer wing sections, top panel assemblies, fin and outrigger units by itself and which also furnished rear fuselage sections in conjunction with Temco.

Smaller contributions came from Cessna (horizontal tail surfaces); Rohr (aft fuselage and gunners compartment, flap tracks, auxiliary fuel tanks and engine pylon struts and nacelles); A O Smith (landing gear bulkheads and main landing gear units); Twin-Coach (flaps, in conjunction with Boeing Wichita) and Zenith Plastics (wing tips). Many other companies chipped in with items such as instruments, actuators, alternators, hydraulic pumps, wiring, anti-icing equipment, braking systems, wheels, tyres, paint, fasteners and all the myriad other bits and pieces needed to transform a collection of parts into a machine capable of taking flight – and the whole exercise was a remarkable demonstration of engineering know-how on the part of the US aerospace industry that was only eclipsed by the space programme of the next decade.

Implementation of that massive effort lay some way off in the future when the time eventually came for the first example to leave the assembly hall and move to the flight test hangar, an event that occurred on 29 November 1951. Although such happenings are now usually surrounded by a snowstorm of publicity, in the early 1950s the USA was most definitely on a war footing and secrecy was the name of the game, hence the decision to move the prototype under cover of darkness on a damp and dreary night when most sensible citizens would be warm and dry indoors. In fact, the desire to keep the newest Boeing bomber under wraps was taken quite literally, for the XB-52 (49-0230) was shrouded when it first emerged and the shape was hard to discern under all that covering material.

In the normal course of events, one would have expected this machine to claim the honour of making the maiden flight of the Stratofortress, but it didn't actually pan out that way. Ground testing and checkout seems to have started satisfactorily but was eventually brought to an abrupt halt when the XB-52's pneumatic system experienced a catastrophic failure during a full pressure trial. The resulting 'blow-out' caused extensive damage to the wing trailing edge, which inevitably necessitated the aircraft's return to the production hall for rectification and repair. For reasons best known to themselves, the company and the Air Force chose to keep a tight rein on this news and instead attributed the further work as being connected with equipment installation. As a direct consequence, the XB-52 did not get airborne for the first time until 2 October 1952.

By then, though, Boeing had already had one Stratofortress flying for several months and was making solid headway with the test effort. This aircraft was the YB-52 (49-0231) which was wheeled out of the assembly hangar on 15 March 1952 and which flew

BELOW Externally virtually indistinguishable from its sistership, the XB-52 prototype (49-0230) was actually the second aircraft to fly. The delay in taking to the skies was caused by a major failure of the pneumatic system during the course of ground trials that were expected to culminate in a successful maiden flight in the early part of 1952 (Boeing)

for the first time from Boeing Field exactly one month later, on 15 April. On board the YB-52 for that auspicious occasion were company test pilot A M Tex Johnston and Lt Col Guy Townsend of the USAF's Air Research and Development Command.

By all accounts, the 2 hr 51 min sortie passed off more or less uneventfully, before culminating in a perfect landing at Moses Lake (later renamed Larson AFB). In fact, by the time that the YB-52 whistled in for its first touch-down, Johnston and Townsend had extended their original plan for the maiden flight and had begun work on formal flight testing.

In summing up that first trip aloft, Johnson volunteered the opinion that Boeing had come up with 'a hell of a good airplane'. About his only gripe concerned control forces, which had deliberately been set high, resulting in the pilots having to work quite hard when manoeuvring the large aircraft. This, however, was easily remedied and adjustments to the system made life much less fatiguing for the test pilots on subsequent sorties. Other relatively minor problems encountered during the maiden flight concerned the failure of one of the main landing gear units to retract properly; defects with the liquid oxygen system; and a leaking engine oil valve.

Five days later, the YB-52 ventured aloft again. During this and subsequent early sorties, it quickly became apparent that Boeing had a potential winner on its hands and that little in the way of 'troubleshooting' would be necessary at the outset of the test effort. This, in turn, allowed the company to curtail the length of time spent at Moses Lake and the YB-52 was back at Boeing Field barely a week after making its first flight. That was certainly contrary to plans, for the Boeing development flight test team had anticipated remaining at Moses Lake for several weeks.

Although the early test effort was generally undertaken from Boeing Field, it should be noted that considerable controversy surrounded the development phase – and, in particular, the centres utilised for flight trials. As the customer, the USAF not surprisingly indicated a desire to concentrate test activity at Edwards AFB, California. This was the home of the Air Force Flight Test Center (AFFTC) and was therefore a logical choice.

Boeing disagreed, arguing that Seattle was far better suited in so far as it would allow defects revealed by testing to be put right far more swiftly and at much less cost. In addition, Boeing also dismissed fears that programme progress would be disrupted by poor weather in the north-western USA.

What made the situation more complicated was that not even the USAF commands involved in the project could reach agreement. Air Research and Development Command (ARDC) backed the use of Edwards, but there's nothing startling about that, for Edwards was the prime ARDC facility and it would have been astonishing if it hadn't pushed the California site for all it was worth. Air Materiel Command (AMC), on the other hand, backed Boeing, apparently being mainly motivated by the understandable desire to avoid facing expensive post-production modifications, but also influenced by the fact that testing at Edwards would automatically be more costly, possibly

BELOW Captured at a later stage in the test programme, this Stratofortress prototype has acquired auxiliary wing-mounted fuel tanks outboard of the outer pair of podded turbojet engines (Boeing)

even to the tune of no less than $20 million. In the end, ARDC reluctantly gave way, although it seems that it didn't have a lot of choice, since AMC evidently refused to release the extra monetary resources to finance testing at Edwards. However, it didn't take long for Boeing's claims about the Seattle weather patterns to be disproved to the extent that the programme begun running into delays in 1953. At this point, the USAF decided to intervene, ordering a change of test site.

Henceforth, the Moses Lake/Larson AFB complex would be used, although the focal point of trials activity was later shifted to Fairchild AFB which also happened to be located in Washington state. Several other USAF installations also figured in the various trials, although the extent of their involvement varied considerably and some were only active in a peripheral capacity. Facilities that played a leading role at some time or another included the AFFTC at Edwards; the Air Proving Ground Command at Eglin AFB, Florida; and the Air Development Center at Wright-Patterson AFB, Ohio.

By the beginning of October 1952, the YB-52 had logged somewhere in the region of 50 hours flight time (it eventually recorded 738 hours in 345 flights) and had been used to get Phase I trials up and running. In the course of that period, it had demonstrated satisfac-

ABOVE YB-52 49-0231 flying over the mountainous terrain near the manufacturer's Seattle headquarters. The black and white cross on a black square immediately behind the wing is a target for the phototheodolite used to track the service-test Stratofortress during take-offs and landings and to determine exact lift-off and touchdown points. The large spoiler on the right wing is serving the role normally filled by an aileron to put the YB-52 in a gentle leftward turn *(Boeing)*

tory performance levels, but the overall test programme was already behind schedule and still worse slippages were to follow.

However, that wasn't apparent on 2 October 1952 when Boeing's up-and-coming bomber project safely negotiated another significant hurdle with the maiden flight of the XB-52 from Seattle. As had been the case with the YB-52, the aircraft remained airborne for more than two hours. With two prototypes now available, the pace of the development effort began to accelerate and the XB-52 was soon put to good use in the Phase II tests that were accomplished by USAF personnel between 3 November 1952 and 15 March 1953. These were already running late and a further delay of nearly two months accrued due to unsuitable weather conditions in the vicinity of Seattle.

Although many aspects were shown to be entirely satisfactory, the Phase II assessment did reveal some deficiencies, as well as a number of disturbing defects. Not least of these was inadequate engine reliability, with the prototype J57s installed in the XB-52 being prone to surge when normal throttle movements were undertaken at high altitude with low engine inlet temperatures – worse still was the risk that they might flame out. Another unwelcome trait was a tendency to pitch up and roll to starboard when approaching the stall, while the braking system was clearly unable to bring the Stratofortress to a halt within distances specified by Boeing.

As far as individual contributions are concerned, there's no doubt that the lion's share of initial test flying was entrusted to the YB-52. As we have seen, this completed its first flight several months before the XB-52 and it was certainly much more active in the early stages, being used almost exclusively for Phase I and carrying the burden of early Phase III efforts. Turning to the XB-52, after bearing sole responsibility for Phase II trials, this was assigned to Phase III contractor development testing which evidently began in late March 1953. However, it was destined to make only a minor contribution, being grounded for attention fairly soon after that task was begun and not regaining flight status until about the middle of 1954.

Subsequent aspects of the formal test programme included a number of distinct phases, each of which was fairly narrowly focussed and each of which could be looked upon as obstacles to be cleared en route to operational squadron service. Today, the terminology has changed and current programmes refer to categories of testing. Then, the preferred term was 'Phases' and there were eight in all.

Mention has already been made of the first three, but it seems sensible to include a brief summary of the objectives of the other five. Phase IV dealt with performance and stability and usually involved around 200 hours flight time, during which all aspects of handling were evaluated throughout the entire flying envelope. Phase V examined all-weather operability and usually included a visit to the McKinley Laboratory at Eglin AFB, Florida where, almost irrespective of type, the aircraft under test could be subjected to extremes of heat and cold in a fully controlled environment.

Moving on to Phase VI functional development testing, this was concerned with evaluating the entire weapon system, for it should be kept in mind that the airframe was only part – albeit a most important part – of a complex package of systems and equipment. In the case of the B-52, that package was designed to ensure the accurate delivery of bombs and other kinds of weapon and it obviously made sound sense to ensure that the various strands meshed together satisfactorily. Phase VI trials were invariably accomplished

BELOW The silvery YB-52 (49-0231) had no armament installed in its tail gun position. The appearance of B-52B-style wingtip tanks (but slightly different in shape from those adopted operationally) suggests that this is a late portrait of the aircraft. The outrigger wheels, the left-side example of which is bearing weight in this view, quickly rose from the ground when the bomber was taxied. Nose radar equipment is covered by moulded, non-metallic material, although the upper radar cover appears to be frayed here *(via Clyde Gerdes)*

with production-configured aircraft by pilots from the designated user agency.

In this instance, that was SAC and crews from the command would also have been responsible for Phase VII Operational Suitability tests and Phase VIII Unit Operational Employment tests, which would be the final trials to be faced before the type was cleared for full-scale service with combat-ready forces. In practice, the last couple of phases often overlapped the initial training and instruction period, so as to ensure that deployment of a new aircraft to frontline echelons could get under way with the minimum of delay.

Although it was obviously desirable to carry a test programme through to its conclusion as swiftly as possible so as to facilitate entry into service, it was equally important not to push ahead too rapidly, since there was always the possibility that development might reveal a major design deficiency or flaw which would require extensive airframe modification. So, making the transition from promising design to combat-ready system could conceivably be likened to walking a tightrope, in as much as the line needs to be sufficiently taut to avoid waste of resources and yet sufficiently flexible to offer adequate support throughout the entire development period.

Boeing seems to have achieved that with the B-52, even though the on-going development that culminated in the much improved short-tailed derivatives meant that test activity related to production and manufacture spanned at least a decade. The bulk of that effort was obviously undertaken in the early stages,

ABOVE The first of three B-52A Stratofortress bombers (52-0001) made its first flight on 5 August 1954, and is seen here over Puget Sound with Mount Rainier and other peaks in the background. Although Boeing senior vice president Wellwood E Beall initially opposed the idea, the B-52A introduced the slightly lengthened and revised nose configuration which permitted side-by-side crew seating. Gen Curtis E LeMay wanted his pilots side-by-side, in part because co-ordination between the two could be achieved more easily, especially during an interphone failure *(Boeing)*

when trials were at their most intensive, but at least half-a-dozen B-52Gs and B-52Hs spent time with specialised test outfits of the USAF.

As has been mentioned, both Stratofortress prototypes were utilised for trials work and it would be fair to say that early progress was solid, if not exactly spectacular. Once production configured aircraft became available, the pace of activity began to accelerate and in that regard the advent of the B-52A model made a huge difference to the programme.

The first of the trio of B-52As was formally rolled out at Seattle in March 1954 and was subsequently accepted by the USAF during June, whereupon it was immediately bailed back to Boeing for use on test tasks. As it transpired, its contribution to the development effort did not get under way until it completed a successful maiden flight on 5 August 1954, but it was soon joined by the other two B-52As and, with effect from December 1954, by the first of several early production RB-52Bs.

ABOVE Revised nose contours arising from the switch in cockpit configuration are all too apparent in this fine head-on study of the first production B-52A Stratofortress (52-0001) in flight over the rugged coastline of the north-western seaboard. Plans to obtain 13 B-52A aircraft were subjected to change, and only three examples were eventually built *(Boeing)*

In addition, ground tests were undertaken with a couple of non-flying vehicles to determine that the production articles would be durable enough to meet design and fatigue-life criteria. For the most part, those objectives were satisfied, although, as will be seen, the use of different materials in concert with the shift from high to low-level operations meant that the final two derivatives (the B-52G and B-52H) soon had to be retrospectively fitted with modified wings. Despite that, many B-52s eventually went on to handsomely exceed the original stipulations with the aid of extensive post-production re-engineering programmes. This process has prompted some observers to draw a parallel between the 'Buff' and the axe that has had seven new handles and four new heads – but which, apart from that, is still the same axe.

Some idea of the magnitude of the effort involved in trials and development flight testing can be gleaned from the knowledge that Boeing's task force eventually numbered more than 600 individuals, many of whom were directly involved in analysing and assessing the mass of data that accumulated as the pace of the test effort accelerated. And, since one two-hour session of flight testing could generate up to eight million items of information, it follows that they would have been kept busy.

So, for that matter, were the aircrew assigned the job of taking the new bomber aloft specifically to assist in obtaining that data – and to establish the B-52's suitability in the role it was earmarked for. As far as determining that suitability was concerned, the three B-52As were primarily assigned to evaluation of more general aspects, like propulsion and secondary electrical power systems as well as aerodynamic characteristics, stability, performance and controllability throughout the entire envelope.

Aspects that were more closely connected with operational suitability were generally entrusted to the RB-52Bs – and, more particularly, to the 10 aircraft that were originally ordered as B-52As (serial numbers 52-0004 to 52-0013). At least two (52-0005 and 52-0006) were assigned to Phase VI objectives, before being passed to the 93rd Bomb Wing at Castle AFB, California, for training duties, while other specific taskings included assessment of the A-3 fire control system (FCS) and its associated quad 0.50 calibre machine gun armament as well as flight loadings (52-0004); assessment of the MD-5 FCS and twin 20 mm cannon armament (52-0009); check-out of the bombing/navigation systems (52-0008); and evaluation of the general purpose reconnaissance capsule and passive defensive systems (52-0010).

Although most flight testing was accomplished from Boeing's facility at Moses Lake, that was far from being the only location used. Reference has already been made to the contribution of other organisations such as the Air Force Flight Test Center at Edwards and this was to include aircraft 52-0004 in its test fleet for several years. Elsewhere, at Eglin, aircraft 52-0011 was subjected to climatic testing in the McKinley Laboratory, while 52-0013 was assigned to the USAF's Special Weapons Center at Kirtland AFB, New Mexico for several years, during which time it undertook many drop tests of inert nuclear 'shapes' to explore weapons separation characteristics at release and also to gather ballistics data.

Of equal significance (but rather more spectacular) was the part played by 52-0013 in Operation *Dominic*. This was a series of atmospheric nuclear tests that took place in the Pacific during 1962, with some 29 of the eventual total of 36 detonations involving B-52 freefall airdrop methods of delivery. Six years before, on 21 May 1956, the distinction of being the first 'Buff' to drop a live nuclear weapon had also fallen to the hardworked 52-0013 in the *Redwing Cherokee* test near Namu Island at Bikini Atoll.

In fact, it was also the first time a US thermonuclear device was air-dropped, but the Mk.15 actually missed its target by nearly four miles as a result of the bombardier releasing it 21 seconds too soon. The pyrotechnic display was no less spectacular for that, but the mistake was costly in so far as the data 'take' was much less than had been hoped for.

In general terms, the original trials programme was probably much more successful than Boeing had anticipated in view of the sheer scale of the effort involved.

By far the most positive aspect was that it was completed without the loss of any of the aircraft that took part, although that's not to say that problems didn't arise. One of the lessons learnt was that ultrasonic noise generated during water-injection augmented take-offs was causing major fatigue damage to flap assemblies, but there were also fuel leaks, problems with icing of the fuel system, difficulties with water injection pumps, defective alternators and inadequate performance of bombing and fire control systems. All of these took time to fix and some were to cause furrowed brows for quite some time after the Stratofortress entered the US arsenal, but Boeing still fared better with the B-52 than it had with the B-47 at a comparable point in its career.

They were far from being the only problems, with reliability of the Pratt & Whitney J57 turbojets falling some way short of desired levels, while the main undercarriage units also gave rise to a few headaches. At least one instance of a truck failing to lower was recorded, although the ensuing landing was accomplished safely, allowing Boeing to claim it had satisfied one of the original design stipulations.

On another occasion, failure of the hydraulic drives resulted in one of the main gears jamming at the 20-degree angle of inclination, resulting in a strong smell

BELOW With the wing clearly already 'flying' before the main wheels have left the ground, the first production example of the B-52A Stratofortress appears to be engaged in a flapless departure from Boeing's home base in Seattle, Washington. Although not destined to be used operationally, the B-52A trio nevertheless made a significant contribution to the eventual success of Boeing's finest and most durable bomber, and unlike the XB- and YB-52s, two of the three jets are still preserved today *(Boeing)*

ABOVE The first genuine production version was the B-52B, also designated RB-52B, the third example of which is the subject of this February 1956 portrait. This jet wears the large 'U. S. AIR FORCE' lettering which came into use in 1955, and replaced the small 'UNITED STATES AIR FORCE' inscription. First flight of the B-52B was on 25 January 1955, and the first delivery was to the 93rd Bomb Wing at Castle AFB, California, on 29 June 1955. Curiously, while the lettering has been added to this B-52 since it emerged from the factory, the white underside paint scheme has not *(USAF)*

on landing, destruction of both tyres and the use of a considerable amount of 'elbow grease' to remove burnt rubber deposits from the aircraft's belly. Less hazardous but probably more exasperating were a few instances in which the forward main units operated independently rather than in unison. Known in the trade as 'split gears', this phenomenon resulted in them swivelling in opposite directions at the same time, an occurrence that effectively rendered the bomber immovable.

By the summer of 1955, however, sufficient progress had been made to permit the start of deliveries to the 'customer', namely Strategic Air Command, which was eager to get to grips with the newest and potentially most capable bomber ever to be conceived and developed in the USA. Boeing's latest 'fortress' had been a long time coming, but shortly before the end of June, that keenly anticipated moment finally arrived. However, before considering the operational deployment of the B-52, it seems best to look more closely at what the USAF got for its money in terms of the aircraft itself, and the weapons that it carried.

BELOW RB-52B 52-0011 on the ramp at Eglin AFB, Florida. This jet has the appearance of early Stratofortresses as they rolled out of the factory, with small lettering on the nose, the absence of a white reflector shield on the underside and a lack of any distinctive unit markings. 52-011 has a standard tail gun position, and the gantry used to give ground personnel access to it illustrates the height of an aircraft which was never terribly easy to either maintain or repair *(USAF)*

THE *DOOMSDAY* DETONATIONS

OPERATION *Redwing* was the detonation of 16 medium and high-yield warheads in the atolls at Eniwetok and Bikini from May to July 1956. The blasts, or 'shots', included large hydrogen bombs; some were detonated from towers, others from barges, and two were air-dropped, including the awesome and nearly catastrophic *Cherokee* shot on 21 May 1956 by a B-52, and the *Osage* shot on 16 June 1956 by a B-36.

Perhaps more important than the method of delivering these warheads, the *Redwing* series tested the weapons' effects on military aircraft in service, including, for the first time, the B-52.

It was neither the first time Americans had gone to the Pacific to unleash the awful fury of the atom, nor was it the last. Several tests of atomic and hydrogen bombs (not usually called nuclear weapons at the time)

came before *Redwing*, but the *latter* series was the first involving the B-52, and included the first aerial drop by Americans of a thermonuclear bomb – Dr Edward Teller's 'Super', or 'Runaway Super', was usually

BELOW B-52C (54-2669) hauling its enlarged 40-ft (12.38-m) external fuel tanks through the sky near Boeing's Seattle plant. The 35 B-52Cs were essentially improved RB-52B models and retained the capability to carry an internal reconnaissance capsule, but were not given an 'R' prefix. SAC was not eager to publicise the thermal-reflecting paint on the underside which first appeared on the B-52C (though retroactively on most B-models), but when a B-52C was displayed at Larson AFB, Washington, no one attending a base dedication ceremony asked a single question about the paint *(Boeing)*

called a hydrogen bomb – although the Soviet Union had air-dropped such a weapon six months earlier. In later years, two subsequent Pacific test series, Operations *Hardtack* and *Dominic*, also involved B-52s.

As part of the tests, the first B-52B (52-0004), nicknamed *The Tender Trap*, was instrumented to evaluate the effects of an atomic blast on the Boeing bomber. Testing the effects of weapons against an aeroplane had begun as early as Operation *Crossroads* in the Marshall Islands in 1946, when drone B-17s were flown near blasts. The XB-47, two B-50s and a B-47B performed the first tests of aircraft structures against new, multi-megaton weapons using atomic fusion in Operations *Ivy* and *Castle* in 1952 and 55 – the *Ivy Mike* shot of 1 November 1952, which all but erased the island of Elugelab from the map, was the world's first thermonuclear detonation, but was a cab-mounted device, not an air-delivered bomb.

To prepare for the Pacific tests, Capt Gene Deatrick, a Wright Field test pilot, went up to Seattle for ground school and flight checkout in the B-52. Deatrick did some training in the third B-52A (52-0003) which usually resided at Boeing as a test ship, though it appeared briefly at Wright-Patterson for icing tests. In later years, 'balls three' found employment at Edwards AFB, California, serving as a mother-ship for the X-15 rocket research aircraft.

In his first flight in a B-52 in June 1955, Deatrick found the bomber to be heavy on the controls but comfortable, stable, and forgiving. He'd already formed the opinion that the B-47, which he'd flown during the *Castle* atomic tests, was 'the last "fighter" a bomber pilot will ever get to fly'. He now felt that he was moving 'from a sportster to a stretched limousine'. Deatrick was pleased with the crosswind landing gear on the B-52 because the B-47 had been severely limited in such conditions. When well-known test pilot Lt Col Guy M Townsend (who'd made the first flight of the YB-52 on 15 April 1952 with Tex Johnston) 'signed off' Deatrick on the B-52 type in August 1955, the latter felt he was now qualified in the 'Cadillac of the skies'.

The bomber was far from perfected, however. In Deatrick's view, the worst error was putting the Stratofort's four bleed-air driven alternators in the bomb bay. This controversial arrangement used pneumatic power for operation of major accessories, bleeding air from the engines and piping it through the aircraft to energise the hydraulics, electrics, air-conditioning,

water injection and de-icing. Originally, the alternators were to have been positioned on the engine nacelles, where logic said they belonged. There were two kinds made by two manufacturers, and neither worked well.

The more cantankerous of the two alternator models had turbine blades which routinely froze – blamed for the early loss of a bomber which killed a much-liked pilot, Col Pat Fleming, vice commander of the 93rd Bomb Wing at Castle AFB, California. Deatrick remembers Gen Bill Irvine at the Pentagon passing along a quote from somebody even higher up in the top brass – 'The Secretary (of the Air Force) says we're not spending another dime for this B-52 aeroplane until I can assure him it won't blow up'. The less troublesome alternator was adopted, still in the fuselage, but it was not until the advent of the B-52F that shaft-power from the engines was used to directly drive alternators mounted in the nacelles and energise the hydraulics.

In March 1956, with Wright Field test pilot Maj Charles G 'Andy' Anderson as pilot and Deatrick as co-pilot, and with a new designation as a JB-52B, *The Tender Trap* left Seattle for Eniwetok. Deatrick believes it may have been the first B-52 to leave the USA.

'0004 made its Pacific journey (together with its maintenance crew in a C-97 Stratofreighter) by way of Honolulu. On arrival at Eniwetok, the short runway and limited ramp space had drawn a crowd. Wright Field had despatched the B-52, a B-47E, a B-57, a B-66, an F-101 and two F-84Fs. From Albuquerque had come no fewer than a dozen more B-57 Canberras to be used in gathering nuclear samples. More F-101 Voodoos were also in attendance. There were also C-47s, C-54s and SA-16s at tiny Eniwetok. Here, in this tropical paradise, it seemed the industrial age was suddenly everywhere. Odd-shaped buildings sprang up. Towers, tunnels and antennas littered the atoll. The barges used for some weapon detonations looked as if plumbers and metalworkers had joined up with cartoonist Rube Goldberg to create a 19th century jumble of tubes, corners and angles.

But amid the palm trees and soothing breezes, a newer age was upon the world and there were no words for it. Physicist Robert Oppenheimer, during the first atomic detonation in July 1945, had sought for words and was able to find them nowhere but in the *Bhagavad-Gita*, the 700-stanza devotional poem in Sanskrit which pre-dates civilisation in the West. Moments after that first blast at New Mexico's Trinity Site, while a few people laughed, many wept, and most stood silent, Oppenheimer had uttered a clause from the Hindu scripture where the warrior Vishnu speaks of change, and of duty – *'I am become death, the destroyer of worlds. . .'*

WEAPONS EFFECTS

The job done by Anderson, Deatrick and the crew of *The Tender Trap* seems, in retrospect, prosaic enough. 'We had a pretty unscientific estimate of the bomb's yield', Deatrick recalls. 'Our job was to position the aircraft to test three major effects – radiation, which was local and limited so long as you stayed out of the cloud – heat and the shock wave.' The crew of another B-52B (52-0013) coming from Albuquerque had the more interesting job, and one about which little has been published even a half century later – releasing the air-dropped weapon known as *Cherokee* on that incredible date, 21 May 1956, when the United States took the extraordinary step of detonating two bombs in a single day.

Albuquerque was then, and is today, a distinct culture. In the secluded village of Los Alamos, an hour's drive north in New Mexico mountains, Oppenheimer and his scientists had developed the first bomb in isolation and secrecy. Though the B-29s which razed Hiroshima and Nagasaki did their work-ups at Wendover, Utah – a dismally lonely expanse of salt-flat – much of the science and most of the aircraft involved in atomic tests were positioned at Kirtland Air Force Base in Albuquerque. It was from Kirtland that 52-0013 and a very tight-lipped Stratofortress crew (of what became known as the 4925th Nuclear Test Group) deployed to actually drop 'The Bomb'.

With the bomb-drop B-52B and Deatrick's effects-test JB-52B located at the crowded Eniwetok airstrip, ground crews were relieved to find the Stratofortress easier to handle than they'd expected. 'With those wide, drooping wings, we wondered if we could turn the plane around and manoeuvre it easily on the ramp', remembers Chief Master Sergeant Edward Hardin, who occasionally pitched in to help, although he belonged to a unit with a different aircraft type. 'I never heard about a serious mechanical problem, which was good because we had bare-bones maintenance facilities on the island. Most new aircraft have glitches, but the B-52 was easy to operate on the

ABOVE The inscription on the nose of this aircraft helps to identify it as RB-52B 52-0004. This was the first true production Stratofortress, and it was employed to obtain weapon effects data as described fully in this chapter. It was finally retired to MASDC on 12 January 1966

ground and to maintain.' Pilots argue that the B-52 is much easier to fly than to taxy, especially at a small aerodrome, but in any event there were no mishaps.

No one associated with the B-52 – pilots, navigator, bombardier, maintenance people – seems to have interpreted the presence of the Stratofortress on Eniwetok as anything but logical for aircraft entering the inventory. An atomic war with the Soviet Union seemed fairly likely. In fact, *Air Force* magazine had frightened the hell out of many Americans with a cover painting of a new invention, known as an ICBM (intercontinental ballistic missile), which its editorial staff called an 'Ik-boom' in shorthand, saying that if such a weapon could be perfected it would make war even more likely. In the circumstance, flying around amid blasts of radiation or through mushroom clouds was a job to be pretty much taken for granted.

Certainly for Anderson, Deatrick, and *The Tender Trap*'s crew, flying near an H-bomb was not nearly as scary as giving a ride to the Pentagon's chief. Secretary of Defense Charles Wilson, known as 'Engine Charlie' from his days at General Motors, arrived at Eniwetok. Wilson, who was not a young man, wanted more than just a look around. He wanted a B-52 ride. The date appears to have been 8 May 1956.

CREW COMFORTS

Aboard Deatrick's B-52, as on all 744 Stratofortresses built (save only the two prototypes), a fold-down jump seat was located behind the two pilots even though there was not adequate space for it in the narrow aisle behind the flight deck. It's really a partial seat, on which an instructor pilot or passenger can never really take the weight off his legs (the helmet, oxygen, survival pack, and parachute aboard a B-52 weigh more than 75 lb, or 34 kg).

One of the few features of the aircraft which seem more an afterthought than an integral part of its design, the seat is never really comfortable or, in event of a mishap, safe. It was certainly not the kind of seating arrangement customary for 'Engine Charlie' Wilson, the number two man, behind the president, in what became known in later years as the National Command Authority (NCA), the United States' chain of command.

Deatrick and his fellow JB-52B fliers took Wilson out on a trip to the calibration area for a planned thermonuclear shot, knowing that if even a minor flight emergency arose in their bomber, 'We would have no way to save him'. Fortunately, nothing went wrong. Another *Redwing* participant believes that a 'fly-by' was made that same day for a group of visiting senators. Meanwhile, plans continued for the *Cherokee* shot.

All but two of the 16 detonations in Operation *Redwing* were of weapons specifically created to be tested. The bomb dropped on 21 May 1956 by B-52B 52-0013, however, was a Mk 15 'Zombie' thermonuclear bomb which could be made available only when President Eisenhower authorised its release from the national warfighting stockpile (the weapon was not a Mk 17, parachute-retarded bomb and was not expected to deliver yields varying from 10 to 25 megatons, as has been reported). Properly released after careful navigation by the B-52's excellent radar navigation/bombing system, the *Cherokee* shot, as this drop was known, should have detonated above Ground Zero (in this case, an illuminated asphalt slab on Namu Island at Bikini atoll, some 200 miles (320 km) east of Eniwetok) with clinical precision.

OFF TARGET

A selected group of reporters aboard USS *Mount McKinley* (AGC-7) watched not only the *Cherokee* drop but the ground-detonated *Lacrosse* shot on the same day. Not since the first postwar tests a decade earlier in 1946 had civilian observers been on the scene. None were permitted near, let alone to fly on, either the Albuquerque B-52 or Deatrick's Wright Field bomber.

52-0013 dropped its Mk 15 'Zombie' from 40,000 ft (12,384 m) and detonated it at an altitude of 4350 ft (1347 m), producing a 3.75 megaton blast.

Capt Michael P Curphey, a participant in the *Cherokee* shot, claims that the B-52B's radar navigator (the term for the bombardier on the Stratofortress) made an error by reading navigational figures in reverse and that the bomb was dropped a considerable, but unknown, distance from the intended spot. Records show that at detonation, the bomb missed its target by 19,000 ft (5882 m) because it was dropped 21 seconds too soon when the bombardier mistook another lighted island for the Ground Zero site.

Curphey remembers, 'The drop B-52B's bombardier made a major mistake in sighting his target by locking on to another set of lights in the Bikini atoll. In addition to the target's large cross-shape of lights, there was also another small island in the flight path that had a small light on, not a cross but a single point of light. On his final run-in the bombardier sighted on this single point, located well beyond the proper target. He realised his mistake and moved the crosshairs of his telescope from the wrong target to the correct one, but he made an additional mistake by not disconnecting the bombing system's computer during this large and rapid movement of the telescope. The bombing system interpreted this as a sudden increase in ground speed and dropped the weapon early, before the (rest of the) crew discovered the error'.

Capt Tom Sumner was aircraft commander of the Wright Field B-47E effects-test aircraft (52-2389), nicknamed *Bubba Boy* after an endearment for Sumner's son, Timothy. Capt Sumner remembers that the 'drop B-52B crew practiced very little, and we never had a full-scale dress rehearsal'. Others on the scene observed that the B-52B drop crew, as Sgt Fred Newman put it, 'were pretty stuck up. It was a small island, with few diversions, and it was no place for a five-man clique to keep to themselves. But these guys were snooty and arrogant'.

Tom Sumner continues, 'The target could be easily seen on radar in any weather, or with optics in clear weather (but) the drop crew bombardier, upon whom we all depended, relied almost entirely on his optical system for sighting the target, rather than using the radar to line up with, then refine, the sighting with the optics in the last few seconds.

'After two attempts to make a live drop were cancelled due to weather, the morning came when the weather was satisfactory. The drop was scheduled for about 0600, some 30 minutes before sunrise. It was desirable that the detonation occur in darkness in order to obtain the contrast of a dark sky against the fireball, to help in analysis of the yield. The drop crew was instructed to abort the drop if things did not go as planned and try for a secondary H-Hour 20 minutes later'.

It was not for nothing that Deatrick's JB-52B, a remarkable gaggle of other Air Force aircraft, and some Navy A3D Skywarriors and P2V Neptunes were aloft near Bikini. During World War 2, the effect of a bomb on the B-29 which dropped it was of no concern. That changed when the shock waves at Hiroshima and Nagasaki stirred up worries about what might happen to airframes amid combat in a nuclear environment, and the effects/test aircraft were on the scene to find out the facts.

Every Pentagon contingency plan for the expected war with the Soviet Union called for flying and fighting near, or even inside, mushroom clouds. Deatrick and many others were guinea pigs, in a sense, charged with finding out how the next war would be fought. As *The Tender Trap* flew its prescribed course near the *Cherokee* detonation, Anderson, Deatrick, radar navigator Maj Charles Gilmore and others all felt that what they were doing was important – in many ways, more important than dropping the weapon.

Tom Sumner's account of how the *Cherokee* drop went awry is evidence that the 'fog of war' can enshroud men even when peacetime tests are being carried out.

When B-52B 52-0013, the Albuquerque Stratofort, started its final run-in and began the countdown over UHF radio, 'the vocal signals became garbled and not understandable. The call contained the phrase and code word, "SAD SACK" followed by "X number of seconds", with X being the time to go to drop. The crews of aeroplanes in the test area planned to compare these calls with the time of day the call was scheduled and to determine if the drop would be early or late, and by how much. When the B-66 pilot heard these garbled calls he sensibly aborted. His direction was opposite from the drop aircraft and though he did not realise it, his decision to abort saved his life.

'Both the B-47E and (Deatrick's) JB-52B requested a clarification of the countdown but that, too, was garbled. Assuming the drop would be on schedule and in place, we (in the B-47E) continued. We assumed that if the drop crew had a problem they would have advised the test force, discontinued their run-in, and gone for the alternate H-Hour. Little did we realise the mistake the drop crew had made.

'The call to indicate the drop was completed was the code word "COMPLETE". This meant the weapon was out of the bay and falling. To the horror of the B-47E and JB-52B crews we heard this call, loud and clear, not garbled, and it came 30 seconds *before* it was scheduled.

'This meant the weapon would detonate 30 seconds too early and we'd be 30 seconds too damn close, which was way too near. Anything closer than three or four seconds meant destruction (of our aircraft) with no escape possible. All I could do was increase speed as much as possible, up to the Mach limit of the B-47E, about Mach 0.81. In the time remaining, that wasn't enough.

'It took the *Cherokee* weapon 54 seconds to fall before exploding. We knew we could not survive and there were very frightened crew members in the air that morning, five in the JB-52B and four in my B-47E.

'When it exploded the heat was felt inside the aeroplane and the light was very bright in spite of the blast curtains made of asbestos. I was certain our aeroplane was on fire and expected it to come apart at any moment, but I ruled out ejection as that seemed an even worse fate – and this turned out to be a wise decision.' The B-47E and RB-52B were both badly beaten about, but survived.

One participant remembers that after the *Cherokee* shot, the Albuquerque crew set their B-52B down on Eniwetok, grabbed their suitcases, and departed for home. On arrival in New Mexico, they were given a sudden, nasty order to go back to Eniwetok – minus Stratofort – for an investigation.

OSAGE SHOT

The effects-test JB-52B, *The Tender Trap*, was now the only Stratofortress in the Pacific. The low-yield *Osage* shot was dropped by a B-36 over Runit island at Eniwetok on 16 June 1956. *The Tender Trap* was aloft when the 70-kiloton *Osage* shot detonated accurately and produced a cloud 21,000 ft (6501 m) high.

Until now, men cavorting through the skies almost within shouting distance of the awesome power of the atom seemed, so they thought, to have proven that

ABOVE The eyes have it! At a later stage in its career, RB-52B 52-0004 acquired a different coloured radome and a pair of eyes that gave it a most distinctive appearance. It ultimately joined the 93rd BW before its eventual retirement to Davis-Monthan

aeroplanes could fight in a nuclear environment. Mishaps occurred, including a navigational error amid a detonation which nearly killed an F-84F pilot. No serious harm was actually inflicted on any aircraft.

Disastrous, however, was the word for the weapons test effects which resulted when the *Dakota* shot was detonated in Bikini lagoon south of Yurochi island (after several delays caused by weather) on 26 June 1956. This thermonuclear blast of several hundred kilotons – by no means the most powerful device detonated during the tests – produced a radioactive cloud rising to 82,000 ft (25,387 m) which was nearly twenty miles wide.

Deatrick and his crewmates from *The Tender Trap* knew that they needed full flaps to stop a Stratofortress on Eniwetok's short runway, which was a mere 6500 ft (2012 m) in length. If anything abnormal happened during a flight, the pilots were afraid to put the flaps down, however. If the flaps jammed, the men would be committed to Eniwetok and unable to divert elsewhere in the vast Pacific.

Flying five miles from an aquatic Ground Zero when the *Dakota* shot went off, a B-47E (apparently not Sumner's) suffered overpressure damage to its bomb bay doors and forward landing gear doors and thermal damage to its control surfaces. Aboard *The Tender Trap*, bomb bay doors, flaps, landing gear, brakes and braking chute were damaged by thermal effects and over-

pressure. Anderson, Deatrick and the rest of the B-52's crew were diverted to Hickam Air Force Base in Hawaii, where they landed without brakes or braking chute.

The evidence was in. There were more shots to come in the *Redwing* series, with appellations like *Navajo*, *Mohawk* and *Tewa*, but now it was known that a B-52 bomber could be five miles from a nuclear detonation and could be damaged. It was luck that the damage was not more severe (or fatal), and that a divert location at Hickam lay within reach. But the evidence was compelling – if airmen were to fight in a nuclear war, they had to expect conditions which were different not merely in degree but in kind. Maybe a SAC B-52 would drop one or more weapons on Moscow some day but it was not going to be possible for a B-52, or any other aircraft, to fly in "business as usual" fashion in the midst of Armageddon.

It's important to emphasise that the *Redwing* test series *did* prove that a hydrogen bomb could be dropped from a B-52. Effects tests carried out by aircraft like *The Tender Trap* and *Bubba Boy*, although not without mishap, proved that other aircraft could operate in the region. The effects tests also provided a wealth of information on how to equip future aircraft for a nuclear environment – for example, with Plizit shrouds carried by SAC crews. However, loads on the B-52B during *Redwing* had been delivered with the tail of the bomber pointed toward the point of detonation. Experts wanted to expose a Stratofort to a nuclear blast from its front and side.

HARDTACK

Operation *Hardtack* was the next series of Pacific detonations, carried out at Eniwetok, Bikini and Johnston Island between 28 April and 18 August 1958. The Atomic Energy Commission (AEC) sought to evaluate 'clean' thermonuclear warheads which produced less harmful fallout than those tested previously. AEC planned to fire two of them at very high altitude, where they would be lofted by *Redstone* missiles, partly to test them as a defense against the intercontinental ballistic missile, which the US and the Soviet Union were now developing in earnest.

Plans called for an ambitious 25 'shots', which was eventually raised to 35, even though the risks of atmospheric testing were now understood and both Washington and Moscow were under pressure to accept a test moratorium or ban. Early plans for *Hardtack* included a drop by a B-52 Stratofortress of a 25,000-lb (11,340-kg) thermonuclear test article expected to yield 25 megatons, and to be the largest detonation ever made by the United States. This was changed and, in the end, *Hardtack* did not include airdrops. As a result, only one B-52 was on the scene.

In the earlier *Redwing* test series, weapons effects on aircraft had been carried out using a gaggle of fighters and bombers. In *Hardtack*, there was just one effects-test aircraft – the sole Stratofortress in attendance.

At Wright Field, experts felt they had enough data on all operational aircraft except the B-52. A new model of the Stratofortress, the B-52D, was chosen to be exposed to the blasts.

Hardtack began with the *Yucca* shot on 28 April 1958, a balloon-lofted hydrogen weapon detonated at 86,000 ft (26,625 m) near Runit, the tortured island near Eniwetok which was repeatedly scarred, blasted, and radiated by the bomb testers.

Capt Tom Sumner was aircraft commander of the B-52D (56-0591) nicknamed *Tommy's Tigator*. The appellation came from a joke about 'a very mean animal that was half tiger and half alligator', and the B-52D had a painting of a green tiger's head on its nose. Sumner and his crew picked up *Tommy's Tigator* at the Boeing Seattle plant, and underwent training sessions in the rainy American northwest. Sumner recalls that 'most of the time it was raining and we were supposed to not get the aeroplane wet because of the glue used to attach the strain gauges in place. We were not able to do this, and the jet got wet lots of times, but the strain gauges were unharmed by the moisture'.

Sumner and crew took the B-52D to Eniwetok. The decision had now been reached not to include a B-52 bomb drop in *Hardtack*, and Sumner's effects-test B-52D crew apparently flew in just nine of the series' of 35 ground-based detonations, not including one which was taken to 252,000 ft (78,080 m) by a *Redstone* launched from the eastern end of Johnston Island.

Included in the very experienced crew of *Tommy's Tigator* were co-pilot Charlie Harr, Lt George Lewis, lead bombardier (who had been the assistant on *Redwing*'s B-52B) Capt John Doyle, assistant bombardier Capt Bill Lounsberry, Lt Bob Mercer, the test engineer (Mercer had been a test engineer at *Redwing*), and finally civilian Ivan Clower, crew chief, who had performed the same function on Sumner's B-47E during *Redwing*.

At Eniwetok, on the island code-named *Fred* where the airfield was located, the runway had been lengthened to 8500 ft (2632 m), an increase of 2000 ft (619 m). Allowing some margin for error, it was determined that this was still not enough space to land a B-52 without full flaps. If any in-flight mishap created doubt as to whether flaps and parabrake would work properly, the B-52D crew would have to divert.

Capt Sumner recalls the *Hardtack* shots, with names like *Koa*, *Holly*, and *Yellowwood*, 'gave us excellent data at various angles, direct side load, at nine o'clock positions relative to the fuselage plus the ten and seven o'clock positions. We also repeated some tail-on loads to verify the data gathered during *Redwing*.

'We were the only weapons effects aircraft in the series so we had the sky to ourselves during the time up to and immediately after the shot. The usual photo, cloud sampler, weather, search and rescue aircraft, plus some SAC jets testing equipment, were also there as they had been on *Redwing*, but their airspace was not in our arena. They were all well out of the area we flew in. This was very different from *Redwing* when we had nine weapons effects aeroplanes clustered around Ground Zero at Time Zero.'

Sumner's most memorable experience came during the last shot in which his crew flew. The record is unclear as to which test in the *Hardtack* series this was; it may have been the *Juniper* shot at Bikini on 22 July 1958 which was detonated from a barge and sent up a cloud rising to 40,000 ft (12,384 m). As Sumner relates, the crew learned something fundamental about the Boeing B-52 Stratofortress.

'We were asked to perform one mission at low altitude. All others, including those in the previous *Redwing* series, had been done above 20,000 ft (6192 m). The flight profile called for flying at 500 ft (155 m) above the surface, which was the ocean, and at maximum air speed which at that time was 425 kts IAS (indicated air speed). We had very little time to plan and prepare for this shot. However, we did have enough time to make one practice flight which we thought ought to be enough. In fact, it was almost too much.

'This shot was made during daylight in the mid-afternoon, not in the early morning darkness. Daylight was welcome as flying around at limit speed only 500 ft (155 m) above the surface left little tolerance for error. This was before the era of low-level equipment, so eyeballs were the best thing going for us then. We flew a practice mission the day before the live shot with a simulated H-Hour of about 1400. Our flight time to H-Hour was about two-and-a-half hours. We had to do some calibration manoeuvres and then enter the race track pattern to pin down our arrival time at the desired location.

'The day of the practice flight the air was exceptionally turbulent and we bounced all around the pattern at 425 kts IAS giving the airframe a hell of a beating. We ran all of the instrumentation that measured anything and even though there was no heat or overpressure input from a bomb blast there was plenty of airframe loading due to the turbulence. After landing we discovered large pieces of skin missing from the upper surface of both the left and right horizontal stabilisers. Each section had lost pieces two by three feet in dimension – very sizeable portions.

'This caused concern. What had happened? A fast review of the data from the loads-measuring instrumentation was conducted to determine if any of the structural members had been overloaded. The analysis of the data, conducted in consultation with the structural engineers in Seattle and the Aircraft Laboratory at Wright-Patterson AFB by telephone via HF radio indicated the airframe had not been overloaded.

'The team of engineers with us was made up of many representatives from the Boeing Company, and they were all experienced analysts. We also had representatives from the Aircraft Laboratory who were engineers as well. The final analysis was that the damage we experienced on that practice flight was only of a superficial nature and the airframe had not been in danger. The recommendation and request to me was, "Fly the profile as planned". As it turned out this was the wrong recommendation, but this was not discovered for nearly a year.

'I flew the profile as planned, somewhat against my better judgment but not enough against it to stop me. My sheet metal maintenance men worked all night repairing the damage and the next day we were ready to go. That day was different, the air was smooth. The mission went as planned. The device gave a yield of about 10 MT (megatons). We experienced from the explosion the effects predicted and received no damage from turbulence. I thought I had done the correct thing. I was also wrong but did not yet know it.

'After this last shot we flew the B-52D, AF # 056-591, back to the Boeing factory in Seattle. The aeroplane was turned over to Boeing on a bailment contract to conduct a lengthy series of flight investigations at low altitudes and high speed. This particular jet was selected because of the elaborate loads-measuring instrumentation that had been installed for *Hardtack*.

'After several weeks of re-calibration and some repairs on the instrumentation system, Boeing began the flight tests. They made several flights at the limit speed of 425 kts IAS and at low altitudes, usually about 500 feet (155 m) above the ground. These flights continued until one day in June 1959 when on such a profile the aeroplane crashed near Burns, Oregon, in a forest. All crew members – Boeing personnel – were killed.

'An investigation, in which I participated, revealed both horizontal stabilisers had broken off and thus flight control was completely lost. Being at very low altitude the crew had no opportunity to eject.'

This is where Sumner, and the US Air Force, reached some fundamental conclusions about the B-52 bomber, which was rapidly entering service in SAC squadrons. The knowledge led to changes in training and tactics, and almost certainly prevented some deaths or injuries to the dedicated men of SAC who were waging the Cold War in the Stratofortress.

'A lengthy review of the data (on 56-0591, the late *Tommy's Tigator*) from all missions flown, including that obtained during *Hardtack*, revealed that the method of predicting structural failure had been in error. It had been believed the failure speed of the B-52 was much higher than 425 kts IAS, but the review indicated it was much closer to about 430, give or take a few kts depending on turbulence. The day we flew the practice mission on *Hardtack* was such a very turbulent day, and we had nearly lost the stabilisers on the flight, but had not realised it. After all this came out, the placard speed of the B-52 was lowered to about 350 knots IAS.'

The loss of a Boeing crew in a B-52D hung heavily on the minds of everyone associated with it. The fact that the Stratofort had previously been battered by nine nuclear and thermonuclear detonations makes the loss even more poignant. Tom Sumner is sombre as he thinks back to it:

'*Redwing* and *Hardtack* were very exciting tests in my career as a test pilot. I am very glad I was able to participate in them, in spite of the close calls we had. I do wish though, for the sake of the Boeing crew killed in the crash of the B-52D, that I had refused to fly that high-speed profile after incurring that skin damage on the practice mission. That was a definite sign that something was really wrong and I elected to ignore it and accepted the explanation that it had only been "superficial damage". I should have insisted on doing it at some lower speed and also insisted on a more thorough analysis before deciding what the placard speed should be. I had the authority as aircraft commander to do just that. No one forced me to make that flight. The decision was mine.'

The late 1950s was a time of enormous fear over the atomic weapons designed to be carried by the B-52. There was no thought that the Stratofort could have any other purpose, and even token tests with conventional bombs were discouraged. It was the era when the USSR's belligerent Premier Nikita Khrushchev banged his shoe on his desk at a United Nations meeting and threatened to explode a 100-megaton weapon.

The US Navy argued vociferously that the Soviet atomic threat could only be met with an enlarged fleet of aircraft carriers. Back in 1953-54 on the editorial pages of Washington's three newspapers, letters from naval officers demanding more carriers had been repeatedly refuted by letters from a teenager, Robert F Dorr, who argued that the planned purchase of 600 B-52s was insufficient.

By 1960, the Navy was arguing with much greater credibility that the Soviet Union could be deterred only with an undersea force of submarines armed with sea-launched ballistic missiles (SLBMs). Thus began the concept of the strategic triad – a three-pronged force of SLBMs, ICBMs and B-52s.

In 1958, a Washington analyst predicted that the Soviets would reach nuclear 'parity' with the United States within two years and that World War 3 would follow, probably in 1961. 'Parity' became a buzz word in the American capital. Debate raged as to whether the United States could reduce itself to being merely 'equal' in doing its part toward Mutually Assured Destruction or whether the US needed nuclear 'superiority'. The young letter-writer, now a USAF veteran, was still bombarding the capital's newspapers, arguing that the increased purchase of B-52s, now 744, still wasn't enough.

Even with the addition of the B-52, SAC's bomber force was dwindling. In the early to mid-1950s there had been as many as 2500 bombers, mostly B-47s now

BELOW Resplendent in dayglo trim, B-52D 56-0591 *Tommy's Tigator* heads a line-up of Boeing products that includes the very first KC-135A Stratotanker. This Stratofortress was destroyed near Burns, Oregon, not long after this photograph was taken *(Boeing)*

being retired. At the same time, Western intelligence overestimated the size and readiness of the Soviets' two principal nuclear strike forces – Long Range Aviation, which had the bombers, and the Strategic Rocket Force, which was beginning to field ballistic missiles.

It is difficult to believe today, but nuclear war was deemed almost inevitable. No one had any thought of using the B-52 in the brushfire wars flaring up around the world. When John F Kennedy replaced Eisenhower as president in 1961, he spoke of defending freedom around the globe ('freedom', in this context, embracing such libertarians as Nicaragua's Anastio Somoza, Formosa's Chiang Kai-shek and South Korea's Park Chung Hee!).

Americans believed they would soon be fighting in conventional wars: in 1961, it seemed certain US soldiers would soon be in combat in the Congo. Few paid any heed to another place no one could quite remember the name of – Vietnam. Kennedy spoke of fighting, if necessary, to free Cuba or the Congo, but believed that atomic war with the Soviets was the gravest danger he'd face during the two terms he expected to serve, 1961 to 1969.

It was taken for granted that some time soon B-52s and Soviet bombers might well obliterate Washington and Moscow – exactly what happened in the 1960 novel *Fail Safe* by Gene Burdick and William Lederer. That year, 16 Soviet Tu-16 bombers with atomic weapons on board took off from Andyr, flew hundreds of miles, and orbited for hours off the Soviet coast. Unlike the United States, the USSR did not then have the practice of flying airborne alert missions with 'nukes' on board.

Fortunately, the Tu-16s ended their unexplained and enigmatic mission, and instead of bombing the West, they turned for home. But what would happen the next day, or the day after?

Though the prospect of atomic war was immediate and real, Congress, press and public were losing their enthusiasm for setting off *Doomsday* weapons in the open atmosphere in the Pacific. Paramount in the public mind was fear of Strontium-90, one of many harmful by-products released into the air and said to cause bone cancer. From what we know today, the blasting of those Pacific atolls seems excessive. Even more frightening was a test series by the Soviet Union in which higher-yield, 'dirtier', hydrogen bombs were exploded in large numbers.

Without talking to each other about it, immediately after *Hardtack*, while continuing to manufacture bombs, bombers and missiles, the two superpowers began a moratorium on weapons testing. It was a kind of unspoken, unwritten agreement and it continued for 34 months.

DOMINIC

The B-52 Stratofortress' third and final series of Pacific nuclear tests was code-named Operation *Dominic*. These tests came after the 34-month moratorium was scuttled. Bomb detonations had resumed in the Soviet Union and (by the United States) in Nevada. Operation *Dominic* included 36 shots, an incredible 29 of them airdropped from B-52s. Some of the shots were to test effects, others to validate stockpiled weapons. The primary purpose of *Dominic* was to provide data for development, rather than information on blast effects.

One B-52 pilot who flew in *Dominic* was Capt Walter J Boyne of the 4925th Nuclear Test Group at Kirtland. Boyne had previously logged many hours in, and was fond of, the B-47. His first impressions of the B-52 were typical.

'When you took off, the wings flew before the fuselage, so the flight surfaces had to be used while the wheels were still on the ground. The crosswind landing gear took some getting used to. You could be looking out the side window while landing. The control surfaces were small so you used trim a lot and it had a stabiliser trim not found on the B-47. Visibility was better than the B-47. Side-by-side seating was a hell of a lot better.

'It gave you a very good ride at altitude. The wings flexed. Turbulence was readily dampened. But at low-level in the B-52 we were restricted to 300 kts IAS (for the reasons explained earlier by Capt Sumner). When you were at 300 ft (93 m), it was like being hammered. You'd really get thrown around in your harness. You'd get knocked around. The aeroplane responded to more than one gust variation at a time and hence was never in synch. If the B-47 was a truck, the B-52 was an 18-wheeler.

'Put it this way. The Buff (as the B-52 later became known) pounded along while the B-47 cleaved the air. The spoilers took some getting used to. It wasn't like having conventional aileron control.

'The B-52 was not difficult to land. You had a lot of

mass coming down out of the sky for a reunion with the ground. When you were lined up, you didn't have any trouble landing on the spot where you intended. You did *not* want to land nosewheel-first because the aircraft could porpoise; that could ruin your whole day, but it was almost impossible to do. Normally, the rear trucks landed first.'

In early days, anyone who wanted to be checked out in the B-52 had to go to the Boeing facility in Seattle. No longer. Capt Boyne followed the now-established procedure of going to the RTU (replacement training unit) at Castle AFB, California. He, like Deatrick before him, knew too well that B-52s had crashed before the alternators were moved back to the engine nacelles. Memories lingered of the loss of Pat Fleming.

While at Castle, Boyne observed a dramatic response to an aerial mishap: a B-52 came in to land with a right outrigger strut that wouldn't extend. The base commander scrambled into a Jeep, raced out to meet the bomber at the moment of touchdown, and drove along beneath the right wing, ready to prevent it from scraping the ground if necessary. The incident ended without serious damage.

TEST FLYING

At Kirtland, Boyne's recollection is that the 4925th Nuclear Test Group had two B-47s and two B-52s (a B-52A and a B-52C). The first of this Stratofort pair was almost certainly the familiar B-52B 52-0013.

'Everybody flew everything. We had short missions. We'd go out to the range for telemetry. We'd put down the gear and fly up and down mountains.' The New Mexico terrain around Albuquerque was almost free of other air traffic, a great place for a pilot to wring out an eight-engined bomber and test his skills. Capt Boyne liked this kind of experimental flying, which sometimes included deployments to Edwards AFB.

'We dropped missile-capsule "shapes". We probed high-altitude performance. We'd test the absolute ceiling of the aircraft; wearing pressure suits we'd go up with a light fuel load to 52,000 ft (16,100 m) and hang there until the fuel warning lights came on.' He remembers that 'this was the very best way to fly a B-52. Flying frontline within SAC was vastly different. It was onerous'.

The mesquite-strewn deserts in the south of New Mexico and the highlands in the north concealed New

Mexico's most remunerative industry – design of nuclear weapons and development of nuclear tactics for aerial warfare.

In the Pacific during *Dominic*, Capt Boyne discovered that 'being amid a vast armada of telemetry-equipped aircraft was like being the centre cog in a huge clock'. The bomb-drop missions were being flown from, and the detonations were visible from, Johnston Island.

The men from Albuquerque went to the Pacific to bring the atmospheric-testing era to an end. This time, they brought at least two B-52s, employed as drop aircraft, although the exact identities of the bombers is difficult to confirm. Because they were flying from Johnston rather than Eniwetok, security was tighter. Boyne recalls one occasion when he needed to land at Christmas Island, was denied permission, and diverted to Naval Air Station Barbers Point near Honolulu, where they were greeted with tremendous hospitality by Navy people.

The 29 airdrops of atomic and hydrogen bombs during *Dominic* were a kind of anticlimax. There were few serious problems, no major mishaps. Most of the *Dominic* blasts were of relatively low yield. The bombs were parachute-retarded (of various models), giving the B-52 crews time to clear the area. B-52 crews were impressed with the flash of a weapon, which could be brighter than daylight, and with its duration, which could be a minute or more. Of four participants who were interviewed many years later, all agreed that the world's politicians should be required to watch the terrible beauty of a nuclear blast before making any concrete decisions about how nuclear weapons might be used in a time of war.

The *Dominic* shots were the last tests conducted in open air by the United States before the 1963 atmospheric test treaty. Other nuclear tests continued underground in Nevada, and B-52s flew *Chromedome* aerial alert missions until 1968, when the atomic alert function was moved to runway's end.

More than three decades after the Pacific nuclear tests, the Berlin Wall, the Cold War and the Soviet Union have become history. In 1992, a B-52 visited Russia on a good-will visit. The American colonel who stepped out of the bomber was greeted with a handshake and grin by a Russian host, who praised the Stratofortress crew on its excellent navigation. 'No problem', the colonel shrugged. 'We've been practicing flying to your country for 30 years'.

TECHNICAL FEATURES

TODAY, THE B-52 looks positively antiquated when compared with later generations of US bomber aircraft such as the Rockwell B-1B Lancer and the Northrop B-2A, but it wasn't always thus. Indeed, when the Stratofortress first appeared in the early 1950s, it lay at the cutting edge of aeronautical progress in many respects, combining its fair share of innovative features in the areas of design and construction with technology that was well proven.

So, while much of the credit for Boeing's pioneering work in producing jet-powered aircraft deservedly belongs to the largely unheralded B-47 Stratojet, there's no doubt that the B-52 also made a major contribution to the family of commercial jetliners that includes the B.707, 737 and 747. Those hugely suc-

cessful airliners might well be almost entirely responsible for transforming the name of Boeing into one that is instantly recognisable around the world – but it was the bombers, and, in particular, the B-52, that made it all possible in the first place.

When it comes to considering the technical attributes of the B-52, the fuselage seems as good a place as any with which to start, although it should be kept in mind that the process of design evolution exerted no

BELOW Structural testing is an essential part of the process of bringing any aircraft into service these days, and the B-52 was no exception, with several representative airframes being tested to destruction throughout the 1950s and 60s *(Boeing)*

little influence on both the external appearance and the internal layout. Nowhere was this process more evident than in the cockpit accommodation, which changed from the tandem-seating arrangement utilised by the XB-52 and YB-52 to the more conventional configuration which made its debut on the B-52A and which was adopted as standard by all subsequent models.

This revision came about primarily as a result of Gen Curtis E LeMay's dislike of the original tandem layout as featured on the XB-52 mock-up. After examining that mock-up for himself, LeMay didn't disguise his lack of enthusiasm from Boeing, being particularly critical of the flight instrument panels and the division of duties between pilot and co-pilot. Two of his major concerns were that with only limited space available, the former inevitably had to make use of small and hard-to-read instruments, while the latter essentially relegated the co-pilot to the status of being little more than a flight engineer with a set of emergency flight controls.

In LeMay's view, that was always likely to compromise safety considerations and he argued forcefully for side-by-side seating. At a stroke, this would allow more room for instrument displays and at the same time permit a much greater degree of crew co-ordination between pilot and co-pilot. Eventually, after considering both options, the Air Staff backed LeMay and the now familiar cockpit layout was formally adopted in August 1951.

By then, of course, construction of the XB-52 and YB-52 was far advanced and nothing could be done to alter the prototypes. However, it isn't widely realised that the layout change was not originally destined to be introduced until after the first few production aircraft had been completed. In the end, aware that a delay in getting production underway was inevitable due to problems in securing necessary tooling, materials and other items, Boeing went to the Air Force with a recommendation that the altered cockpit be incorporated on production airframes from the outset – not surprisingly, the Air Force agreed.

Despite the fact that the B-52 is far from being a small aircraft, the cockpit accommodation is surprisingly cramped. Access to the pressurised cockpit is gained via a door located on the fuselage underside – on the tall-tailed models, this is offset to starboard and hinged at the rear; on B-52G/H models, it is situated on the centreline and hinged at the front. On all ver-

ABOVE In a scene reminiscent of the roll-out of the first prototype, a production B-52 Stratofortress emerges from the Seattle factory with its fin folded over so as to allow adequate clearance to extract it from the assembly hall *(Boeing)*

sions, the forward fuselage section embodies a twin-deck arrangement, with the pilot and co-pilot occupying the upper deck, while crew stations for the navigator and radar navigator are on the lower deck in an area that is irreverently referred to as either the 'black hole' or the 'hell hole'.

Accommodation for the remaining two crew members varies according to model. On the B-52A through B-52F versions, the Electronic Warfare Officer (EWO) sat alone in a tiny cubicle at the right-hand aft extremity of the upper deck, while the gunner had his own pressurised compartment just behind the base of the rudder. This had its own entry door in the starboard aft fuselage side below the horizontal tail surface. Although isolated from the rest of the crew, a crawl-way gave access to the weapons bay which was linked to the main crew compartment via a small access door in the aft cabin pressure bulkhead. This meant it was possible for the gunner to move forward and join the rest of the crew, although depressurisation was necessary in the event of him wishing to make use of this facility.

On the final two versions, as part of a weight-saving programme, the gunner's aft accommodation was deleted and he was positioned with the rest of the crew at the front of the aircraft, seated alongside the EWO at the rear of the upper deck.

Weber ejection seats were provided for five of the six crew members on the B-52A through B-52F and for all of them on both the B-52G and B-52H. Those occupied by pilot, co-pilot, EWO and gunner fired

ABOVE B-52E 56-0637 ready for flight at Boeing's Seattle plant. The 100 B-52Es were almost identical, except for internal systems, to the better-known B-52D model, but enjoyed a much shorter career (ending in 1970), and were used only for the strategic nuclear mission *(Boeing)*

upwards, with those of the two navigators firing downwards, a factor that may well have resulted in frequent reminders to the pilot to half-roll the aircraft in the event of an emergency on take-off or landing. When on board, supernumary crew members, such as instructor pilots and navigators, would evacuate the aircraft via the holes left after departure of the navigators' ejection seats. On the B-52F and earlier versions, the escape procedure for the gunner involved jettisoning the entire turret assembly, unfastening the safety belt and simply rolling out into space before deploying his parachute.

Before leaving the subject of crew accommodation, reference should also be made to the general purpose capsule that could be installed in the weapons bay of both the RB-52B and B-52C models. Irrespective of capsule configuration, this was a fully pressurised device with work stations for two operators. In the event of an emergency making a hasty departure necessary, both of the systems operators had downward-firing ejection seats.

Having alluded to the weapons bay, further discussion seems appropriate. Situated directly below the wing, it occupies almost the entire section of fuselage between the main undercarriage members and measures some 28 ft long and 6 ft wide, being enclosed by double-panel doors. Three interconnected and

hydraulically-actuated lower panels on each side make up the section of the bomb bay doors that can be opened in flight to release weapons. On the ground, loading and unloading of those weapons is facilitated by additional clearance obtained through swinging back the hinged upper panels.

In the early days, the only weapons carried would have been bombs and the large and unwieldy nuclear devices of the 1950s no doubt exerted influence on the generous physical characteristics of the bay. Later, there was good reason to be thankful for its capacious nature, for it proved capable of accepting a variety of missiles as well as newer thermonuclear bombs. More details of the various weapons combinations may be found elsewhere, but one specific modification does merit attention here.

This was the so-called *Big Belly* configuration which was introduced in the mid-1960s and which significantly enhanced the conventional warfare payload of the B-52D model. Almost all of the B-52Ds were eventually given the high-density capability, which resulted in the normal internal load of 27 bombs rising to no fewer than 84 Mk 82 500-lb or 42 M117 750-lb bombs. In conjunction with a further two dozen M117s carried underwing, this gave the modified B-52D a total payload of about 60,000 lbs. This was considerably in excess of the 38,250 lbs achieved by conventionally-armed B-52Fs and almost three times the payload of the B-52G, which wasn't configured to take conventional weapons externally until much later in its service life.

Apart from the weapons bay, the fuselage also contained the main landing gear, with the B-52 featuring

RIGHT Technicians watch anxiously as the two-man reconnaissance capsule is fitted into place in the weapons bay area of an RB-52B of the 93rd BW at Castle AFB. Identical capsules could also be installed in the succeeding B-52C derivative *(USAF)*

a distinctive quadricycle arrangement composed of four two-wheeled main units and two much smaller, single-wheeled, outrigger units positioned just inboard of the external fuel tanks. Initially, this unusual arrangement was given a high security classification and early photographs of the B-52 prototypes invariably had the undercarriage airbrushed out.

The retraction process involves fairly complex geometry, with the wheels swivelling through almost 90 degrees, before folding to lie flat within the stowage bays. Those units sited to port fold forwards for stowage, with the starboard units folding aft. Outriggers fold sideways and are housed within the wing itself. In theory, it is possible for the B-52 to land safely with only two of the four main units deployed – although, obviously, those two units must include one fore and one aft if an expensive scraping noise isn't to be the end result.

Another particularly interesting aspect of the undercarriage is the cross-wind steering facility which allows the main units to be offset by up to 20 degrees of the direction of flight. This facilitates take-off and landing in high cross-wind components by allowing the aircraft to point directly into wind while the wheels remain aligned with the runway. In addition, any one of the four main units can be lowered independently.

Space in the fuselage was also given over to the carriage of fuel, with the upper sections from directly behind the cockpit to just aft of the rear main undercarriage units being used for this purpose on all Stratofortress versions, although capacities varied. On the

B-52C to B-52F derivatives, fuselage fuel cells contained some 15,378 US gallons, while the internal wing tanks held a further 20,175 gallons and the jettisonable drop tanks 6000 gallons, giving a total capacity of 41,553 gallons.

On the B-52G and B-52H, which were fitted with a

BELOW Some idea of the nacelle size of the TF33-powered B-52H can be gleaned from this examination of groundcrew gathered around the bomber's engine intakes. Assistant crew chief, Airman First Class Dick LaFuze, is carrying out an inspection under the supervision of Senior Master Sergeant Dale VanCamp. Both men were maintenance personnel in the 319th Bomb Wing at Grand Forks on 18 June 1981 *(USAF)*

greatly revised wing making use of lighter materials and incorporating integral tanks as opposed to the bladder-type cells of earlier versions, fuel capacity was substantially improved. Fuselage tanks now accommodated 17,680 gallons and wing tanks 28,950 gallons. Finally, the much smaller, fixed, external wing tanks between them accounted for another 1400 gallons, raising the total capacity to a suitably impressive 48,030 gallons.

That was more than enough to bestow intercontinental range. However, since the Stratofortress has always been capable of being refuelled in flight, range limitation factors have more to do with crew fatigue and oil capacity than with stocks of JP4 fuel. As described elsewhere, missions lasting in excess of 24 hours have been commonplace events throughout the B-52's service career, but those are actually quite short when compared with the 1957 circumnavigation of the world by three B-52Bs of the 93rd Bomb Wing, since that epic transit involved an airborne time of over 45 hours. Clearly, recourse to air-to-air refuelling meant that nowhere on earth was out of reach, something that would almost certainly have caused consternation within the Kremlin.

Returning to the wing, although a change of materials occurred with the final two production models, the basic dimensions of span and area remained constant for all versions, at 185 ft and 4000 sq ft respectively. Compared with the B-47 wing, which spanned 116 ft and had an area of 1428 sq ft, the B-52 wing was

a massive structure and posed engineering problems of some complexity, in as much as it had to be relatively light and yet sufficiently robust to cope with flight loadings.

Boeing managed to reconcile these very different requirements and opted for a shoulder-mounted wing that was very slender at the extremities and yet sufficiently thick near the root to accommodate main undercarriage units. Such an arrangement was unnecessary for the B-52 but was adopted for the Boeing 367-80 which paved the way for the commercial 707 series and the KC-135 Stratotanker. The wing also featured 35 degrees of sweep and was set at an angle of incidence of six degrees. The latter aspect was an inevitable by-product of the choice of a tandem main undercarriage layout, which would not permit the new bomber to rotate on take-off. Instead, the B-52 has to be flown off the runway in a level attitude and often assumes a slightly 'nose low' appearance when climbing away.

The generous span of the wing was also directly responsible for another characteristic feature, namely wing-droop. This is always apparent when the aircraft is at rest on the ground, although the extent of the droop is conditional upon the amount of fuel carried. On lightly-laden machines, the outrigger wheels seldom touch the ground. On aircraft with full tanks, they always do, only rising clear of the surface as lifting force is generated during the take-off roll, when the wing flexes and moves upwards. This flexing is quite

LEFT A mechanic or a pilot breezing through a pre-flight check can stand almost upright beneath a B-52, whose forward main wheel trucks are shown to good advantage here. Crew chief, Senior Airman Jeffrey S Ryan, is inspecting the tyres of a B-52H belonging to the 319th Bomb Wing at Grand Forks AFB, North Dakota, on 18 June 1981. Grand Forks later became one of the USAF's four B-1B Lancer bases *(USAF)*

LEFT Boeing engineers are dwarfed by the imposing bulk of the underwing auxiliary fuel tank as they put the finishing touches to a brand-new aircraft at Seattle, while other members of the work force are busy in the vicinity of the weapons bay doors. Production at the home of Boeing terminated with the B-52F, leaving Wichita to be the sole source of the B-52G and H *(Boeing)*

ABOVE The quad 0.50 calibre M-3 machine gun installation at the rear extremity of a B-52D provided a modicum of defensive capability against rear-quarter attackers and was eventually to account for two MiG-21s during *Linebacker II (Boeing)*

normal and ground static testing demonstrated that the wing tip was capable of movement through a 32 ft arc without failing.

The wing also embodied moveable control surfaces and flaps, although the arrangement was modified during the production run. Ailerons and spoilers were fitted as standard on all models up to and including the B-52F, with the ailerons located between the inner and outer flap sections, while the seven-segment spoilers were sited slightly further outboard on the wing upper surface. On these versions, differential operation of the ailerons provided adequate roll control during normal flight regimes, but for landing, in-flight refuelling and combat situations, an additional measure of control could be had by resorting to the spoilers, which could also function as air brakes when operated symmetrically. This did away with the need for a deceleration parachute, such as used by the B-47 on final approach. However, on the B-52G/H, the ailerons were deleted, with roll control provided by differential actuation of the spoilers.

Turning to the Fowler-type flaps, all B-52 models were fitted with four segments (two per wing), offering a total flap area of 797 sq ft. When selected, these slide aft and extend down, but only two settings are avail-

LEFT The tail gun armament package, and associated radar, had still to be added by Boeing when these company technicians enlisted the aid of a large gantry device to perform some work on the tall fin of the seventh production RB-52B at Seattle (Boeing)

BELOW The first true B-52B was 53-0373 which featured an alternative tail gun armament package in the form of the MD-5 fire control system allied to a pair of M-24A-1 20 mm cannon. As it turned out, this system was not adopted as standard and was only fitted to 33 B/RB-52B aircraft (Boeing)

able – up or down, with the latter corresponding to 35 degrees of deflection.

Mention has already been made of external fuel tanks, but these were far from being the only items that dangled below the wing, since it also provided an anchor point for the powerplants. As with the B-47, these were suspended on pylons, with the pairs of podded engines slung beneath and ahead of the wing. Careful positioning helped to limit the drag rise at high speed and to alleviate load factors. In addition, the pylons doubled as wing fences and thus helped to delay the onset of the stall.

When it comes to considering the type of powerplant chosen to power the 'Buff', Pratt & Whitney's J57 merits description as being the standard engine, in so far as variants of this noisy and smoky 'stovepipe' turbojet were fitted to both prototypes and seven of the eight production sub-types. However, development of the J57 closely paralleled that of the Stratofortress itself and significant increases were made in terms of thrust which rose from a meagre 8700 lbs on the YB-52 to 13,750 lbs on the B-52F/G.

Even more impressive gains accrued from Pratt & Whitney's TF33 turbofan adaptation of the J57. First evaluated on the fourth production B-52G (57-6471) during 1960, this was subsequently fitted to the final production model, namely the B-52H. Benefits were immediately apparent across the board, for the TF33 was significantly more powerful, while simultaneously being a lot quieter and a heck of a lot cleaner. That essentially translated into a 30 per cent increase in thrust, which rose to 17,000 lbs, but that spectacular gain wasn't offset by a comparable reduction in range. Indeed, one of the real advantages of the TF33 was that it also offered a 13 per cent improvement in specific fuel consumption.

Items of armament such as missiles and bombs were also destined to be carried underwing by almost all versions of the Stratofortress family at some time or another. The actual weapons are discussed in greater detail elsewhere, but brief mention should be made of facilities that existed for the carriage of external stores. These were limited, to say the least, with the first such application involving the provision of pylons, inboard of the inner pair of engines, for the AGM-28 Hound

ABOVE Although the identity of this aircraft is clearly not in doubt, B-52A 52-0001 is unusual in featuring the shortened tail surfaces that were such a characteristic feature of the ultimate B-52G and B-52H models. Testing of the cut-down fin is known to have been conducted with this aircraft, but close study of the tail poses a mystery in that the number 923X (final digit not visible) can be faintly discerned. This seems to confirm that the fin had once been installed on one of the original prototypes, before being drastically cut down in size and fitted to 52-0001 for test purposes *(Boeing)*

Dog nuclear tipped missile. All versions from the B-52D onwards are known to have carried the AGM-28, and the B-52C also had this capability. Later, of course, the external stations were adapted for the carriage of conventional munitions.

Two other external hardpoints were incorporated on the B-52G and B-52H versions, but these had defensive rather than offensive applications in so far as they were used to carry AN/ALE-25 chaff dispenser pods. Positioned at about the mid-span point between the pairs of engines, each pod was about 13 ft long, weighed 1100 lbs and contained 20 Tracor AN/ADR-8 2.5 in folding-fin chaff rockets which could be fired manually or automatically by the AN/ASG-21 fire-control system. Installed from the outset on the final 18 B-52Hs, the AN/ALE-25 system was retrofitted to earlier aircraft but was eventually retired from use at the start of the 1970s when the more sophisticated Phase VI suite of electronic countermeasures equipment began to be installed on the B-52G/H.

Moving to the rear of the B-52, the vertical tail came in for quite noticeable redesign, this being one of the main recognition features between early and late production versions. On models up to and including the B-52F, the fin tip was an impressive 48 ft 3 in above ground. Then, as part of the weight saving programme implemented for the B-52G, the vertical tail was reduced in size, with the tip henceforth being just 40 ft 7 in above ground. Although Boeing engineers were confident that the new arrangement would provide adequate directional stability, it was nevertheless subjected to evaluation on the first B-52A during the latter part of the 1950s. Subsequently, it was also adopted as standard by the B-52H model.

Regardless of model, the entire fin assembly is hinged at the base and can be folded sideways so as to allow the aircraft to fit into low hangar accommodation. In addition, the rear of the fin incorporates a near full-length rudder of quite narrow chord.

The horizontal tail surfaces have a span of some 52 ft and an area of 900 sq ft and represented a fairly radical feature of the B-52 from the outset, for these were of the fully-variable type, pivoting through an arc of 13 degrees (+9/-4) measured at the leading edge. This arrangement has, in fact, caused problems on occasions, for the small elevators that are provided lack enough control authority to overcome the stabilisers. In view of that, great care must be taken to ensure that the stabilisers are properly set – at least two B-52s are known to have been destroyed in take-off accidents due to incorrect stabiliser positioning, and an ensuing loss of control.

Lastly, the aft fuselage section also serves as the location for the 44 ft diameter braking parachute that is invariably deployed on landing. On the tall-tailed models (B-52A to B-52F), the presence of the gunner's cockpit meant that the parachute had to be stowed beneath the fuselage – on the B-52G and B-52H, however, it was repositioned to a new location directly aft of the vertical tail.

VARIATIONS ON A THEME – THE 'BUFF' FROM A TO H

When it comes to examining the production history of the Stratofortress, a succession of improvements and refinements to the design resulted in eight basic variants and one sub-variant appearing before manufacture finally terminated in the autumn of 1962. By then, exactly 742 production-configured examples had been completed by the two assembly lines and, not surprisingly, every succeeding model introduced new features of one kind or another. Some of them stemmed from lessons learnt during the development and manufacturing process. Some came about as a result of improvements to essential component parts, such as the engines and avionics. And some were prompted by the availability of new weapons like the North American Hound Dog missile.

In attempting to recount the production saga, it is perhaps simplest to consider the different models individually, in the order in which they appeared and paying particularly close attention to the key variations that existed. Before turning to that, though, it is worth emphasising that the production quantities mentioned here relate to the aircraft as they were built and that this did not always correspond to original planning. By way of illustration, one need look no further than the initial production version – at one time, it was expected that 13 B-52As would be completed, but amendments to the contract eventually resulted in 10 of these aircraft emerging from the Seattle assembly hall as RB-52Bs. Similarly, a late 1956 increase in the size of the SAC force anticipated that the batch of B-52Gs purchased with Fiscal Year 1957 funding would be built as B-52Es. No account is taken of such changes in the following text.

B-52A

Rolled-out at Seattle on 18 March 1954 amidst a certain amount of fanfare in the presence of the USAF Chief of Staff Gen Nathan F Twining, the first B-52A (serial number 52-0001) eventually made a successful maiden flight on 5 August 1954. Three examples of this derivative were completed and delivered to the USAF in the summer of 1954, whereupon they were immediately bailed back to Boeing and assigned to flight test duties.

While these three machines were considered as true

production specimens and while they did approximate much more closely to the definitive Stratofortress, they lacked certain vital items of equipment and never saw service with operational or training elements of the Strategic Air Command, although they were flown by SAC pilots assigned to the test force. In view of that, it is fair to describe them as equating to pre-production research, development, test and evaluation airframes.

When compared with the XB-52 and YB-52 prototypes, the most visible evidence of change related to the forward fuselage section. This had been extensively redesigned, with the result that the original rather grotesque bubble canopy and tandem seating arrangement for pilot and co-pilot had been abandoned. As has been described, Curtis E LeMay was largely responsible for this alteration, voicing his disapproval and indicating a preference for side-by-side seating. His was probably not the only dissenting voice, but it may have been the most influential.

Boeing duly redesigned the forward compartment, which was actually extended by some 21 inches so as to accommodate additional equipment and an extra crew member. Henceforth, the Stratofortress crew would total six – pilot, co-pilot, navigator, radar navigator, electronic warfare officer and tail gunner – with the latter isolated from his colleagues by virtually the entire length of the fuselage. The process of redesign resulted in the Stratofortress taking on a rather more conventional and much more aesthetically pleasing appearance.

Another change made to the B-52A related to the powerplants, with the Pratt & Whitney J57-P-1W being fitted as standard. This version was already more powerful than that fitted to the pair of prototypes, but further benefits accrued from the fact that it was also configured for water-injection, a process that allowed significantly increased thrust levels to be achieved. When operating 'dry', output was some 10,000 lb st, whereas the 'wet' rating was 11,000 lb st. The latter could, however, only be sustained for a limited duration, but the extra 'kick' came in useful, particularly in hot weather when anything that would help get a heavily-laden B-52 off the ground and into the air was welcome.

Provision of the water for injection was accompanied by a slight penalty in terms of fuel and the capacity of the B-52A was less than that of the prototypes. To some extent, this was offset by fitment of 1000-gallon auxiliary tanks outboard of the outrigger wheels, although it should be noted that these could also be installed on both prototypes and, in fact, the B-52As seem to have dispensed with them more often than not. Where the B-52A did possess an advantage was in being fitted with an in-flight refuelling receptacle. This

BELOW Photographic reference markings similar to those applied to the pair of Stratofortress prototypes are visible on the upper fuselage of the first B-52A. This machine actually ended its days as a ground instruction aid at Chanute AFB, Illinois *(Boeing)*

was, of course, a standard feature of all succeeding Stratofortresses.

The B-52A was also the first model to possess armament, being fitted with four M-3 0.50 calibre machine guns (each with a magazine containing 600 rounds of ammunition) in a tail barbette. Equipment associated with the defensive armament consisted of an A-3A Fire Control System (FCS), which embodied search and tracking radar antennae and which could automatically aim and fire the battery of guns. In addition, the tail gunner was also able to utilise a periscopic gun sight for manual operation. However, no bombing/navigation system was installed and other mission-specific items of avionics were also omitted from the three aircraft, since they were primarily concerned with exploration of the flight envelope and performance.

By 1960, with that work complete, two of the trio were assigned to other tasks. One (52-0003) was modified to NB-52A standard and used as a 'mother ship' for the rocket-powered X-15 research project until shortly before the end of the decade. Another (52-0001) was flown to Chanute AFB, Illinois and permanently grounded as a teaching aid with the Technical Training Center, while the remaining example (52-0002) was scrapped at Tinker AFB, Oklahoma in 1961.

B-52B/RB-52B

This was the first production version of the Stratofortress to enter service with Strategic Air Command. That important milestone was passed with the delivery of an RB-52B to the 93rd Bomb Wing at Castle AFB, California, in late June 1955, barely six months after the maiden flight which took place from Seattle on 25 January 1955. A total of 50 aircraft was eventually completed, with 23 emerging from the Seattle line as pure bomber B-52Bs and the remaining 27 as dual-capable reconnaissance/bomber RB-52Bs.

Operating weights, fuel capacity and unrefuelled combat radius of both the B-52B and RB-52B were identical to the B-52A. So, at the outset, was the engine, with about half the B-52Bs and RB-52Bs being delivered with J57-P-1W turbojets, while efforts were made to improve the reliability of the water injection system. This was expected to lead to the J57-P-9W, which embodied titanium compressor blades and which would have been somewhat lighter.

Unfortunately, defects in the manufacturing process posed severe problems and forced a return to steel components on the J57-P-29W and J57-P-29WA. These engine variants were installed on the bulk of the remaining aircraft before difficulties encountered with the titanium components were overcome in the summer of 1956, in time to allow yet another version of the engine (the J57-P-19W, which did make use of titanium) to be fitted to the final five aircraft. Despite the differences in designation, thrust ratings for the '19W, '29W and '29WA engines were identical, at 10,500 lb st 'dry' and 12,100 lb st 'wet'.

Difficulties were also being experienced with the bombing and navigation and fire control systems. In the case of the former, it had been hoped that a package of equipment known as the MA-2 would be available but shortcomings encountered in development proved particularly hard to fix and SAC was quite adamant that it had no use for an unproven system. In the end, it was decided to equip some early production aircraft with the K-3A as used by the B-36. Even though this was far from ideal, it was better than nothing, or, at least, it was when operating at altitudes below about 35,000 ft.

Unfortunately, the B-52 was expected and designed to spend most of its time at altitudes well in excess of that – and at heights of around 45,000 ft, the K-3A was revealed to be almost totally ineffective. Poor resolution qualities and a loss of definition made it more or less impossible to identify targets with any degree of certainty. A temporary 'fix' developed by Philco increased power output by a factor of about half and this undoubtedly helped to alleviate the worst of the problems, but it wasn't much of a solution and things didn't really improve until the MA-6A system (itself fundamentally just an updated K-3A) was adopted during production of the B-model.

At the same time, efforts were being made to rectify shortcomings experienced with the FCS that was associated with the tail-mounted defensive armament. This led to two different units being installed in the B-52B and RB-52B models. Nine of the first 10 RB-52Bs (52-0004/0008 and 52-0010/0013) retained the original A-3A set as used by the B-52A in concert with the quartet of 0.50 calibre machine guns. However, one early RB-52B (52-0009) was fitted with the alternative MD-5 Fire Control System (FCS), which incorporated rather different armament in the form of a pair of M-24A-1 20 mm cannon.

The MD-5 FCS and twin-cannon installation was also adopted as standard equipment on the remaining 17 RB-52Bs and 16 B-52Bs (52-8710/8716 and 53-0366/0391). However, this eventually proved to offer no real improvement by virtue of possessing more than its fair share of defects. In consequence, the last seven B-52Bs (53-0392/0398) reverted to the original armament package of four machine guns in conjunction with a version of the A-3A FCS that had supposedly been 'perfected'. In reality, those claims proved to be much too optimistic.

Other problems stemmed from the earlier debate about the precise nature of the mission to be undertaken by the Stratofortress, a debate that had culminated in the Air Staff's October 1951 directive that the mission should primarily be one of reconnaissance, with a secondary capability as a bomber. That decision was not destined to be overturned for some time, with the result that the first two major Stratofortress production models were both configured for the reconnaissance role.

However, at the start of January 1955, just two weeks before the maiden flight of the initial B-series aircraft, the Air Force performed a dramatic about-turn when it decided that in future, the Stratofortress was to be first and foremost a bomber with a secondary reconnaissance capability. At this point, one might be excused for interjecting that the left hand didn't seem to have too much idea of what the right hand was doing, and it is interesting to note that little more than half of the 50 B-model aircraft were configured for the reconnaissance task, whereas all of the B-52Cs could perform this mission.

When employed for reconnaissance, the RB-52B crew was augmented by two mission specialists occupying a pressurised capsule inserted in the weapons bay area. In fact, reconfiguring the aircraft was a quite straightforward process and could usually be accom-

BELOW Small outboard wing tanks and a tall tail help confirm that the 'Buff' shown here flying above a snowy landscape is a B-52B. This was the first version to achieve operational status, and was introduced to service by the 93rd BW in mid 1955 (Boeing)

plished in about four hours. Equipment could be optimised for different types of intelligence gathering and
included long-focal length and panoramic cameras
plus photoflash bombs for photographic reconnaissance; mapping radars, receivers, pulse analysers and
recorders for electronic reconnaissance; and other
equipment for weather reconnaissance along the flight
tracks most frequently used by SAC bombers.

Apart from a number of aircraft utilised for development and test taskings, virtually all of the B/RB-
52Bs were delivered to the 93rd Bomb Wing at Castle
AFB. Some remained with that unit on training duties
until well into the 1960s, but the implementation of
dispersal resulted in a proportion of the fleet being
redistributed to other units at Biggs AFB, Texas (the
95th BW) and March AFB, California (the 22nd BW).
Retirement was accomplished in 1965-66, apart from
one aircraft. Redesignated as an NB-52B, this
machine (52-0008) served alongside the sole NB-52A
as a 'mother-ship' for the X-15 and Lifting Body projects. It was later passed to NASA and is still active at
Edwards AFB, California, as an airborne launch platform.

B-52C

Built in fewer numbers than any of the other production versions that attained operational status with
SAC, the B-52C flew for the first time on 9 March
1956 and began to enter service with the 42nd Bomb
Wing at Loring AFB, Maine, just over three months

later, in mid-June. A total of 35 aircraft was eventually
completed during 1956. Like the RB-52Bs, they all
possessed dual bomber and reconnaissance capability
by virtue of being able to accommodate the capsule
system in the weapons bay area. Unlike the RB-52B,
however, this was not reflected by the aircraft's designation.

There were a number of major differences from the
previous model, although by no means all were obvious. However, there were two features which immediately set the B-52C apart when it first saw the light of
day on 7 December 1955. One was the adoption of
much larger auxiliary fuel tanks, with the 1000-gallon
type of the B-52A and B-52B being replaced by a truly
massive 3000-gallon type. The other, which was retrospectively applied to the B-model and adopted as standard by all subsequent versions of the Stratofortress,
was the external finish. Natural metal was still pre-
dominant, but the undersides of the fuselage and wings
were covered in gloss white anti-flash paint that was
intended to reflect thermal radiation resulting from a
nuclear detonation.

With extra fuel and now adorned with a coat of
paint, it should come as no surprise to learn that maximum take-off weight had risen quite substantially. In

BELOW The second major production model was the B-52C,
which introduced larger external fuel tanks and was also the
first to have white undersides. 53-0400 was the second B-
52C to be completed, and soon joined the 42nd BW at
Loring AFB, Maine, after this photograph was taken (Boeing)

ABOVE Bearing a suitable inscription, B-52D 55-0049 was
the first aircraft to be completed by the production source
established by Boeing in Kansas. It was also the first B-52D
to venture aloft, making a successful maiden flight from
Wichita on 14 May 1956 (Boeing)

fact, this was now 450,000 lbs, but there was no compensatory increase in available thrust, for the B-52C
retained the J57-P-19W or J57-P-29WA engines as
used by late production B-52Bs.

Changes to the avionics suite were far from extensive at this time, although the B-52C did undergo
updating of the bombing and navigation system at a
later date in its service career, acquiring the AN/ASQ-
48 package at the same time as this equipment was fitted across the B-52D fleet. Defensive armament was
also unchanged and comprised four 0.50 calibre
machine guns, while all but one B-52C relied on the
'improved' A-3A FCS as installed on the last seven B-
52Bs.

Operational experience soon showed that efforts to
address the failings of the A-3A FCS had not achieved
anything like the desired result and the generally poor
levels of reliability eventually culminated in a decision
to fit yet another type on the last B-52C (54-2688).
This was the MD-9 and it was similar in appearance to
the earlier package. However, the resemblance was
only skin deep, for it featured many improvements and
succeeded in at last giving the B-52 a trustworthy
defensive capability.

After several years of service with two squadrons of
the 99th Bomb Wing, in the latter half of the 1960s the
B-52C fleet was redistributed amongst a number of B-
52D units, with which they remained active until consigned to storage in 1971.

B-52D

This was the first of three Stratofortress variants to be
produced on two separate assembly lines and a total of
170 was completed in 1956-57, making it second only
to the B-52G in terms of quantity built. As the original
source, Seattle made the dominant contribution and
was responsible for 101 aircraft, while Wichita
weighed in with the remaining 69. It was, in fact, a
Wichita-built B-52D that made the initial flight on 14
May 1956, with the first Seattle example not getting
airborne until 28 September.

As originally produced, the B-52D was more or less
identical to the B-52C in terms of structure, equipment and appearance. However, by the time the B-
52D appeared, any lingering doubt over the precise
nature of the Stratofortress mission had been dispelled
and it was looked upon as a dedicated bomber from
the outset. It therefore lacked the reconnaissance
capability of its predecessors, with the only other
notable difference concerning adoption of the MD-9
FCS as fitted to the final B-52C.

Deliveries were very quick to get underway, with
the first examples starting to reach SAC in the autumn

ABOVE Seen on a murky day at Fairford, England, B-52D 56-0616 carries a 4128th SW badge, despite belonging to the 461st BW at Amarillo (Aviation Photo News)

of 1956 and some remained operational until well into the 1980s, outliving both the later B-52E and B-52F versions. In the meantime, as described more fully elsewhere, the B-52D had been extensively modified for conventional bombing duty, a task it retained until retirement in 1983. It should be noted that this change in emphasis was not accomplished at the expense of the nuclear role, for suitably armed B-52Ds continued to pull their fair share of alert duty until just before the last examples were withdrawn from service.

B-52E

With the B-52E, the second-source production centre at Wichita began to assume the leading role, accounting for 58 aircraft, while Seattle completed 42. The maiden flight of this version was made by a Seattle-built example on 3 October 1957, with the first deliveries to SAC taking place not long afterwards, during December 1957. Wichita's initial B-52E got airborne for the first time on 17 October 1957.

Externally identical to the B-52D, the B-52E did nonetheless differ in several important aspects, although these were by no means apparent to the casual observer. Such changes as were made related principally to the internal equipment fit and were prompted by SAC's acceptance that new tactics would henceforth have to be employed in the event of a thermonuclear exchange with the Soviet Union. A huge increase in the extent and capabilities of the Soviet air defence network effectively meant that bomber aircraft would be vulnerable to attack by fighters and/or missiles at high altitude.

Recognising that the days of high-level immunity

LEFT In its original guise, the lines of the Stratofortress were quite elegant, as exemplified by a pristine B-52E as it banks gently for the benefit of the cameraman during the course of a pre-delivery test flight (Boeing)

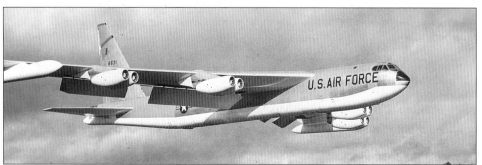

LEFT B-52E (56-631) in the standard markings in which 'Stratoforts' were being delivered in the late 1950s and early 1960s, hoisting itself skyward at Seattle (Boeing)

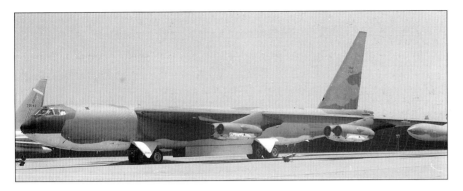

LEFT The USAF began experimenting with tactical camouflage in 1965 and tried numerous variations before settling on the T.O.1-1-4 scheme, named after a set of technical orders. This 93rd BW aircraft (57-0153) was one of about 30 B-52Fs that eventually donned camouflage battledress and was seen at Castle AFB in the summer of 1969. Note that the Stratofortress retains the familiar white thermal-reflecting paint on the undersides of the fuselage, wing, engine pods and fuel tanks *(Arnold Swanberg)*

ABOVE Another 93rd BW aircraft, B-52F 57-0039 accompanied a pair of B-52Hs to Marham, England, to take part in the 1967 RAF Bombing Competition *(Brian Service)*

were at an end, SAC had little option but to set about training its crews in the considerably more demanding and potentially more hazardous low-level penetration tactics. This, in turn, dictated the adoption of a more sophisticated suite of bombing and navigation avionics in the guise of the AN/ASQ-38 system, which was installed in the B-52E and all subsequent models.

In theory, this was a more reliable and accurate package. In reality, as is often the case, it wasn't quite as simple as that, for the new system revealed deficiencies in performance and also proved to be far from easy to maintain. These failings were, of course, eradicated in time, but incorporation of a number of modifications to the AN/ASQ-38 was a costly process and had to be implemented in the form of a special project that was given the code-name *Jolly Well*. By 1964, when this effort was finally completed, the resultant 'fixes' had been incorporated in several models (B-52E to B-52H) and affected no fewer than 480 aircraft.

Apart from a few time-expired examples that were withdrawn from use in 1967, the majority of the B-52Es were phased-out of SAC service and committed to long-term storage during 1969-70.

B-52F

Production at Seattle finally came to an end with the B-52F which flew for the first time on 6 May 1958, with the first example from Wichita following suit eight days later. In addition, it proved to be the last of the 'tall-tailed' variants, Seattle completing 44 examples while Wichita contributed the remaining 45. All 89 aircraft were delivered to the USAF between June 1958 and February 1959.

The principal difference between the B-52F and the previous model concerned the engine installation, with the rather more powerful J57-P-43W, J57-P-43WA or J57-P-43WB being fitted as standard. Normal military rating was 11,200 lb st, but all three versions of the 'dash 43' were able to push out 13,750 lb st with the aid of water injection.

Another notable feature of the new engines was that these incorporated alternators to supply electrical power to the aircraft. These were attached to the left-hand example of each podded pair of engines and replaced the often troublesome air driven turbines and alternators situated in the fuselage of earlier versions. Fitment of the alternator necessitated some redesign of the engine cowling cover, which resulted in the appearance of a very noticeable bulge on the lower left-hand side. Small ram air intakes also appeared in

ABOVE Key recognition features of the hugely improved B-52G were the short fin and much smaller fixed external fuel tanks. The aircraft seen here (57-6468) was the first of 193 examples to be built for SAC by Boeing at Wichita between 1958 and 1961 *(Boeing)*

the lower lip of each intake, with these being intended to provide cooling air for engine oil and constant speed drive units.

Subsequent modifications gave the B-52F an increased conventional warfare payload capability and this model was in fact the first to undertake combat, when aircraft from the 7th and 320th Bomb Wings were sent to bomb targets in South Vietnam in June 1965. In the event, they were replaced by B-52Ds in the spring of 1966 and played no further part in the Vietnam War. Several time-expired examples were withdrawn from service in 1967-68, but the majority continued in operation until retired in fits and starts during 1969-73 and 1978.

B-52G

The penultimate version of the Stratofortress flew for the first time on 31 August 1958 and turned out to be far and away the most numerous member of the family, with 193 examples being completed by the Wichita factory between 1958 and 1961. When compared to previous models, the B-52G was also radically different, with considerable attention being devoted to reduction in structural weight. In view of that, it is something of a paradox to report that maximum take-

off weight actually rose, to an awesome 488,000 lbs. Much of the extra weight stemmed from a marked increase in fuel capacity, for the B-52G featured a 'wet wing' which resulted in it carrying 48,030 gallons, as opposed to the 41,553 gallons of the B-52F. Not surprisingly, this offered worthwhile increases in unrefuelled ferry range and combat radius.

The weight reduction was partly achieved by use of different materials in construction and partly by redesign, such as that which resulted in the vertical fin being much reduced in size. The latter was the most visible manifestation of change, but far from the only one. The familiar jettisonable 3000 gallon auxiliary fuel tanks provided further evidence, having given way to smaller, fixed 700-gallon tanks.

Other weight savings accrued from a decision to move the gunner from the extreme rear of the aircraft to a new position alongside the electronic warfare officer in the forward fuselage crew compartment. Henceforth, like his colleagues, the gunner would also have recourse to an ejection seat in the event of an emergency. At the same time, a new FCS was adopted in the form of the Avco-Crosley AN/ASG-15 set. Like earlier systems, this embodied different radar dishes for search and track functions, but it also included a TV camera although the latter was eventually replaced by ALQ-117 countermeasures gear. Even though the FCS was itself changed, the armament and ammunition capacity remained unaltered, but the chance was taken to move the stowage location for the 44-foot diameter braking parachute from below to above the extreme aft fuselage section.

Use of different materials such as aluminium alloy offered benefits in terms of reduced weight, but it later became evident that the degree of stress experienced by the redesigned wing structure of the B-52G (and, incidentally, of the B-52H as well) was considerably greater than that of earlier models in a comparable flight regime. This inevitably meant that fatigue very soon began to present serious problems.

Those problems were manifested in dramatic fashion by the loss of a 4241st Strategic Wing aircraft in January 1961 during the course of an airborne alert mission. The aircraft concerned (B-52G 58-0187) first developed a severe fuel leak at altitude, although it remained flyable throughout the emergency descent that followed – tragically, when almost within sight of home base, the act of selecting full flaps for landing placed still further stress on the already weakened wing and precipitated a catastrophic failure that culminated in the aircraft crashing to earth near Goldsboro, North Carolina.

At around this time, SAC placed a number of flight restrictions on the B-52G and B-52H models, pending incorporation of a satisfactory 'fix' that involved substituting a modified wing box fabricated from thicker aluminium as well as other measures intended to provide greater strength. Authorisation to proceed with what became known as Engineering Change Proposal 1050 was forthcoming in May 1961 and implementation was eventually accomplished on a fleet-wide basis at a cost of $139 million during 1962-64. In most cases, the aircraft were given modified wings as they fell due for routine IRAN (Inspect and Repair As Necessary) visits – however, the final 18 production examples of the B-52H were actually fitted with modified wings during construction at Wichita.

As well as improved range characteristics, the B-52G was also markedly superior to its predecessors in terms of offensive potential, for it was actually the first version of the Stratofortress to possess a stand-off capability. This came in the form of the North American GAM-77 (later AGM-28) Hound Dog, fundamentally an early form of cruise missile featuring a nuclear warhead. In fact, as built, the first batch of B-52Gs were unable to carry Hound Dog and it was only with effect from the 55th example (58-0159) that it became a regular addition to the Stratofortress arsenal. Post-production modification resulted in Hound Dog capability being added to the first 54 B-52Gs as well as to some earlier aircraft.

Another missile that was routinely carried by the B-52G was the GAM-72 (later AGM-20) Quail. This was a decoy device which produced an identical radar image to the Stratofortress, thus making life exceedingly difficult for defensive forces. Unlike Hound Dog, the Quail was housed internally, with four being the usual complement per aircraft, although by no means all B-52 Bomb Wings were compatible with Quail and/or Hound Dog.

Production examples of the B-52G began to enter service with SAC's 5th Bomb Wing at Travis AFB, California in February 1959 and by the time the last example was delivered in February 1961, sufficient aircraft had been received to equip a total of 11 squadrons. Apart from attrition, no aircraft were withdrawn until May 1989. Thereafter, disposition proceeded fitfully until it was eventually completed during May 1994 when the 93rd Bomb Wing despatched its very last example to storage at Davis-Monthan AFB, Arizona.

B-52H

Known colloquially as the 'Cadillac', this was the ultimate version of the Stratofortress in both a literal and metaphorical sense of the term. Making its maiden flight on 6 March 1961, a total of 102 examples had been delivered to SAC by 26 October 1962 when production terminated. Although it bore a distinct similarity to the previous model, with which it shared several features in common, the B-52H was markedly superior in a number of respects, not least of which was the powerplant installation.

Instead of the familiar J57 'stovepipe' turbojets which pumped out clouds of noxious black smoke while at the same time generating a fearsome din, the B-52H was rather more environmentally friendly as a result of the switch to the TF33-P-3 turbofan. This was significantly more powerful, being rated at 17,000 lb st, and bestowed worthwhile benefits in terms of field performance. At the same time, it was much cleaner and much, much quieter when operating at full throttle, an aspect that was obviously greeted with delight by those who happened to live within earshot of the half-a-dozen bases earmarked to operate the final variant of the Stratofortress family.

At the same time, it was also much more economical, which translated into a notable improvement in range – indeed, when configured for the basic mission

with a 10,000-lb bomb load, the combat radius of the B-52H was an impressive 4176 nautical miles as opposed to just 3550 nautical miles for the B-52G. Of course, with air refuelling, such considerations were generally academic, but SAC wasted little time in demonstrating the B-52H's long reach by staging operation *Persian Rug* at the beginning of 1962. On 10-11 January, an aircraft of the 4136th Strategic Wing from Minot AFB (60-0040) set a new 'distance in a straight line' world record by completing an unrefuelled 12,532.28-mile flight from Kadena, Okinawa, to Torrejon, Spain.

The revised engine arrangement was far from being the only change introduced on the B-52H. Closer study of the extreme tail section revealed that defensive armament was also very different, with the Emerson AN/ASG-21 system being installed as standard. Gone was the familiar quad 0.50-calibre nest of machine guns – in their place was a single General Electric M61 multi-barrelled Gatling-type 20 mm rotary cannon.

This had a maximum firing rate of 4000 rounds per minute and came with a magazine containing 1242 rounds of ammunition. Key elements are the dual radar sub-systems, each of which was capable of searching for and tracking targets – however, the fire control system can only track a single target at any given time. As with the B-52G, the gunner was positioned in the main crew compartment forward of the wing, occupying an upward-firing, aft-facing ejection seat alongside the electronic warfare officer.

The B-52H was initially expected to rely on four GAM-87 Skybolts as its main offensive weapon, but cancellation of this project resulted in it being given identical capability to the B-52G in the form of the AGM-28 Hound Dog and gravity thermonuclear

ABOVE There was no B-52H prototype in the truest sense of the word, but the Stratofortress illustrated here (57-6471) came close to meriting that description. It began life as a B-52G and was then fitted with TF33 turbofans to evaluate the engine installation earmarked for the B-52H, before reverting to basic B-52G configuration *(Boeing)*

bombs. Later, of course, it acquired newer weapons such as the AGM-69 Short-Range Attack Missile and AGM-86 Air Launched Cruise Missile.

Delivery of the B-52H to operational elements of SAC began on 9 May 1961 when the 379th Bomb Wing at Wurtsmith AFB, Michigan received its first aircraft. Production finally ended in the autumn of 1962 and the last 'Cadillac' was formally accepted by SAC's 4136th Strategic Wing at Minot AFB, North Dakota. Today, 32 years on, attrition has made few inroads into the size of the fleet and all but eight of the B-52Hs remain in service with elements of Air Combat Command and the Air Force Reserve.

MODS AND SODS - UPGRADING THE BEAST

As far as military aircraft are concerned, the process of modification may accurately be described as both a boon and a bane. In the former case, the benefits arising from efforts to enhance capability are obviously to be welcomed, but there is a down-side in as much as it is necessary to remove aircraft from the operational inventory specifically to accomplish the upgrade project, which can often be a lengthy procedure. And, of course, there is always the matter of cost, something that keenly exercises the minds of the accountants, as well as those that control the purse strings of the military budget.

In the case of the B-52, four decades of frontline service inevitably mean that it has been subjected to many improvement initiatives. Some were driven by the need to retain its combat capability in the face of developments elsewhere – some arose out of flaws in the basic design – and some had their origins in nothing more than the ageing process. Irrespective of the motives that prompted their implementation, they were nearly all costly exercises in terms of both time and money. However, with forty years of service under its belt, the Stratofortress has undergone more projects of this kind than most other aircraft and a full catalogue of these would merit a book in itself. In consequence, only the more ambitious, significant and intriguing ones are examined here, using the code names and/or project numbers that were assigned where these are known. Since some of these ran concurrently, details are presented in alphabetical rather than chronological order so as to facilitate reference.

ALCM INTEGRATION

While the AGM-69A SRAM and gravity nuclear weapons bestowed considerable firepower on the B-52, in the latter half of the 1970s SAC began to doubt its survivability as a manned penetrator in the face of the formidable Soviet defensive network. The Command therefore directed its attention to finding ways and means of ensuring the 'Buff' would remain a viable and effective weapon system. This eventually culminated in deployment of the ALCM (Air-Launched Cruise Missile) which gave genuine stand-off capability and which could also be employed in a 'shoot-and-penetrate' mode, with ALCM-armed aircraft expending missiles from a position of safety before pressing on into hostile territory to deliver gravity bombs.

Two contractors fought for the plum $1.34 billion ALCM contract, with Boeing's AGM-86B eventually emerging victorious in a competitive fly-off staged during 1979. Adaptation to carry this new weapon began in the early 1980s and the first unit to be declared operational with the AGM-86B was the B-52G equipped 416th Bomb Wing at Griffiss AFB, New York, in December 1982. Eventually, some 98 B-52Gs and 96 B-52Hs were adapted to carry ALCM, with the B-52Gs all featuring a distinctive leading-edge wing root fairing that allowed them to be identified as 'cruise missile carriers' by satellite as per the requirements of the SALT II (Strategic Arms Limitation Treaty) agreement.

The B-52Hs were already considered distinctive enough, by virtue of possessing turbofan engines rather than turbojets. B-52Gs that were given compatibility with the AGM-86B were able to carry 12 missiles underwing – B-52Hs were additionally able to accommodate eight more missiles internally, courtesy of the Common Strategic Rotary Launcher (CSRL) which was not fitted to the B-52G.

Paradoxically, while complying with some of the

LEFT Upgrading of the defensive avionics systems resulted in the final two production versions gaining an extra 40-inches in length in the form of an extended aft fuselage section. This was accomplished from the late 1970s on, and is readily apparent in this view of the back end of a B-52G following modification

ABOVE The first excrescences to mar the clean lines of the B-52's nose appeared between 1971 and 1976 when the EVS system was installed on all existing B-52G and B-52H aircraft at a cost of some $248.5 million. Later, more wart-like additions appeared *(Boeing)*

stipulations of the unratified SALT II agreement, the USA proceeded to break others, foremost of which was the deployment of more than 130 ALCM-armed bombers. Delivery of the 131st ALCM-capable aircraft (B-52H 60-0055, appropriately named *Salt Shaker*) occurred on 28 November 1986 and put the USA over the permitted 1320 strategic nuclear delivery systems. Despite that, ALCM integration continued until the USA was eventually able to field no fewer than 194 Stratofortresses with this weapon system. Later, as mentioned elsewhere, some ALCMs were adapted for conventional warfare missions and used to knock out key targets in the initial phases of the air war against Iraq.

BIG BELLY

Combat use in Vietnam was the motivating factor behind this modification which was aimed at vastly enhancing the conventional warfare capability of the B-52D model. The *Big Belly* project was begun during December 1965 and increased the internal bomb-carrying capacity from just 27 weapons to a maximum of 84 500-lb Mk 82s or 42 750-lb M117s. In addition, a further 24 bombs of either type could be carried on modified wing racks, giving a maximum payload of the order of 60,000 lbs. All of the surviving B-52Ds (approximately 150 aircraft) were subjected to this change and a number of them were further adapted to carry and deliver aerial mines in 1969-71.

BIG FOUR

Also referred to as 'Mod 1000', this arose out of a radical change in operating procedure that saw the Stratofortress move from high to low-level and got under way in earnest during 1959. All models apart from the B-52B were affected, although some aspects of *Big Four* were incorporated in the B-52H during the production process. At one time, it was to include fitment of the AN/ALQ-27 ECM system on no fewer than 572 'Buffs', but the high cost of this equipment (estimated at $1 billion) forced a change to a QRC (Quick Reaction Capability) package that was installed in new-build B-52Hs on the line at Wichita and retrospectively fitted to earlier versions.

Cost was a major stumbling block in carrying out the low-level modifications and forced the Air Staff to withhold funds for a while in the summer of 1960 after successive rises from $192 million to $241 million and on to $265 million between November 1959 and July 1960. In the event, despite assurances from the Oklahoma City Air Materiel Area (which was responsible for implementing *Big Four*) that the project could be completed within the $265 million ceiling, the bill finally came to just over $313 million.

Big Four was also plagued by a succession of technical difficulties, for the switch to low level operation was actually much more complex than had been anticipated. Part of the reason for that lay with the fact that several different models of aircraft were involved, each of which required a uniquely tailored suite of equipment. This included modifications to existing 'kit' such as the bomb/nav system and Doppler radar, as well as installation of terrain clearance radar and radar altimeters.

Furthermore, a considerable amount of structural strengthening was necessary to cope with the greater stresses to be found at low level and the aircraft also had to be adapted to carry and launch Hound Dog 'side-arms'. All of this added to the complexity, and the cost, but *Big Four* was concluded during 1963.

BLUE BAND

This was the first effort to eradicate the fuel leaks which affected early models of the Stratofortress, such as the B-52B, B-52C and B-52D. It was accomplished with great rapidity during September 1957 and basically involved the fitment of new CF-14 clamps in place of the Marman devices originally used on interconnecting fuel lines between the various fuel cells. Rather than ferry the aircraft to a single depot for attention, the job of installing the new clamps was accomplished at the B-52 bases.

As it transpired, *Blue Band* proved ineffective, with the aluminium clamps very quickly showing evidence of stress. Moreover, there was the possibility of failure after barely three months of service, with potentially disastrous consequences. As a result, another project known as *Hard Shell* (which see) was implemented in short order.

ECP1050

Specific to the B-52G and B-52H models, ECP1050 (Engineering Change Proposal) was a wing structure improvement project that was completed between February 1962 and September 1964 at a cost of $219 million. It arose in the wake of an earlier design change to the wing structure that rendered these versions of the 'Buff' more, rather than less, vulnerable to fatigue damage and stress-induced failure.

Indeed, a couple of instances of disastrous wing failure had forced SAC to implement flight restrictions pending a 'fix' that essentially entailed replacing the existing wing box beam with a new unit incorporating thicker aluminium as well as substituting stronger steel taper lock fasteners for the titanium ones used previously. Additional brackets and clamps were also used on wing skins along with extra panel stiffeners, while a new protective coating was used on the interior of the integral wing fuel tanks.

Rather than remove the aircraft from service, SAC instead opted to allow the modification work to be undertaken during routine IRAN depot visits, although the final 18 B-52Hs to be built received their new wings during the production process.

ECP2126

Also specific to the B-52G and B-52H, ECP2126 was the project that resulted in these two models being given AGM-69A SRAM (Short-Range Attack Missile) compatibility in the 1970s. This was a complex and costly effort ($400 million plus) and involved the addition of modified wing pylons and launch gear as well as weapons bay rotary launchers and associated avionics equipment.

Work began on 15 October 1971 when the first B-52G arrived at the Oklahoma City AMA – following adaptation, it was returned to the 42nd Bomb Wing at Loring AFB, Maine, in March 1972, and this outfit

BELOW This view of the nose of a B-52H reveals how its contours have been changed by EVS installation. This 'Buff' is participating in an exercise called *Glad Customer* in Darwin, Australia, in 1982. The groundcrewman is 'on the headset' talking to the two pilots and holds a device, essentially a pole with a spike at one end, that is used to pass them last-minute flight manifest documents through the open window on the left side *(USAF)*

became operational with SRAM during August of that year. The Oklahoma City AMA had sole responsibility for adapting B-52Gs while the San Antonio AMA looked after the B-52H.

Approximately 270 surviving B-52Gs and B-52Hs eventually received SRAM capability, with each being able to carry 12 of the missiles externally and eight more internally.

EVS MODIFICATION

More properly known as the AN/ASQ-151 Electro-Optical Viewing System, this useful system had its origins in the mid-1960s when Boeing's Chief of Flight Test Jack Funk arranged for a Sony TV camera to be installed on the fin of a B-52 during an unconnected test. Experience with this rather unsophisticated sensor showed promising results and these were very soon brought to the attention of the USAF representative, Col Rick Hudlow.

He in turn mentioned the idea to SAC and they responded by issuing a requirement in 1965 to examine the possibility of using visual sensors to improve damage assessment and strike capability as well as to augment existing terrain avoidance equipment. At that time, the intention was to limit this capability to just the final two models and that is what happened,

although it took five years of testing before a production contract was placed in 1970.

That contract paved the way for the modification of all surviving B-52Gs and B-52Hs (roughly 270 aircraft) between 1971 and 1976 at a cost of $248.5 million. As installed, the equipment is contained in prominent fairings beneath the nose section, rather than on the fin, as per the arrangement adopted by Funk. That to port contains a steerable Westinghouse AN/AVQ-22 low-light-level TV unit (LLL-TV) capable of operating by starlight, while the starboard element consists of a Hughes AN/AAQ-6 forward-looking infra-red (FLIR) sensor. Other associated equipment comprises a video distribution unit; a symbol signal generator; a servo control unit and display screens for the pilot, co-pilot and both navigators.

BELOW Close-up of a B-52H (60-0013) taken in the early 1980s provides excellent detail of bumps and bulges associated with the AN/ASQ-151 EVS (Electro-Optical Viewing System), conceived by Boeing's Jack Funk to give the B-52G/H low-level eyes in the night. The 'Buff's' two pilots have EVS displays which give them a picture of terrain-avoidance at work; the system relies on both television and forward-looking infrared, and tells the pilots their radar altitude, time to bomb drop, air speed and other key items of information (USAF)

Data that may be presented on these screens includes overlaid terrain avoidance profile trace in either TV or FLIR mode; alpha-numeric symbology which includes a height reading from the radar altimeter and time-to-go before weapons release, as well as indicated airspeed, heading error and bank steering, artificial horizon overlay and attitude and position of the sensor in use.

GIANT FISH

This unique adaptation of the B-52H provided it with the ability to undertake atmospheric sampling missions by using a special pod installed in the forward section of the capacious weapons bay. Controls associated with operation of the *Giant Fish* device are situated at the gunner's work station and the pod itself has five forward-facing scoops which permit it to capture particulate and radiation samples.

At least four B-52Hs have been utilised on *Giant Fish* missions, with 60-0024 and 60-0033 being the first to be adapted, although they were later replaced by 60-0051 and 60-0052. The latter two aircraft were both assigned to the 7th Bomb Wing at Carswell AFB, Texas, for some considerable time and are known to have conducted sampling missions in the immediate aftermath of the 1986 reactor explosion at Chernobyl. Following the cessation of B-52 operations by the 7th Bomb Wing, at least one of the pair (60-0052) joined the 92nd Bomb Wing at Fairchild AFB, Washington, although it has since moved again, being noted in use with the 5th Bomb Wing at Minot AFB, North Dakota, during 1994.

HARD SHELL

The failure of *Blue Band* (as previously mentioned) to overcome the fuel leak problems forced Boeing to take another look at this troublesome failing. The outcome was *Hard Shell*, which was a modification programme that involved replacement of CF-14 clamps by Boeing-developed CF-17 stainless steel strap clamps. The work was undertaken by Boeing and the Air Force and was completed in January 1958.

Within a very short time, however, it became evident that it had failed to solve the problem and fresh restrictions were soon placed on B-52 operations, pending the development of a definitive 'fix'. In the first instance, this resulted in a switch to modified CF-

17A couplings which used strengthened latch pins, but neither the company nor the customer appear to have had much faith in this solution – and it wasn't too long before a further attempt was made to resolve the leaks in a project known as *Quickclip*.

HI-STRESS

Involved fleet-wide structural fixes intended to alleviate fatigue arising from the switch from high altitude to low altitude. It was accomplished concurrently with *Big Four* but was an additional three-phase programme, with the first two phases completed in 1960-62 and the final phase by about 1964.

Phase One took place as aircraft neared 2000 flying hours and included strengthening of the fuselage bulkhead and aileron bay area plus reinforcement of boost pump panels and wing foot splice plates. Phase Two took place as aircraft neared 2500 flying hours and was more extensive, with areas that received attention including upper wing splices inboard of the inner engine pods; lower wing panels supporting inner and outer engine pods; upper wing surface fuel probe access doors and the lower portion of the fuselage bulkhead. In most cases, work was limited to reinforcement.

Phase Three was an IRAN (Inspect and Repair As Necessary) project that involved early model B-52s and was intended to deal with wing cracks. As with some other modification efforts, it was basically accomplished in the field, usually by the *Sky Speed* contractor maintenance teams that supported operations from each bomber base. For Phase Three, however, they were augmented by technicians from the Oklahoma City and San Antonio Air Materiel Areas, which specialised in B-52s.

HOT FAN

Although it offered considerable benefits, the Pratt & Whitney TF33 turbofan did not enjoy entirely trouble-free operation in the early years of service, with these difficulties evidently reaching a head during the closing months of 1961. Among the problems that made themselves manifest at that time were throttle 'creep', 'hang' or 'slow start', flame-outs, uneven throttle alignment, excessive oil consumption, turbine blade failure and inlet case cracks. *Hot Fan* was an initiative aimed at eradicating these shortcomings and, at a mere $15

LEFT A view of the 'front office' of a B-52H participating in the *Glad Customer* exercise in Darwin, Australia, in late 1982. Crew members in the B-52 wear the same equipment as those in fighters (except for G-suits): helmets, oxygen, flight suits, and survival packs. These views show the EVS television-style display, analog flight instruments and throttles for eight engines *(USAF)*

million, was clearly a relatively low-cost exercise.

It had two primary objectives, specifically to increase engine reliability and eliminate the possibility of failure before 600 hours of operation. This was to be achieved via a depot maintenance and overhaul programme to be undertaken by the Oklahoma City AMA. Work began in mid-1962, but was interrupted by the Cuban Missile Crisis when all B-52s were put on alert. A resumption came in January 1963 and by the time *Hot Fan* was completed in late 1964, some 894 engines had been dealt with.

JOLLY WELL

This concerned the replacement of major components of the AN/ASQ-38 bomb/nav system as fitted to the B-52E to H models. By the time *Jolly Well* was completed in 1964, a total of 480 aircraft had been modified, with this project encompassing some engineering changes to improve low level terrain avoidance as well as replacement of the terrain computer.

MADREC

This refers to Malfunction Detection and Recording, a modification that was accomplished across the entire B-52 fleet during the first half of the 1960s. It involved the installation of monitoring equipment in the bomb/nav and autopilot systems, so as to alert aircrews to actual and potential malfunctions.

It was also closely linked to the ambitious *Big Four* project, with MADREC equipment being used to check out the AGM-28 Hound Dog missiles.

The requirement for this capability was conceived during 1961, with the subsequent installation being a two-pronged effort as a direct result of different 'kit' being fitted to the various Stratofortress models. Phase One affected the B-52B, B-52C and B-52D and was completed by the summer of 1963. Phase Two concerned the B-52E and subsequent versions and was essentially all but complete in 1965.

OAS MODIFICATION

Yet another upgrade effort that applied only to the B-52G and B-52H, the AN/ASQ-176 Offensive Avionics System evolved out of the desire to replace the AN/ASQ-38 bomb/nav equipment initially fitted to these models. By the mid-1970s, this was evidently proving prone to malfunctions and the task of rectification was becoming increasingly difficult. As a result, the Air Force began casting around for a number of modifications to overcome these difficulties in 1975 and these eventually led to the OAS, which made extensive use of digital technology.

The OAS 'kit' was first tested in prototype form aboard a suitably adapted B-52G on 3 September 1980, with the process of weapons integration following from June 1981 when it was successfully used to launch an AGM-69A SRAM. At the heart of the system is the now almost obligatory Mil-Std-1553A digital data bus and the package includes new controls and displays as well as a new radar altimeter, an attitude heading reference system, an inertial navigation system, plus missile interface units and major modifications to the primary attack radar.

As well as being considerably more reliable than the AN/ASQ-38 it replaced, it was specially configured for low-level use and embodied hardening against electro-magnetic pulse effects.

Updating was accomplished during the first half of the 1980s, with the last of 168 B-52Gs and 96 B-52Hs emerging from this process by the end of 1986. Although it greatly enhanced the effectiveness of the 'Buff', it proved to be a hugely expensive project, costing somewhere in the region of $1.66 billion.

PACER PLANK

This involved a total of 80 B-52Ds and was undertaken as ECP1581 (Engineering Change Proposal) by Boe-

ing's factory at Wichita, Kansas. The main objective was to ensure that SAC retained the B-52D's impressive conventional warfare capability for the near to mid-term future and the work entailed redesign and replacement of the lower wing skin, using new alloys with greater resistance to fatigue.

In addition, *Pacer Plank* called for the wing centre panel to be redesigned and replaced; for new upper longerons to be incorporated; for some fuselage side skins to be replaced and for fitment of a new pressure bulkhead in the forward fuselage section. Authorisation to proceed with *Pacer Plank* was received in late 1972 and the work was completed in 1977 at a cost of some $219 million.

QUICKCLIP

Yet another modification aimed at eliminating the fuel leak problem, *Quickclip* affected the B-52B through B-52E versions as well as some B-52Fs and related to the installation of safety straps around the CF-17A clamps. It began in the summer of 1958 and was completed swiftly, being judged successful in as much as it prevented fuel from leaking in the event of clamp failure. Those B-52Fs that were delivered from Boeing's two production centres at Wichita and Seattle after *Quickclip* began were fitted with the safety straps during manufacture.

QUICK START

The desire to launch alert-dedicated bombers in the minimum time possible was at the heart of this modification programme, which received approval during 1974 and which added cartridge starters to each engine on the B-52G and H models by July 1976 at a cost of $35 million. *Quick Start* permitted instantaneous ignition of all eight engines and greatly reduced the amount of time needed before the aircraft could begin rolling towards the runway.

In fact, not every engine needed to be modified, for a similar exercise had been undertaken during 1963-64, which resulted in every 'Buff' being fitted with two of these devices. These reduced reaction time by some two minutes and also greatly facilitated the use of dispersed operating sites by eliminating the need for specialised ground support equipment. In SAC's eyes, however, that still wasn't enough and persistent lobbying eventually culminated in *Quick Start.*

RIVET ACE

Also known as the Phase VI ECM Defensive Avionics Systems (ECP2519), this project involved only the B-52G and H models and was launched in the early 1970s. Externally, the most visible evidence of change concerned the extreme aft fuselage section which was extended by some 40-inches in order to house extra equipment, but many other assorted protuberances were also added, giving the finished article more than its fair share of 'warts' when compared with the original fairly clean lines of both models. Initially projected to cost $362.5 million, the final bill came to a cool $1.5 billion.

The go-ahead decision was taken in December 1971, but it required several years development and testing before the final configuration was settled upon,

BELOW Over the years, various proposals have been put forth to 're-engine' operational B-52s with new powerplants. This 1975 concept based on the B-52H shows a four-engined Stratofortress, powered by what were then imaginary high-powered turbofan engines of the near future, and with four external fuel tanks. Although frontline 'Buffs' have benefitted from numerous other kinds of equipment upgrades, none ever had an engine change to enhance their operational capability *(USAF)*

followed by several years more to modify surviving aircraft. Even then, updating continued as Phase VI+ until at least the late 1980s.

Equipment installed as part of Phase VI consisted of an AN/ALR-20A countermeasures receiving set; AN/ALR-46(V) digital radar warning receiver set; AN/ALQ-117 active countermeasures set; AN/ALQ-122 false-target generator system or Smart Noise Operation Equipment; AN/ALT-28 noise jammers; AN/ALQ-153 tail warning radar set; AN/ALT-32H and AN/ALT-32L high and low-band jamming sets; AN/ALT-16A barrage-jamming system; 12 AN/ALE-20 flare dispensers (192 flares) and eight AN/ALE-24 chaff dispensers (1125 bundles).

Subsequent refinement of the above suite of equipment led to the Phase VI+, which entailed substitution of an AN/ALQ-172 countermeasures set in lieu of the AN/ALQ-117 unit. Evolved under the *Pave Mint* project, two different configurations exist, with the B-52G model utilising an AN/ALQ-172(V)1 unit in conjunction with antennae associated with the original AN/ALQ-117. This is reported to have become operational during September 1986, whereas the B-52H has the 'all-singing, all-dancing' AN/ALQ-172(V)2 system with an electronically steerable phased-array antennae farm. This was declared operational in mid-1988.

RIVET RAMBLER

An EW capability update that was specifically developed for the B-52D model, this was also known as the Phase V ECM fit. Installation occurred during 1967-69, with some (perhaps all) items of equipment apparently also being added to B-52Gs assigned to conventional warfare missions in South-East Asia.

As fitted to the B-52D, it comprised one AN/ALR-18 automated set-on receiving set; one AN/ALR-20 panoramic receiver set; one AN/APR-25 radar homing and warning system; four AN/ALT-6B or AN/ALT-22 continuous wave jamming transmitters; two AN/ALT-16 barrage-jamming systems; two AN/ALT-32H and one AN/ALT-32L high and low-band jamming sets; six AN/ALE-20 flare dispensers (96 flares) and eight AN/ALE-24 chaff dispensers (1125 bundles).

Some of the B-52Gs that were given this apparatus also had AN/ALE-25 forward-firing chaff dispenser rocket pods suspended on pylons between the engine pods and a number of Guam-based B-52Gs were observed with AN/ALQ-119(V) ECM pods in lieu of AN/ALE-25 during the *Linebacker* campaign of 1972.

SENIOR BOWL

This little publicised code name is understood to have related to a CIA-managed intelligence gathering operation that involved two specially adapted B-52Hs (possibly 60-0021 and 60-0036) during the latter half of the 1960s. Essentially, it concerned carriage and launch of the D-21 pilotless drone that was originally developed for use with the M-12 version of Lockheed's amazing A-12, the precursor to the SR-71.

Unfortunately, the loss of one of the M-12s with its observer on 31 July 1966 following a collision during the third launch attempt resulted in Lockheed's Kelly Johnson calling a halt to further development of the M-12/D-21 pairing and it was at this point that the B-52H was chosen to act as the 'mother-ship'.

Modification work on at least one of the Stratofortresses was apparently undertaken by the Oklahoma City Air Materiel Area at Tinker AFB in the spring of 1967. At around the same time, the 'Skunk Works' at Burbank was busy adapting the D-21 for carriage by the B-52 using pylons mounted in the same locations as those which normally held Hound Dog missiles. As a result, the 'Buff' was able to operate with

two of the drones. Following launch, a jettisonable booster rocket motor accelerated the D-21B drone until its integral ramjet could be started and it could sustain flight unassisted.

Turning to operational matters, published sources state that missions using the D-21B were mounted from Beale AFB, California, by a rather shadowy organisation known as the 4200th Test Wing. However, it appears possible that the parent was actually the 4200th Support Squadron which is known to have been resident at Beale between 2 April 1968 and 31 October 1971.

Regardless of the identity of the parent unit, the procedure employed evidently entailed departure from Beale under cover of darkness and a transit to Andersen AFB, Guam, from where the operational sorties were staged. In the event, it appears that less than five missions were accomplished during the period in question - and all of those are alleged to have involved illicit overflights of China. As for the nature of the intelligence being sought, nothing is known, but China's nuclear weapons development programme could well have been a likely target.

As already noted, the missions were reportedly under CIA control, although use of the word *Senior* in the code name appears to imply that this operation was run by USAF Headquarters from the Pentagon.

SOUTH BAY

This was the first project specifically aimed at increasing the conventional warfare capability of the Stratofortress and resulted in some 28 B-52Fs being adapted to carry up to 24 750lb M117 bombs externally, on modified wing racks. Air Staff approval was forthcoming during June 1964 and all 28 aircraft had been adapted by October of that year, with these being amongst the first 'Buffs' to see combat in Vietnam just a few months later.

SUN BATH

Fundamentally similar to *South Bay*, this project was accomplished during June and July 1965 and affected a total of 46 B-52Fs. Modifications were virtually identical to those of the *South Bay* bombers, although a shortage of equipment forced the Oklahoma City AMA to draw upon war reserve material and Tactical Air Command resources to satisfy the deadline set by

Defense Secretary Robert McNamara, at whose behest the project was implemented. Like the earlier B-52Fs, the *Sun Bath* aircraft were soon despatched to the war zone.

STRATEGIC RADAR MODIFICATION

The most recent upgrading of the Stratofortress radar came during 1985 when work began on modifying all surviving B-52Hs and some B-52Gs, with the ASQ-176 unit being removed and replaced by the Norden AN/APQ-156 Strategic Radar (or 'Strat Radar' as it is more familiarly known). The modification wasn't simply a case of ripping out one antenna and sticking in a new one, however, for it also encompassed the fitment of associated controls and displays, as well as a new antenna electronics unit and an improved radar processor.

Furthermore, new software was part of the package, which was intended to enhance targeting capability and simultaneously ease the workload on navigator/bombardiers aboard the 'Buff'. Almost inevitably, it was far from being an inexpensive undertaking, for the estimated cost of the revamp was around the $700 million mark.

SUNFLOWER

Accomplished by Boeing at Wichita between the summer of 1956 and December 1957, this involved bringing a total of seven B-52Bs to a configuration that closely approximated to the B-52C, a process that entailed the installation of about 150 kits. The aircraft involved were all early production examples that had been used for various aspects of development flight testing, but which were eventually destined to be refurbished and assigned to SAC on the completion of that effort.

BELOW One of the secrets of the Cold War was the D-21 reconnaissance drone, code-named *Tagboard*, developed for air launch from the Lockheed M-12 and B-52H. Under the *Senior Bowl* programme, this B-52H tested the drone, which had a range of 1200 miles (1930 km), and was later employed on fewer than half a dozen reconnaissance missions over mainland China. A fatal mishap involving the loss of an M-12, coupled with the absence of any pressing need for a drone launched from a jet (a C-130 could do the same job) spelled an early end to the D-21 programme *(USAF)*

BUILDING THE FORCE – INTRODUCING THE **B-52B/C/D** MODELS

AFTER MONTHS OF PLANNING and preparation, SAC formally accepted its initial example of the mighty Stratofortress at Boeing's Seattle factory on 29 June 1955 and promptly flew it away to its new home. At the controls for the ferry flight of RB-52B 52-8711 to Castle AFB, California, was the commanding officer of the unit that had been selected to be the first to receive SAC's latest bomber, namely Brig Gen William E Eubank, Jnr, of the 93rd Bomb Wing. It was, in anyone's book, a significant moment, but few of those who attended the ceremony at Seattle or who turned out to greet the new arrival at Castle can have contemplated the possibility that later versions of the B-52 would still be an important part of the USAF inventory some 40 years later – or that Boeing's creation would face the very real likelihood of remaining in operation until the next millenium.

Things like that just didn't happen. Or, at least, they didn't in the world of military aviation as it was in the 1950s, since technological strides were coming thick and fast, with the result that today's hottest hardware was quite likely to be superseded by something hotter next week – or next month – or next year. In the B-52, Boeing broke the mould and succeeded in creat-ing a machine that proved both durable and, perhaps more important, adaptable. In the beginning, it functioned solely as a vehicle to carry and drop gravity nuclear (and, if need arose, conventional) weapons from high altitude. Subsequently, it demonstrated the capability to operate at low altitude and to accommodate new weapons such as the AGM-28 and AGM-69 nuclear-tipped missiles. It is precisely that adaptability which has enabled it to remain an indispensable tool for such a long time.

In the summer of 1955, of course, the primary consideration was that of introducing the new type into service as smoothly and quickly as possible. It was a tall order by almost any yardstick you cared to name or imagine. The aircraft was an awfully complex one, by

BELOW RB-52B 52-8711 seen from the right following retirement to the SAC Museum at Offutt AFB. As compared with earlier views of this same airframe, the aircraft now carries the SAC *Milky Way* (the star-spangled nose band named for a candy bar), a bomb wing emblem and a non-standard white upper surface aimed at reducing the effect of heat on the flightdeck crew. The aircraft has a standard tail gun position (*via Robert F Dorr*)

ABOVE B-52B and RB-52B bombers (52-8716, foreground) of the 93rd Bomb Wing on the line at Castle AFB on 16 July 1956. It was routine practice in the late 1950s and early 1960s for some of these bombers to fly *Chromedome* air alert missions with hydrogen bombs on board. Others stood on runway alert with nuclear bombs loaded, ready to go at very short notice *(USAF)*

the standards that then prevailed. That complexity was matched by the infrastructure required to operate it effectively, since specialised support equipment had to be obtained. In addition, the B-52 was a real heavyweight, tipping the scales well in excess of 400,000 lbs, and that necessitated a massive construction effort which involved such work as the strengthening of hard-standings, taxiways and runways at most of the bases chosen to accommodate the new bomber.

It was in many ways a logistical nightmare and the situation wasn't exactly helped by the fact that SAC still had no clear idea just how many B-52s it would ultimately possess at the time the first example was delivered. In the summer of 1953, official Air Force endorsement had been given to a plan based on the procurement of 282 aircraft, which was deemed sufficient to equip a total of seven Bomb Wings. Allowing for extra resources to satisfy maintenance and servicing requirements, that would probably have resulted in each of those Wings possessing a Unit Establishment (UE) of about 30 aircraft, split evenly between three subordinate squadrons.

By 1955, however, the procurement target had risen to slightly in excess of 400 aircraft and SAC was pushing hard to increase that number still further, towards the 600 mark. In September of that year, following Air Force Council recommendations to acquire

at least 576 examples of the latest bomber, SAC drew up a much more ambitious plan for its deployment. This basically envisaged equipping a total of 11 Bomb Wings, each with a UE of 45 aircraft in three squadrons, and it was duly promulgated in the December 1956 defence budget, when the programme was formally set at 11 Wings and 603 aircraft.

As already noted, the first SAC unit to acquire the B-52 was the 93rd Bomb Wing at Castle. This had, in fact, undergone the fairly momentous transition from piston to jet power little more than a year before, when it traded the B-50 Superfortress for the B-47 Stratojet in the first half of 1954. In the event, the latter type remained on strength for barely a year, but played a vital role in allowing the Castle-based personnel to gain jet experience as a sort of 'stepping stone' to the rather more awe inspiring B-52.

For the remaining 10 Wings, the acquisition of new hardware was a considerably more ambitious undertaking, in that all were originally equipped with the Convair B-36. Initial planning evidently envisaged organisation along similar lines to those used when operating with the 'Aluminium Overcast' (as the B-36 was facetiously known). Each Wing would therefore possess a total of three tactical echelons (Bomb Squadrons), although it should be noted that the UE was increased by some 50 per cent, rising from 10 to 15 aircraft per squadron.

Thus, while a three-squadron B-36 Wing had 30 aircraft, transition to the B-52 would be accompanied by an increase in fleet size to no fewer than 45. In addition, it was intended to add a further five command support aircraft at a later date, this action being expected to raise nominal Wing strength to exactly 50. As it transpired, subsequent events had far-reaching

ABOVE Dating from about mid-1955, this previously unpublished portrait depicts RB-52B 52-8713 with wheels, flaps and spoilers extended. Note that the white undersides to reflect the heat of an atomic blast include the engine pods, pylons and wing tanks *(via Robert F Dorr)*

BELOW The colour scheme and markings applied to the B-52B seen here are virtually standard for the period from around 1956 through to the adoption of camouflage, although it has yet to acquire SAC's familiar star-spangled sash, as well as the SAC shield and a Bomb Wing badge. This jet (53-0394) was soon issued to the 95th BW's 334th BS at Biggs AFB, Texas, from where it was retired to the USAF Museum at Wright-Patterson AFB in 1966 *(via USAF)*

consequences for SAC's heavy bomber force and only a handful of units ever operated as fully-fledged three-squadron organisations following the process of conversion to the B-52.

All that lay in the future, however, and the most urgent task for the 93rd BW was that of getting 'up to speed' with the new bomber. In the first instance, that required the Wing's three tactical squadrons (the 328th, 329th and 330th BSs) to reach combat ready status and this was duly achieved on 12 March 1956, albeit with a UE of just 30 aircraft, made up of a mix of pure bomber B-52Bs and bomber/reconnaissance RB-52Bs. A couple of months later, an increase in establishment to the definitive quantity of 45 signalled

the loss of combat ready status and the Wing was not deemed operational again until June 1957, coincident with a change in primary mission.

Throughout the same interlude, another important element of the Wing was busy preparing the formal training syllabus, since the 93rd had already been selected to function as SAC's 'Stratofortress College', a mission it was to fulfil for almost 40 years. Initially, the instructional task was entrusted to the 4017th Combat Crew Training Squadron which formed on 8 January 1955, several months before the first 'Buff' reached Castle.

Subsequently, the training task became the overriding concern of the entire Wing, with the 4017th CCTS henceforth being responsible for dealing with administrative aspects and running the five-week ground instruction course, while the three tactical squadrons looked after airborne phases of the training programme. Broadly speaking, that required each 'student' crew to log somewhere in the region of 35 to 50 hours flying time during a four-week period.

Not everything went smoothly, but that's hardly surprising, given the nature and extent of the enterprise. Some of the difficulties that affected the programme – such as fuel leaks and defective water injection pumps – inevitably interrupted flight operations. Others, like shortages of key items of spares and ground equipment, had a similar impact, as indeed did delays in construction work at Castle.

An even more serious setback occurred on 16 February 1956 when the 93rd suffered its first attrition loss during the course of a routine training mission. Departure of B-52B 53-0384 from Castle occurred in the early morning and all proceeded pretty much as normal until about half-way through the mission, when it appears that the aircraft caught fire, with disastrous consequences for its crew. Within a very short time, the fire increased in severity and eventually resulted in a loss of control, at which point the stricken B-52 entered a terminal dive, breaking into several sections as it passed through about 10,000 ft. Of the eight individuals on board, only four were able to exit the doomed machine safely and use their parachutes before the wreckage fell to earth near the town of Tracy, California.

Subsequent investigations isolated an alternator as being the most likely culprit for the fire and subsequent destruction of the B-52. Action to rectify the fault was instigated more or less immediately, with the Air Force

placing a grounding order on 20 B-52Bs known to be fitted with similar alternators. At the same time, it moved to suspend further deliveries of new aircraft and these did not resume until the middle of May, once Boeing had professed itself happy that the fault was fixed. In that, it soon became clear that the manufacturer was overly optimistic, since the alternators continued to pose problems in both the B-52B and B-52C models until about the end of 1957.

Yet another unwelcome grounding order came into effect in July 1956, arising this time from faults with fuel and hydraulic systems. Of short duration only, it did nonetheless have a damaging effect on the training of personnel for SAC's next B-52 unit, specifically the 42nd Bomb Wing which was resident at Loring AFB, Maine – about as far away from Castle as it was possible to be and yet still remain within the confines of the Continental USA.

The 42nd was also the first of the former B-36 units to trade up to the Stratofortress, disposing of the B-36H by the start of 1956 and accepting its first B-52C on 16 June of that year. Like the RB-52B, this version was compatible with the reconnaissance-dedicated capsule system, but its maximum take-off weight was considerably greater, at 450,000 lbs compared to the 420,000 lbs of the B-52B series. In addition, the C-model was fitted with the more powerful J57-P-19W turbojets from the outset and it also introduced a couple of other notable new features. Most visible was the thermal-reflecting white underside paint scheme, which was standard on all succeeding versions and which was retrospectively applied to the B/RB-52B. Less obvious, but no less welcome for that, was the fact that fuel capacity was increased by virtue of fitment of larger auxiliary tanks, outboard of the outer pair of podded J57s.

Produced in fewer numbers than any of the other operational versions of the Stratofortress, only 35 B-52Cs were destined to be completed and all of these were accepted by the USAF during the course of 1956, with the majority handed over between June and December. Almost all of them initially found their way to the 42nd BW, although they were not destined to remain with that unit for long, being passed on to the 99th BW during 1957.

Thus far, all of the B-52s delivered to the USAF had come from Boeing's Seattle factory. However, with procurement set for a major increase, it had been decided in mid-1953 that a second factory was essen-

ABOVE AND LEFT RB-52B 52-8716 in flight near Mount Rainier in Washington state. This jet was the last of three 'Stratoforts' lost by the 93rd BW during the B-52's first year of service, crashing near Castle AFB soon after a night take-off on 30 November 1956 *(Boeing)*

tial to allow for greatly accelerated production rates. In consequence, the next three versions of the B-52 to be acquired by SAC originated from two widely separated locations. Seattle was one – Wichita, the other, with Boeing's Kansas-based operation having plenty of production capacity to spare now that the long-running B-47 Stratojet programme was winding down.

The change came into effect with the B-52D and it was actually a Wichita-built example (55-0049) that was first to fly (in May 1956), as well as first to be formally accepted by the Air Force (in June 1956). As for Seattle, this was still busy churning out the B-52C and some four months were to elapse before the initial B-52D from this source got airborne for its maiden flight, an event that took place in late September 1956.

Even though it lagged behind slightly, Seattle soon made up the leeway and eventually took responsibility for the lion's share of B-52D production. Perhaps the best evidence of the accelerated nature of the programme can be gleaned from the fact that all 170 aircraft were delivered to the USAF between June 1956 and November 1957.

As usual, a period of flight testing presaged entry into the SAC inventory and the command did not receive its first B-52D until the autumn of 1956. Initial deliveries were made to the 42nd BW at Loring, which was still busily acquiring B-52Cs – however, as already mentioned, the 42nd very quickly disposed of the 'C-model, with the three assigned Bomb Squadrons (69th, 70th and 75th BSs) all standardising on the B-52D during the course of 1957. Another early operator of this version was Castle's 93rd BW, which accepted its first examples in December 1957, although these were earmarked specifically for training duties.

The next unit to enter the transition process was the 99th BW, which ceased B-36 operations at Fairchild AFB, Washington, in the summer of 1956, thereafter moving a few thousand miles east to occupy new quarters at Westover AFB, Massachusetts, with effect from September 1956. Once there, it awaited the arrival of its first Stratofortress and this duly materialised in December 1956, almost certainly being a B-52C transferred from the 42nd BW. Within a very short period, the 99th was fully equipped and was noteworthy in possessing a mixed fleet of aircraft for the next few years, in as much as it operated the equivalent of two squadrons worth of B-52Cs plus one of B-52Ds.

Two more Wings were slated to convert from the B-36 to the B-52D during the course of 1957. Fairchild's 92nd BW led the way, picking up its first aircraft in March 1957 and it was followed in June by the 28th BW at Ellsworth AFB, South Dakota.

Both conformed to the now well-established pattern, in that they were three-squadron organisations with a UE of 45 aircraft. So, by the end of that year, SAC could claim solid progress in building its B-52 force.

In the first instance, it had taken delivery of close to 250 Stratofortresses. Secondly, it possessed five units that were fully-equipped with B/RB-52Bs, B-52Cs and B-52Ds, although it should be noted that only three of them were considered to be combat-ready. Finally, a further three units were well advanced with preparations to operate the Stratofortress – and one of them had already begun accepting the first few examples of the fourth sub-type to enter service with SAC, namely the B-52E which made a successful maiden flight in early October 1957.

No less important was the fact that the blueprint for the future had begun to be drawn up and this signposted an end for the so-called 'big Wings' and a shift towards smaller and less vulnerable concentrations of air power. In time, it would result in the Stratofortress operating from many more air bases than was at first anticipated, for 'dispersal' of the manned bomber force was at last on the verge of moving from theory to reality.

B-52 UNITS AS AT DECEMBER 1957

Number	Base	Squadrons	Model	UE
6th BW	Walker AFB, NM	24/39/40 BS	Getting B-52E	45
11th BW	Altus AFB, Ok	26/42 BS	To get B-52E	30
28th BW	Ellsworth AFB, SD	77/717/718 BS	B-52D	45
42nd BW	Loring AFB, Me	69/70/75 BS	B-52D	45
92nd BW	Fairchild AFB, Wa	325/326/327 BS	B-52D	45
93rd BW	Castle AFB, Ca	328/329/330 BS	B/RB-52B, B-52D	45
99th BW	Westover AFB, Ma	346/347/348 BS	B-52C, B-52D	45
4123rd SW	Carswell AFB, Tx	98 BS	To get B-52E	15

BELOW RB-52B 52-8716 may well have been one of the most photographed of all Stratofortresses, but as previously related it was also one of the earliest examples to be destroyed (Boeing)

EXPANDING THE FORCE

At the end of 1957, substantial progress had been made in deploying SAC's latest and most potent bomber. Deliveries of three versions of the Strato-fortress were already complete and a fourth, the B-52E, was beginning to appear in increasing numbers. In addition, the B-52F was expected to join the force during the coming year and contractual negotiations for the B-52G were making headway, with action in hand to complete the projected procurement of 603 aircraft at the start of the 1960s.

That figure was sufficient to equip 11 bomb wings, in accordance with SAC planning of the mid-fifties. However, as it transpired, the final distribution and shape of the B-52 force bore little resemblance to the command's original intent.

There were a couple of reasons for that. First and foremost, a programme of dispersal intervened. Sec-ondly, procurement of the B-52 was significantly increased, with follow-on contracts placed during the 1958-60 period causing the total buy to rise from 603 to 744. So, while the command eventually received sufficient aircraft to equip no fewer than 42 squadrons, not too many of these were destined to operate as part of a full-sized, three-squadron, Wing. Indeed, by the close of 1957, SAC had already established the first of a number of new organisations that would eventually acquire the B-52.

This was the 4123rd Strategic Wing (SW), which came into existence on 10 December 1957 at Carswell AFB, Texas. Its creation sign-posted the impending demise of the so-called 'big Wings' and it was joined by

another 13 SWs during 1958, with a further eight completing the roster during the course of 1959. In the event, by no means all of these were immediately equipped and it wasn't until the spring of 1962 that the last of the 22 'Strat Wings' organised specifically to facilitate B-52 dispersal began to accept its allotted complement of aircraft.

The logic that drove the desire for dispersal was impeccable in theory, although it is probably fair to observe that it was flawed in reality, hindsight reveal-ing that it was based upon an erroneous perception of Soviet capability, particularly in the missile sphere. Hindsight is, of course, an exact science, which is more than can be said of the intelligence estimates of the time. These repeatedly referred to a developing 'mis-sile gap', whereby Soviet strategic rocket forces would enjoy a quantitative advantage over their US counter-parts. As later events confirmed, that 'missile gap' was vastly exaggerated – but nobody knew that in 1957. More importantly, nobody was prepared to bet on it either, hence the decision to distribute the expanding B-52 force much more widely.

Although dispersal may have been undertaken somewhat earlier than was really necessary, the moti-vation for this action was undeniably valid and there can be no doubt that it would have become essential at some point. A more leisured approach might have made the task easier to accomplish and might also have resulted in a very different final picture – in 1957, though, the SAC commanders simply didn't feel that they had sufficient time to take time.

The primary objectives of dispersal were two-fold. In the first instance, it was apparent that concentrating 45 bombers (plus about 20 associated tankers) on a single base made it a fat target indeed and one that would be hugely vulnerable to a single well-aimed missile or bomb. Dispersing those 45 bombers into three equal-sized packages of 15 immediately meant that the Soviets would have to employ more weapons to achieve the same result (i.e. the destruction or immobilisation of 45 aircraft). Thus, at one stroke, it increased the difficulty of ensuring that first-strike objectives would be satisfied. At the same time, it put an increasing strain on the Soviet economy and it shouldn't be forgotten that the Cold War was as much an economic battle as anything else. In simple terms, more B-52 bases would result in more targets and more targets would require more missiles, raising the financial stakes considerably in the process.

One is, however, inclined to wonder how much, if any, consideration was given to the reverse of that argument, for each extra Soviet missile silo was an extra target that the US forces would have to hit in the event of nuclear war. Probably not too much, in view of the fact that the US nuclear arsenal mushroomed more than ten-fold in just seven years, rising from about 2250 weapons in 1955 to over 26,000 in 1962, before eventually peaking at around 32,000 in 1967.

Once on the treadmill of proliferation, it clearly wasn't easy to get off again. Paying for all this hardware must have been a heavy burden for the USA but the world's wealthiest nation state was better able than most to afford it. In the Soviet Union, however, the authorities were less able to simply throw money at the problems they faced until they went away – but they could always print some more.

Getting back to the reasons that prompted dispersal, it must be obvious to even the meanest intelligence that the decreased warning time arising from a missile attack will naturally result in reaction time being much reduced. Henceforth, the margin was only ever likely to be measured in minutes, rather than hours and this inevitably raised the unwelcome possibility of incoming warheads bursting overhead before all the bombers could get airborne, especially at some of the dual-Wing Stratojet bases which were home to as many as 90 B-47s and 40 KC-97 tankers.

With SAC in the process of introducing the one-third ground alert programme on a global basis during

LEFT Boeing test pilots Tex Johnston (left) and Art Curren (centre) join Lt Col Guy Townsend of the Air Force Flight Test Center in modelling the new T-1 high altitude pressure suit prior to getting airborne for another sortie during the course of the test programme. In time, with the switch to low level methods of operation, this complex and costly item of equipment fell into disuse, to the relief of all, but it was a necessary evil to be endured by SAC personnel in the early years of the B-52's long career (Boeing)

LEFT More conventional flying kit is worn by the co-pilot aboard this B-52G as he runs through pre-departure checks at one of SAC's many bomber bases in the early 1960s. Study of the instruments visible on the panel in front of him confirm that all eight engines are fired up, and this particular 'Buff' may shortly have got airborne, possibly for a routine training mission or perhaps to participate in the air alert programme that ran for more than a decade from the late 1950s onwards (USAF)

1957-58, it made sound sense to explore any option that held out the promise of ensuring that alert-dedicated aircraft would be able to launch in time. Breaking up the major concentrations of bombers was one such option and in the case of the B-52, which was fast becoming the prime strategic weapon delivery system, it was pursued in a quite relentless way. Just how relentless is perhaps best illustrated by mentioning that 30 additional air bases welcomed Stratofortress-equipped outfits between 1958 and 1962.

When it comes to considering just how dispersal was actually accomplished, the first thing to bear in mind is that all of the squadron identities were taken from those Bomb Wings that were initially earmarked to acquire the B-52. In essence, it was achieved by stripping away squadrons from their original parent Wings; moving them to a new base, usually as a tenant of another major USAF command; and assigning them to newly-constituted Strategic Wings.

Reference has already been made to the 11-Wing plan of the mid-1950s. It was these Wings that pro-

vided the core of the dispersal programme, being made up of one that had briefly used the B-47 (93rd BW) plus 10 B-36 units (5th, 6th, 7th, 11th, 28th, 42nd, 72nd, 92nd, 95th and 99th BWs). Between them, they contributed 33 squadrons to the eventual line-up – with the balance coming from the decision to up B-52 acquisition to 744.

This resulted in sufficient extra aircraft becoming available to equip the equivalent of three more Wings (i.e. nine squadrons). In selecting these, SAC looked to its dwindling medium bomber force, choosing to convert a trio of B-47 outfits.

Even though it was actually an on-going undertaking, dispersal might in some ways be considered as having three distinct 'phases', although one should note there was some overlapping. The first 'phase' affected Wings that remained to be equipped under the original 11-Wing plan; the second concerned the Wings that were equipped during 1956 and 1957 in the pre-dispersal era; and the third involved the former B-47 Wings added to the programme in 1958. In discussing how it was done, it seems best to consider the actions 'phase' by 'phase', starting with units that had still to be equipped at the beginning of 1958.

At that moment in time, the 6th BW at Walker AFB, New Mexico, had already begun to take delivery of the Stratofortress and it duly became the last unit to be equipped and operated as a full sized Wing of three squadrons. In fact, for reasons that will be explained later, the 6th BW was not directly involved in the dispersal effort at all and continued in existence as a 45 UE organisation until well into the 1960s, latterly being redesignated as a Strategic Aerospace Wing (SAW) on acquiring an Atlas ICBM squadron.

Going back in time, another unit accepted its first example of the Stratofortress within weeks of the 6th BW. This was the 11th BW which had moved home from Carswell AFB, Texas, to Altus AFB, Oklahoma, in December 1957. Like the 6th BW, it was equipped with the B-52E, but the 11th BW merits special mention for a couple of reasons.

In the first instance, extensive construction work at Altus meant that it was unsuitable for immediate use. Rather than delay the equipping and training process, flight operations by elements of the 11th BW actually started at Clinton-Sherman AFB, Oklahoma.

Second, and of much greater importance, was the fact that the 11th was the first SAC Wing to shed a squadron in accordance with the newly-implemented dispersal doctrine. As a consequence, it began operations as a two-squadron organisation with a unit establishment (UE) of 30 aircraft, distributed equally between the 26th BS and the 42nd BS. Eventually, the 42nd BS also departed, being transferred along with 15 B-52Es to the control of the 4043rd SW at Wright-Patterson AFB, Ohio, in June 1960.

With regard to the third squadron (the 98th BS), this was left behind at Carswell at the time of the parent Wing's move to Altus. It experienced a very brief period of attachment to the co-located 7th BW (from 1 to 10 December 1957), before being officially reassigned from the 11th BW to the 4123rd SW with effect from 10 December 1957. Shortly thereafter, in early 1958, it began to take delivery of the B-52E and continued to operate from Carswell until February 1959 when it moved to Clinton-Sherman AFB, where it took over the facilities that had been used by 11th BW aircraft and personnel while they awaited completion of the work in progress at Altus.

While all that was going on, production of the next version was also proceeding apace and the first of 89

LEFT No self-respecting photo-journalist in the America of the mid-1950s would be seen dead without his hat. Here, a member of this elite breed covers the triumphant return of three 93rd Bomb Wing B-52Bs to Castle AFB after their epic 45-hour globe-circling flight in January 1957

ABOVE With KC-97 tankers at the ready in the background, B-52B 53-0376 taxies out for take-off from Castle AFB in the mid-1950s. The distinctive main landing gear is clearly visible in this near head-on view, and it should be noted that pilots generally spoke highly of this unique attribute. Although it cannot be discerned in this picture, the B-52B and RB-52B models featured alternative tail armament arrangements, with some aircraft using the standard four machine guns while others relied on twin 20 mm cannon coupled to the MD-5 fire control system *(Boeing)*

B-52Fs was accepted by SAC in June 1958. Manufacturing responsibility was split almost equally between Wichita and Seattle, with the final example from Seattle (57-0073) also being the 277th and last Stratofortress to be built at the home of Boeing. Henceforth, all new B-52s would originate from Wichita.

Delivery of the F-model was completed by February 1959, with the first few joining the 93rd BW for training tasks at Castle. As far as operational employment was concerned, this began with the 7th BW at Carswell AFB, Texas. Like the 11th BW, this emerged from the B-36 to B-52 conversion process with two operational squadrons (9th/492nd BSs) and a UE of 30 aircraft.

Equipping these two squadrons got under way in June 1958, but the 492nd didn't stay at Carswell for long, splitting away to constitute the bomber-equipped element of the 4228th SW at Columbus AFB, Mississippi, with effect from 15 June 1959. As for the third squadron (436th BS), this was still assigned to the 7th BW when the first B-52F arrived in June 1958 - however, it had been non-operational since April and remained so until after reassignment to the 4238th SW at Barksdale AFB, Louisiana, on 1 August 1958. Only then did it begin accepting the B-52F.

One other squadron obtained the B-52F model during the course of 1958, but this had originally been part of the 5th BW at Travis AFB, California, and actually began operating the Stratofortress some months in advance of its former parent. I refer to the 72nd BS, which transferred from 5th BW to 4134th SW control on 1 July 1958, subsequently receiving its first F-model at Mather AFB, California, a few months later, in October.

Such an action was by no means unknown during the course of implementing the dispersal. However, it was noteworthy in as much as the 72nd BS obtained a different version of the B-52 to that assigned to its former 'sister' squadrons in the 5th BW. While this was unusual, it was not unique, since the 95th BW was treated in a similar fashion, although in that instance the three squadrons involved received what might best be called 'hand-me down' aircraft.

Re-equipment of the other two 5th BW squadrons coincided with deployment of the newest version of the Stratofortress. This was ultimately also to become the most numerous sub-type, with no fewer than 193 B-52Gs being completed and flown by the Wichita factory between August 1958 and February 1961. Of that figure, the first 154 were obtained with Fiscal Year 1957/58 appropriations under original procurement plans, with the last 39 funded in FY 1959 mainly due to cuts in the B-58 programme.

Despite that, delivery of the B-52G to SAC kicked-off on 13 February 1959 when the 5th BW received its first example at Travis AFB, California. As mentioned a few moments ago, the 5th had already lost one squadron to the 4134th SW in 1958, but it flew B-52Gs as a two-squadron Wing for a short period in

ABOVE The second B-52C off the production line (53-0400) flies near Seattle not long after the first jet was rolled out on 7 December 1955. The B-52C can be distinguished by elongated 3000 US gal wing tanks in place of the 1000 US gal tanks associated with the B-52B version. B-52s of the 42nd Bomb Wing ar Loring AFB, Maine, took part in Operation *Quick Kick*, a 13,000-mile (20,921-km) record flight around the periphery of the continental United States in November 1956. The increased fuel load made the B-52C heavier than previous Stratofortresses *(Boeing)*

1959, controlling the 23rd and 31st BSs until 1 October. On that date, the 31st BS was officially transferred to the 4126th SW, but this action doesn't appear to have been accompanied by an immediate change of base. In fact, it looks very much as if the squadron did not leave Travis for Beale AFB, California, until after the start of the new decade, being attached to the 5th BW throughout this period. Authoritative sources indicate that the transfer was officially undertaken on 18 January 1960, when the attachment to the 5th BW terminated.

If the situation regarding dispersal of 5th BW elements is somewhat vague, that most certainly isn't true of the 72nd BW, which ceased flying the B-36 from Ramey AFB, Puerto Rico, in the autumn of 1958, an action that made its three squadrons available to receive B-52Gs. Two of them were relieved from assignment to the 72nd BW in 1959, with the 73rd BS coming under control of the 4241st SW at Seymour Johnson AFB, North Carolina, with effect from 5 January and the 301st BS joining the 4135th SW at Eglin AFB, Florida, on 17 June.

In both instances, delivery of the B-52G com-

menced in the summer of 1959, with the 4135th SW being of particular interest in that it later shared responsibility with the Air Research and Development Command's Air Proving Ground Center (also at Eglin) for conducting much of the Category III testing of Hound Dog and Quail missiles.

As far as its former parent was concerned, the 72nd BW didn't have much longer to wait before it too got its hands on the B-52G. This event took place in August 1959, with delivery of the initial example to the 60th BS also marking the first occasion on which the Stratofortress was based outside the USA.

Re-equipment of the 72nd was accomplished more or less concurrently with conversion of another former B-36 unit, specifically the 95th BW at Biggs AFB, Texas. Bringing up the rear of the original 11-Wing programme, the 95th still had some B-36s on hand at the start of 1959 and is historically significant by virtue of being the last SAC unit to operate propeller-driven bombers. Little time was wasted in disposing of the few 'Peacemakers' that lingered at Biggs and an era officially ended on 12 February 1959 when the last B-36J droned its way into the sky and headed for preservation at Fort Worth.

Mention has already been made of the fact that the 95th BW fared less well than other B-52 Wings in that it didn't receive a complement of shiny new aircraft more or less fresh from the factory. In fact, that statement is true of all three of the squadrons that had previously been assigned to this Wing, for all of them obtained their new equipment 'second-hand' from existing units.

As it transpired, the process of dispersing the 95th BW predated final withdrawal of the B-36 by about a month, with the 335th BS splitting away to be reassigned to the 4130th SW at Bergstrom AFB, Texas, on 15 January 1959. Within days of arriving at its new home, the 335th began accepting B-52Ds and it appears likely that most of the aircraft came from Loring AFB, where the 42nd BW was on the brink of transition to the newer B-52G.

The Loring-based unit was almost certainly also the source of new equipment for the second 95th BW element to be dispersed, since the 336th BS acquired B-52Ds upon being transferred to the control of the 4138th SW at Turner AFB, Georgia, on 1 July 1959. Departure of these two squadrons left just one in residence at Biggs, this being the 334th BS which was also equipped with the Stratofortress in 1959. In this instance, the aircrews that were eventually assigned to the 334th BS might well have been excused for thinking they'd got the worst end of the deal when the time came to receive a replacement bomber, for it was equipped with a number of even older B-52Bs.

By June 1960, what I have described as the first 'phase' of dispersal was complete, and the second 'phase' was already under way, having begun shortly before the end of 1959. This actually concerned half-a-dozen squadrons drawn from four of the five Bomb Wings that had been equipped during the 1955-57 time-frame. Only the 93rd BW was unaffected, almost

certainly by virtue of its primary role of crew training, and it continued to function as a three-squadron outfit until well into 1963.

The first of the four original Wings to face reorganisation through dispersal was the 42nd BW, which lost one squadron on 15 October 1959 when the 75th BS was reassigned to the 4039th SW at Griffiss AFB, New York. This squadron had been non-operational since about June 1959 and was almost certainly involved in the transfer of B-52Ds to elements of the 95th BW. In the event, even though it came under 4039th SW control in late 1959, it did not begin operating the B-52G from Griffiss until January 1960.

Dispersal of elements of the 28th BW at Ellsworth appears to have commenced in the same month, with the 717th BS starting to move its authorised complement of B-52Ds to Sheppard AFB, Texas. In this case,

BELOW B-52C 54-2686 of the 99th Bomb Wing landing at Westover AFB, Massachusetts, in 1968. The B-52C remained in service until 29 September 1971 when the final example was consigned to the boneyard at Davis-Monthan AFB, Arizona. This machine is becoming a bit frayed, as its paint scheme struggles to keep up with wear and tear, and the flaps and spoilers reveal charring from the J57 turbojet engines, renowned for their ability to generate enormous plumes of black smoke (R W Harrison)

though, it was officially reassigned from the 28th BW to the 4245th SW with effect from 1 February 1960. Less than three weeks later, on 20 February, the 28th BW was reduced still further, shedding another 15 B-52Ds of the 718th BS which henceforth reported to the 4128th SW at Amarillo AFB, Texas.

There was then a lull of a few months, before attention turned to the 92nd BW at Fairchild. Like the 28th, this was eventually fated to lose two of its three squadrons. First to leave was the 327th BS, which did not have far to go in order to join up with its new parent at Larson AFB, Washington. Transfer to the 4170th SW took place on 1 June 1960, leaving the 92nd BW to operate as a two-squadron Wing until 1 April 1961 when the 326th BS left to join the 4141st SW at Glasgow AFB, Montana. In this instance, it appears that the physical shift of 326th BS resources began ahead of formal transfer, since the squadron was detached from 92nd BW control with effect from 1 March 1961 and may have begun moving to its new home as early as February 1961.

One more of the originally-planned 33 squadrons remained to be moved to a new base and this event was officially accomplished on 1 September 1961. On that date, the 99th BW surrendered control of the 347th BS to the 4047th SW at McCoy AFB, Florida, although once again it appears that the process of relocation may have begun a few weeks earlier, during August.

Irrespective of that, this action brought to a close the second 'phase' of dispersal and in September 1961 the reality of B-52 distribution bore little comparison to the initial intent. Squadrons that had once formed part of the first 11 Wings were now spread across some 27 air bases in 17 states and one overseas location (see table for details). In consequence, the once large concentrations of B-52s were now virtually at an end, since only two bases – Castle and Walker – still hosted three-squadron Wings with 45 or so examples of the Stratofortress.

There was a good reason for that, since the hugely expanded force meant that the 93rd BW was no longer able to meet the demand for personnel on its own. Driven entirely by the need for additional training resources, the Walker-based 6th BW was selected to augment the 93rd BW. This at first entailed the assignment of two squadrons (the 24th and 39th BSs) to training duties in September 1959. Subsequently, in June 1960, the 40th BS followed suit, although its

period of employment in the training role was relatively short-lived and it eventually regained operational status at the start of December 1961.

Concurrent with the final stages of dispersal of the original units, SAC was also busy with the third and last 'phase' of the programme. Implementation of this would bring the force to the peak level of 42 squadrons and would also witness deployment of the latest and most advanced version of the Stratofortress. Colloquially known as the 'Cadillac', the B-52H began to join SAC in May 1961 and eventually equipped six of the nine squadrons that were added to the overall programme in 1958.

Just where they originated and how they were distributed will be described in the next chapter. This examines the completion of deployment and dispersal and also considers the motives that lay behind the demise of all 22 of the Strategic Wings in 1963, just a matter of months after the final one had accepted its full complement of aircraft.

FINALISING THE FORCE

As has already been mentioned, the size and extent of the B-52 programme was progressively expanded over a period of several years. This process of expansion witnessed an incremental rise in the size of the planned force from seven to 11 Wings in the mid 1950s, before being increased yet again to the equivalent of 14 Wings in 1958. That resulted in a total of 42 squadrons, each with an authorised Unit Establishment of 15 aircraft, plus one or two 'spares' in almost all cases. By 1958, however, for reasons alluded to in the previous chapter, SAC had also arrived at the decision to disperse its fast growing fleet of B-52s and this action exerted considerable influence on existing units, as well as those that had still to be equipped.

Delivery of the first of the additional 141 Stratofortresses (39 B-52Gs and 102 B-52Hs) occurred in June 1960, but was inevitably preceded by the selection of three more Wings to provide the extra nine squadrons that would be needed by the time that the final examples of the B-52H were handed over. With all of the former B-36 heavy Bomb Wings having already been chosen, SAC had no option but to look elsewhere to find these Wings – and it turned to the Stratojet medium bomber community.

Two bases were involved. One was Biggs AFB, Texas, which was a particularly appropriate selection

POST-DISPERSAL DISTRIBUTION OF
THE ORIGINAL 33 B-52 SQUADRONS

Wing	Base	Squadrons	Model
5th BW	Travis AFB, Ca	23 BS	B-52G
6th BW	Walker AFB, NM	24/39/40 BS	B-52E
7th BW	Carswell AFB, Tx	9 BS	B-52F
11th BW	Altus AFB, Ok	26 BS	B-52E
28th BW	Ellsworth AFB, SD	77 BS	B-52D
42nd BW	Loring AFB, Me	69/70 BS	B-52G
72nd BW	Ramey AFB, PR	60 BS	B-52G
92nd BW	Fairchild AFB, Wa	325 BS	B-52D
93rd BW	Castle AFB, Ca	328/329/330 BS	B-52B/F
95th BW	Biggs AFB, Tx	334 BS	B-52B
99th BW	Westover AFB, Ma	346/348 BS	B-52C
4039th SW	Griffiss AFB, NY	75 BS	B-52G
4043rd SW	Wright-Patterson AFB, Oh	42 BS	B-52E
4047th SW	McCoy AFB, Fl	347 BS	B-52D
4123rd SW	Clinton-Sherman AFB, Ok	98 BS	B-52E
4126th SW	Beale AFB, Ca	31 BS	B-52G
4128th SW	Amarillo AFB, Tx	718 BS	B-52D
4130th SW	Bergstrom AFB, Tx	335 BS	B-52D
4134th SW	Mather AFB, Ca	72 BS	B-52F
4135th SW	Eglin AFB, Fl	301 BS	B-52G
4138th SW	Turner AFB, Ga	336 BS	B-52D
4141st SW	Glasgow AFB, Mt	326 BS	B-52D
4170th SW	Larson AFB, Wa	327 BS	B-52D
4228th SW	Columbus AFB, Ms	492 BS	B-52F
4238th SW	Barksdale AFB, La	436 BS	B-52F
4241st SW	Seymour Johnson AFB, NC	73 BS	B-52G
4245th SW	Sheppard AFB, Tx	717 BS	B-52D

BELOW This fine study of B-52C 54-2669 was probably taken prior to delivery, since the aircraft has still to acquire SAC and unit insignia below the cockpit windows. Initially assigned to the 42nd BW at Loring, the greater part of the B-52C's operational career was actually spent with the 99th BW at Westover, which retained its status as a two-squadron outfit until shortly before it was inactivated in 1974 (Boeing)

as well as a uniquely unusual one, in as much as it had previously hosted a heavy Bomb Wing equipped with B-36s (the 95th) and a medium Bomb Wing with B-47s (the 97th). Now, following the example set by its former stablemate, the 97th BW was chosen to provide three of the nine additional squadrons.

The second base was that at Homestead, a few miles to the south of the sprawling mass of Miami, Florida. At the end of the 1950s, this was occupied by the 823rd Air Division, which directed the activities of two B-47 Wings. These consisted of the 19th and 379th Bomb Wings, each having the usual complement of about 45 aircraft, although a slightly different approach to alert operations meant that they differed

from the large B-52 outfits in having four rather than three bomber-equipped squadrons. In addition, the 19th BW controlled a tanker element with about 20 examples of the KC-97.

Between them, these two units added the six squadrons that were required by SAC to complete the B-52 re-equipment programme at the revised level of 42 squadrons. Not surprisingly, in view of the fact that they were added to the programme at a much later stage, the nine squadrons involved were also the last to undergo conversion.

This process was launched by the 97th BW which phased-out its final few B-47 Stratojets at Biggs AFB in January 1959, prior to moving in non-operational status to Blytheville AFB, Arkansas, with effect from 1 July 1959. Concurrent with the shift of Wing headquarters, three tactical squadrons (340th, 341st and 342nd Bomb Squadrons) also transferred to the Arkansas base, where the 340th BS became the first to regain operational status. That event technically took place at the end of September 1959, although it did not acquire its first B-52G until January 1960, henceforth continuing to operate as part of the 97th BW.

With regard to the other two squadrons, these adhered to the well-established procedure of dispersal and were reassigned to other locations shortly before also being equipped with B-52Gs. In the case of the 341st BS, this moved to the north-eastern USA, occupying its new home at Dow AFB, Maine, with effect from 15 February 1960. Once in place, command jurisdiction passed to the 4038th SW, which began accepting B-52Gs in May 1960, at about the same time as the 342nd BS left Blytheville.

The destination for this squadron was Robins AFB, Georgia, where the 4137th SW had already been in residence for more than a year, albeit on a minimally-manned basis. Transition to the status of a fully-operational unit began with the arrival of the 342nd BS on 1 May 1960, but some three months were to pass before the first B-52G flew in to join the Wing during August 1960. In the meantime, a 'prototype' B-52H (actually a re-engined B-52G) made its maiden flight on 10 July 1960 and with the production article due to follow suit in early 1961, it was apparent that the final stage of deployment was now not far off in the future.

The pair of Homestead-based Bomb Wings assigned to the 823rd Air Division were chosen to receive the B-52H and the process of re-equipment was to start with the 379th BW. It began phasing out the B-47 in October 1960 and clearly wasted little time in disposing of its aircraft, for it was redesignated as a Bomb Wing, Heavy and reassigned to Wurtsmith AFB, Michigan, on 9 January 1961. Of the squadrons previously assigned, the 524th BS also went north to Michigan on 9 January 1961, subsequently accepting its (and SAC's) first B-52H on 9 May of the same year.

The departure of the 379th BW and one tactical squadron left three others behind at Homestead. Two of them (525th BS and 526th BS) were immediately transferred to the control of the co-located 19th BW.

ABOVE All eight engines are clearly operating in this classic study of B-52D 56-0584 contrailing at altitude while being used for test purposes. Unlike the JB-52C shown earlier, this aircraft did join SAC *(Boeing)*

The third squadron (527th BS) was much less fortunate and was discontinued with immediate effect.

These changes resulted in the 19th BW briefly becoming one of SAC's largest bomber units, on paper at least, since it now possessed no less than six Bomb Squadrons. However, it should be borne in mind that two of those squadrons had transferred from the 379th BW without aircraft and were thus effectively non-operational. As for the other four, these continued to utilise the B-47 until the Spring of 1961, when the process of withdrawal began. Within a very short space of time, the faithful Stratojets had all departed, which paved the way for the 659th BS to be discontinued on 1 July 1961.

By then, the pair of former 379th BW squadrons had also left Homestead for good, although they fared rather better than the 659th BS and did remain in existence for a little while longer. First out was the 525th BS which was transferred to the control of the 4136th SW at Minot AFB, North Dakota, in March 1961 and it began accepting B-52Hs in July. Next to go was the 526th BS, which also travelled northwards, to K I Sawyer AFB, Michigan, at the beginning of June 1961. Its new parent command was the 4042nd SW and it acquired the B-52H from August onwards.

Departure of those squadrons left just three in residence at the Florida base and it fell to them to round out the long process of initial deployment of the

BELOW Another shot from the sequence of pictures portraying B-52D 56-0584. This 'Buff' ultimately spent many years with SAC, but was destroyed at U-Tapao after being hit by a SAM over Kinh No, North Vietnam, in 1972 *(Boeing)*

Stratofortress. They were all 'traditional' 19th BW elements, but it didn't take too much time before two of them severed their links with Homestead and moved out to new quarters. The first to leave – at the beginning of August 1961 – was the 93rd BS, which was reassigned to the 4239th SW at Kincheloe AFB, Michigan, where it took delivery of its initial B-52H in November 1961.

Attention then shifted to equipping the squadron that was destined to continue operating from Homestead as part of the 19th BW. This was the 28th BS and it picked up its first B-52H in February 1962, just a few weeks after the 19th BW had been reduced to the status of a single-squadron Wing, with the departure of the 30th BS to Grand Forks AFB, North

BELOW The six-man crew of a SAC B-52 outfit stand in front of their aircraft with personal kit neatly laid out ready for inspection, possibly during one of the dreaded operational readiness evaluations *(USAF)*

ABOVE Wichita's first 'Buff' cleans up as it heads skywards for its first flight. Although it does carry SAC insignia, this has been applied incorrectly, with the sash extending down into the white anti-flash paint. The B-52E on the facing page shows the correct presentation *(Boeing)*

Dakota. Now part of the 4133rd SW, the 30th BS could be described as being almost the final piece to be slotted into its appointed place in the puzzle that represented the 42-squadron plan.

Personnel at Grand Forks turned out to greet the first B-52H to reach this northern base in April 1962, just six months before Boeing formally delivered the 744th example. By then, most units had their full complement and the very last B-52H (61-0040) actually went to the 4136th SW at Minot on 26 October 1962, although it wasn't clear at the time that it would turn out to be the final 'Buff'. The reason for doubt stemmed from an Air Force request that Boeing store B-52H tooling at Wichita until July 1963 while it considered the possibility of additional orders. As it transpired, no further contracts ensued and the delivery of 61-0040 thus marked the termination of a production run that had been launched almost a decade earlier.

Not long after it finally became clear that B-52 production had indeed ended for good, SAC undertook the final actions to complete the dispersal project. In so doing, it also eliminated the last of the impressive but vulnerable 'big Wings', for both of the units involved still possessed three squadrons. On 15 September 1963, however, recognition that the training workload was now greatly diminished permitted them to be reduced in size.

Each was accordingly directed to inactivate a single squadron, which freed approximately 30 B-52s for reassignment to a pair of former B-47 Stratojet-equipped units. At Walker AFB, the 6th SAW lost the 39th BS, which broke with previous dispersal procedure in that it was inactivated rather than relocated, for reasons that will soon become clear. As for the 15 or so B-52Es made available by this move, these joined the 337th BS, 96th SAW at Dyess AFB, Texas – and it is also worth mentioning that the cutback in 6th SAW establishment was accompanied by an end of training duty and a return to tactical operations.

Elsewhere, at Castle AFB, the 93rd BW's 330th BS was also inactivated, although the remaining two squadrons continued to function as SAC's B-52 crew training 'university'. The demise of the 330th BS freed a number of long-serving B-52Bs to be transferred to the 2nd BS, 22nd BW at March AFB, California.

These were the final acts in the dispersal programme that had begun some six years earlier. It culminated in the 42 squadron B-52 force being distributed amongst no less than 38 air bases. In most cases, these installations hosted Wings composed of a single bomber squadron plus an accompanying tanker squadron, but four continued to operate as two-squadron organisations with just over 30 examples of the Stratofortress on charge.

Elimination of the last of the 'big Wings' was far from being the only noteworthy change that took place in 1963. This is reflected most clearly in the accompanying listing of B-52 distribution as it stood at the end of September and also provides an explanation for the logic behind the decision to inactivate the 6th SAW's 39th BS, rather than simply move it to another base. I refer to the decision to discontinue the 22 Strategic Wings created in the late 1950s specifically to facilitate

the dispersal process – and replace them with Bomb Wings that were deemed to be historically significant.

It was, in fact, a fairly major reorganisation on paper at least, in as much as it was extended in scope to also embrace three Air Refueling Wings and the 4321st Strategic Wing at Offutt AFB, Nebraska. It was not, as is often stated, simply a redesignation exercise, for the rules and regulations pertaining to USAF lineage do not permit histories, awards and battle honours to be transferred from MajCon (major command controlled) units to AFCon (Air Force controlled) units.

Before turning to consider the changes that occurred in 1963, it makes sense to provide a brief explanation of the differences in status between Maj-Con and AFCon units. In essence, MajCon units are those that use four-digit numerical identities and it is also worth mentioning that separate and specific blocks of numbers were allocated to the individual USAF commands. In the case of SAC, the allocation extended from 3900 to 4399. So, any organisation that

BELOW This B-52E (56-0646) is getting a good ogling by citizens at an airshow. B-52Es were used as carriers for the North American AGM-28 (originally GAM-77) Hound Dog inertial-guidance, air-to-ground, thermonuclear missile powered by a Pratt & Whitney J52 engine. Not shown here because the Hound Dog was at first not cleared for public exhibit, the missile was an early precursor to what became known as an air-launched cruise missile (ALCM) in later years *(via Glyde Gerdes)*

LEFT The advent of the surface-to-air missile forced SAC to reconsider tactics and switch to low-level as a means of ensuring survivability in the event of being called upon to go to war. Here, the first B-52E off the Seattle production line shows how it should be done *(Boeing)*

used a numerical designation in this range must, by definition, have been a SAC-controlled organisation.

MajCon units are also viewed as temporary organisations, although one might well be advised to take a large pinch of salt when contemplating the meaning of the word 'temporary' – since some of these units have been particularly long-lived. The key point to bear in mind when considering these units is that each use of a four-digit number stands alone as far as history is concerned. So, while there is nothing to prevent a number from being used again, there can be no linkage between successive uses of a specific number.

AFCon units (squadrons and wings with one, two or three digit numbers) conform to different criteria. For a start, they may be assigned to any command organisation and can also be switched from the control of one command to another. Furthermore, they are allowed to retain lineage, awards and battle honours through a succession of inactivations and activations. For obvious reasons, the USAF is acutely aware of its history and tradition and it was precisely the desire to perpetuate a number of inactive World War 2 units that prompted SAC's action.

It is also worth bearing in mind that while MajCon

LEFT Small underwing tanks and a chopped-down fin identify this aircraft as a B-52G, but these were far from being the only changes incorporated into what eventually became the most numerous version, with some 193 aircraft completed by Wichita in the late 1950s and early 1960s. The aircraft seen here (57-6468) was in fact both the first to emerge and the first to be retired. It is now preserved at Offutt AFB, Nebraska *(Boeing)*

Wings usually exercise control over MajCon squadrons, it is not unknown for them to 'parent' AFCon squadrons. This was, in fact, exactly the situation that existed with regard to SAC's Strategic Wings. As a matter of interest, the reverse situation is also true, for AFCon Wings may 'parent' MajCon squadrons.

To explain what happened to the Strategic Wings (and their constituent squadrons), it will probably be best to refer to a typical example of the changes that took place during the course of 1963 and Eglin AFB seems as good as any. On 1 February, the resident 4135th SW and the 301st BS were both discontinued. In the case of the 4135th SW (a MajCon unit), it effectively ceased to exist and its history ended with it. In the case of the 301st BS (an AFCon unit), it reverted to the control of USAF Headquarters in inactive status so it could be reactivated at some future date, with its history (including the period of assignment to a MajCon 'parent') being perpetuated.

Concurrent with the demise of the 4135th SW and 301st BS, replacement units were organised at Eglin and these assumed jurisdiction over the aircraft and personnel resources that were already in place. The new 'parent' was the 39th BW, which directed the operations of the subordinate 62nd BS, which had been chosen for assignment by virtue of past association with the Wing. Both were AFCon units and both had been activated by USAF Headquarters on 15 November 1962 and immediately assigned to SAC control in readiness for the change. Thus, operations were able to continue more or less uninterrupted as a result of what was fundamentally little more than a 'paper' exercise in the change of command.

A similar procedure was adopted for the bulk of the Strategic Wings, 18 of which were eliminated with

ABOVE The unit badge visible on the nose section of B-52G 58-0212 confirms assignment to the 380th Strategic Aerospace Wing at Plattsburgh AFB, New York. A former B-47 outfit, the 380th came late to the 'Buff', receiving its first example of the B-52G in June 1966 and retaining this model until January 1971, when it began preparing to operate the General Dynamics FB-111A. This aircraft was captured on film at Plattsburgh in May 196, and features colours and markings that were typical of the pre-camouflage era *(R W Harrison)*

their assigned squadrons on 1 February 1963, and simultaneously replaced by recently activated AFCon units. When it comes to considering the other four Strategic Wings that operated the B-52, a slightly different policy was employed so as to ensure the survival of some existing Bomb Wings that were on the verge of retiring the B-47 Stratojet.

In each case, inactivation of the Strategic Wing and its subordinate squadron coincided with the assignment of a replacement Bomb Wing (and squadron) from another base. In technical terms, these were 'WOPE' (without personnel or equipment) transfers and they also enabled operations to continue without a break using resources that had been assigned to the now defunct Strategic Wing. This phase of the programme took slightly longer to implement – and resulted in two Strategic Wings disappearing on 1 April 1963, with a third following suit on 15 April. This left just one in existence (the 4130th SW at Bergstrom) and it hung on for a few more months, until 1 September 1963, when it was replaced by the 340th BW. Full details of the changes made during the course of 1963 are presented in an accompanying table.

B-52 DISTRIBUTION AS AT 30 SEPTEMBER 1963

Wing	Base	Squadron(s)	Model(s)
2nd BW	Barksdale AFB, La	20 BS	B-52F
5th BW	Travis AFB, Ca	23 BS	B-52G
6th SAW	Walker AFB, NM	24/40 BS	B-52E
7th BW	Carswell AFB, Tx	9 BS	B-52F
11th SAW	Altus AFB, Ok	26 BS	B-52E
17th BW	Wright-Patterson AFB, Oh	34 BS	B-52E
19th BW	Homestead AFB, Fl	28 BS	B-52H
22nd BW	March AFB, Ca	2 BS	B-52B
28th BW	Ellsworth AFB, SD	77 BS	B-52D
39th BW	Eglin AFB, Fl	62 BS	B-52G
42nd BW	Loring AFB, Me	69/70 BS	B-52G
68th BW	Seymour Johnson AFB, NC	51 BS	B-52G
70th BW	Clinton-Sherman AFB, Ok	6 BS	B-52E
72nd BW	Ramey AFB, PR	60 BS	B-52G
91st BW	Glasgow AFB, Mt	322 BS	B-52D
92nd SAW	Fairchild AFB, Wa	325 BS	B-52D
93rd BW	Castle AFB, Ca	328/329 BS	B-52B/F
95th BW	Biggs AFB, Tx	334 BS	B-52B
96th SAW	Dyess AFB, Tx	337 BS	B-52E
97th BW	Blytheville AFB, Ar	340 BS	B-52G
99th BW	Westover AFB, Ma	346/348 BS	B-52C
306th BW	McCoy AFB, Fl	367 BS	B-52D
319th BW	Grand Forks AFB, ND	46 BS	B-52H
320th BW	Mather AFB, Ca	441 BS	B-52F
340th BW	Bergstrom AFB, Tx	486 BS	B-52D
379th BW	Wurtsmith AFB, Mi	524 BS	B-52H
397th BW	Dow AFB, Me	596 BS	B-52G
410th BW	K I Sawyer AFB, Mi	644 BS	B-52H
416th BW	Griffiss AFB, NY	668 BS	B-52G
449th BW	Kincheloe AFB, Mi	716 BS	B-52H
450th BW	Minot AFB, ND	720 BS	B-52H
454th BW	Columbus AFB, Ms	736 BS	B-52F
456th SAW	Beale AFB, Ca	744 BS	B-52G
461st BW	Amarillo AFB, Tx	764 BS	B-52D
462nd SAW	Larson AFB, Wa	768 BS	B-52D
465th BW	Robins AFB, Ga	781 BS	B-52G
484th BW	Turner AFB, Ga	824 BS	B-52D
494th BW	Sheppard AFB, Tx	864 BS	B-52D

BELOW Variations in skin tone are readily visible in this view of the premier B-52H (60-0001) as it emerges from the assembly hall at Wichita for the first time. Still to be given USAF insignia and a coat of thermal-reflecting white paint, the new TF33 turbofan engines are the most noteworthy change introduced by the B-52H which soon won the nickname 'Cadillac'. In the right background are two of the GAM-87 Skybolt air-launched ballistic missiles that would have been the primary armament of the final 'Buff' model had this weapon not been cancelled *(Boeing)*

ABOVE A B-52H (51-0010) landing with its parabrake shortly after delivery of the first H-model to SAC on 9 May 1961. The B-52H was originally conceived as a carrier for the Douglas GAM-87A Skybolt, a two-stage, solid-propellant, stand-off ballistic missile with a nuclear warhead developed as a joint US-British project. The Skybolt was not successful and the B-52H ended up carrying AGM-28 Hound Dogs, AGM-69 SRAMS and AGM-129 Advanced Cruise Missiles instead *(Boeing)*

POST-DISPERSAL DISTRIBUTION OF FINAL B-52 SQUADRONS

Wing	Base	Squadron	Model
19th BW	Homestead AFB, Fl	28 BS	B-52H
97th BW	Blytheville AFB, Ar	340 BS	B-52G
379th BW	Wurtsmith AFB, Mi	524 BS	B-52H
4038th SW	Dow AFB, Me	341 BS (ex-97 BW)	B-52G
4042nd SW	K I Sawyer AFB, Mi	526 BS (ex-379 BW)	B-52H
4133rd SW	Grand Forks AFB, ND	30 BS (ex-19 BW)	B-52H
4136th SW	Minot AFB, ND	525 BS (ex 379 BW)	B 52H
4137th SW	Robins AFB, Ga	342 BS (ex-97 BW)	B-52G
4239th SW	Kincheloe AFB, Mi	93 BS (ex-19 BW)	B-52H

STRATEGIC WING ELIMINATION ACTIONS
(FEBRUARY-SEPTEMBER 1963)

Original Units	Replacements	Effective	
4038th SW/341 BS	397 BW/596 BS	1/2/63	
4039th SW/75 BS	416 BW/668 BS	1/2/63	
4042nd SW/526 BS	410 BW/644 BS	1/2/63	
4043rd SW/42 BS	17 BW/34 BS	1/2/63	
4047th SW/347 BS	306 BW/367 BS	1/4/63	(WOPE, ex-MacDill, Fl)
4123rd SW/98 BS	70 BW/6 BS	1/2/63	
4126th SW/31 BS	456 SAW/744 BS	1/2/63	
4128th SW/718 BS	461 BW/764 BS	1/2/63	
4130th SW/335 BS	340 BW/486 BS	1/9/63	(WOPE, ex-Whiteman, Mo)
4133rd SW/30 BS	319 BW/46 BS	1/2/63	
4134th SW/72 BS	320 BW/441 BS	1/2/63	
4135th SW/301 BS	39 BW/62 BS	1/2/63	
4136th SW/525 BS	450 BW/720 BS	1/2/63	
4137th SW/342 BS	465 BW/781 BS	1/2/63	
4138th SW/336 BS	484 BW/824 BS	1/2/63	
4141st SW/326 BS	91 BW/322 BS	1/2/63	
4170th SW/327 BS	462 SAW/768 BS	1/2/63	
4228th SW/492 BS	454 BW/736 BS	1/2/63	
4238th SW/436 BS	2 BW/20 BS	1/4/63	(WOPE, ex-Hunter, Ga)
4239th SW/93 BS	449 BW/716 BS	1/2/63	
4241st SW/73 BS	68 BW/51 BS	15/4/63	(WOPE, ex-Chennault, La)
4245th SW/717 BS	494 BW/864 BS	1/2/63	

NOTES: WOPE signifies moved without personnel or equipment from the base mentioned in parenthesis. All of the units which accomplished the change of command on 1 February 1963 had been activated on 15 November 1962 and assigned to SAC in anticipation of the re-organisation.

GROUND ALERT OPERATIONS

COINCIDENTAL WITH WIDE-SCALE deployment of the B-52, the latter half of the 1950s was a time when SAC was also kept busy as it strove to introduce other new aircraft and missile systems, as well as implement radically different plans and policies. The latter came about partly as a result of the desire to enhance its already impressive combat capability and partly to counteract what was perceived to be an increasing threat from the armed forces of the Soviet Union. This manifested itself in what became known as the 'bomber gap' and the 'missile gap', whereby poor US intelligence and over-generous estimates of Soviet military production capabilities conspired to bring about a belief in certain circles that the Soviet forces had attained a position of numerical superiority. In consequence, SAC began giving serious consideration to finding ways and means of improving the survivability of the bomber and tanker forces at its disposal.

Dispersal of the available forces was one of the methods used to resolve concerns about vulnerability to surprise attack and its effect on the B-52 fleet in particular is examined in considerably greater detail elsewhere. However, dispersal was by no means the only far-reaching change made to operating doctrine in the late 1950s.

Of much greater significance was the decision to introduce a concept whereby a number of fully-armed bombers and their supporting tankers would be maintained on alert at major SAC installations in the USA and overseas. These resources would be held in readiness along with their crews, the idea being that they would get airborne within 15 minutes of the order to

LEFT B-52B 52-8711 was the very first Stratofortress to be delivered to SAC, and was still giving good service at the time of this early 1960s photograph of a bomber crew engaged in a practice alert. By then, however, the 'Buff' had moved on from Castle and was assigned to the 22nd Bomb Wing at March AFB, as evidenced by the badge and Latin motto which is most appropriate for this aircraft, since it translates as 'We Lead' *(USAF)*

take-off being given. This, it was felt, would be a sufficient margin of time to allow an effective nuclear response in the event of a surprise missile attack. While that response may not have involved overwhelming force, it would certainly have been quite capable of bringing devastating consequences to bear on any aggressor.

As per usual, SAC directed a number of tests and trials during 1956-57 before moving to introduce this concept on a force-wide basis. Three such evaluation projects – given the code names *Try Out*, *Watchtower* and *Fresh Approach* – were undertaken by B-47 and KC-97 units within the USA and these highlighted areas where reorganisation would be necessary if the alert scheme was to be truly viable. Eventually, having gone as far as it could to refine the concept, ground alert was introduced at certain US and overseas bases with effect from 1 October 1957. Subsequently, it was progressively extended to other SAC installations over the next year or so.

In the USA, of course, maintaining an alert force posed few serious difficulties, but the situation was slightly more complex when it came to overseas bases, such as those which were located in North Africa and the United Kingdom. Before 1958, these airfields had routinely supported SAC's rotational training programme, whereby combat-rated echelons deployed for 60 or 90 day tours of duty.

These deployments often involved Wing-strength movements and since a typical B-47 Stratojet Wing was composed of three squadrons (45 aircraft) and a supporting KC-97 Stratofreighter squadron (20 aircraft) plus several hundred personnel, it follows that deployment was something of a logistical nightmare, with the transit overseas being a fairly complex exercise. What made it worse was the fact that an incoming unit was usually (though not inevitably) required to relieve an outgoing one – in those circumstances, a single rotation to the UK would involve transatlantic flights by up to 90 bombers and 40 tankers.

In the spring of 1958, however, SAC's long-established 'rote' training policy was terminated with the completion of the 100th Bomb Wing's tour in England. A few months earlier, at Sidi Slimane in French Morocco, an entirely new method of basing bombers overseas had been trialled and this henceforth provided the standard deployment plan for the B-47 force.

It was known as *Reflex Action* and was fundamentally a system in which smaller numbers of aircraft were despatched overseas to stand nuclear-armed alert duty on a three-week cycle. In the case of the Sidi Slimane test, this involved a total of 20 bombers drawn in equal numbers from four US-based Wings. Since the powers-that-be instituted *Reflex* on a constantly-rotating basis, it follows that roughly a third of the aircraft and manpower resources would be replaced by fresh aircraft and personnel in any given week. Only when the newly-arrived bombers had been postured for alert duty with nuclear weapons would the aircraft they

LEFT Alert! The klaxon sounds as members of a SAC B-52H combat crew race for their primed bomber at K I Sawyer AFB during the 1962 Cuban Missile Crisis. During normal periods of readiness throughout the Cold War 40 per cent of the SAC bomber and tanker force was on continuous alert. One of the bomber's two AGM-28 Hound Dog missiles is shown in the foreground of this photograph *(via USAF)*

were to replace be taken off alert and flown home.

Since responsibility for bearing the brunt of *Reflex Action* fell to the B-47, it should come as no surprise to learn that the introduction of this concept had a most profound effect on SAC's sizeable force of medium bomber units. In fact, apart from a few B-52s that participated in the broadly similar *Air Mail* operation at Andersen AFB, Guam, from April 1964, *Reflex Action* was only ever undertaken by the B-47 throughout eight years of operation that terminated in the spring of 1965.

For the fast-expanding B-52 Stratofortress community, the idea of *Reflex Action* doesn't appear to have been seriously contemplated in the mid-to-late 1950s – and later proposals to implement it with B-52s (and B-58s) in Europe were shelved in 1963 when the US Department of Defense initiated major cuts on a global basis under Project *Clearwater*. However, some Stratofortresses did stand alert at Andersen AFB with effect from April 1964, when B-52Bs drawn from the 22nd and 95th Bomb Wings took over responsibility for *Air Mail* from the Stratojet.

In the USA, the alert operation made its debut on 1 October 1957 and the initial objective was to keep a third of the bomber and tanker force primed for near-immediate action. Irrespective of whether the alert duty was undertaken at home or overseas, it was by all accounts a pretty tedious experience and one that featured its fair share of inactivity. The tedium was, however, occasionally interrupted by no-notice practice alert exercises which could be called at any time, day or night.

Such exercises usually seem to have occurred at least once during each tour of alert duty. It was also usual for them to involve bomber and tanker crews starting their aircraft and heading towards the runway, before the stand-down order was passed – and many of these exercises culminated in a simulated MITO (minimum-interval take-off) departure, which was curtailed before lift-off. Although the plan was based upon getting alert aircraft into the sky within 15 minutes, frequent drills meant that the launch would normally have been completed comfortably inside that time, with engine start occurring in under two minutes and with the bombers beginning to move towards the runway within five minutes.

Aircrews engaged in alert duty at most US bomber bases passed their time in specially constructed facilities. In the normal course of events, a bomber crew could expect to pull a tour of alert duty at monthly intervals and each tour usually required the crew to spend a week in one of these facilities, although some

units opted for shorter three- or four-day tours. For fairly obvious reasons, the alert accommodation was invariably positioned close to the alert-dedicated aircraft. They, in turn, were located near the runway threshhold, well away from other flightline areas, and the quite distinctive physical appearance of the hard-standing areas at many bomber bases resulted in them quickly picking up the nickname 'Christmas trees'.

If the foregoing remarks seem to imply that bomber and tanker crews engaged on alert duty were virtual prisoners, it should be emphasised that this certainly wasn't the case, for they were free to leave the alert complex if they wished. However, it was imperative that they remain together and it should also be noted that freedom of movement extended only as far as visiting selected on-base areas within close proximity to the alert line. Furthermore, crew members were

expected at all times to remain well within earshot of the klaxon horn and to carry two-way radios, so as to ensure that contact was maintained with the alert facility command post at all times. Finally, in the event of the order to launch being given, special routes existed on base to speed the movement of personnel hastening to their aircraft. These were marked at intervals by flashing yellow lights and signs that directed all non-essential traffic to pull over to the side.

As to how they spent their time at the alert facility, the normal procedure was for each crew to begin the duty tour by reviewing details of SAC's positive control procedures and the specific Emergency War Order (EWO) mission allocated to them, a process that usually required several hours of quite intensive

RIGHT With Hound Dog 'side-arms' suspended from the underwing pylons, a B-52G maintains close formation with a tanker after topping off its fuel tanks. As many as a dozen bomb and missile-armed examples of the Stratofortress undertook 24-hour airborne alert missions continuously for about 10 years, until this activity terminated in early 1968 after the loss of an aircraft and its weapons in Greenland (USAF)

study. After that, the time was passed in a number of ways, but daily weather briefings on routes to be flown may well have helped focus the mind on the purpose of each alert tour. Other activities usually included routine on-going training, mission planning for the next post-alert sortie, academic studies and exercise. In addition, recreational facilities also existed in the form of a library, games room and TV lounge and there was even a regular film show to break the monotony, although there was always a chance that SAC Headquarters would time a no-notice drill to interfere with the movie.

Even though the first bomber and tanker aircraft were placed on alert in October 1957, it took quite some time to reach the target of keeping one-third of the available assets primed and ready for nuclear warfare. SAC finally reported that it had achieved this objective in May 1960, but not long after, in March 1961, President Kennedy directed that it be further increased to encompass half the B-47s and B-52s. According to SAC, this new level was attained just four months later, in July.

There does, however, appear to be good reason for scepticism about both of these claims or, at the very least, for doubt over some of the figures that were used in calculating them. At the end of 1960, for example, SAC admits to possessing 1735 bombers (1178 B-47s, 538 B-52s and 19 B-58s), of which 428 were on alert duty. Unless my calculations have gone seriously awry, this equates to about 24.6 per cent, which falls some way short of the 33 per cent claimed. A year later, the size of the bomber force had diminished in numbers to 1526 (889 B-47s, 571 B-52s and 66 B-58s), with 519 on alert duty. Another arithmetical exercise gives a figure of 34 per cent, which is significantly less than the 50 per cent claimed.

There is, quite clearly, a major discrepancy here and one that I am unable to explain, beyond observing that SAC calculations must have used different figures. For the record, my estimates have been based on data released by SAC – but I still find it impossible to reconcile the quoted alert levels and suspect that some other unidentified criteria must be involved in the calculation.

Playing around with numbers and, in particular, with percentages may be a fascinating exercise for statisticians and there's no doubt that it confirms SAC's ability to keep a formidable (and formidably large) proportion of its total resources ready for nuclear war on a 24-hour basis, year-in, year-out. But, when all is said and done, it doesn't present the whole picture, as study of the following few figures confirms. Expressed in purely percentage terms based on the total bomber force numbers, the peak level appears to have been attained in 1966 when almost 45 per cent stood alert. That figure is impressive, but it disguises the fact that the number of aircraft involved was 301 – a far cry from the 625 bombers that were committed to alert duty in December 1962 when the B-47 still figured in the inventory.

By 1966, of course, SAC bombers and tankers were heavily committed to the war in South-East Asia – and

LEFT Securely strapped in, the pilot and co-pilot of a B-52 crew run through the first of an almost bewildering number of predeparture checks aboard a 'Buff' at a typical SAC base. Behind and below them, in the 'black hole', the two navigators will also be busily preparing for the upcoming mission, whilst elsewhere the gunner and electronic warfare officer will be checking out their equipment *(USAF)*

ABOVE The massive yet slender wing of the Stratofortress is displayed to advantage in this study of a Hound Dog-toting B-52G breaking gently away from the camera-ship, as is the gloss white underside paint scheme that was applied to reflect thermal energy from a nuclear detonation. At this time, the 'Buff' still had to acquire the many 'add-ons' that marred its lines *(USAF)*

this conflict had a dramatic impact on alert posture. This was particularly true of the period from about 1968 onwards, when the demand for combat ready crews imposed a serious drain on US-based resources.

In 1968 and 1969, for instance, required alert rates for the bomber force were 202 and 190 aircraft respectively, whereas the corresponding rates achieved were 166 and 100. Similar shortfalls were experienced during 1970-71, but the most serious reduction occurred in 1972, when the demands of the *Linebacker* campaign cut the number of alert-dedicated bombers from the planned figure of 174 to 49 – which was just under 11 per cent of the total force of 462 aircraft (402 B-52s and 60 FB-111As).

This obviously had quite damaging effects and undoubtedly meant that it would have been virtually impossible to execute the Single Integrated Operational Plan (SIOP) – basically the plan for nuclear war

with the Soviet Union – in its entirety. The discrepancy was, to some extent, offset by the availability of intercontinental ballistic missiles and submarine-launched ballistic missiles and there's no doubt that the USA still possessed an awesome potential to inflict damage. But, those systems lacked the flexibility and responsiveness that were always perceived as being key facets of the manned bomber force.

Thereafter, the end of the conflict in Vietnam meant that the situation improved as B-52s which had been deployed to Guam and Thailand returned home in the latter half of 1973. Nevertheless, shortfalls were still very much in evidence in 1973-74 and it was only when SAC substantially lowered its alert requirement in 1974-75 that the required figures were actually attained. In essence, while the number of bombers fell only slightly (from 493 in December 1973 to 489 in December 1975), the alert requirement was drastically reduced, declining from 34 per cent to just under 22 per cent over the same period. Expressed in more literal terms, that involved cutting the number of alert dedicated bombers from 170 to 107.

This change meant that for the first time in more than a decade, SAC was able to meet its obligations and the number of alert aircraft was held at slightly above the 100 mark until 1982, despite more than 75

ABOVE An early proving flight by a B-52G (58-0159) wearing a SAC shield and carrying two North American AGM-28 Hound Dog air-launched cruise missiles. SAC's enormous investment in the ungainly Hound Dog, which was smaller and more nimble, but no faster, than a jet aircraft, reflects the emphasis on strategic bombing from stand-off distances which resulted from the appearance of radar-guided surface-to-air missiles like the Soviet SA-2 *Guideline* that shot down an American U-2 reconnaissance aircraft on 1 May 1960 *(Boeing)*

B-52s being retired from service during this interval. This effectively meant that about 25 per cent of the force stood alert at any given time until the early part of 1982.

The next noteworthy reduction came in 1982-83 when another 80 B-52s were taken out of service and this coincided with a fall in alert resources to just 76 bombers at the end of 1983. This represented 23.5 per cent of the total strength of 323 and one might reasonably have expected that percentage level to be sustained with the advent of the B-1B in 1986-87. Curiously, though, the reality was rather different and the opposite happened. So, while the delivery of the B-1B was directly responsible for a rise in total bomber numbers to 396 at the end of 1987, there was no corresponding increase in alert resources. Indeed, the latter actually fell to 69 (17.4 per cent) over the same period and further decline followed, to just 63 at the end of 1988, when the total number of bombers in the SAC inventory was 411.

Thereafter, progressive disposal of the B-52G model was the signal for still more reductions in alert strength. This in fact resulted in a decline to the point

where just 53 bombers were on guard at the close of 1990, a figure that may well have dipped sharply in the first two months of 1991, when roughly two-thirds of the B-52Gs that remained in the active inventory were committed to combat against Iraq and when the B-1B Lancer was itself subject to a grounding order in the wake of the latest accident.

For the bombers and crews that returned from the Gulf with fresh battle honours during March, it was a case of very quickly getting back to 'business as usual' but the full-scale resumption of alert duty was not destined to last long. Six months later, with the 'Cold War' over and the threat from the former Soviet Union apparently at an end, it was evident that the need to continue with alert had all but ceased to exist. In view of that, President George Bush directed that the long-running programme be formally terminated with immediate effect.

By this time, following the removal of the FB-111A from alert status in June 1991, only about 40 B-52s and B-1Bs were still being kept in 'cocked' configuration at a dozen SAC bases. Removal of Air Launched Cruise Missiles and gravity bombs from these aircraft began on the morning of 18 September 1991 and was completed in the early afternoon. Closely monitoring the stand down of the bombers and 450 Minuteman II missiles at his Omaha headquarters, CinCSAC Gen George L Butler received word at 1459 hours that the process had been completed and that, for the first time in just under 34 years, no SAC bomber was on alert.

This did not mean that SAC was not prepared for nuclear war, for the Minuteman III and Peacekeeper ICBMs did remain ready for launch at a moment's notice – and the command was quite capable of returning a proportion of its bomber resources to alert status if the international situation dictated such a course of action. So far, that hasn't been necessary and if it does ever come about, responsibility for managing the force will no longer be entrusted to SAC, which ceased to exist in June 1992.

SAC itself may have gone, overtaken by events and victim to a major USAF reorganisation - but the bomber that was synonymous with the command for all but the first decade kept on trucking as part of the newly-created Air Combat Command. Alert may have ended as a formal part of day-to-day operations, but the capability remains – and who is to say categorically that the Stratofortress may not again find itself held in readiness for nuclear war at some future date.

While they may not have been called upon to engage in ground alert at overseas locations to any great extent, B-52s most definitely pulled their fair share of this often tedious duty at a host of stateside bases for more than three decades, until President Bush ordered a stand-down with effect from 18 September 1991. That aspect of operations was quite well publicised by SAC and so was the *Looking Glass* airborne command post KC/EC-135 Stratotanker which began continuous operations from the command's headquarters at Offutt AFB on 3 February 1961.

Even though the idea of maintaining aircraft aloft on a 24-hour basis may have appeared revolutionary, the concept was in fact far from new, since B-52s had already been doing exactly that on pretty much a daily footing for more than two years. And, unlike the KC-135s that functioned in the command post role, the B-52s weren't replaced at eight-hour intervals. Far from it, for an airborne alert mission as flown by the Stratofortress must have been a quite fatiguing experience, in that each mission typically lasted somewhere in the region of 24 hours 30 minutes, included two in-flight refuelling hook-ups and covered at least 10,000 miles.

It is also perhaps not widely realised that this operation ran for the best part of a decade before it came to an abrupt halt in January 1968 following the loss of a B-52G that was attempting an emergency landing at Thule Air Base, Greenland. Prior to that, the airborne alert had been officially known by the code-names *Steeltrap* and *Chrome Dome* at different times.

Like most innovative SAC ideas, it was first subjected to test and evaluation, before being adopted as standard operating procedure. In fact, it appears pos-

sible that the first experiments were conducted at around the same time as ground alert was introduced, for CinCSAC Gen Thomas S Power's revelation of ground alert in November 1957 also included a rather mysterious reference to having 'a certain percentage of my command in the air'.

Due to political concerns which had their origins in Washington, he was unable to expand on that observation, but there is reason to believe that he was most probably referring to a trial project involving the B-36, for a SAC historical study indicates that aircraft of this type were exploring the concept of airborne alert during February 1958. Power's deliberately vague choice of words masked what was in reality no more than a token effort, for the same study states that only one bomber was involved at any given time. There's no denying that this aircraft represented a 'certain percentage', nor that it possessed considerable destructive power, but a clearer perspective of its worth can be gained from the knowledge that SAC possessed about 1650 bombers at the end of 1957.

Subsequently, a more exhaustive examination of the practicalities and pitfalls of airborne alert was undertaken by at least two Stratofortress outfits in 1958-59. Responsibility for the first trial – appropriately given the code-name *Head Start I* – was entrusted to the 42nd Bomb Wing at Loring AFB, Maine, which

BELOW Armourers replenish the magazines associated with the quartet of 0.5 cal machine guns that constituted the sole defence against rear-quarter attacks by hostile fighter aircraft on most versions of the B-52 *(USAF)*

kept several B-52Ds airborne on a round-the-clock basis between 15 September and 15 December 1958. The second trial (*Head Start II*) was accomplished between 2 March and 30 June 1959 and required the 92nd Bomb Wing at Fairchild AFB, Washington, to keep five B-52Ds airborne at all times.

Between them, these tests proved that the concept was indeed viable, while also indicating that centralised servicing was essential if it was to be successful. Having confirmed the feasibility of airborne alert, SAC next directed its attention to what it was forced to refer to as an 'indoctrination period' when it went public with news of these operations in mid-January 1961. In reality, this euphemism disguised the fact that B-52s were now engaged in a genuine airborne alert programme which had been extended in scope and which required a number of other units to take turns in keeping a proportion of their bomber resources in the air around the clock.

SAC's original desire – as put forward to the Joint Chiefs of Staff and the Secretary of Defense in the spring of 1959 – was nothing if not ambitious and anticipated developing the ability to keep no less than a quarter of the B-52 fleet in the air at any given time. With the size of that force surpassing the 600 mark in the early 1960s, it doesn't require too much brainpower to realise that we are talking of at least 150 bombers and there can be no doubt that an airborne alert of that extent would have placed an enormous strain on human resources. As for purely financial aspects, only the wealthiest nation on earth could have contemplated such an idea, since the annual bill was

BELOW The larger diameter of the TF33 engine intakes is clearly seen in this head-on study of a B-52H cruising at altitude. Also worthy of note is the application of white paint above the forward and rear fuselage sections, with that above the cockpit almost certainly intended to provide a more comfortable working environment for the crew during often tedious missions *(USAF)*

confidently expected to run into hundreds of millions of dollars.

In the end, a compromise was reached that allowed the command to draw up plans for an airborne alert force of half that size – one-eighth of the fleet or somewhere in the region of 75 aircraft. Even then, it was recognised that this capability could not be maintained indefinitely, but sufficient spares and manpower resources were acquired to permit it to be continued for one year - and then only on a contingency basis in the event of an emergency. As will be seen, such an emergency wasn't long in arriving.

In the meantime, SAC continued training, but the extent of the effort was low-key and largely dictated by appropriations of $15 million in FY 1960 and $25 million in FY 1961. That was sufficient to support barely 10 aircraft on a year-round basis, while cost projections in the early 1960s indicated that at least $225 million would be required to cover annual operating costs to sustain one-eighth of the force. If other factors such as spares, fuel, personnel and training were taken into account, those costs would rise to the order of $800 million once the programme was up and running. And that was in 1961 dollars, at a time when fuel was plentiful – and plenty cheap. . .

While cost considerations may have prohibited implementation of airborne alert on the grand scale suggested by SAC, the command did elect to keep a token force in the sky on a 24-hour basis. By the time that Gen Power revealed this activity to the public, more than 6000 sorties had been completed and it was now part and parcel of routine operations. Eventually, almost all SAC B-52 units underwent spells of airborne

ABOVE Plugged in and with fuel flowing, the tanks of the fifth Seattle-built B-52E (56-0635) are replenished by a KC-135A Stratotanker in a scene replayed countless times since the mighty 'Buff' entered service. This shot almost certainly dates from the late 1950s, for the KC-135 still has the short fin that was originally fitted to the Stratotanker when it entered the inventory *(USAF)*

alert duty, although it seems that by no means all of them emerged from the experience with their reputations enhanced.

One unit that was involved at a fairly early stage was the 4228th Strategic Wing at Columbus AFB, Mississippi. This began operating the B-52F model in May 1959 and was subsequently tasked with keeping a total of four aircraft aloft around-the-clock from October 1959 to July 1960, while simultaneously satisfying its normal ground alert commitments.

Normal procedure with the 4228th was probably representative of the other units involved at that time and this Wing basically split the operation in half, launching its four aircraft as two pairs at different times of the day. Once the replacement bombers were airborne and had checked in with SAC's command post, the previous pair was stood down and permitted to recover at Columbus, typically after just over 24 hours in the air. In the case of the 4228th, its contribution to *Steeltrap* and *Chrome Dome* got off to what can only be called an inauspicious start, for the unit lost a B-52F (57-0036) in a mid-air collision with a KC-135A Stratotanker on 15 October, barely a week after launching its first sorties.

After that, things appear to have improved somewhat, since the 4228th eventually won a Presidential Outstanding Unit Award for its achievement in supporting airborne alert – and, in company with Barksdale's 4238th SW, it was allegedly the only SAC unit to 'survive' the rigours and pressures involved in keeping four aircraft airborne day-in, day-out, for nine months. Of itself, that achievement may not sound too startling, but the effort involved probably comes into stark focus if you consider that the Wing possessed just 16 B-52Fs; that it had to keep about a third of those on ground alert throughout the same interval and that each and every member of aircrew accumulated over 2000 flight hours during the nine-month period in question.

Even though the airborne alert operation was ostensibly still a purely training activity at this time, it should be emphasised that nuclear weapons were routinely carried by B-52s assigned to this duty. That was most certainly the case in the accident referred to above, for two weapons of an unknown type (possibly Mk.15s) were subsequently recovered from the wreckage that fell to earth about 20 miles south of Hardinsburg, Kentucky.

In both cases, the external casings survived unbroken and there was thus no hazard from radiation. In later accidents, the consequences were much more serious – and much, much more embarrassing, since the wreckage fell on foreign soil.

Turning to consider the the number of aircraft involved, this seems to have fluctuated somewhat throughout the period of time that airborne alert was undertaken. Freely available statistics indicate that as few as six were active at the end of 1960 and that the quantity declined still further to just three or four in the last two years of the operation, presumably because of increased cost against a background of escalating involvement in the war in South-East Asia.

For much of the time, though, the usual figure hovered around 10 to 12 aircraft, hence the unofficial nickname of 'SAC's Dirty Dozen' that was applied to the airborne alert force. Not too much is known about specific routes that were used, although these were apparently designed to ensure that aircraft remained within reach of nominated targets for the bulk of the mission. One such route regularly brought B-52s over the northern United Kingdom; another lay further south in the vicinity of Spain; and still others involved transits of the Arctic landmass.

Although airborne alert was generally limited in extent, there was one brief interlude when it was vastly expanded – and when, for a few days, the world appeared to be hovering on the brink of the unthinkable, namely a full-scale thermonuclear exchange between the USA and the Soviet Union. The catalyst for this was the basing of Soviet SS-4 'Sandal' medium-range and SS-5 'Skean' intermediate-range ballistic missiles (IRBMs) and Ilyushin Il-28 'Beagle' medium bombers in Cuba in the autumn of 1962. In view of the fact that this placed an offensive Soviet capability less than 100 miles from Florida, in what the USA liked to think of as its own back-yard, it was hardly surprising that it precipitated a major crisis between the two superpowers.

President Kennedy wasn't slow in demanding removal of both the missiles and the bombers, going public with news of the growing crisis on 22 October, when he informed the world that a naval blockade of the island would come into effect two days later. At about the same time as Kennedy was speaking, SAC was shifting into a heightened state of readiness. This was accomplished in a number of ways. One was the expansion and dispersal of ground-based alert bomber and tanker resources. Another entailed bringing the small but increasingly important intercontinental ballistic missile (ICBM) force to alert configuration. In addition, the command instigated a full-blown airborne alert for the first (and last) time in its history.

As it turned out, that alert was to last for almost exactly a month, even though evidence that the message had been received and understood by the Soviets was apparent as early as 24 October when shipping bound for Cuba came to a halt in mid-Atlantic and even though Premier Krushchev announced on 28 October that the offending missiles would be withdrawn.

Undeterred by that admission, Stratofortresses continued to roam the skies until 21 November 1962, when a B-52H of the 379th Bomb Wing returned to its home base at Wurtsmith AFB, Michigan and brought the airborne alert to an end, after the Russians had agreed to also remove the Il-28 medium bombers from Cuba. Henceforth, SAC progressively resumed normal peacetime levels of activity.

Over the period in question, B-52s engaged in the airborne alert operation completed more than 2000 sorties, which equates to a daily average rate of about 70. This was very close to the desired target of keeping an eighth of the fleet on alert in times of emergency - and proved beyond doubt that it was a workable concept, as well as an inordinately expensive one, since that month-long operation resulted in the consumption of around 70 million gallons of fuel.

For airborne alert, that was in many ways the apex. The nadir came a few years later, with the loss of a couple of aircraft in unfortunate circumstances. The first of those losses involved B-52G 58-0256 from the 68th Bomb Wing's 51st Bomb Squadron at Seymour Johnson AFB, North Carolina. On 17 January 1966, this collided with a KC-135 while refuelling, with wreckage from both aircraft falling to earth near Palomares in Spain.

That was bad enough. What made matters much worse was that conventional explosive in two of the four nuclear weapons being carried by the B-52 detonated on impact with the ground, spreading radioactive material and contaminating the immediate vicinity of the crash site. Even more embarrassingly, one of the weapons went missing for the best part of two months and was only discovered on 15 March when a US Navy submarine engaged in the hunt found the device in 2500 feet of water about five miles offshore. Attempts to recover the B28RI bomb ultimately proved successful on 7 April, but not before it had been dislodged and allowed to sink deeper. In the meantime, US efforts to clean up the crash site and eliminate any vestiges of contamination resulted in the removal of some 1400 tons of soil and vegetation for transfer to a storage site in the USA.

A little over two years later, in late January 1968, B-52G 58-0188 of the 528th Bomb Squadron, 380th Strategic Aerospace Wing at Plattsburgh AFB, New York, was destroyed when it crashed on ice in North Star Bay while trying to make an emergency landing at Thule Air Base, Greenland. Once again, four nuclear weapons were involved and, as with the incident in Spain, some contamination resulted. This was evidently confined mainly to the area of the wreckage, with all four weapons being consumed by fire.

The ensuing clean-up operation necessitated removal of more than 200,000 cubic feet of ice, snow and water as well as aircraft wreckage to a storage facility in the United States and was evidently not completed until 13 September.

This accident effectively signalled an end to airborne alert operations, for they were immediately suspended and, as far as is known, were never resumed.

BELOW Loaded on its handling trolley, and with the wing attachment pylon in place, an AGM-28 Hound Dog missile is gingerly guided from the cavernous hold of a Military Air Transport Service Douglas C-124C Globemaster II. Missile and pylon were usually left mated to facilitate rapid armament of the B-52 *(USAF)*

STRATOFORTRESS WEAPONS

IN THE COURSE of its long career, the Stratofortress has outlived almost all of the weapons that it was expected to employ when it first entered service with SAC, apart from one or two types of conventional 'iron' bomb. That's hardly surprising, when one recalls that the only nuclear weapons available at the time of the B-52's maiden flight were little more than refined versions of the somewhat primitive devices that had been dropped on Japan in the summer of 1945. What has perhaps been more surprising is that Boeing's long-serving bomber proved sufficiently adaptable over the years to take advantage of much more sophisticated weaponry, including some devices which hadn't even progressed as far as the conceptual stage when the 'Buff' made its debut and which only evolved long after it entered service.

Considered purely and simply as a bomber, the ability of the B-52 to accept a succession of new weapons has undoubtedly been an important factor in its longevity and no survey of the Stratofortress would be complete without some reference to the weaponry that has been carried over the years. Unfortunately, the nature of some of those weapons is such that relatively little information is freely available.

Since the *raison d'etre* of the B-52 was strategic deterrence, it should come as no surprise to learn that thermonuclear weapons were regularly carried by the bombers of Strategic Air Command. If proof of that is needed, one need look no further than the two airborne collisions with KC-135 tanker aircraft in 1959 and 1966 and the accident at North Star Bay in Greenland in 1968. These much publicised incidents

LEFT This close-in view of a B-52G in flight shows the neat carriage arrangement adopted for the AGM-28 Hound Dog. Also visible are the missile's engine bay, main flying surfaces and smaller canard surfaces near the nose of the needle-like device. In the final years of service, many Hound Dogs also gained camouflage paint schemes like those of the bombers that carried them *(USAF)*

ABOVE The third production B-52H (60-0003) was used to test carriage of the ill-fated GAM-87A Skybolt ALBM. Had this immensely powerful weapon attained operational service, it was intended that each 'Buff' would carry four missiles. Initial deployment was to have been on the 'Cadillac,' but the B-52G may also have been destined to operate with Skybolt

certainly confirmed the presence of nuclear devices – or, at least, the massive clean-up operations that went on afterwards did.

As for ground alert, it was common knowledge that the aircraft involved were loaded with 'nukes', even though one couldn't always tell from just a casual glance at B-52s on alert pads, since they didn't always carry missiles. But, it was obvious that without nuclear weapons on board, the alert concept would be completely and utterly meaningless. The trouble was that nobody in a position of authority would admit it – nor, for that matter, would they deny it. A polite 'I can't discuss that' was about the only response one would get, raising the tantalising thought that the whole edifice of nuclear deterrence might conceivably have been built upon a huge game of bluff.

Leaving aside such diverting possibilities, secrecy surrounding the status of alert aircraft was, if anything, surpassed by the secrecy relating to nuclear weapons and it is only in the past few years that the veil has slipped slightly. Nevertheless, personnel who served with the now-defunct SAC and its successor, Air Combat Command, generally choose to say little or nothing about these weapons. In view of that, the following

has been based on information drawn from a variety of freely available sources. Suffice it to say that it probably isn't anything like the complete picture, but it at least provides a guide to the various weapons options available to the B-52 over the past four decades.

NUCLEAR-TIPPED MISSILE SYSTEMS

GAM-77/AGM-28 HOUND DOG

Four different types of nuclear-tipped missile have seen service on B-52s at different times, with a fifth falling victim to cancellation in the early 1960s. The first such weapon was also far and away the largest, with the North American Hound Dog actually meriting classification as a fairly unsophisticated cruise missile. It was certainly no lightweight, tipping the scales at an impressive 10,150 lbs when fully fuelled. Dimensionally, it was slightly over 42 ft long and some 9 ft high with a wing span of more than 12 ft. It was powered by a single Pratt & Whitney J52-P-3 engine rated at 7500 lb st. This was sufficient to propel the Hound Dog to a maximum speed of Mach 2.1 and the J52 could be used to augment the B-52's own clutch of eight turbojets, transforming it into a ten-engined machine during take-off and climb regimes of flight. Fuel burnt in this way could be replaced by drawing upon the parent aircraft's own stock. The Hound Dog's maximum range at altitude was somewhere in the region of 700 nautical miles, although this fell to little more than 200 nautical miles when at low level.

Two basic models of the Hound Dog were pro-

ABOVE If it is possible to describe a nuclear weapon as having an elegant appearance, that appellation most definitely applies to the GAM-87 Skybolt, as this view of two test missiles suspended from the wing of a Stratofortress clearly portrays. Cancellation meant that the B-52H eventually had to make do with the older and less potent Hound Dog, only two of which could be carried

duced. These were the GAM-77 (later AGM-28A) and GAM-77A (later AGM-28B), but the differences between the two were mainly intended to improve accuracy of the inertial guidance system and included repositioning the KS-120 astrotracker device from the missile pylon to the missile body. Both Hound Dog sub-types featured a common warhead in the form of a single W28 device which reportedly possessed a one megaton yield. This was basically identical to the warhead of the Mk 28 bomb and was one of three candidates considered for installation in the Hound Dog. Selection of the W28 occurred in 1959 and approximately 600 warheads were eventually stockpiled. In the same year, the USAF determined that sufficient missiles would be acquired for 29 B-52 squadrons and this eventually culminated in the production of about 700 by North American's plant at Downey, California.

Operational deployment began in December 1959 with the first unit to accept the Hound Dog being the 4135th Strategic Wing at Eglin AFB, Florida. Equipped with the B-52G model, this outfit was rather unusual in being tasked with supporting Category III tests of the GAM-77 and worked closely with the

Eglin-based Air Proving Ground Center in smoothing the path of full operational deployment of this weapon and the Quail decoy missile.

Following its introduction into service, those Bomb and Strategic Wings that were equipped with the Hound Dog eventually organised specialist subordinate elements to handle these weapons and the Quail decoy. Known as Airborne Missile Maintenance Squadrons (AMMS), 28 such units were created and these invariably used the same numerical designation as the parent Wing – thus, the squadron assigned to the 5th Bomb Wing at Travis AFB was the 5th AMMS; similarly, the 4130th SW at Bergstrom AFB had the 4130th AMMS. In virtually every case, the date of AMMS formation was 1 November 1962, with the only known exception being the 4135th AMMS which came into existence on 10 November 1962.

Incidentally, alert readers may have noticed that 29 B-52 squadrons were quoted as being in receipt of Hound Dog, but only 28 AMMSs are mentioned as having been formed. The discrepancy is explained by the 42nd Bomb Wing which possessed two subordinate B-52 squadrons (the 69th and 70th), rather than the more usual one. In this instance, the 42nd AMMS was responsible for looking after Hound Dog missiles carried by aircraft flown by crews from either of the two bomb squadrons.

At peak strength, attained during the latter half of 1963, SAC's operational Hound Dog force numbered around the 600 mark. However, this weapon wasn't so much concerned with knocking out specific strategic targets as with ensuring the successful execution of strategic bombing operations. Since accuracy evidently left more than a bit to be desired, the Hound Dog would not merit description as a pin-point weapon. Instead, it would most probably have been sent on ahead of penetrating bombers so as to eliminate concentrated defences along the ingress routes and in the vicinity of key targets. In this way, the AGM-28 was expected to give the bombers a greater probability of reaching their targets and delivering gravity nuclear weapons accurately. In later years, of course, the smaller Boeing AGM-69 SRAM was employed for a similar task.

Although carriage of the Hound Dog by the Stratofortress began with the penultimate production variant and was later extended to the B-52H in lieu of the abortive Skybolt, these were far from being the only models that acquired compatibility with this bulky missile. Eventually, as is evident from the table detailing Hound Dog deployment, other B-52 sub-types also carried the familiar shape beneath each inner wing section.

However, in the case of the B-52E and B-52F, it seems that these relinquished this capability with effect from about the mid-1960s. The draw-down in fact began in earnest in 1967, with the number of AGM-28s on charge falling from 550 or so to about 475. Still further cuts followed in 1968 and by the end of that year only just over 300 were still on hand. These were mainly assigned to B-52G/H units although some B-52Ds carried on standing alert duty with the Hound Dog until well into the 1970s, when not needed for conventional bombing operations in South-East Asia.

The number of missiles thereafter fluctuated, rising to about 350 at the close of 1969, before slowly dwindling to just over 300 in December 1975. By then,

BELOW In addition to being rather more aesthetically pleasing than the Hound Dog, Skybolt also made use of a much neater method of carriage, with the 'inverted-Y' pylon attachment being shown to advantage in this close-up view of two test weapons

however, the Hound Dog was essentially part of SAC's history, for some six months had passed since the last missiles had been taken off alert duty at the end of June. They were not, however, disposed of immediately and the Hound Dog seems to have been retained in non-operational status for a little while longer. In fact, it was not until June 1978 that personnel assigned to the Loring-based 42nd Bomb Wing finally scrapped the last AGM-28.

GAM-87A SKYBOLT

Arguably the most ambitious weapon to be considered for carriage by the Stratofortress, the Douglas GAM-87A Skybolt was an air-launched ballistic missile (ALBM) system which would have carried a W59 nuclear warhead in a Mk 7 re-entry vehicle (RV). Development was initiated in the latter half of the 1950s and Douglas was selected as prime contractor, with Aerojet looking after propulsion aspects, General Dynamics working on the RV and Nortronics taking care of the complex guidance system.

The decision to proceed with Skybolt was reached in February 1960, with the initial operational capability expected in 1964. It was also revealed that the B-52 would be the launch platform, with four such weapons being carried on specially adapted pylons located between the inner engine pods and the fuselage. Four months later, in June, British interest culminated in an order for 100 missiles to be carried by the Avro Vulcan.

At this time, the US anticipated buying 1000 missiles and procurement of the final B-52H model was undertaken with the Skybolt very much in mind, as indeed was the trials programme which used several examples of the B-52H. However, since the total B-52H buy only numbered 102 aircraft of which roughly 90 would be operational at any given time, it's pretty obvious that the 'Cadillac' would not have been the only version of the Stratofortress to carry the Skybolt ALBM. The B-52G appears to be the most likely candidate to have upped the numbers and was closely involved in captive-carry and inert drop testing. In view of that, it's not unreasonable to assume that all of the 11 B-52G Wings would have been given this weapon as well.

As it turned out, political and economic factors forced President Kennedy to call a halt in December 1962, rather ironically at about the same time as the

LEFT The second missile to be carried externally by the 'Buff' was the AGM-69A Short-Range Attack Missile, or SRAM. Smaller and lighter than Hound Dog, up to six SRAMs could be accommodated beneath each wing, with eight more on a special rotary launcher inside the weapons bay to give a maximum load of 20 (Boeing)

first truly successful air-launch of a test specimen took place. Cancellation made little difference to the B-52G, but had rather more significant consequences for the B-52H, which would now carry only half the number of 'side-arms'. And those would be the Hound Dog, a system unable to match the potential of Skybolt, even though it was a proven weapon.

AGM-69 SHORT-RANGE ATTACK MISSILE (SRAM)

The next missile to be associated with the B-52 was much smaller than the Hound Dog and also much more numerous. This was Boeing's AGM-69A SRAM which was originally visualised as being a kind of super defence-suppression system, although it eventually became rather more than that, by virtue of possessing similar accuracy and yield characteristics to those of the Boeing LGM-30G Minuteman III ICBM. In fact, the W69 warhead yield was of the order of 170 KT.

SAC first identified a requirement for a new missile during the course of 1963, but it was not until the end of October 1966 that Boeing was formally authorised to press ahead with what eventually became the SRAM. The finished article was a surprisingly small device measuring some 14 ft in length, 17.5 inches in diameter and weighing about a ton. Propulsion was by means of a Thiokol SR-75-LP-1 restartable solid-fuelled two-pulse rocket motor, which gave a maximum speed of about Mach 2.5 and range varied from 30 to 100 miles. A General Precision/Kearfott inertial guidance system was installed.

Flight testing of the new missile began in July 1969,

with the first launch by an all-SAC crew taking place in September 1970. Results of the trials programme were sufficiently promising to result in Boeing securing the first production contract in January 1971. About 15 months later, on 1 March 1972, the first SRAM to reach a SAC unit was delivered to the Loring-based 42nd BW, which went on to attain operational status with the AGM-69A on 4 August of the same year.

Thereafter, deployment of SRAM was limited to the final two versions of the Stratofortress family and the FB-111A, with some 1521 missiles eventually being completed before production ended in July 1975. The final missile to be delivered was assigned to the 320th BW at Mather just one month later and as far as is known, all of the SAC units that were current with the B-52G and B-52H at that time were ultimately to be equipped with the new missile. In addition, both FB-111A Wings received this weapon and at a later stage, it was also assigned to those units equipped with the B-1B Lancer.

In the case of the B-52G/H, at the start of its service career, the number of SRAMs that could be carried was 20. Of these, a maximum of eight could be accommodated internally, on a specially designed rotary launcher situated at the aft end of the weapons bay area. In addition, a further dozen missiles were carried underwing, with six being positioned on each of two pylons.

In the early 1980s, however, external carriage was abandoned. Eventually, following concerns over the continued safety of the warheads installed in SRAM, this weapon was removed from the operational inventory in 1990.

AGM-86B AIR-LAUNCHED CRUISE MISSILE (ALCM)

Beginning life as the Subsonic Cruise Armed Decoy (SCAD) missile in the mid-1960s, subsequent developments affecting this concept were nothing if not convoluted, but eventually led to a decision in June 1973 to use surplus SCAD funds to finance fresh research into a new study of cruise missile technology. It was this study that eventually culminated in the 1979 competitive fly-off between two ALCM contenders, with Boeing's AGM-86B eventually emerging victorious over the General Dynamics AGM-109H Tomahawk, itself a derivative of the US Navy's submarine-launched cruise missile.

Not long afterwards, in May 1980, Boeing was awarded its first production contract, for a batch of 225 missiles. Deliveries began in 1982 and the first unit to acquire this new weapon was the 416th BW which achieved an initial operational capability with ALCM in December 1982. Production eventually ended in October 1986 with the delivery of the 1815th missile.

ALCM is carried with the wings, elevons and vertical tail folded. Deployment of these surfaces takes just two seconds to accomplish after release, while the Williams International Corporation F107-WR-100 turbofan reaches its full rated output of 600 lb st just a second or so later, by which time the AGM-86B will have fallen about 450 ft.

When configured for flight, the ALCM spans 12 ft, is 20 ft 9 in long and has a body diameter of 24.5 in., which is more than enough to accommodate a single W80-1 nuclear warhead with a selectable yield in the 150-170 KT range, as well as TERCOM (terrain contour matching) navigation equipment and sufficient fuel to fly for about 1500 miles. Gross weight is 3200 lbs and the AGM-86B has a maximum speed of about 500 mph.

Operational deployment eventually encompassed about a dozen units, including those equipped with the B-1B. Of the B-52 force, approximately 190 aircraft were configured to carry ALCM, with this number embracing all 96 surviving B-52Hs as well as 98 examples of the B-52G. So as to permit satellite identification of the ALCM-compatible B-52Gs, fairings known as 'strakelets' were fitted at the leading edge of the wing roots – B-52Hs did not require these, since the turbofan engines provided a clear recognition feature. On the B-52G, the AGM-86B has only ever been mounted externally, with six missiles being carried on each of two wing pylons. An identical arrangement is used for external carriage by the B-52H, which can also accommodate up to eight more ALCMs on the Common Strategic Rotary Launcher (CSRL) in the weapons bay.

As is recounted elsewhere, some ALCMs were modified in the late 1980s for conventional warfare purposes. These featured a 1000-lb blast fragmentation device in place of the W80 warhead and also embodied Global Positioning System satellite receiver equipment in lieu of TERCOM. In this guise, as the AGM-86C, they are the only ALCMs ever to have been used in anger, with some three dozen missiles being expended against Iraq in the Gulf War.

RIGHT Utilised to test *Rivet Ace* Phase VI defensive avionics, B-52G 58-0204 featured an appropriate emblem on its forward fuselage section, and was also employed to verify compatibility with the AGM-69A SRAM. Just visible on the far tailplane is the fairing that apparently housed AN/ALQ-127 tail warning radar antenna, which was not adopted *(Boeing)*

AGM-129A ADVANCED CRUISE MISSILE
(ACM)

Development of the Convair AGM-129A ACM began in the latter half of the 1980s, culminating in airborne trials getting under way in the spring of 1989. Dimensionally similar to its ALCM predecessor, the ACM is somewhat lighter, at 2750 lbs, but possesses greater range and survivability as well as enhanced accuracy. Power is furnished by a Williams F112 turbofan engine rated at 900lbst and this weapon also capitalises on experience gained in the field of low-observable or 'stealth' technology. Warhead details are not known, but a version of the W80 appears to be the most likely candidate.

BELOW Looking more akin to an oversized revolver, the internal carriage of SRAM relied upon a rotary launcher device that was able to carry a maximum load of eight missiles.SRAMs were usually positioned at the aft extremity of the weapons bay, thus allowing the same aircraft to carry up to four parachute-retarded gravity nuclear bombs – this fit applied to both the B-52G and H *(Boeing)*

By the end of Fiscal Year 1991, somewhere in the region of 650 ACMs had been manufactured, but plans to obtain 1461 specifically to arm the B-52H force were shelved by President George Bush at the beginning of 1992. Details of current deployment are not available, but it is known that the B-52Hs of the 410th BW at K I Sawyer AFB were modified to carry ACM in the late 1980s, although there is no evidence to confirm that they received it. In addition, the 7th BW at Carswell was also identified in 1989 as being earmarked to be an early recipient of the AGM-129A.

However, the 7th BW ceased operating the B-52H during 1992 and the 410th BW is slated to follow suit in 1994. In view of that, it is likely that AGM-129 deployment has actually involved other units, with the 2nd BW at Barksdale and the 5th BW at Minot being good possibilities. Maximum B-52H load is almost certainly 20 missiles, comprising eight in the bomb bay CSRL and six on each of the two wing stations.

DECOY MISSILE SYSTEMS

GAM-72/ADM-20 QUAIL

Of broadly similar vintage to the Hound Dog in terms of its frontline service career, if not its development timescale, the McDonnell GAM-72 (later ADM-20) Quail decoy missile was housed internally at the extreme rear of the B-52's weapons bay. The installation was in fact surprisingly compact and comprised four missiles, along with a pair of retractable launcher devices that lowered the decoys into the slipstream, where the flying surfaces were spread and the engine was started, prior to launch command by the radar navigator. It was usual practice to pre-build missile 'packages' for installation as a complete unit of four, but any one or all of the missiles could be jettisoned in the event of malfunction and it was also possible to dump the whole package in major emergency situations.

A much smaller device than Hound Dog, the Quail measured some 12 ft 10.6 ins in length; had a span of 5 ft 4.5 in with the wings spread for flight; and was some 3 ft 3.5 ins high with the vertical tail surfaces deployed. In stowed form, it took up rather less space, being just 2 ft 1.7 in high. Like the Hound Dog, it relied upon a jet engine for propulsion, being fitted with a single General Electric J85-GE-7. This enabled it to attain a maximum speed of Mach 0.85 and a

range of some 460 nautical miles at 50,000 ft. At 35,000 ft, the corresponding figures were 393 nautical miles range at Mach 0.8.

While it may have looked somewhat boxy and unsophisticated, the Quail was deceptive, for careful design and the use of radar reflectors, electronic repeaters, chaff and infra-red simulators resulted in it producing a radar and infra-red image that closely approximated to that of the B-52 'mother ship'. It was, in simple terms, the exact reverse of today's much-vaunted stealth technology – and the confusion it

ABOVE Emerging victorious in the fly-off against the General Dynamics AGM-109H Tomahawk, Boeing's AGM-86B Air-Launched Cruise Missile or ALCM was ordered in large quantities for service with SAC's B-52 force *(Boeing)*

would have sown in the mind of enemy air defences was compounded by the fact that Quail could be programmed to perform at least one change of cruising speed and two turns.

Three basic versions existed, although only two were produced in new-build form. The first model was

RIGHT Extensive trials were undertaken with both ALCM contenders before the USAF opted to purchase the Boeing missile from 1980 onwards. Here, one of the development rounds is caught a split second after being dropped from the wing station of a B-52G. Within moments, the flying surfaces will deploy and the small Williams F107-WR-100 turbofan engine will have reached full power, allowing the ALCM to proceed under its own steam to the target *(Boeing)*

the basic GAM-72 (later ADM-20A) but only 24 were built and these were mainly expended on trials and tests. Therefter, manufacture switched to the GAM-72A (later ADM-20B), with more than 500 of this derivative being completed before production ended on 28 May 1962 when McDonnell handed over the final missile. Subsequent modification to adapt the Quail for low-level operation resulted in the GAM-72B (later ADM-20C) making its debut in 1963. Most of the GAM-72As were so modified, through fitment of a barometric switch for terrain avoidance and alterations to the wiring.

Development of the Quail in fact predated the Hound Dog and was initiated in October 1952 when SAC advised the USAF headquarters that it had a requirement for a decoy device that could be carried and launched from bomber aircraft prior to them pen-

BELOW Although rather larger than the AGM-69A SRAM, the Boeing AGM-86B ALCM makes use of an equally neat pylon attachment that allows up to six weapons to be carried under each wing. In addition, the B-52H can take a further eight missiles on the Common Strategic Rotary Launcher in the weapons bay, an option that was not available to the B-52G (Boeing)

etrating enemy territory. More than three years later, after extensive study by the Air Research and Development Command, McDonnell was alerted in February 1956 that it had been chosen to be the prime contractor for a decoy system known as Quail. Flight trials of the XGAM-72 began in November 1958 and events moved far more swiftly thereafter, with McDonnell being awarded a production contract on the very last day of December 1958.

Production configured missiles began to join the 4135th Strategic Wing at Eglin in mid-September 1960 and SAC formally declared this unit operational with the Quail on 1 February 1961. By this time, it had been determined that 14 Stratofortress squadrons (drawn from 13 Wings) would eventually utilise the decoy missile and these were fully equipped and operational with effect from 15 April 1962. It remained in service until 1978, when a shortage of spares forced its retirement, even though it was still felt to be effective. Details of those units that were initially equipped with the ADM-20 can be found in the table listing AGM-28 Hound Dog assignments and it is worth noting that while all Quail-equipped Wings had Hound Dog, not all Hound Dog-equipped Wings had Quail.

SUBSONIC CRUISE ARMED DECOY (SCAD)

For a time, it looked very much as if the Quail would be supplanted and eventually replaced by another system known the Subsonic Cruise Armed Decoy (SCAD). This proposal was put forward in 1966 and there's no doubt that SCAD would have made life much more difficult for the Soviet defence network by virtue of adding a measure of nuclear attack capability to a decoy. Thus, even if the USSR managed to develop the means to determine which was the bomber and which the decoy, they would still find it necessary to divert valuable resources to destroy the latter.

At that time, two versions were considered, with SCAD-A being earmarked for carriage by the B-52 and SCAD-B by the B-1A. In the event, after much debate, the SCAD concept was abandoned in the summer of 1973, but development and design work undertaken by Boeing in connection with the project led, via a tortuous and time-consuming route, to a device that fared much better in frontline service, namely the AGM-86B ALCM.

AGM-28 HOUND DOG OPERATING UNITS – INITIAL DEPLOYMENT

Wing	Squadron	Base	Model	
5th BW	23 BS	Travis AFB, Ca	B-52G	(ADM-20 also)
6th BW	40 BS	Walker AFB, NM	B-52E	
11th BW	26 BS	Altus AFB, Ok	B-52E	(ADM-20 also)
19th BW	28 BS	Homestead AFB, Fl	B-52H	
28th BW	77 BS	Ellsworth AFB, SD	B-52D	
42nd BW	69 BS	Loring AFB, Me	B-52G	(ADM-20 also)
	70 BS	Loring AFB, Me	B-52G	(ADM-20 also)
72nd BW	60 BS	Ramey AFB, PR	B-52G	(ADM-20 also)
92nd BW	325 BS	Fairchild AFB, Wa	B-52D	
97th BW	340 BS	Blytheville AFB, Ar	B-52G	(ADM-20 also)
379th BW	524 BS	Wurtsmith AFB, Mi	B-52H	
4038th SW	341 BS	Dow AFB, Me	B-52G	(ADM-20 also)
4039th SW	75 BS	Griffiss AFB, NY	B-52G	(ADM-20 also)
4042nd SW	526 BS	K I Sawyer AFB, Mi	B-52H	
4043rd SW	42 BS	Wright-Patterson AFB, Oh	B-52E	(ADM-20 also)
4047th SW	347 BS	McCoy AFB, Fl	B-52D	
4123rd SW	98 BS	Clinton-Sherman AFB, Ok	B-52E	
4126th SW	31 BS	Beale AFB, Ca	B-52G	(ADM-20 also)
4130th SW	335 BS	Bergstrom AFB, Tx	B-52D	
4133rd SW	30 BS	Grand Forks AFB, ND	B-52H	
4134th SW	72 BS	Mather AFB, Ca	B-52F	
4135th SW	301 BS	Eglin AFB, Fl	B-52G	(ADM-20 also)
4136th SW	525 BS	Minot AFB, ND	B-52H	(ADM-20 also)
4137th SW	342 BS	Robins AFB, Ga	B-52G	(ADM-20 also)
4138th SW	336 BS	Turner AFB, Ga	B-52D	
4228th SW	492 BS	Columbus AFB, Ms	B-52F	
4238th SW	436 BS	Barksdale AFB, La	B-52F	
4239th SW	93 BS	Kincheloe AFB, Mi	B-52H	
4241st SW	73 BS	Seymour Johnson AFB, NC	B-52G	(ADM-20 also)

BELOW A test example of the AGM-86B falls clear of the weapons bay during trials of the Air-Launched Cruise Missile in the latter part of the 1970s. An adaptation of this weapon optimised for conventional warfare was successfully employed in the Gulf War of 1991, when more than 30 AGM-86Cs were launched against targets in Iraq *(Boeing)*

NUCLEAR BOMBS

About a dozen different types of nuclear and thermonuclear bomb have been carried by the B-52 throughout its service career, ranging in terms of explosive power from the Mk.6 fission bomb which had a relatively low yield of between 30-60 kilotons up to the awesome B53 nine-megaton monster. Those figures might well seem pretty meaningless, but a better perspective of their destructive power may result if one recalls that one kiloton (KT) is the equivalent of 1000 tons of TNT whereas one megaton (MT) equates to 1,000,000 tons of TNT.

Mathematicians may well be able to come up with an estimate of how much more powerful the B53 is when compared with the Mk.6 but such abstruse considerations are probably of interest only to nuclear physicists and experts in demolition. After all, if you happened to be hanging around anywhere in the vicinity of ground zero, either one of these weapons is

clearly going to spoil your day. So, for that matter, would any of the other bombs carried by the 'Buff' had thermonuclear war become reality. Happily, it hasn't – or, at least, it hasn't yet.

Improvements in weapons design and engineering combined with advances in the field of nuclear physics have not surprisingly exerted a considerable impact on

ABOVE Missile shapes approximating the size and weight of the Boeing AGM-86B air launched cruise missile (ALCM) hang beneath a B-52G (58-0204) used as a trials vehicle in ALCM tests. This 1979 view shows preparation for captive-carry and separation trials for the AGM-86B. At the time, a competitive fly-off was slated between the AGM-86B and the General Dynamics AGM-109, a contest which was won by the Boeing design *(USAF)*

BELOW Another view of the aircraft used for trials in connection with the AGM-86B ALCM, this time with the main undercarriage just starting the retraction cycle as the 'Buff' takes-off from Wichita, Kansas. Evidence of previous ownership is provided by the 320th BW badge *(Boeing)*

the physical attributes of these bombs. In the early days, when attention was focussed more on maximising the already fearsome destructive potential, these weapons were large and unwieldy, relying on the 'sledgehammer and nut' principal of using excessive force to achieve the objective.

Subsequent developments benefited from a process that was almost akin to miniaturisation. In reality, while the length of these weapons may not have changed much, they have certainly become slimmer and lighter. This, in turn, allows more weapons to be carried by each bomber and those weapons could also be referred to as more 'user-friendly'.

This is best exemplified by late production versions

of the B61 bomb. These have a variable-yield capacity that can be selected in flight, as well as 'FUFO' capability. The latter acronym actually signifies 'Full-Fuzing Option', which allows bomber crews to select the desired mode prior to weapons delivery. For the record, the options are retarded or free-fall airburst; retarded or free-fall surface burst and delayed detonation after lay-down delivery from altitudes as low as 50 ft.

Brief details of the nuclear and thermonuclear bombs known to have been applicable to the B-52 follow. Before considering them, it should be pointed out that weapon designation practice changed in 1968. Prior to that, production examples of these devices were given Mark numbers (commonly abbreviated as Mk) which corresponded to the warhead identification number – hence, a bomb based on the W8 warhead would be known as the Mk 8. In 1968, however, the 'Mk' prefix was replaced by 'B' (for bomb, as in B83), with the numerical portion still correlating with the warhead number. In the following text, weapons that were still in the stockpile after 1968 are referred to as 'Bxx', whereas those removed from inventory before that are referred to as 'Mk xx'.

At the time the B-52 made its maiden flight in April 1952, the US nuclear arsenal contained only fission weapons, with the newest additions being the Mk.5 and Mk.6. The former actually entered the stockpile in 1952, but was not widely deployed, for production ended after less than 150 had been built. The latter began reaching the stockpile a little earlier, in 1951,

and was the first such weapon to undergo mass production, with approximately 1100 examples being completed by 1955, coincidentally the year in which the B-52 began to join SAC.

Both of these devices were destined to remain in the stockpile until 1962-63 and both were also deployed with B-52 units during that time. However, they were soon supplanted and eventually replaced by more potent devices, starting with the Mk.14. This was the first US thermonuclear bomb as well as the shortest-lived, being part of the arsenal for just a few months in 1954, before being replaced by the Mk 17 and the Mk 24. As a matter of interest, the latter was identical to the Mk 14 save for using a different primary or fission trigger.

The Mk 17 was a seriously impressive item of ordnance, measuring almost 25 ft in length and weighing almost 19 tons. It was also the most powerful nuclear device ever built by the US, with a yield in the region

BELOW At altitude over upstate New York in November 1982, B-52G 68-0170 bores its way through the sky with a lethal payload of AGM-86B Air-Launched Cruise Missile suspended beneath its wings – this weaponry packs six times the punch of the earlier Hound Dog missiles. The bomber was assigned to the Griffiss-based 416th Bomb Wing which operated the B-52G model for many years before eventually converting to the B-52H. More recently still, it disposed of its aircraft during 1994 as a prelude to being inactivated *(USAF/SSgt Ernie Sealing)*

of 15 to 20 MT, but was so large that it could only be carried by the B-36. However, that shortcoming was offset slightly by the fact that the B-36 could accommodate two of these monsters, although it probably wouldn't have been able to take them very far.

In between the Mk 14 and the Mk 17, there was the Mk 15 which was a much more practical weapon. It also had much wider applications, by virtue of being a much smaller device, for it was just under 12 ft long and weighed some 7600 lbs. Those dimensions and weights could easily be accommodated by the B-47 and it was also the first of the so-called 'hydrogen'

BELOW When released in the early 1990s, this in-flight portrait of a B-52H (60-0020) was the first photo showing the bomber carrying the AGM-129A Advanced Cruise Missile (ACM). Although the external appearance is little different from the AGM-86B ALCM, the package containing the advanced versions gives the bomber much greater reach *(USAF)*

bombs to be compatible with the B-52. Delivery of production examples of the Mk 15 to weapons storage bunkers began in April 1955 and about 1200 had been completed when stockpiling terminated in early 1957. Two Mk 15s could be accommodated in the B-52 weapons bay and yield was in the low megaton range.

As a matter of interest, a Mk 15 was the first US thermonuclear bomb ever dropped, an event that occurred on 21 May 1956 during the *Redwing Cherokee* test in the Pacific Ocean. The delivery aircraft was a B-52 (52-0013) and the estimated yield of this test was 3.75 MT. Frustratingly for the scientists, the data take from the *Cherokee* drop was meagre since it undershot the target area by some 19,000 ft. This was due to the bombardier failing to correctly identify the target and releasing the weapon 21 seconds too early.

Further development of this design resulted in the advent of the Mk 39, which was basically a Mk 15 that embodied a drogue parachute retardation system, giving the delivery aircraft more time to make good its

RIGHT In one of the later colour schemes, and toting a clutch of M117 750 lb bombs, B-52G 58-0182 *What's Up Doc* of the 806th Bomb Wing (Provisional) stands ready for combat action at RAF Fairford during the Gulf War with Iraq. The 'Buff' enhanced an already impressive reputation during the conflict by hauling a greater weight of bombs than any other single type committed to the battle to liberate Kuwait *(API/J Flack)*

escape. At between 9-10,000 lbs, it was somewhat heavier than the Mk 15, but it was dimensionally more or less identical and the final Mod 2 weapon was compatible with the 'laydown' method of delivery forced upon SAC by the switch to low-level penetration methods. Stockpile entry came in 1957 and about 700 Mk 39s were produced between then and the spring of 1959. Retirement of the last Mk 15s occurred during 1965, with the Mk 39 following suit in 1966.

In the interval that elapsed between deployment of the Mk 15 and the improved Mk 39, another type of bomb also appeared in the stockpile. This was the Mk 36, a 17,500 lb 9-10 MT high-yield 'monster' that was some 12 ft 6 ins long and almost five feet in diameter. It was based on the Mk 21 which may itself have figured in B-52 payloads when this weapon formed part of the stockpile between December 1955 and November 1957. Eventually, all of the Mk 21s (approximately 275 bombs) were modified to Mk 36 standard, with production of new-build Mk 36s raising the number procured by the summer of 1958 to around the 950 mark. In definitive form as the Mk 36, this bomb featured parachute-retardation as well as fusing options for air or surface detonation and the B-52 weapons bay was sufficiently capacious to accommodate two of these immensely powerful devices. Retirement occurred between August 1961 and January 1962, when they were replaced by the B41.

The next type of bomb to enter the stockpile was the B28, which made its debut in 1958 and which ultimately became the most numerous of all the air-delivered weapons, with both tactical and strategic applications that resulted in about 4500 examples of five basic types being completed by mid-1966. It was also an entirely new weapon, rather than an adaptation of an existing design, hence the failure to reach the stockpile until after the Mk 36 and Mk 39. Five different yields between 70 KT and 1.45 MT are understood to have existed, with low-yield devices earmarked for delivery by fighter-bombers.

Versions compatible with the B-52 comprised the B28IN, B28RI and B28FI, but it should also be noted that the W28 warhead was also fitted to the Hound Dog air-to-surface missile. The B28IN was the first bomb to be deployed, starting in 1958. Dimensionally, it was the smallest, measuring some 8 ft in length and weighing about 1980 lbs. It was also the least sophisticated, lacking parachutes and capable of being fuzed for only ground or airburst.

The next model was the B28RI which began to enter the stockpile in 1960 and which evolved in response to SAC's change of operating doctrine. In consequence, the B28RI was longer and heavier, this 11 ft 1 in, 2320 lb device being a parachute-retarded version that could be dropped from low-altitude. Fuzing options were identical to the B28IN version.

ABOVE Literally covered with scores of chalked-on messages, a fresh load of 750 lb 'iron bombs' are manoeuvred into place prior to loading aboard the wing rack of one of the B-52Gs that flew missions to Iraq from RAF Fairford, England. A total of eight examples of the 'Buf'f were temporarily based at Fairford during the Gulf War of 1991, with four aircraft making the long haul to the war zone on most days *(API/J Flack)*

The final strategic model was the B28FI, which weighed more or less the same as the B28RI, despite being a foot longer. Improvements in this case mainly concerned incorporation of a 'FUFO' capability and deliveries of this sub-type began in the summer of 1962. These three models were a major element of the US nuclear arsenal throughout the 1960s and 1970s, but the advent of newer weapons (notably the B61 and B83) permitted progressive retirement. This resulted in the last few examples of the B28IN and B28RI being withdrawn from the stockpile in 1980. The B28FI was destined to survive rather longer, but retirement began in 1984 and was set for completion by 1990.

A maximum of eight B28s could be carried, with these being loaded on two so-called 'clips'. Each of the MHU-14/C assemblies was able to accommodate four weapons and there's no doubt that they greatly facilitated the handling of these weapons, since the 'clips' could be built-up in bomb storage facilities and then towed direct to the bombers for loading. Although the B-52 could easily have taken a pair of 'clips', it seems that the more usual load was just one,

for a total of four bombs. In many cases these would have shared weapons bay space with Quail decoy missiles or the AGM-69A SRAM rotary launcher.

Further proliferation followed at the start of the 1960s, with no less than three new bombs – the B41, B53 and B57 – being added to the B-52's list of nuclear options in the space of just four years. The first two were extremely powerful devices, with the *Hardtack Oak* test shot demonstrating just how powerful. Involving a development TX41 bomb, this test took place at Eniwetok atoll in the Pacific Ocean on 29 June 1958 and demonstrated a yield of 8.9 MT, considerably in excess of the predicted 7.5 MT. The B53 bomb is understood to have been rated at 9 MT and was similar in size to the B41, albeit somewhat lighter, with respective weights being 10,670 lbs and 8850 lbs.

Approximately 500 examples of the B41 were produced by the summer of 1962 and the last was deleted from the inventory in 1976. Fewer B53s were completed, with about 340 assembled between August 1962 and June 1965. Most had been retired by the summer of 1987, when the unprecedented step was taken of returning some to the stockpile, apparently in order to retain a high-yield weapon for use against particularly deeply-buried targets that could not be eliminated by less powerful but more accurate devices.

The third weapon to appear in the early 1960s was the B57. This had its origins in the US Navy's wish to obtain a lightweight, air-delivered, nuclear depth bomb and the separate Air Force request for a low-yield device with tactical applications in what is euphemistically called 'limited' nuclear warfare. A merger of the two requirements eventually culminated in the B57, which measured just under 10ft in length, had a diameter of about 15ins and weighed 500 lbs. Yield was in the 5-20 KT range and stockpile entry occurred in 1963, with just over 3000 of these devices being produced by the spring of 1967.

Fuzing options permitted free-fall or parachute-retarded airburst; retarded laydown delivery for delayed surface detonation and retarded depth bomb, with the B57 having a wide range of applications, as well as compatibility with other aircraft such as the F-101 Voodoo, F-104 Starfighter and F-105 Thunderchief. When utilised as a depth bomb, it could even be dropped by helicopter. Although some examples apparently still figure in the Navy arsenal, the B57 has evidently been retired by the Air Force, following replacement by the B61.

Of these 1960s-vintage weapons, it is conceivable that some B53s do still form part of the US stockpile. However, apart from ALCM and ACM, the two principal nuclear weapons now available to the dwindling B-52 fleet are the B61 and B83.

Development of the former was launched at the start of the 1960s, when the USAF expressed interest in the concept of using drogue-retarded weapons that could safely be delivered at high speed and low altitude. Work on this project eventually led to the B61, which is a versatile weapon indeed, with both tactical and strategic applications by virtue of having four selectable yields. Three fall within the 100-500 KT band and there is also a special low 10 KT option. On early weapons, it was necessary to 'program' the yield before take-off, but later B61s have a facility that allows both the yield and fuzing option to be selected while in flight. Entry into the stockpile of early versions of the B61 occurred in late 1966 and more than 3100 have since been assembled, with improved models still being in development and production until quite recently.

When compared with earlier bombs carried by the B-52, the B61 most definitely merits classification as a lightweight weapon, for it typically weighs around 700 lbs, is just under 11 ft long and has a diameter of 13.4 ins. In conjunction with a basically natural metal fin-

ABOVE A B-52G (59-2572) from the 43rd Strategic Wing, Andersen AFB, Guam, drops an aerial mine during an exercise called *Minex 85*, part of 1985's annual *Team Spirit* joint exercise in Korea. In the mid-1980s, SAC emphasised the 'Stratofort's' maritime capabilities as a competitive move against its principal adversary which was, of course, not the Russians, but the US Navy! In this 26 March 1985 study, the 'Buff' is being paced by an F-16B Fighting Falcon wearing the WP (for 'Wolfpack') tail code of the 8th Tactical Fighter Wing, based at Kunsan, Korea *(USAF)*

ish, those physical attributes have earned the B61 the nickname 'silver bullet'. Configuration appears identical irrespective of whether the weapon is carried internally, as on the B-52 and other bombers, or externally, as on tactical fighter and attack aircraft like the F-16 Fighting Falcon and A-7 Corsair.

In the case of the B-52, the 'clip' concept was employed at the outset, with a usual load comprising four B61s in conjunction with SRAM and/or ALCM. More recently, development of the Common Strategic Rotary Launcher (CSRL) and fitment of this accessory to some B-52Hs allows up to eight such bombs to be accommodated within the weapons bay.

The B83 is the latest and conceivably the last in a long line of nuclear bombs to enter the stockpile. Development engineering started at the beginning of

ABOVE B-52G 58-0225 of the 43rd Strategic Wing from Guam dropping a parachute-retarded mine on a practice mission in the early 1980s. Mines are an especially lethal weapon against shipping and amphibious operations because countermeasures against them always lag behind the development of newer and better mines. When 'Maritime Strategy' was the working paper which set forth US Navy policy in the 1980s, the B-52 suddenly acquired this maritime duty. When that paper was replaced by 'From the Sea', emphasising sea power in littoral regions, the potential of the B-52 for minelaying and anti-shipping work suddenly lost its emphasis. By defining its job as it chose, the Navy won a rare victory over the Air Force, which normally came out ahead in the ongoing conflict between the two servies *(USAF)*

1979, with initial drop trials being accomplished later that year, leading up to a start on production engineering in the autumn of 1980. Stockpile entry followed in June 1983 and by the middle of 1987, about 1000 B83s had been completed, with a further 1500 to come as replacements for the B28, B43 and B53 devices. However, with the ending of the Cold War, it

is possible that procurement has been curtailed.

Unlike the B61, the B83 is first and foremost a strategic weapon system, with a yield of between one and two megatons. It is some 12 ft long, has a diameter of 18 ins and weighs 2400 lbs. Four fuzing options exist, these being free-fall or parachute retarded airburst; contact burst and laydown. Between them, they allow delivery to be undertaken at all altitudes from 150 ft to 50,000 ft and at speeds of up to Mach 2.

Loading arrangements for the B83 are identical to those of the B61, with the CSRL able to accept a total of eight bombs and with four-weapon 'clips' also applicable.

NON-NUCLEAR MUNITIONS

A variety of types of conventional weapon are compatible with the B-52, which possesses the ability to carry a substantial payload, although the B-52D's remarkable *Big Belly* capacity has not been matched by any other derivative. Today, of course, only the B-52H is still operated and there is some doubt as to whether this has been modified to carry all of the weapons available to those B-52Gs that were assigned conventional and maritime attack taskings.

Dealing first with internal carriage, the weapons bay has the ability to accommodate a maximum of 27 bombs, although its capacity is obviously influenced by the weight and size of the munitions in question. Two basic configurations are employed, with the 27-bomb rig involving the use of three cluster racks, each of which carries nine weapons. These may include SUU-30, SUU-64 and SUU-65 Cluster Bomb Units (CBUs); M117 750lb general purpose (GP) bombs; Mk 82 500 lb GP bombs and Mk 36 Destructor underwater mines.

The second configuration is employed for much heavier items of ordnance and involves use of a pair of 'clips', with each carrying four weapons. These include Mk 84 2,000lb GP bombs and Mk 55, Mk 56 and Mk 60 mines, each of which is also in the 2000-lb class.

With regard to external carriage, three configurations have been observed in recent times, with these being dependent upon the stores pylon fitted to the aircraft in question. For many years, when carrying conventional munitions, various marks of Stratofortress (notably the B-52D/F/G/H models) made use of the original AGM-28 Hound Dog pylon, in conjunction with an 'I-beam' rack adapter and a pair of multiple ejection racks (MERs). This arrangement gives a total capacity of 12 bombs (CBUs, Mk 82s, M117s and Mk 36s) per pylon. As far as is known, this rig is still in use at the time of writing.

In more recent times, coincident with the decision to place more emphasis on non-nuclear applications and the concurrent modification of the B-52G for conventional missions, the much shorter 'stub' pylon appeared on non-ALCM B-52Gs. It is here that the variations occur, for the 'stub' pylon is compatible with the original 'I-beam' arrangement as well as with a newer item of equipment known as the Heavy Stores Adapter Beam (HSAB). When used in concert with the 'I-beam', external payload capacity is identical to that of aircraft retaining the AGM-28 pylon.

When employed with the HSAB, however, only nine M117s (or similar weapons) may be carried on each pylon. That shortcoming is more than offset by the fact that use of the HSAB permits much heavier items of ordnance to be slung externally. By way of illustration, typical loads per pylon include five Mk 84 2000-lb bombs or Mk 60 mines; six Mk 55 or Mk 56 mines; and six AGM-84 Harpoons. Alternatively, they

can accommodate up to four examples of the AGM-142 Popeye 3300-lb stand-off attack missile.

Finally, as discussed earlier in this chapter, a variation on the ALCM theme has been fitted with a conventional warhead. Designated AGM-86C, this made its operational debut during the Gulf War with Iraq when 35 missiles were fired by crews from Barksdale's 2nd Bomb Wing at a number of targets in and around Baghdad. Since the 2nd BW was still equipped with the B-52G at that time, it follows that these weapons must have been carried externally.

BELOW Suspended from the wing rack of a black-painted B-52D, the TV-guided GBU-15 modular glide bomb married modern miniaturised guidance systems to high explosive. In so doing, it provided the Stratofortress with the ability to utilise precision munitions for the first time. The GBU-15 seen here has planar wings, but a version with cruciform wings was also available for use *(Hughes)*

'BUFF' INTO BATTLE

ALTHOUGH THE MIGHTY STRATOFORTRESS eventually clocked up more than eight years of combat duty in the Vietnam War, 1964 contingency plans concerning the use of SAC bombers in that conflict evidently anticipated the deployment of a mixed force of B-47s and B-52s. As it turned out, the only Stratojets to see operational duty in support of US forces in the Vietnam theatre were the handful of RB-47Hs of the 55th Strategic Reconnaissance Wing that were used to gather electronic intelligence at the outset of the war. However, when the time came to base conventional bombers in the Pacific region, the B-47 had been almost entirely retired from SAC's inventory, which meant that the B-52 was the only option available.

The event that actually precipitated deployment of the B-52 came on 7 February 1965 when Viet Cong guerillas staged a mortar attack on a US facility near Pleiku in the central highlands of South Vietnam. US reaction was swift, with the most visible evidence being provided by Operation *Flaming Dart*. This was the code name given to a series of retaliatory strikes staged in early February by Navy aircraft against targets in the vicinity of Dong Hoi and Vinh.

Even as the Navy aircraft were committed to combat, the civilian-staffed National Security Council (NSC) was considering other measures and actions. These were partly intended to bolster the US presence in the South-East Asia theatre and partly to signal US resolve to support the South Vietnamese administration until such time as their counterparts in the North indicated willingness to enter into meaningful negotiations and settle the impasse.

In later years, the strength of that resolve waned, but in early 1965 there were no such qualms and one of the actions the NSC agreed to take was the immediate transfer of 30 B-52s to Guam. It is perhaps ironic to consider the significance and timing of this movement. Had they but known it, the arrival of those B-52s in Guam put the weapon in place that would ultimately have a legitimate claim to bringing about the ceasefire – eight long and bloody years later. At the time, of course, nobody was aware of how things would turn out. And nor, as will become apparent, does there appear to have been much clarity of thought on the matter of just how the Stratofortress should or could be employed in Vietnam.

The decision to despatch bombers was conveyed to the operating forces involved via the Joint Chiefs of Staff on 11 February 1965 and within a matter of hours they were on their way west to the Pacific island base. Movement was accomplished as a '30/30 contingency force', whereby the number of B-52s was supposed to be matched by an equal number of KC-135s. In this instance, though, the number of tankers was actually 32, since two extra aircraft were used to airlift personnel and equipment.

Two B-52F bases provided the necessary resources, namely Barksdale, Louisiana, and Mather, California. Virtually the entire complement of bombers from the 20th BS, 2nd BW (at Barksdale) and the 441st BS, 320th BW (at Mather) flew west to Andersen AFB, with the accompanying tankers going to Kadena AB, Okinawa. From there, they would be handily positioned to provide in-flight refuelling support to the B-52Fs when and if they were called into action.

It appears probable that virtually all of the B-52Fs which were despatched to Andersen in February 1965 had been subjected to the *South Bay* modification project a few months earlier. This actually received Air Staff approval in June 1964 and was specifically intended to enhance the conventional warfare capability of the B-52F. A total of 28 aircraft had been modified in this fashion when the programme ended in October 1964 – and each of them was able to accommodate 27 750-lb bombs internally and 24 more externally, making use of racks fitted to the pylon mountings used to carry the Hound Dog missile. External carriage in this way almost doubled the payload, which rose from 20,250 lbs to 38,250 lbs.

Subsequently, in June 1965, Secretary of Defense Robert S McNamara asked for 46 more B-52Fs to be brought to a similar configuration. The request was approved but the deadline of just one month meant that it had to be executed in extreme haste. Despite running into difficulties in obtaining the necessary equipment, project *Sun Bath* alterations were accomplished ahead of schedule by the Oklahoma City Air Materiel Area and the first of the freshly modified aircraft were operating from Andersen within weeks of the request being made.

By then, a change had occurred in the composition of the force at Andersen, with the 20th BS, 2nd BW having given way to the 9th BS, 7th BW in early May 1965. At that time, of course, only the *South Bay* aircraft had the extra payload capacity. In view of that, there is good reason to believe that the changeover which took place in May was limited to personnel only – and that the 2nd BW left its B-52Fs behind for the 7th BW. Irrespective of that, within a few weeks of returning to Barksdale, the 20th BS had been reassigned from the 2nd BW to the 7th BW.

Having moved in haste, the B-52Fs that reached Andersen in February 1965 then sat around leisurely for more than four months while the politicians and the military commanders figured out what to do with them. A number of options were considered – and rejected. One early proposal raised by the Joint Chiefs of Staff in March envisaged despatching them against North Vietnam as part of *Rolling Thunder* and it is perhaps not widely realised that plans existed to strike no less than 20 targets in the North.

Technological aspects were one obstacle, but doubts about the potential accuracy of any bombing that might ensue could have been (and later were) overcome. Of greater import was the fact that the whole idea was viewed with grave misgivings by the State Department, which held the view that it would represent a significant escalation of the war effort and might prompt an over-reaction on the part of China and the Soviet Union.

Yet another aspect that militated against using the B-52 to bomb targets in the North was the consequences that might follow the loss of an aircraft and its crew to enemy fire. Then, as now, what could be referred to as the 'wimp factor' held sway amongst the political hierarchy, which appeared anxious to convey an impression of steely resolve – but which had a distressing tendency to back off when it came to demonstrating that resolve.

BELOW More than a decade into its service life, the 'Buff' finally drew blood when the B-52F model went into action in South-East Asia in 1965. This jet (57-0144) is carrying 750-lb (340-kg) bombs across the South Vietnamese coast in October 1965. Following a tragic beginning in which two bombers collided in mid-air, the B-52Fs waged an ambitious campaign against Viet Cong strongholds south of the 17th Parallel. Note that this aircraft has been given a freshly-applied black underside paint job to help reduce its reflectivity during night missions *(USAF)*

Had they actually chosen to 'go for it' and made use of the B-52s at the earliest opportunity, it is possible that the course of history might have taken a different path. They didn't, with the result that the USA became ever more deeply embroiled in a war it didn't want – and, perhaps more importantly, didn't understand. As much as anything else, that stemmed from a failure to fully comprehend the nature of the enemy, who were always clear-sighted and who sought only victory. It was a misjudgement that was to cost the USA dearly.

If the authorities in Washington were uncertain as to what use they should make of the Guam-based bombers, no such doubts existed in the mind of Gen William Westmoreland, commanding officer of the United States Military Assistance Command Vietnam (ComUSMACV). He very quickly began pressing for them to be used against Viet Cong enclaves in the South, raising this possibility in a conference to consider future actions and strategy that took place in Honolulu, Hawaii during April. This conference sign posted a major shift in US priorities to that of supporting assets and forces in the South – and eventually paved the way for use of the B-52Fs.

Authorisation wasn't immediately forthcoming, largely due to the fact that SAC and the Pacific Command objected to employing the bombers in South Vietnam, albeit for quite different reasons. SAC misgivings had more to do with a natural and ingrained opposition to using a strategic weapon system for tactical operations and it remained to be convinced that there was a need for them to even be in the region in

ABOVE The USAF's art programme has given the world provocative images including *One Dozen Eggs for Charley* (sic), by Al Muenchen, which shows a B-52F carrying 12 pylon-mounted bombs intended for the Viet Cong, known to Americans as 'Charlie' *(USAF Art Program)*

the first place. In addition, it had already made clear a desire to return some of the B-52Fs to nuclear alert duty in the USA. Pacific Command, on the other hand, was not opposed to using B-52s, but did feel that if they were going to be employed anywhere, it should be against the North. Not surprisingly, in view of these conflicts of opinion, continued inactivity was about the only outcome.

Undeterred, Westmoreland persisted in seeking clearance to use the B-52Fs – supporting his case by citing his doubts about the effectiveness of tactical fighter-bombers, especially in pattern bombing. His persistence eventually won the day and the approval of the Joint Chiefs of Staff back in Washington, with the result that SAC was soon directed to prepare an operations plan, while 2nd Air Division intelligence personnel in Vietnam nominated a number of potential target areas.

After consideration of the four areas suggested, it was agreed that Kontum Province appeared most suitable, with intelligence sources indicating that this was a major Viet Cong base area. So as to ensure accurate weapons delivery, the B-52Fs would use a helicopter-borne radar beacon as an aid to bombing and this was flown to Tan Son Nhut during May to be installed, tested and made ready. Soon afterwards, on 24 May

ABOVE B-52F 57-0164 seen during an early mission to Vietnam, before the application of black undersides *(USAF)*

1965, a single Stratofortress left Guam bound for South Vietnam, where this unarmed aircraft flew over the unfamiliar terrain to verify the beacon worked and obtain imagery of the designated target area.

On that first visit, everything functioned more or less as advertised and orders were therefore cut for the first attack to take place on the very next day. In the event, the latest intelligence estimates reported that the Viet Cong had left the area and this news resulted in the mission being scrubbed at the eleventh hour. The long wait continued.

Three weeks later, it came to an end when the B-52 force finally went into action with a raid on a Viet Cong enclave near Ben Cat, roughly 40 miles to the north of Saigon. Reconnaissance of the area revealed the presence of a number of buildings, but their dispersal pattern was such that it would require a prohibitively high number of fighter-bomber sorties to inflict a worthwhile degree of damage. So, while concluding it was not a suitable target for tactical aircraft, the planning staff in Saigon opined that was almost tailor-made for pattern bombing by the B-52s. A request to use the Guam-based bombers was duly forwarded by Westmoreland on the morning of 15 June and this met with prompt approval from the Joint Chiefs in Washington – *Arc Light I* would go ahead on 18 June.

By then, as noted earlier, composition of the bomber force on Guam had changed as a result of unit rotation and responsibility for introducing the Strato-fortress to combat would be entrusted to the 9th BS, 7th BW and the 441st BS, 320th BW.

Even at this late stage, with some important details still to be ironed out between the various command agencies involved in ordering and executing the attack, the mission was not immune from political interference. One particularly unwelcome manifestation of this arose when the command authorities in Washington forwarded a request to Andersen to advance the timing of the attack by 24 hours – barely 26 hours before it was scheduled to take place.

This was rejected, ostensibly on the grounds that it allowed insufficient time to deploy the ground forces that were to enter the area after the bombing. Just who was behind this idea isn't known, but it must have been someone fairly high up in the civilian administration, since the Joint Chiefs would surely have been aware of the complex nature of the mission – and could have been expected to forestall any attempts at rescheduling other than those from the very highest office.

Meanwhile, at Andersen, preparations forged ahead in readiness for the launch. Weapons bays and racks were loaded and ammunition for the tail guns was installed, even as the crews finalised their mission planning and briefed for the upcoming raid. Of the 30 aircraft scheduled to take part, 24 had the full 'bag' of 51 750-lb bombs while the other six carried just internal weapons in the form of 27 armour-piercing thousand pounders. Elsewhere, at Kadena, on the island of Okinawa, an identical number of KC-135A Strato-tankers were also made ready to pass fuel to the bombers on the outbound leg of the mission.

Departure began on schedule and within less than 30 minutes, all of the bombers had got away safely, climbing to altitude for the first leg of the six-hour journey to Vietnam. All seems to have gone smoothly until the time came to meet the tanker force in the *Parcel Post* refuelling area which lay over the ocean just to the west of Luzon in the Philippines. Arriving several minutes earlier than anticipated due to a strong tailwind, elements of the bomber stream began manoeuvring for a rendezvous.

In so doing, the three aircraft that comprised 'Green' cell (each of the 10 cells of three B-52Fs was allocated a different colour) began a 360-degree turn. This resulted in them leaving their designated track, meandering across the track being used by 'Blue' cell and continuing on to end up flying a reciprocal course to that of 'Yellow' cell, roughly 40 nautical miles south of where they should have been.

BELOW Taking off from Andersen AFB, Guam – the Pacific island which is American soil and which was a bastion of Stratofortress combat operations – this B-52F (57-0153) is heading for targets in South Vietnam in June 1965, carrying 750-lb (340-kg) iron bombs in its bay and on inboard pylons. Though it was first to carry bombs on conventional missions, the B-52F model had a lesser capacity than the B-52D, which was converted under the *Big Belly* programme specifically for Vietnam fighting *(USAF)*

The consequences were disastrous, for two bombers collided, with the wreckage plunging thousands of feet to end up in the South China Sea. Eight of the 12 crew members died in the accident, which prompted SAC to consider and modify its air refuelling procedures - in that, it was evidently successful, for there was only one other instance of a collision between bombers during the eight years that followed. Nevertheless, it was far from an auspicious start and matters weren't helped when one of the remaining B-52Fs experienced the failure of a hydraulic pump and the loss of its radar. Unable to effect a hook-up and get its fuel, it was forced to divert to Kadena, leaving the other 27 to press on to the target area.

Going 'feet dry' (crossing the coast) at 0630 hours local time, the first of the bombers began disgorging its weapons some 15 minutes later with the assistance of the radar beacon. Drop altitude varied from 19,000 to 22,000 ft and the entire force required about 30 minutes to scatter its ordnance throughout a target box that measured one mile in width and two miles in length. After that, they turned south, skirted the Cambodian border and then headed east towards Guam, shedding another jet which was forced to divert to Clark AB, in the Philippines, with an electrical glitch. Some 13 hours after the first B-52F took off, the last of 26 bombers recovered at Andersen. *Arc Light I* was over, and the post-strike analysis was about to begin.

As far as the bombing was concerned, questions were soon being asked, with the press being particularly quick to criticise and cast aspersions about 'sledgehammers' and 'gnats'. Some of their remarks appear to have been justified, for the accuracy of the bombing appears to have been less than spectacular, with only just over half of the weapons landing in the target area. Worse still was the news that those bombs which did succeed in hitting the right spot caused surprisingly little damage.

Worst of all, inspection by the reconnaissance teams sent in by helicopter soon afterwards found evidence of occupation by the Viet Cong, but also discovered that the birds had evidently flown the coop before the bombing started. It later became apparent that they had been warned in advance of the impending raid and were able to withdraw in good time.

Arc Light II was scheduled to take place just over a week later, with the target area being situated not far from the air base at Bien Hoa. However, a preliminary reconnaissance by US Special Forces personnel again produced evidence that Viet Cong guerillas had been present but had departed. In consequence, the B-52 attack was cancelled and it was not until July that the Buff returned to action. In that month, some 140 sorties were recorded in five raids and a roughly similar pattern followed in August, when 165 sorties were flown by the Guam-based bombers.

During that period, increasing familiarity with the terrain resulted in the B-52F's own radar being used to pinpoint the target for the first time on 2 August. By then, a unit rotation had also occurred, with the 441st BS, 320th BW being replaced by the 20th BS, 7th BW and heading back to Mather AFB, California. For the next four months, *Arc Light* missions were the sole prerogative of the 7th BW, which had both of its subordinate bomber squadrons on Guam.

Subsequently, at about the beginning of December 1965, the pair of squadrons went home to Barksdale, with their respective places at Andersen being filled by a newcomer and a veteran. The debutante was the 736th BS, 454th BW from Columbus AFB, Mississippi – the veteran was the 441st BS, 320th BW, back for its second tour of duty. Between them, these two saw out the brief era when the B-52F model was involved in *Arc Light* bombing operations.

While the B-52F may have been responsible for less than one per cent of the total number of sorties flown by the Stratofortress during the war years, it did nevertheless play an important role. This was particularly true with regard to establishing methods of employment, which changed quite noticeably during the first nine months of *Arc Light* operations.

As has already been mentioned, the first few raids were rather large, involving as many as 30 aircraft. While this may have looked spectacular, there's no doubt that the results were of questionable value. If proof of that is needed, one has to go no further than the opening mission, which achieved nothing of military significance. So, even as the first few missions were being flown, there were already doubts about the wisdom of using large formations. During August, those doubts resulted in the decision to continue flying missions with fewer bombers but at more frequent intervals. At the same time, five so-called free bomb zones were created in South Vietnam, with available intelligence being utilised in the preparation of a target folder for each.

Two of the zones lay to the north of Saigon; two more were in the extreme south of the country and the fifth was located to the south-east of Da Nang. In setting up the free bomb zones, it was hoped that the B-52 force could be more responsive to the needs of local commanders, although that would also require changes to the somewhat unwieldy process that existed for ordering *Arc Light* strikes.

Thus far, the only individual able to authorise these missions was the President, whose orders were relayed to local commanders via the Joint Chiefs of Staff in Washington. This, not surprisingly, caused a considerable amount of 'heartburn' on the part of local commanders, since it took time to submit requests for heavy bomber support – and even more time for those requests to be approved or refused. And, even in instances where approval was forthcoming, it's apparent that US intentions were often known by the Viet Cong well in advance of a raid being staged, with the result that many missions were little more than a pointless waste of bombs.

The local commanders weren't the only ones who didn't much care for the situation. SAC's hierarchy was definitely unhappy, since it was virtually excluded from the decision-making process and actually had little say in the use of the bomber and tanker resources it had so reluctantly provided. A change for the better did occur in the latter part of August, in as much as the responsibility for authorising missions was relinquished by the President – henceforth, the Joint Chiefs were the final arbiters. This was better, for it put control in the hands of the professionals, but it still required a considerable amount of message traffic. Nevertheless, the first of the smaller missions to be made following these changes occurred on 26 August.

From this point on, strike packages varied in size quite markedly. The day of the mass attack was certainly not over and 30-bomber missions were still flown from time to time. Generally speaking, though, more use was made of smaller quantities of bombers and this did indeed result in greater flexibility, to the point where two or three targets could be attacked more or less simultaneously.

Implemented in late August, the benefit was apparent almost from the outset. Evidence of this is provided by the sortie rate which jumped quite markedly, rising from 165 in August to 322 in September. Thereafter, the number of *Arc Light* sorties flown against targets in South Vietnam hovered around the 300 per month level for the remainder of the B-52F era. That era came to a close in March 1966, with deployment of the so-called *Big Belly* B-52Ds of the 28th and 484th Bomb Wings. From here on in, even greater tonnages of bombs would be carried across the Pacific.

EXPANSION AND CONTRACTION 1966-71

Modification of the Stratofortress to increase its conventional payload got under way within six months of the type making its combat debut and resulted in the B-52D shouldering the burden of SAC's offensive operations in South-East Asia with effect from the spring of 1966, when it took over from the B-52F model. Although nobody can have been aware of it at the time, this marked the start of a six-year period during which the B-52D was to carry the burden single-handedly, before being joined by the B-52G for the final stages of the conflict.

Save for the adoption of a sinister new paint scheme of black undersides and camouflaged top surfaces, there were few clues to indicate the change in capability. Nevertheless, in its revised *Big Belly* form, the B-52D now possessed unequalled qualities as a bomb carrier and was unmatched in the sheer weight of ordnance it could bring to bear upon a target box. However, when operating in high density configuration with the external racks fitted, it could accommodate a maximum of 108 weapons.

The majority of that load was housed internally, with the capacious weapons bay able to carry either 84 Mk 82 500-lb or 42 M117 750-lb bombs. As for external capacity, this was identical to that of the B-52F, at 24 M117 750lb bombs. In the *Big Belly* configuration, therefore, the maximum ordnance payload was an impressive 60,000lbs or close to 27 tons – and loads of that magnitude were soon being hauled daily across the Pacific Ocean from the island base on Guam to distant Vietnam and Laos.

Aircraft of this sub-type began to enter the modification programme during the closing staged of 1965 and little time was wasted in committing the first reconfigured examples to combat, with the B-52Ds of the 28th BW being deployed to Andersen to replace the B-52Fs of the 320th BW in early March 1966. Less than a month later, a second rotation saw the 484th BW depart from Turner AFB, Georgia to relieve the 454th BW. The arrival of these B-52Ds must have been welcomed with enthusiasm by General Westmoreland, who was already an avowed admirer of the 'Buff' and who would have been eager to make use of the significantly increased weight of weapons at his disposal.

Shortly before the switch in the Stratofortress model took place, a notable change occurred with regard to the organisation and management of the force assembled at Andersen. This resulted in the establishment of the 4133rd Bomb Wing (Provisional) on 1 February 1966 and bomber units that deployed from SAC bases in the USA were invariably attached to this unit during their period of residence at Andersen. In the normal course of events, such spells of duty lasted for about six months, whereupon a unit rotation occurred, with fresh aircraft and crews from another SAC Wing arriving to relieve those whose tour was complete.

Over the next few years, the rotational policy resulted in a total of 11 more B-52D Wings experiencing their share of combat duty in Vietnam. For the record, these comprised the 7th BW, 22nd BW, 70th BW, 91st BW, 92nd SAW, 96th SAW, 99th BW, 306th BW, 454th BW, 461st BW and 509th BW – and some of those Wings eventually completed three tours of duty in support of the war.

Later, possibly more or less coincident with the base at U-Tapao in Thailand acquiring sole responsibility for the *Arc Light* mission, it appears that the force of about 42 B-52Ds needed to meet operational requirements was drawn from across the fleet. In consequence, all SAC B-52D units were required to contribute small numbers of aircraft which were attached to the resident Wing while deployed overseas for combat duty. In the case of aircraft flying from U-Tapao, such responsibility was initially vested in the 4258th Strategic Wing (SW) until 1 April 1970, when it was eliminated and replaced by the 307th SW in a major reorganisation of SAC's Pacific-based resources.

Irrespective of the basing mode employed, throughout this long period, efforts were made to spread the load as equitably as possible among the aircrew, for it was obviously unfair to expect the B-52D community to alone carry the responsibility. Thus, while this was the only bomber version to be involved in combat during the period from April 1966 until April 1972, the crews tasked with taking the B-52D into battle on an almost daily basis were actually obtained from across the length and breadth of SAC.

Not surprisingly, in view of the subtle and not-so-subtle differences that existed between the various models, this necessitated the establishment of a cross-training programme within SAC's 'Stratofortress School' at Castle AFB. This was specifically tasked with instructing personnel who were more familiar with the B-52E to B-52H models in the unique attributes and idiosyncrasies of the B-52D. On completion of the course, which lasted for two weeks, graduates would soon find themselves heading west to any one of the three bases that eventually housed Stratofortress combat echelons at different times, namely Andersen, Kadena and U-Tapao.

The advent of the B-52D with its voracious appetite for bombs was quite timely, in so far as its arrival on the scene dovetailed fairly neatly with expansion of the target areas covered by *Arc Light*; a broadening of the missions undertaken by the Guam-based bombers and the introduction of the *Combat Skyspot* radar-assisted, ground-directed bombing system. As noted in the previous chapter, the initial targets were primarily those suspected of harbouring Vietcong and North Vietnamese forces, with the first sorties being concentrated in South Vietnam. Subsequently, as the level of activity rose, the 'Buff' acquired a wider role and began to play a part in the interdiction effort as well as being used to support friendly forces engaged in the ground battle against a foe that was nothing, if not elusive.

Thus, operations against targets in the South were stepped up in line with the increasing US ground pres-

ABOVE This is the view of Boeing's biggest bomber, known by mid-way in its career as the 'Buff', seen by thousands of SAC boom operators, those vital members of tanker crews who look at the world backwards and pump the gas to keep 'em flying. This B-52F returning from a bombing mission is taking on JP-4 aviation fuel from the Boeing-developed 'flying boom', designed by the manufacturer for the KC-97 and KC-135 *(USAF)*

ence, but the B-52 also began to range somewhat further afield. One manifestation of this involved interdiction, which entailed bombing the celebrated Ho Chi Minh trail where it exited into South Vietnam. However, as described more fully elsewhere, the interdiction effort was most certainly not confined to South Vietnam, for neighbouring Laos also came under the hammer, with the first *Arc Light* strikes being staged there as early as December 1965. Later still, when Nixon was in the White House, Cambodia was bombed with increasing frequency from March 1969 onwards.

Moreover, not long after the B-52D took over from

the B-52F, the offensive was carried across the demilitarised zone for the first time, albeit not all that far, since such activity seems to have been confined to Route Pack One (RP1) for most of the time. This covered the southernmost portion of North Vietnam, an area that included the strategically important Mu Gia, Ban Karai and Ban Raving passes, through which flowed much of the traffic that eventually debouched from the various strands of the Ho Chi Minh trail into South Vietnam.

Following vigorous debate, responsibility for directing use of air power assets in RP1 came under General Westmoreland's jurisdiction and it didn't take long for him to consider calling SAC's heavyweight into action. As was the case in Laos, the objective was interdiction of the supply routes that were used to infiltrate men and materiel – but this time, the target was one of the entry points to the labyrinthine network of trails, specifically the Mu Gia Pass. The first mission took place on 11 April 1966 and the B-52 was back again a couple of weeks later, on the 26th. Between them, these two attacks involved a total of 44 sorties, but it was to be another five months before any further Stratofortress strikes were staged against the North.

When they returned, the targets were concentrated in the southern part of RP1, in an area that had been christened *Tally Ho* in late July. This extended about 30 miles north of the demilitarised zone and was perceived as a major North Vietnamese rear base complex. It was first struck on a regular basis by tactical aircraft flying from airfields in the South such as Cam Ranh Bay, Chu Lai and Da Nang, but Westmoreland was eager to make ever greater use of the B-52 and wasted little or no time in pushing for them to be employed against targets in the *Tally Ho* interdiction area.

Initial requests were turned down, but Westmoreland's persistence – coupled with regular warnings of an expected major North Vietnamese offensive – eventually wore down the opposition and he was reluctantly given permission in early September. In the event, eight missions were flown during 15-26 September and the 'Buffs' returned ten times in October. During that interval, some 150 sorties were flown, before operations were suspended following the discovery in late October of SA-2 *Guideline* surface-to-air missile (SAM) sites to the north of the *Tally Ho* area and along the Laotian border. If there was one thing everyone involved in *Arc Light* agreed on, it was that

the loss of a B-52 would provide the North with a major propaganda coup.

With regard to operations carried out in direct support of friendly forces, the first such mission took place on 16 November 1965, when elements of the US Army's 1st Air Cavalry Division engaged in hot pursuit of Vietcong guerillas that had been reported in the vicinity of a Special Forces camp at Plei Me. During the course of this pursuit, the US troops stumbled upon a major base area near the Chu Phong mountains and found themselves caught up in a keenly fought battle for survival against two regular North Vietnamese Army regiments and numerous Vietcong.

Air power came to the rescue, with the initial *Arc Light* mission involving 18 B-52Fs which deposited more than 300 tons of bombs on the enemy. Later strikes by the B-52s raised the number of sorties to just under 100 and these, in concert with 400 more sorties by tactical fighters, helped to save the day – and, in so doing, inflicted a telling blow on the opposition.

Further use of B-52s in this way occurred in December, but there was a certain amount of justifiable nervousness about calling B-52s in to bomb from high altitude within reasonably close proximity to friendly forces. In view of that, such employment was sporadic at first and it took a little while before such missions became routine. As a result, less than 10 per cent of the sorties staged over South Vietnam in 1965 were allocated to support of this kind.

In 1966, increasing confidence and the advent of *Skyspot* resulted in greater trust being placed in B-52 crews and greater use being made of its support capabilities by ground force commanders who came to rely ever more heavily on its support, using the bomber almost as a kind of 'airborne artillery'. The increasing confidence may best be gauged from the knowledge that about 27 per cent of the total number of sorties flown in 1966 were in support of ground operations involving three or more battalions. In 1967, the figure rose still higher, to just over 34 per cent.

However, the close air support mission as performed by the 'Buff' was perhaps best exemplified by the part played in defence of the beleaguered Marine base at Khe Sanh between 14 January and 31 March 1968. During that period, no fewer than 2707 sorties were flown as part of Operation *Niagara*. In the process, B-52s dumped an awesome amount of ordnance on the surrounding countryside – and the bomb fall line crept ever closer to the base, as the besieging forces continued to turn the screw and applied ever greater pressure on the defenders.

At the start, bombing never encroached within 3300 yards of friendly positions. By late February, with the enemy almost encamped on the wire and the general situation looking exceedingly grave, bombs released by the B-52s far above were often falling as close as 300 yards from the perimeter and these frequently set off secondary explosions when caches of weapons and ammunition were hit. Thereafter, B-52 support strikes regularly occurred within 1000 yards of friendly troops and could come even closer if the situation demanded it.

By the close of 1966, then, the B-52 was a major player in the continuing war effort and the patterns and procedures that were to be followed over the next five years had been well established. At the same time, the amount of effort expended had also risen, in line with the general intensification of the war. For the B-52 community, this can best be judged by considering the sortie rate, which rose from about 300 per month at the start of 1966 to about 450 a month in August and then to 600 at the end of the year. Those increases were matched by the deployment of extra bombers and approximately 50 B-52Ds were in temporary residence at Andersen during December. By then, the 28th and 484th BWs had both rotated home and the core of the Guam-based force was now provided by the 91st and 306th BWs, augmented by aircraft and crews drawn from other US-based Wings.

The ante was upped still further in the opening months of 1967, when the sortie rate rose to 800 and the number of bombers to 61. The same year also witnessed the addition of another base, with U-Tapao in Thailand welcoming its first bombers on 10 April when three B-52Ds recovered there at the end of a mission staged in support of the *Junction City* ground operation.

A great deal of thought had been devoted to finding a second base for the B-52 throughout 1966, with numerous candidates being considered and rejected before U-Tapao was chosen. The original idea was simply to expand the facilities at Guam so that Andersen could accommodate up to 70 bombers, but that soon fell by the wayside, almost certainly because of the distance involved, which militated against increased responsiveness. After all, even in an emergency situation, the Guam-based bombers couldn't reach Vietnam in anything less than six hours.

Attention then turned to Taiwan, the Philippines, Okinawa and Thailand, all of which were much closer to the scene of the action. In the event, political factors and cost considerations conspired to bring about rejection of the first two and it then looked as if Kadena would get the nod. Yet again though, politics came into the debate, for the US was anxious to avoid doing anything that would embarrass Japan, even though it clearly had the authority to base bombers on Okinawa. At this point, the recently opened KC-135 base at U-Tapao assumed more prominence and soon became the most favoured option, particularly in the view of USAF Chief of Staff, Gen John P McConnell.

RIGHT The guard on sentry duty in the foreground of this photograph appears to be paying little attention as a sinister black-painted B-52D rumbles its way in for landing at Andersen AFB, Guam, after successfully concluding yet another long haul across the Pacific Ocean to distant Vietnam. However, since this scene was an almost daily occurrence on the tropical island, he'd probably seen it all before *(USAF)*

He subsequently asked the US Ambassador to Thailand to look into the possibility during September 1966, but that was pretty much where the matter rested until November. In that month, Secretary of Defense Robert McNamara attended a meeting of senior military commanders at Guam and promptly threw a spanner in the works by ordering the Joint Chiefs to prepare plans for updating the facilities at Andersen and for basing a force of up to 15 B-52s at Tuy Hoa, South Vietnam.

Not surprisingly, the latter proposal met vigorous opposition and may well have been greeted with incredulity. Cost of construction of support facilities was undoubtedly a factor in prompting opposition, but was far outweighed by the question of security, since there can be absolutely no doubt that the Vietcong would have made determined efforts to stage one of their 'spectaculars' had Tuy Hoa ever welcomed B-52s. In the face of that resistance, McNamara relented and in January 1967 he backed McConnell's earlier request to the US Ambassador to seek approval from the Thai government for stationing B-52s at U-Tapao.

Thai approval was forthcoming in March and hardly any time was wasted in getting operations under way. Within four months of receiving the go ahead, 15 B-52s were regularly flying from U-Tapao, but it is worth mentioning that the Thai airfield initially functioned as a forward operating base, rather than as a main operating base. In essence, this meant that responsibility for scheduling missions rested firmly with the planners on Guam.

As for the bombers, when missions from U-Tapao commenced, the usual procedure was to launch from Andersen and bomb a target in Vietnam (or Laos) in the normal way. However, rather than make the long transit back to Guam, the crew would then proceed to Thailand. Once in temporary residence, a B-52 would then fly eight 'round-robin' sorties, before launching on another mission that would culminate in a return to Andersen. In this way, the Thai base was able to achieve a high level of productivity, with its 15 aircraft comfortably able to account for 450 of the 800 sorties that were being flown every month. Furthermore, this continually rotating method meant that anything more complex than routine servicing of the aircraft was normally undertaken on Guam which possessed much more comprehensive maintenance facilities.

In due course, U-Tapao's assumption of sole responsibility for the *Arc Light* campaign in September 1970 resulted in it becoming home for just over 40 B-52Ds. That change was accompanied by new status as a main operating base and there's little doubt that the maintenance set-up was expanded to provide a much greater degree of self-sufficiency.

Having alluded to sortie rates, it is worth paying a little more attention to these, since they provide the clearest indication of the magnitude of the operation as well as clues to the size of the force committed in support of the war effort. Mention has already been made of increases in the rate to a level of about 800 per month with effect from March 1967, but it should be noted that achievement of this was actually delayed by a shortage of bombs that also affected other operations, particularly those by tactical fighters.

The revised level was destined to be held for the best part of a year, before the siege of Khe Sanh and the opening of the Tet offensive on 30 January 1968 prompted a further hike, to around 1200 sorties per month with effect from the beginning of February. In fact, some of the assets that allowed this 50 per cent increase to be implemented were actually deployed to the region for a quite different reason.

One of those reasons was North Korea's seizure of the US Navy intelligence-gathering vessel USS *Pueblo* on 23 January 1968. As part of the US reaction to this occurrence, SAC was directed to despatch a sizeable bomber and tanker task force to the theatre. Code-named *Port Bow*, this was composed of some 26 B-52Ds and 10 KC-135As. Looking more closely at the bombers, 11 of them went to augment those already in place on Guam, with the remainder (drawn mostly from the 91st BW) ending up at Kadena AB, Okinawa. While there, they were attached to the 4252nd SW.

Movement of the *Port Bow* contingent was accomplished between 3-7 February and raised the total number of B-52Ds in the Pacific region to 105, which was handsomely in excess of the 79 needed to achieve the 1200 sortie rate. However, faced with a determined offensive and with the Marine garrison at Khe Sanh also under threat, Westmoreland was soon requesting that the latest arrivals be committed to *Arc Light*. This time, the powers-that-be in Washington agreed with alacrity, authorising the transfer on 11 February and this new increment of bomber resources allowed the sortie rate to shoot up still further, to an unprecedented level of 1800 per month with effect from 15 February.

On the following day, Kadena's first *Arc Light* mission took place, inaugurating a 30-month period when three bases were involved in hosting *Arc Light* bombers. In fact, the revised sortie rate was originally intended to be merely a temporary expedient, but it remained in force throughout the rest of 1968 and well into 1969, only being curtailed by economic factors associated with the cost of running the war. Some idea of that cost

may be gained by mentioning that projections for 1967 (when the sortie rate was just 800) anticipated that the sum total of all expenditures associated with the *Arc Light* force would consume in the region of $750-800 million dollars. Clearly, it was in every way an awesomely expensive undertaking... but it ws only a part of the overall picture.

Following the imposition of economies, the sortie rate declined initially to 1600 on 18 July 1969, with a further reduction to 1400 occurring on 6 October. Despite the cut-back, the bombers continued to fly regularly from Andersen, Kadena and U-Tapao until 16 August 1970 when a more significant curtailment saw the sortie rate fall to 1000 per month.

At this point, Andersen was relieved from providing direct support to the ongoing war and Kadena duly followed suit little more than a month later, on 19 September. Not long before, the reorganisation of SAC had resulted in the 4133rd BW(P) turning over responsibility for tasks associated with B-52 operations from Guam to the 43rd SW on 1 July 1970, while control of the Kadena based element had passed from the 4252nd SW to the 376th SW on 1 April 1970.

Cessation of bomber operations from these two airfields left *Arc Light* solely in the hands of the base at U-Tapao, which was able to accomplish the task with a total of about 42 aircraft. That number was easily able to cope with a rate of 1000 sorties per month and also proved equal to accommodating a slight increase that came into effect in February 1971 when it rose to 1200.

Those extra sorties were largely prompted by the need for close support during the *Lam Son 719* incursion into Laos – and the end of that military adventure was accompanied by a return to the previous rate, which was held until early in 1972 when a dramatic worsening of the military situation prompted deployment of additional aircraft to the theatre.

That process was launched at the beginning of February and culminated in the number of bombers available for combat in the war zone multiplying almost fivefold in the space of just a few months. Inevitably, with such a hugely expanded force available for combat, the bombing campaign against targets in South-East Asia was also stepped up to an extraordinary degree and rose over the same period to an unprecedented 3150 sorties per month.

The stage was clearly set for the final denouement, which went by the name of *Linebacker*...

THE OTHER THEATRES – LAOS AND CAMBODIA

ONE PARTICULARLY INTERESTING aspect of the B-52's combat record in South-East Asia concerns the fact that the *Linebacker II* operation is by far the best known, even though it covered a period that spanned just 12 days and despite that concentrated effort accounting for well under one per cent of the total number of combat sorties flown by the B-52 during eight years of war. In distinct contrast, precious little publicity was ever given to two other major theatres in which the B-52's unique bomb-carrying talents were employed, specifically Laos and Cambodia.

Operations in these two areas eventually accounted for close to 40 per cent of all the sorties recorded between December 1965 and August 1973. In Cambodia's case, that equated to over 380,000 tons of ordnance, while Laos may well have been battered by upwards of three-quarters of a million tons. That's an awful lot of bombs and quite extraordinary efforts were made to disguise extension of the bombing campaign into these areas by successive occupants of the highest office in the US political arena.

That policy of secrecy first manifested itself in early operations against targets in Laos during Lyndon Johnson's term as president, but was taken even further in Cambodia by Richard Nixon. Within weeks of occupying the Oval Office in the White House in 1969, he authorised bombing of the so-called 'sanctuary' bases and simultaneously issued a directive that this bombing be kept secret. In accordance with that directive, officials in the Department of Defense announced that the B-52 strikes were actually being aimed at targets in South Vietnam, while some rather peculiar operating procedures were invoked for the aircrew tasked with carrying out the bombing and the operators of radar sites associated with directing that bombing.

It didn't take too long before the story broke in the press and the clandestine operation was unmasked, but the full extent of what was going on didn't become public knowledge for several more years. However, the early press reports prompted a furious Nixon to instigate a search for those responsible for leaking information. Illegal wire-taps of government officials and reporters followed and the atmosphere of paranoia that beset much of the later period of Nixon's presidency led more or less directly to the creation of the notorious 'White House Plumbers' – and, ultimately, to the Watergate scandal which forced him out of office in disgrace in August 1974, not long before the final chapter of US involvement in South-East Asia was written with the helicopter-borne evacuations of Cambodia and South Vietnam.

Initial use of the B-52 in both theatres was predominantly in an interdiction capacity, with the objective of staunching the flow of supplies that passed along the Ho Chi Minh and Sihanouk trails into South Vietnam. In the later stages, when the fighting had spread to both countries and when Communist-backed Pathet Lao and Khmer Rouge forces began to gain the upper hand in the respective ground wars, the 'Buff' was employed as a kind of 'airborne artillery'. That was certainly not the mission it was designed for – and there's good reason to question the effectiveness of these attacks, especially in view of the lack of friendly ground troops to occupy territory in the disputed areas.

In reviewing operations conducted in these theatres, it seems best to consider them separately, starting with Laos. This actually absorbed its first load of B-52 bombs in December 1965 and was eventually to be the target for just over a quarter of all the 124,532 B-52 sorties that culminated in weapons release. That meant it was probably hit with five times the tonnage dropped on Japan in the whole of World War 2.

For Laos, the bombing in general finally ended in mid-April 1973, with a B-52 strike in the vicinity of the

Plain of Jars. This was prompted by a series of violations of the ceasefire agreement, but whether this or any of the thousands of other missions achieved much beyond turning the local terrain into something that more closely approximated to the surface of the moon is a matter for speculation.

It's unarguable that eight years of bombing certainly caused a tremendous amount of damage. What is equally clear is that the bombing was ultimately militarily unsuccessful in so far as neither of the objectives of that bombing was accomplished. Interdiction of the Ho Chi Minh trail may well have slowed the pace of infiltration and made it more difficult for the communists but it didn't prevent them from achieving the ultimate victory. In much the same way, bombing of Pathet Lao and North Vietnamese forces in Laos may have helped to stave off the eventual defeat of the legitimate government but, once again, it certainly didn't prevent it. This, of course, was not the fault of the bomber or its crews, for both performed well. However, one could not make the same claim for the politicians in Washington who were responsible for the conduct of the war.

As already remarked, the first B-52 strikes against targets in Laos were fundamentally an extension of the *Arc Light* campaign in adjacent South Vietnam – and were intended to interdict men and materiel heading for the northernmost provinces of South Vietnam. The initial request by General Westmoreland to extend the area of B-52 operations into neighbouring border regions was made in November 1965 and met with the approval of the US Ambassador to Laos, William H Sullivan, on the strict understanding that these strikes were not publicised.

For their part, the Joint Chiefs of Staff (JCS) also agreed to back use of the SAC bombers in this way and Westmoreland then recommended that the initial attack be made against an area bounded by Thac Hiet province in Laos and Quang Tin province in South Vietnam. This was known to be free of villages and clear of friendly troops and was understood to be harbouring substantial quantities of the enemy. A formal request for an *Arc Light* strike was submitted on 23 November, but the US State and Defense Departments were slow to authorise use of the heavy bombers.

That inability to respond quickly meant the first strike did not actually take place until well into December. As manager of the bomber force at Andersen,

responsibility for undertaking this strike fell to the Guam-based Third Air Division, which duly despatched two dozen B-52Fs to Laos on the 12th. They were laden with M117 750-lb general purpose bombs and cluster bomb units containing BLU-3B sub-munitions, it being considered that this mix of ordnance would cause the maximum possible damage to structures and personnel in the target areas.

Unfortunately, it appears that no serious attempt was made at post-strike assessment, with the result that the effectiveness or otherwise of the bombing remained an unknown quantity. Part of the reason for that failure was that the area that came under attack was heavily forested. This naturally precluded damage assessment from the air by means of photography, since the jungle canopy formed an effective screen. In addition, there was also no attempt to insert a ground reconnaissance team to take a first-hand look at the objective. Putting friendly forces on the ground in an area known or suspected to house hostile forces might well sound like a fairly hare-brained idea, but was far from being an improbable one. Indeed, if truth be known, the capability existed in the form of the *Shining Brass* programme, whereby teams of US and South Vietnamese Special Forces infiltrated Laos to monitor activity in the *Tiger Hound* sector of the Ho Chi Minh Trail.

If the success of the mission was questionable, no such doubts existed over the effectiveness of the veil of secrecy, for this was breached within a couple of weeks, much to the chagrin of Ambassador Sullivan. News of the bombing of Laos by B-52s was first made public knowledge in the USA by the *Washington Post* on 28 December and the same report stated that further missions were almost certain to follow.

In that assumption, the *Post* journalists were soon proved to be correct, but the revelation was a source of grave embarrassment to Ambassador Sullivan who very quickly requested Washington not to authorise further missions by the B-52s until he was able to reassure the Laotian Prime Minister, Souvanna Phouma, that no more publicity would be forthcoming. At least, that was the reason given, although the Ambassador's worries seem to have been based more on the fear that Souvanna Phouma would not agree to further B-52 missions.

That isn't altogether surprising, since the Prime Minister of Laos hadn't exactly been well informed about the first such raid, which had been carried out

ABOVE B-52Ds being readied for action during the Vietnam war. During *Arc Light* missions against communist forces, 'Buffs' typically flew in three-ship formations known as cells. A cell could unleash no fewer than 324 bombs, cutting a three-laned swath of explosions two miles wide and three miles long *(USAF)*

without the government being consulted – or even officially informed. Nor, for that matter, was he told of subsequent B-52 strikes in Laos until as late as September 1966 and by that time well over 500 sorties had been staged from Guam.

Irrespective of such diplomatic niceties, resumption of *Arc Light* strikes against Laos came in January 1966 after further planning again identified areas in the vicinity of the border that were suspected to be harbouring enemy troops, equipment stockpiles and rest areas. Westmoreland was again an influential figure in the target selection process but it was far from being a case of simply choosing an area to attack, calling up the B-52s and then waiting for the bombs to start dropping.

For a start, the choice of target had first to win the approval of Ambassador Sullivan, while responsibility for giving the go-ahead to execute a particular strike was shared between Sullivan and the JCS. And, even then, SAC's 3rd Air Division at Andersen still required clearance from CinCSAC at Offutt AFB before launching the B-52s from Guam and the supporting

KC-135A Stratotankers from Kadena AB, Okinawa. All in all, it was a complex pie, with many ingredients to be blended together before the bombers were able to drop any weapons.

All of those ingredients next came together on 14 January 1966 when 24 B-52Fs (each laden with 24 750-lb and 27 500-lb bombs) conducted operation *Ocean Wave*. This entailed a strike on the border area adjacent to Quang Nam province in South Vietnam and some of the bombers were diverted to perform cover strikes on the edge of the province. In this instance, mission effectiveness again remained undetermined, but there was some good news for the US authorities in that security wasn't compromised.

Two more missions followed during February and one of these did at last feature efforts to establish just what, if anything, was being achieved by the raids. The first mission was code named *West Stream* and took place early in the month. It was also smaller than the two previous raids, involving just a dozen aircraft which worked over a target box adjacent to Quang Tri province. As with *Ocean Wave*, cover strikes were performed, although in this case they took place some 90 minutes after the main attack.

The next raid, staged on 27 February, was also the largest to date and hit a target area next to Kontum province. A total of 27 B-52Fs was involved in operation *Back Road* and the subsequent ground probe by a *Shining Brass* team into the area that had been attacked

ABOVE A trio of B-52Ds (55-0054, foreground) runway-bound at U-Tapao airfield, Thailand, in October 1968. The *Rolling Thunder* campaign against North Vietnam had just been replaced by a bombing halt, but gruelling missions against Viet Cong forces in South Vietnam were continuing. The Stratofortress, then becoming more familiarly known as the 'Buff' (the acronym for 'Big Ugly Fat F.....') was now attired in a variation of wartime TO 1-1-4 camouflage with flat black undersides *(USAF)*

must have been rather disquieting in a number of ways. Most disturbing was the matter of accuracy – or, to be more precise, the lack of it, for only about a third of the bombs that had been dropped had actually landed within the designated target area.

That was far from satisfactory and the news that even those bombs which did fall in the right spot caused little damage was almost certainly even more distressing. One thing the *Shining Brass* team did report was a surprising lack of craters and the reason for that was the dense nature of the jungle canopy. Study of the trees in the target area quickly confirmed that many bombs actually detonated well above ground level.

Despite evidence that the B-52 force was achieving little more than the destruction of trees, Westmoreland and other officers in the Military Assistance Command Vietnam chose to ignore the findings of the *Shining Brass* team and continued to press for more bombing attacks. They certainly got them, for the raids continued and intensified throughout the rest of 1966.

In March, for instance, three 12-aircraft and two 15 aircraft attacks took place. In April, the number of monthly sorties exceeded 100 for the first time and the weight of ordnance would also have risen markedly, since this same month witnessed the first appearance of the B-52D model. By the close of the year, Laos had been on the receiving end of just under 650 sorties. That equated to about 12 per cent of the 5217 *Arc Light* sorties flown in 1966 but worse followed, for in 1967,

resources targeted on Laos rose even more, to almost 18 per cent of the total (ie, 1711 of 9686 sorties).

The *Tiger Hound* interdiction area continued to bear the brunt of the B-52 strikes throughout this period, but ever more determined efforts to staunch the flow of men and equipment down the Ho Chi Minh Trail were made from 1968 onwards and the end of the bombing of North Vietnam had far-reaching effects on Laos. This stemmed in part from the fact that the US was no longer making any effort to damage the North's war-making capability by bombing. In consequence, many of the US warplanes that had previously been operating against North Vietnam were now diverted to find fresh targets – and many of those targets were in Laos.

At the same time, freed from the attentions of US tactical air power, the North now found itself in the happy position of being able to channel many more resources into the pipeline that ran south, via the Ho

Chi Minh Trail, into South Vietnam. This, not surprisingly, meant that infiltration through Laos was stepped up by a quite dramatic degree during the course of 1968-69.

In turn, these factors had disastrous consequences for Laos, which now assumed front-line status in the fight to ensure the survival of South Vietnam and which very soon began to soak up bombs like blotting paper. The campaign known as *Commando Hunt* was one manifestation of the interdiction effort and made great use of the tactical fighters that were no longer permitted to go 'downtown' (to Hanoi). In addition, B-52s also began to range much more widely over Laotian territory and this, not surprisingly, resulted in a further hike in the number of sorties flown, which reached a new record of 3377 during 1968.

Almost all of those sorties were apparently concentrated within the the so-called Laotian 'panhandle' which lay in the southern part of the country, where the various strands of the trail exited into South Vietnam. However, in 1969 and later years, operations expanded northwards to cover the trail's entry points, particularly those in the vicinity of the Mu Gia, Ban Karai and Ban Raving passes which linked Laos to the southern part of North Vietnam.

At the same time, the fortunes of war within Laos also began to turn in favour of the Pathet Lao and North Vietnamese and this culminated in a decision to expand air operations over the *Barrel Roll* area of Northern Laos. In fact, it was more a case of massive escalation rather than expansion, for the amount of ordnance expended by tactical fighters shot up from around 22,000 tons in 1968 to somewhere in the region of 189,000 tons in the following year.

As for the B-52, although some sources suggest that it was first committed to action in the *Barrel Roll* area during 1969, freely available USAF historical studies of the various conflicts in South-East Asia state that the first raid in Northern Laos did not take place until mid-February 1970. That wasn't for lack of asking, since requests to employ the 'Buff' had been made a number of times, most notably when the town of Muong Soui had been attacked in the previous summer. On that occasion, permission was denied by the Washington authorities and the town was soon captured by Communist forces. In early 1970, however, with the enemy again on the rampage and very much in the ascendancy, authorisation was forthcoming for B-52 strikes on the Plain of Jars – and the first such

raids took place on 17-18 February, when more than 1000 tons of bombs were dropped. These were reported to have sparked off many secondary explosions and to have caused many casualties.

Inevitably, many more sorties followed and by the end of the year it appears that B-52s had deposited about 28,000 tons of ordnance on targets in the *Barrel Roll* area. While impressive, that quantity paled into insignificance when compared with the level of activity further south in the *Steel Tiger/Tiger Hound* zones, where the effort to cut off the flow of men and materiel continued unabated – and where, during 1970, the B-52s are reported to have disgorged four times the weight of bombs that had been used on *Barrel Roll* (ie, 112,000 tons).

Corresponding estimates for 1971 show further increases, to 41,000 and 126,000 tons respectively, with a substantial amount of the latter being expended in support of the *Lam Son 719* incursion into Laos that took place between 8 February and 6 April. This was primarily intended to forestall an anticipated Communist offensive into the two northernmost provinces of South Vietnam, namely Quang Tri and Thau Thien.

A Congressional edict prohibiting the use of American troops in Laos dictated that only South Vietnamese forces were involved in the ground battle, which essentially took the form of a major push by troops and mechanised units across the Ho Chi Minh trail towards Tchepone. However, the US more than compensated by committing massive air power resources to the action. These were drawn from all of all the services and included over 8000 sorties by Air Force, Navy and Marine Corps tactical fighters as well as thousands more by Army helicopters which were used to move men and supplies around the area being fought over. In addition, some 1358 B-52 sorties were recorded, the majority of which were in direct support of friendly soldiers.

Initially, the Vietnamese forces made good headway, but a determined counter-attack and increasingly stubborn resistance eventually caused the South Vietnamese commander, Lt Gen Hoang Xuan Lam, to curtail the operation. At the same time, he ordered his forces to withdraw, but the retreat was far from orderly and much valuable military equipment was simply abandoned where it stood. So, even though *Lam Son 719* inflicted a considerable amount of damage on the enemy, it is undeniable that it also cost the South Vietnamese dear. More significantly, it boded ill for the future, when the South would have to fight alone, for Nixon's 'Vietnamization' policy was now in process of implementation.

As for Laos, this had more than enough trouble of its own and it continued to feel the impact of B-52 strikes for another two years. Much of the bombing that took place during that time was involved with interdiction of the Ho Chi Minh trail, but Northern Laos also came increasingly under attack as the tide of the ground war turned irrevocably against the Laotian Army and Gen Vang Pao's Meo forces in 1972. Indeed, it was only the availability of US air power (including B-52s and F-111s) that prevented the fall of Vang Pao's bastion and stronghold at Long Tieng in November 1972.

By then, however, the end was in sight, for it was in that same month that negotiations between the existing Laotian government and representatives of the Pathet Lao got under way. These eventually culminated in a ceasefire being agreed between the various factions and it duly came into effect on 21 February 1973, simultaneously bringing a halt to the US bombing of Laos.

Two days later, in the wake of ceasefire infringements by the Communists and a request for assistance from the Laotian government in Vientiane, the B-52 was back, engaging in a very heavy attack on enemy positions close to Paksong in the south. Yet more strikes followed during 15-17 April, when the Plain of Jars was targeted in the aftermath of further violations.

They, however, proved to be the last missions against Laos, which is said to have been the target for about 27 per cent of the 124,532 B-52 sorties that culminated in weapons release between 1965 and 1973. That equates to more than 33,000 sorties, but a better understanding of the destructive power unleashed over that eight-year period may be had if one considers that those 33,000 sorties could conceivably have resulted in approximately 800,000 tons of bombs being dropped.

In mid-April 1973, as mentioned a few moments ago, Laos was declared firmly off limits as a target and the focus of attention turned to Cambodia which was now 'the only game in town'.

CAMBODIA

South Vietnam's other neighbouring state was Cambodia and this also came under attack by B-52, although the first raids did not take place until the spring of 1969. Prior to that time, President Johnson had persistently denied requests by US military commanders to extend the bombing into the so-called 'sanctuary' areas that adjoined South Vietnam. In this, it seems apparent that his principal motive was fear of further escalation of the fighting in South-East Asia.

Cambodian neutrality may also have been another restraining factor, even though there is evidence to support a belief that this neutrality was somewhat elastic in nature, to the point where Cambodia's head of state, Prince Norodom Sihanouk, apparently favoured whichever side appeared to be winning. Thus, North Vietnam was given access to port facilities at Kompong Som (also known as Sihanoukville) to ship in military supplies for much of the 1960s. This culminated in the Cambodian leader unwittingly giving his name to the 'Sihanouk Trail' – which was one of the major supply lines that fuelled the war effort and headed in a roughly easterly direction towards South Vietnam.

Then, in 1968, when it looked as if the North was heading for defeat, Sihanouk is reported to have experienced a change of heart. Furthermore, he is said to have made it clear in a conversation with US envoy Chester Bowles that he did not want any North Vietnamese in Cambodia and that he would not object to US bombing attacks on the sanctuary areas that had for so long been a thorn in the side of the allied forces in South Vietnam.

But, when all is said and done, there's bombing and there's bombing and later remarks attributed to Sihanouk seem to indicate that the conversation with Bowles was taken out of context at best – and wilfully misinterpreted at worst. There appears little doubt that Sihanouk wanted to rid Eastern Cambodia of the Vietnamese presence. With regard to the bombing, though, it seems that what he actually said was that he 'could not object'.

This appears to indicate that while Sihanouk may have tacitly condoned the use of fighter-bombers against the sanctuaries, he certainly wasn't prepared to agree to missions involving large numbers of B-52s. That, however, is what resulted, and the B-52 raids increased in intensity following Sihanouk's overthrow in March 1970 by Prime Minister Lon Nol and Prince Sirik Matak, both of whom were much more pro-American.

In fact, no attacks were actually mounted in the immediate aftermath of the Sihanouk-Bowles discussion, although it is possible that President Johnson may

ABOVE A 43rd Strategic Wing B-52D (55-0101) at Andersen AFB, Guam, 'bombed up' for an *Arc Light* mission over South Vietnam. During combat operations in the 1960s, 'Buffs' occasionally ventured into the narrow southern area of North Vietnam known as Route Package One, but in neither the *Rolling Thunder* (1965-68) nor the *Linebacker* (May-October 1972) campaigns were they unleashed against Hanoi, Haiphong and the nerve centre of the country known as Route Package Six. Only in Operation *Linebacker II*, better-known as the Eleven Day War (December 1972), did B-52s finally assault strategic targets in the heart of North Vietnam *(USAF)*

well have been planning to take up this option. As it turned out, the North Vietnamese acted first, launching the so-called Tet offensive on South Vietnam in January 1968 – and Johnson's next key move was to call a halt to the bombing of the North and invite representatives of Hanoi to negotiate a peaceful solution to the war. Those negotiations began in Paris in May 1968 and don't appear to have been taken all that seriously by the North Vietnamese since they were still in progress when Johnson left office at the start of 1969.

As noted earlier, the new occupant of the White House showed little or no inclination towards moder-

ation, for one of Richard Nixon's first acts was to approve a request from Gen Creighton W Abrams (who had taken over from Westmoreland as ComUS-MACV in July 1968) for clearance to use the B-52s to bomb a part of Cambodia situated to the north-west of Saigon and known as the *Fish Hook*. According to intelligence reports, this contained a North Vietnamese regional headquarters and what Abrams wanted was a low-key assault, of no more than 60 sorties.

What he actually got was the precursor of more than four years of bombing which only ended in mid-August 1973. By that time, some 16,527 sorties had been flown and 383,851 tons of bombs dropped by B-52s – if one accepts the available figures, which may in fact be seriously in error. This was overkill on a monumental scale, but the clandestine bombing was rationalised by Henry Kissinger's military advisor, Alexander M Haig, who described the area under attack as 'enemy territory'.

In that, he was undoubtedly correct, but the follow-up remark is surely open to debate, since Haig went on to say, 'It was not Cambodian territory and we had every right, legally and morally, to take what action was necessary to protect our forces'. That action included a massive cross-border incursion in late April

1970 by some 90,000 US and Vietnamese troops, supported by US warplanes. In the intervening period between the start of American bombing and the US-led invasion, Sihanouk had been deposed and the tragedy of Cambodia had begun to unfold.

The bombing campaign undertaken before the invasion was given the generic code-name of *Menu*. It began, appropriately enough, with *Breakfast* on 18 March 1969, when Vietcong Base Area 353 was hit. This lay astride the border roughly north of the South Vietnamese town of Tay Ninh. The focus of the B-52 bombing then moved north, with the region around the Cambodian-Laotian border being the target for raids on Base Area 609.

These were collectively known as *Lunch* and were supposedly staged in retaliation for the shooting down of a Navy EC-121 with the loss of 31 crew by North Korean fighters on 14 April 1969. According to President Nixon, the intent was to impress upon the leaders of North Korea and North Vietnam that the USA was determined to support its allies and resist aggression. However, cynics might well be excused for concluding that Nixon's grasp of geography left more than a little to be desired and one might also reasonably question the morality involved in violating the neutrality of a third-party nation state that had played no part in the destruction of the Navy aircraft.

Other even more bizarrely named courses such as *Dinner*, *Dessert*, *Snack* and *Supper* followed and by the time the first phase of bombing ended in late May 1970, some 4308 sorties had been flown and well over 100,000 tons of bombs had been dropped on Cambodia under conditions of great secrecy.

Some rather unusual procedures and practices were employed to disguise what was going on. Mention has already been made of Defense Department collusion in covering up the objective of the strikes by announcing them as being against targets in South Vietnam, but it is worth noting that SAC records were also falsified and that the bombing was actually carried out by night under the direction of ground units using the MSQ-77 radar.

Known as the *Combat Skyspot* system, this relied on bomber crews following instructions from a radar site which guided them to the release point and informed them of the precise moment that weapons should be dropped. *Skyspot* was originally conceived to improve the accuracy of B-52 bombing since the nature of the terrain provided few radar-significant landmarks and most targets could not be discerned on the 'Buff's' own radar. In addition, it was also extensively used to control attacks by fighter-bombers.

Enough MSQ-77 sites were eventually positioned in the war zone to provide coverage of all of South Vietnam, the southern portion of North Vietnam, most of Laos and a good chunk of Cambodia and it became the prime method of directing B-52 attacks after 1965. As far as the heavy bomber force was concerned, *Skyspot* most definitely bolstered operational flexibility by allowing it to hit targets of opportunity and thus be more responsive to the needs of field commanders in South Vietnam.

Combat Skyspot was therefore of great value in attacks on North Vietnamese and Viet Cong elements in Cambodia during the course of operation *Menu*. Moreover, the availability of this system made it possible for the Nixon administration and the Joint Chiefs to conduct a secret bombing campaign and, for the most part, disguise what was going on. The key to the successful subterfuge lay in what the JCS called 'dual reporting'.

Procedures first put into use for *Breakfast* were employed in later strikes, with the bomber crews being briefed in the normal fashion on target areas in Vietnam. After that, however, the pilots and navigators were taken aside and told to expect the MSQ-77 ground operators to direct them to release their weapons on a different set of coordinates. Such alterations didn't entail major revision, for the cover targets in South Vietnam usually lay a short distance from the secret objectives just across the border in Cambodia.

Elsewhere, whenever a *Menu* mission was to be flown, the personnel at Bien Hoa who supervised operation of the MSQ-77 system were given a different set of target coordinates – and it was these that were processed by computer to determine weapons release points which were passed on to the approaching B-52s. On completion of the bomb run, an HF radio message was passed in the normal way from the bomber to home base confirming that the mission had been accomplished.

However, the crew member responsible for sending that message was not in on the secret – and nor were the the individuals who received it. Thus, when it came to preparing the post-strike reports, they simply entered the original target co-ordinates on the paperwork, making it seem that the bombs had actually fallen on South Vietnam.

Meanwhile, back at Bien Hoa, all of the paperwork and computer tape relating to the mission's true target was carefully gathered up and burnt, thus eliminating any tangible evidence of what had taken place. After that, the usual reports were completed and forwarded via normal secure channels to the SAC Advanced Echelon headquarters in Saigon – but these featured the original South Vietnamese coordinates. In this way, official SAC records (which themselves were classified as secret) were distorted, making reference only to bombing of South Vietnam and giving no clue as to the real nature of the night's activity.

Subsequently, with effect from May 1970, when US air power was used to support Cambodian Army personnel in the fight against Pol Pot's much-feared Khmer Rouge guerillas, operation *Menu* evolved into *Freedom Deal*. However, whereas *Menu* specifically targeted areas within close proximity to the border with South Vietnam, *Freedom Deal* encompassed a much greater area of the country. At the outset, coincident with the deployment of friendly troops in the *Fish Hook* and *Parrot's Beak* areas, the B-52 force was kept quite busy, paving the way for the assault with a number of missions and eventually recording some 763 sorties over a period of two months.

Of that quantity, 653 were carried out in direct support of six ground operations, but SAC's heavyweight was allowed to range considerably further afield than the 18-mile limit which applied to forces on the ground and several raids were made on areas thought to contain enemy troops, equipment and munitions. Another military objective was the elusive Communist headquarters although, as far as is known, this was never actually hit.

In the final stages of the war in Cambodia, B-52 strikes ranged much further from the border, with much of the eastern half of the country being targeted at some time or another. Indeed, as the Khmer Rouge moved ever closer towards Phnom Penh, so did the bombing, with Khmer forces within just a few miles of the capital coming under attack by the high-flying bombers.

This naturally called for great care to be taken in order to ensure that the bombs fell in the right place. However, almost inevitably, there were instances of inaccurate bombing causing death and destruction amongst the civilian population and friendly forces. Without doubt one of the most disastrous of these incidents occurred on 7 August 1973, when a B-52 dis-

charged its entire ordnance load on Neak Luong, to the south-east of Phnom Penh. The town's hospital was amongst the buildings destroyed in this tragic episode, which also claimed the lives of 137 people and caused injury to almost twice that number. Just over a week later, on 15 August, the Congressional-imposed ban on funding the bombing in Cambodia became law and effectively brought a halt to the American role in the various wars in South-East Asia.

In the seven months that preceded the ceasefire, the ending of combat operations in other parts of South-East Asia resulted in Cambodia becoming the only target for US air power. In consequence, it found itself on the receiving end of a real battering as the ferocity of the bombing intensified. Eventually, the onslaught did stop, but by then, Cambodia had absorbed no fewer than 539,129 tons of bombs since *Freedom Deal* had been launched in May 1970, although it should be emphasised that by no means all that awesome quantity of ordnance was dropped by B-52s.

Moreover, almost half of that total (257,465 tons, to be precise) had been expended in little more than six months – using the Japanese comparison again, that was about 100,000 tons more than fell on Japan in the whole of World War 2. Unfortunately, in the absence of an effective ground force capable of holding on to the contested territory, the effect of the prolonged bombing may have been no more than to stave off a defeat that increasingly seemed inevitable. So, while it could legitimately be argued that the achievements of US air power were militarily significant, it would perhaps be foolish to ignore the counter-argument that one result of the bombing may well have been to incite the Khmer Rouge to exact even more fearsome retribution than it had been planning.

LINEBACKER

On 30 March 1972, regular North Vietnamese Army troops supported by heavy artillery and armoured fighting vehicles poured across the demilitarised zone and the border with Laos into South Vietnam. Within hours, the invading forces had made significant progress southwards and such was the ferocity of the offensive that they soon succeeded in capturing the provincial capital of Quang Tri as well as most of the surrounding countryside, while laying siege to An Loc and Kontum. Eventually, in the face of determined opposition by South Vietnamese forces, the offensive stalled in June, but it was to take several months bitter fighting and many thousands of sorties by US aircraft before the last North Vietnamese elements were driven back whence they came and the lost territory was retaken.

The operation that was given the code name *Linebacker* was by far the best known manifestation of the massive US air effort in support of its South Vietnamese ally, but bombing of the North in 1972 actually began as *Freedom Train* on 2 April, when the US National Command Authorities authorised air strikes as a response to the invasion. In the first instance, the primary objective was that of providing direct support to South Vietnamese troops tasked with blunting the North Vietnamese advance. Later, the focus of attention shifted to a more strategic standpoint, with interdiction of supply lines following the relaxation of restrictions on the bombing of North Vietnam.

However, rather than opt for the piecemeal approach used during the *Rolling Thunder* campaign of 1965-68, the Washington authorities were much bolder this time and also far more amenable to the needs of force commanders responsible for the conduct of the war in South-East Asia. Evidence of this was provided by the fact that they permitted the scope of operations to be expanded much more rapidly – thus, the cut-off line for air strikes which initially lay just a little way north of the 17th parallel was extended to 18 degrees North on 4 April and then to 19 degrees North on 6 April. Barely a week after that, virtually all of the restrictions had been lifted, with targets close to Hanoi and Haiphong coming under attack by Air Force and Navy aircraft, including B-52s, for the first time in more than three years.

In addition to allowing operations to be conducted over a far wider area, Washington also avoided interfering as much as possible when it came to selecting targets to be attacked. Obviously, there were some political aspects that needed to be taken into consideration and the administration was mindful of the public relations angle. This was most apparent in the determination to avoid hitting civilian areas and causing what was euphemistically known as 'collateral damage'. Other than that, the bombing campaigns of 1972 were for the most part conducted along strict military lines and with military objectives quite rightly taking priority.

In the meantime, senior members of the US administration also pursued diplomatic channels in the search for a solution to more than seven years of war. Unfortunately, North Vietnamese intransigence continued to block any progress with the talks in Paris and 1972 was most notable for a steady increase in military pressure as the Nixon administration sought to tighten the screw. Actions of this kind included a robust response to the Easter invasion; the mining of ports and harbours in May; the expansion of bombing operations through the spring and summer; and, finally and most decisively, the operation known as *Linebacker II*.

Often referred to as the '11-day war', the latter took the bombers to the major population centres of Hanoi and Haiphong in considerable numbers during the second half of December 1972. It was also viewed by many as being the single most influential factor in securing a ceasefire agreement with effect from mid-January 1973. However, even though it may have been the catalyst for the successful conclusion of the long-running peace negotiations, it should not be forgotten that a high price was paid by some of the crews that participated in *Linebacker II*.

At the beginning of 1972, of course, all that lay in the future and there was no way of knowing that within a matter months Andersen AFB would play host to the greatest concentration of operational B-52s ever seen. In fact, as the year opened, Guam wasn't even involved in the war effort, other than as a staging post and rear echelon support facility for bomber aircraft operating from U-Tapao, Thailand. The latter base (often referred to as just 'U-T') had held sole responsibility for *Arc Light* bombing missions for more than 16 months and at the start of the year was tasked with performing approximately 1000 sorties per month. This was a level that could be sustained fairly comfortably more or less indefinitely from the Thai base.

Of the three locations that were used for bomber operations in the Vietnam War, 'U-T' was actually just about the most ideal, since its proximity to the target areas in South Vietnam, Laos and Cambodia meant that missions seldom lasted more than four hours (three-and-a-half hours was a good average) and could be accomplished without the need for in-flight refuelling support. As far as management of the resident bomber force was concerned, this was entrusted to the 307th Strategic Wing, which had a nominal strength of 42 B-52Ds at the start of 1972.

Crews to fly those aircraft were routinely drawn

from US-based bomber units on a constantly rotating basis so as to ensure that the workload was split as fairly and evenly as possible. Cross-training of crews from B-52G and B-52H outfits was provided by a small B-52D cadre that operated as part of the 93rd Bomb Wing at Castle AFB, California.

Within a few weeks of the new year opening, the first action to expand the size of the bomber force occurred with the deployment of eight more B-52Ds to U-Tapao on 5 February. This was one of a number of initiatives taken in advance of the invasion and stemmed from intelligence reports of increased cross-border infiltration activity. The infusion of additional aircraft raised the number of bombers present in Thailand to about 50.

A couple of days later, still more examples of the Stratofortress were ordered to move westward at short notice. This proved to be the first of a succession of *Bullet Shot* deployments that would result in a four-fold increase in the size of the bomber force committed to support of the war in Vietnam. Once again, it was the B-52D model that was involved, but this time the number of bombers was much greater and their destination was also different, no less than 29 aircraft heading for Andersen from the bases at Carswell, Dyess and McCoy. Once in place, *Arc Light* missions resumed from Guam on 15 February 1972.

The revised force level permitted an increase in the monthly sortie level to approximately 1200, but this was still far from enough to discourage further military adventures on the part of the enemy. As already noted, the easter offensive was launched on 30 March 1972 and this prompted massive air power reinforcement by the USA. The Air Force was at the forefront of this effort, with Stateside-based fighters hurriedly deploying under operation *Constant Guard*. At the same time, another wave of *Bullet Shot* bombers also flew west from SAC bases in the USA.

Once again, the destination was Andersen, which welcomed a further 50 Stratofortresses during the first half of April 1972. The first aircraft to arrive consisted of another two dozen or so B-52Ds which raised the number on the 'Rock' to approximately 55, but they were soon followed by a 28-strong contingent of B-52Gs which flew in between 10-16 April. The G-model was not, in fact, anything like as well suited for combat duty in South-East Asia as the 'D, since it was unable to carry bombs externally and also lacked the so-called *Big Belly* modification that gave the older ver-

sion such a fearsome conventional capability. Consequently, the maximum B-52G load was just 27 bombs, whereas the 'D could take four times that amount.

The B-52Gs that reached Guam in April were actually the first of the short-tailed 'Buffs' to move to the war zone, but, as events proved, they were far from being the last, for another 70 followed suit during late May and early June. Directing and supporting operations from the base at Guam – and also from U-Tapao – was now such a daunting task that it became necessary in June to instigate a major reorganisation so as to facilitate the day-to-day business of controlling the vastly expanded fleet of bombers and tankers in the Pacific area.

At Guam, the 57th Air Division (Provisional) was created to serve as an intermediate link in the chain of command between the more rarified level of Eighth Air Force headquarters and the subordinate elements which bore responsibility for actually flying and servicing the aircraft. With somewhere in the region of 150 B-52s now in temporary residence, it follows that the maintenance workload was particularly heavy and this was henceforth entrusted to the 303rd Consolidated Aircraft Maintenance Wing (Provisional) which possessed about 5000 personnel and which routinely performed near-miracles in ensuring that operations went on as smoothly as possible.

Turning to the aircrew, these were divided between two Strategic Wing organisations that were type-orientated. Thus, the original 43rd Strategic Wing was entrusted with the B-52D element. This numbered about 50 aircraft which were allocated to two subordinate squadrons, specifically the 60th BS, which had already existed prior to the start of *Freedom Train*, and the 63rd BS(Prov), which was newly created. As for the B-52G fleet, this came under the 72nd Strategic Wing (Prov) and since this was roughly twice as big, with approximately 100 aircraft, it controlled four provisional Bomb Squadrons, specifically the 64th, 65th, 329th and 486th BSs.

Similar organisational changes took place at U-Tapao, where the 17th Air Division (Prov) was created to oversee operations by the 307th SW; the 310th SW(P) and the 340th CAMW(P). In this case, however, only the 307th managed B-52D operations, exercising control via the 364th BS(P) and 365th BS(P). As for the 310th SW(P), this was a tanker outfit with almost 50 examples of the KC-135A that were dedicated to *Young Tiger* support of tactical fighters.

Gains in the size of the bomber force were matched by increases in the monthly sortie rate. As already noted, this climbed from 1000 to 1200 in February, but that modest boost provided no real clue as to the quite extraordinary levels that would be achieved in the coming summer. In April, the next increment of B-52s brought successive increases in sortie rate to 1500 (on the 8th); 1890 (on the 14th) and 2250 (on the 15th). The latter level equated to some 75 sorties daily and this figure was held throughout the rest of April and virtually all of May. It should, however, be borne in mind that by far the majority of these sorties were *Arc Light* and involved the bombing of targets in South Vietnam, Laos and Cambodia – of the total effort, only a relatively small percentage was directed against targets sited in the North.

This same time frame also witnessed a change in nomenclature for US air operations, with Operation *Freedom Train* evolving into *Linebacker I* on 10 May. In fact, the first attacks to be staged on the 10th were actually accomplished as *Rolling Thunder Alpha*, due to the new code name not being notified to operational elements in sufficient time. Despite that glitch, *Linebacker I* was soon widely used and the B-52 certainly played its part, as the monthly sortie rate continued to climb, rising to 2340 on 30 May after the arrival of more B-52Gs.

The Stratofortress contingent based on Guam continued to expand in size after that date as yet more *Bullet Shot* bombers were flown in. Not surprisingly, this growth permitted further incremental increases in sortie rates. These rose initially to 2430 (on 5 June) and then to 3060 (on 19 June), before eventually peaking at a staggering 3150 with effect from 21 June. The best part of 200 bombers (virtually 50 per cent of SAC's entire B-52 fleet) was necessary to sustain that rate, which equated to 105 sorties daily.

In terms of productivity, there's no doubt that U-Tapao achieved more, since its much closer proximity to the battle area allowed it to furnish 39 sorties daily with a contingent that numbered just 50 bombers, all of which were *Big Belly* B-52Ds. Andersen, on the other hand, had something like three times as many bombers to call upon, but about two-thirds of them were the relatively lightly-laden B-52G. Finally, since missions from here typically lasted around 12 hours, it could only contribute 66 sorties per day.

Even though *Linebacker* was generating a fair amount of publicity (and a fair amount of anti-war feeling as well), it was in fact only one of several operations that placed demands on the B-52 communities at Andersen and U-Tapao. As it had done for some considerable time, *Arc Light* continued to swallow up the lion's share of B-52 offensive operations and it follows that the effort directed against the North was far from large.

In addition, of course, the B-52 was far from being the only US warplane to be committed to combat during the *Freedom Train* and *Linebacker I* operations. Mention has already been made of USAF fighters deploying to the region and they were certainly in the thick of things, with the Phantom being kept particularly busy and scoring some startling success in a sequence of bridge-busting exploits. Phantoms also flew combat air patrols to protect the SAC bombers, since it was evident from an early stage that the North Vietnamese were desperate to shoot-down an example of the mighty 'Buff'. And, of course, there were US Navy carrier-borne attack aircraft and US Marine Corps fighter-bombers, all of which were doing their bit to help repulse the invaders.

For the Stratofortress, the first opportunity to operate north of the demilitarised zone in more than three-and-a-half years came within a week of the decision to hit North Vietnamese targets. On 9 April 1972, 15 B-52Ds were despatched to bomb railway yards and POL (petroleum, oil and lubricants) storage facilities in Vinh. Three days after that, North Vietnam again rocked to a succession of blasts as a total of 18 bombers pulverised the airfield at Bai Thuong and the following weekend (15-16 April) saw SAC's heavyweight move within earshot of the capital city and the main port. Then, in a concerted action with Navy and Air Force fighter-bombers, B-52s were involved in a series of attacks on military storage facilities and POL dumps within close proximity to Hanoi and Haiphong, a pattern that was repeated a week later in and around Ham Rong and Thanh Hoa.

As was the case with *Arc Light* strikes, mission planning was based upon the use of the bomber 'cell', whereby the B-52s almost invariably operated in groups of three. There were a number of reasons for this. Obviously, it allowed the 'Buff's' impressive firepower potential to be concentrated within a confined area, which would maximise damage potential. In addition, it permitted defensive electronic countermeasures equipment to be used more effectively, for cell integrity was a vital factor in minimising the risk

ABOVE B-52D 55-0110 of the 4133rd Bomb Wing in its unsheltered parking spot at Andersen AFB, Guam, with Mk 82 500-lb (227-kg) bombs on its underwing pylons and 'clips' of mines on loading vehicles ready to go into the bomb bay. The double-staged ladder used to give mechanics access to the upper area of the Stratofortress was a stock item of ground equipment *(USAF)*

posed by North Vietnam's ever-increasing network of SAM sites. By concentrating the jamming power, it meant that the area of acquisition of radars associated with the missiles was much reduced.

Although operations against targets in the North continued throughout the summer and on into the autumn, as far as the B-52 force was concerned, *Arc Light* still claimed top priority. Evidence of this is provided by detailing the number of sorties directed into *Linebacker* between July and October, figures for these

succeeding months being 337, 560, 411 and 502 respectively. At its worst, that equates to slightly more than 10 per cent of the overall number of B-52 sorties flown – at best, just under 18 per cent.

Even though the effort targeted against North Vietnam was relatively small, there's no doubt that the North Vietnamese were taking a pasting throughout this period and it should come as no surprise to learn that their negotiating team in Paris was also adopting a more positive line in the on-going peace talks. Regrettably, that attitude didn't last long, for a couple of conciliatory gestures by the US resulted in letting the North off the hook. Indeed, the decision to terminate all air operations beyond the 20th parallel with effect from 23 October gave them a valuable breathing space and allowed air defences in the vicinity of Hanoi and Haiphong to be fortified still further. At the same time, damage to key lines of communication between north and south was also quickly repaired and it didn't take much longer for the flow of supplies to be resumed in earnest.

Thus fortified, the North Vietnamese decided to prolong the conflict in the hope of securing extra concessions from the US and they immediately began to renege on promises and assurances made just a few weeks earlier. So, by the start of December, a golden opportunity had been allowed to slip away and the eagerly anticipated peace deal seemed as far away and elusive as ever.

During the interval when targets to the north of the 20th parallel were off-limits, there was still plenty of scope for the B-52 force and November was actually notable for a significant increase in the proportion of sorties devoted to *Linebacker*. In fact, no fewer than 848 sorties were flown against targets in the North, this comprising almost 27 per cent of the overall bombing effort by the heavy bomber force.

In almost every case, sorties ended satisfactorily, with a safe return to home base of a bomber and its crew. However, as *Linebacker* continued, it became evident that the North Vietnamese were making ever more determined efforts to knock down one of the B-52s and score a major propaganda coup. They had come close in April, when a B-52D from U-Tapao was hit by a SAM during one of the first raids to go north of the demilitarised zone. On that occasion, despite the loss of two engines, fuel leaks and over 400 shrapnel punctures, the aircraft concerned (56-0665) was able

to land at Da Nang, where it was eventually repaired and returned to service. That incident confirmed that the 'Buff' was tough and could take severe punishment as well as mete it out, but the odds against the bomber force continuing unscathed shortened with virtually every passing day, especially in the frequently visited area around Vinh.

This was now far better defended and those responsible for scheduling bomber operations were beginning to recognise that it was only a matter of time before the defences claimed their first victim, if for no other reason than that the law of averages dictated it. While Vinh may not have had the fearsome defence in depth of 'downtown' Hanoi, it was definitely becoming a hot spot and the early part of November resulted in some stressful times for a number of crews as well as some very anxious moments for those on board two aircraft that came under fire. Both sustained battle damage but both landed safely at U-Tapao.

BELOW B-52Ds (55-0087, foreground) and KC-135s operating from U-Tapao during Arc Light operations. U-Tapao was nominally a Royal Thai Navy airfield, but in the late 1960s it became, in effect, a new haven for SAC, which never relinquished control of its bombers and tankers to the local command in the war zone. When the Eleven Day War began in December 1972, 53 B-52Ds and 99 B-52Gs were operating from Guam and 54 B-52Ds from U-Tapao – a total of 206 'Buffs', which amounted to more than half the SAC heavy bomber fleet (USAF)

A third aircraft was less fortunate and the moment that many had been fearing finally came on 22 November when B-52D 55-0110 of the 307th Strategic Wing suddenly and irrevocably ran out of luck whilst operating against Vinh. Flying from U-Tapao as *Olive 2* (B-52 cells were traditionally colour-coded and this practice was adhered to throughout *Linebacker*), the bomber had successfully delivered its load of ordnance when it fell victim to a proximity detonation of an SA-2 *Guideline* missile. Fragments of the SAM penetrated the aircraft's belly, aft fuselage and wings, starting fires in several locations.

Despite the fact that it was well ablaze and steadily losing height, the crippled bomber remained flyable, prompting pilot Capt N J Ostrozny to steer a course towards Thailand, which lay more than 100 miles away. Eventually, as the fires in the wings spread and consumed more of the precious fuel that remained, the engines began to flame-out and the crew realised it would be touch and go as to whether or not the B-52 would hang together long enough to allow them to reach safety.

In the event, it did, but it was a desperately close-run thing, for the last engine failed when the aircraft was still five miles short of the Thai border. Despite that, the 96th Bomb Wing crew remained on board until the last possible moment, which came when the starboard wing tip broke away, inducing a complete loss of control. Only then, as they crossed the Mekong River and reached sanctuary in Thailand, did they abandon the bomber. By good fortune, they came down close to the US base at Nakhon Phanom and were soon being treated for injuries received during the hasty evacuation. Later, some members of the crew returned to U-Tapao to report on the experience of being on the first B-52 to be destroyed by hostile fire in more than seven years of war.

On that day, disaster was narrowly averted, but the loss of the B-52D was a sobering moment for those who would be called upon to take it into combat before the war ground to an end. Had they but known it, it was also the first instance of a scenario that would be re-enacted on no fewer than 16 more occasions during the next six weeks, when the B-52 force played a vital role in forcing the North Vietnamese back to the negotiating table and into accepting a ceasefire.

Linebacker II was the campaign that culminated in President Nixon achieving his much-stated goal of 'peace with honour'. For the SAC crews, though, a high price was paid in satisfying that objective, for by no means all of the 16 losses experienced during December 1972 and January 1973 were to have quite such a fortuitous outcome as *Olive 2*.

LINEBACKER II - THE FIRST PHASE

By early December 1972, the prospect of achieving a peaceful resolution of the long-running war in Vietnam had receded as the Paris-based negotiations broke down yet again amidst the usual acrimony. Exasperated by the inability to attain the desired result through discussion and aware that the North Vietnamese were taking full advantage of curtailment of the bombing offensive to repair damage, bolster defences and generally engage in a military build-up, President Nixon opted for more forceful action. This initially involved lifting the moratorium on bombing operations, although bad weather in the Red River Valley restricted the wide-scale use of tactical air power resources.

Something more was needed. Something that would most assuredly get the attention of the North Vietnamese and signal clearly to them that the USA was at last determined to put an end to the nightmare of the Vietnam War. The weapon that was to play the major role in achieving that had been available from the very onset of the war, although the resolve to utilise it to its maximum effectiveness hadn't previously been apparent.

Now, at last, the resolve was most emphatically present and the curtain was about to be lifted on one of the final chapters of direct US involvement. Even though Nixon may not have actually uttered the oft-mentioned remarks about bombing the North Vietnamese back to the stone age, he did go as far as to observe that, 'the bastards have never been bombed like they're going to be bombed this time'. While the sentiments expressed may have been different, the end result would undeniably be the same, in as much as Hanoi and Haiphong were in for a battering.

It fell to the B-52s present on Guam and in Thailand to be the principal means of carrying out that threat in an operation that became known as *Linebacker II*, although it should be kept in mind that SAC's heavyweight was by no means the only type of warplane committed to this operation, for Air Force, Navy and Marine Corps fighters and fighter-bombers were all involved to some extent or other. The 'Buff', however, was the most impressive weapon, as well as the most contentious one, especially when it became public knowledge that they were operating against major centres of North Vietnamese population.

Authority to proceed with this new offensive was passed via the Joint Chiefs of Staff to the Commander-in-Chief Pacific and other interested parties on 17 December 1972. The original intent was to direct a three-day maximum effort bombing campaign, although the order to execute that campaign alerted the appropriate military commanders to the possibility that it would be extended. At the same time, it stipulated that this new effort was not to be conducted at the expense of other operations in South Vietnam, Laos and Cambodia. In other words, it was business as usual in the remaining theatres of war.

Unlike previous efforts, which were concerned more with interdiction of supply lines, the newest bombing operation was directed against targets that were situated in the military industrial heartland of North Vietnam and particularly in and around the major conurbations of Hanoi and Haiphong. Although the campaign didn't start until mid-December, preparations predated that event by some considerable time and the small number of personnel assigned to the Bombing and Navigation Division at Eighth Air Force headquarters were kept busy from about 10 August working on various planning aspects associated with what eventually became *Linebacker II*. This was in addition to the ongoing effort associated with *Arc Light*.

A vital concern of the planning effort was the job of establishing suitable offset aim-points and attack paths based on the list of targets authorised by the National Command Authorities via the Joint Chiefs of Staff. At the time, of course, there was no certainty this data would ever be used, but the work done then was eventually to prove vital in allowing the B-52 force to successfully execute its part in *Linebacker II*.

The original list provided to Eighth Air Force in August evidently featured about 60 targets, although subsequent expansion and refinement resulted in authorisation being given to attack a total of 103 targets. Of those, 31 were in the immediate vicinity of Hanoi; 19 were close to Haiphong and the rest were more than 10 miles from the centres of the two cities.

In the end, 62 of them were struck, consisting of 27 in Hanoi, 15 in Haiphong and 20 elsewhere. As it transpired, only some 34 of those received the attentions of

the B-52, since some targets were designated for attack by precision munitions such as the laser-guided bomb (LGB). Additionally, had the weather conditions been more favourable, there's no doubt that some of the objectives that were bombed by the 'Buff' would have been hit with precision munitions, rather than 'dumb' bombs dropped with the assistance of radar.

With regard to the nature of the targets, as far as the B-52 force was concerned, these were generally of a specifically military nature and included air bases, missile sites and storage centres, POL (petroleum, oil and lubricants) facilities and ammunition dumps. In addition, key elements of the extensive railroad network were also on the list for attention along with warehouses, power stations and other facilities.

Strict rules of engagement were in force so as to minimise the risk of unwittingly bombing civilian areas and thus providing the North Vietnamese with propaganda opportunities. At the same time, of course, the US had no desire to score an 'own goal' by hitting a prisoner-of-war camp. Between them, these concerns meant that great care had to be taken in selecting offset aim points and in choosing suitable approach paths that would allow those targets to be bombed. This was inevitably a tedious and time-consuming process, which required painstaking study of the available intelligence material, including huge amounts of photographic imagery obtained by *Giant Scale* SR-71 missions flown from Kadena, Okinawa.

In addition, pilots were prohibited from manoeuvring to evade SAMs or fighters once they had passed the initial point and were approaching the bomb release point. Since the IP usually lay several miles from the target, this meant that they had to fly straight and level in a decidedly hostile environment for up to four minutes – and that required nerve, especially when it is realised that several hundred SAMs were fired at the B-52s during the 11-days of *Linebacker II*. On-board ECM equipment provided some protection against the missile threat, but this was far from infallible, particularly in the case of the B-52G model which proved alarmingly vulnerable.

While the SAC bombers were undoubtedly at the very heart of the *Linebacker II* campaign, they were far from being the only aircraft involved in the sustained effort. Mention has already been made of other combatants but there were also many supporting players. At the outset, when B-52 operations against the North Vietnamese heartland were accomplished in wave form with intervals of four to five hours between each wave, the number of supporting aircraft was substantial but far from large. This is illustrated by the first wave on the opening day, when 48 B-52s were given direct support by 39 other USAF aircraft which included F-4 Phantoms to dispense chaff clouds and disrupt defensive radars; more F-4s to escort the 'chaffers' and the bombers; F-105 Thunderchiefs for *Iron Hand* SAM suppression and EB-66 Destroyers to augment the B-52's own jamming capability.

Later, when the bombing raids were more compressed, the ratio of support aircraft to bombers rose significantly. For example, on days five to seven, when only 30 B-52s were in action, the support force numbered 65 to 70 aircraft, whereas the 60 bombers in action on each of the final three days of the campaign were generally accompanied by about 100 aircraft. Once again, Phantoms, Thunderchiefs and Destroyers of the Air Force were heavily committed, but they were often augmented by aircraft from other services. The US Navy, for instance, furnished F-4 fighter escorts; EA-6B Prowler and EA-3B Skywarrior ECM platforms and A-7 Corsair SAM-suppressors, while the Marine Corps contributed to the electronic 'battle' with the EA-6A Intruder.

In addition, a host of other aircraft and helicopters were available to provide less obvious but no less welcome back-up in the form of rescue and recovery support. This capability was spearheaded by the USAF's HC-130 Hercules and HH-53 'Super Jolly Green Giant' which stood-by to co-ordinate recovery efforts and retrieve downed aircrew if their aircraft could be persuaded to remain flyable for long enough to reach a safe area.

Furthermore, the developing aerial scene was monitored by friendly air and surface-based radars in order that timely warning of MiG threats could be provided. As already mentioned, this information was not much help to the B-52s once they had passed the initial point and were committed to bombing, but escorting fighters were certainly in a position to react to anticipated aerial threats and they undoubtedly played a valuable part in ensuring no bomber was lost to any cause other than SAMs.

Last, but by no means least, there were all the tankers, for SAC's KC-135 fleet was kept exceedingly busy in support of *Linebacker II*, partly in refuelling bombers making the long haul from and to Guam, but also in giving similar back-up to the tactical elements

that were more actively involved in associated combat missions.

All of this support meant that the crews aboard the B-52s weren't exactly going in 'alone, unarmed and unafraid', but there's no doubt that they faced considerable risk, especially when tasked against targets in 'downtown' Hanoi, which lay at the centre of a formidable array of defences. Heavy anti-aircraft artillery abounded, but actually caused little concern and there was only one recorded instance of a B-52 involved in *Linebacker II* sustaining flak damage.

Fighters failed to achieve any success against the bombers, although interception attempts were certainly made and several MiGs were shot down during the campaign, including two that were credited to tail gunners on B-52Ds flying from U-Tapao. There is also evidence that North Vietnamese MiG fighters were used to determine bomber operating altitudes for SAM batteries. In fact, as will be seen, such success as was achieved by the defenders was credited wholly to the missiles, with the SA-2 *Guideline* accounting for 15 examples of the B-52 during the period in question.

That period began at Andersen AFB in the early afternoon of 18 December 1972. The force at Guam was earmarked to contribute a total of 27 bombers (18 B-52Gs and 9 B-52Ds) to the first wave, with U-Tapao furnishing the balance of 21. Subsequent waves would follow at periodic intervals and by the time that the night's work ended, a total of 87 Guam-based aircraft (54 B-52Gs and 33 B-52Ds) would have been despatched, along with 42 B-52Ds from the base in Thailand.

Targets for the first wave consisted of a trio of North Vietnamese fighter bases at Kep, Hoa Lac and Phuc Yen, plus the Yen Vien railhead and the Kinh No complex which included storage sites, warehouse facilities and railway yards. Timing was such that all 48 aircraft would bomb in the space of 33 minutes and it fell to the bombers from U-Tapao to open the offensive at 1945 hours local time. During the next 12 minutes, a hail of bombs deposited by the 21 Thai-based B-52Ds would hopefully deter any MiG fighters from interfering with the bombers that were slated to attack the other two targets.

Leading the way was 'Snow' cell, which went into action against Hoa Lac air base at about 1945 hours. Two minutes later, it was the turn of 'Brown' cell. This clearly took the MiG suppression task a bit more seriously, for the tail gunner of 'Brown 3', SSgt Sam

Turner, succeeded in shooting down a pursuing MiG-21 with a particularly well-aimed burst of gunfire. This was the first of five MiGs to be claimed by B-52 gunners during the *Linebacker II* campaign, although only two were destined to be confirmed.

The focus of attention then swung to Kep air base, which lay to the north-west of Hanoi. Bombs began falling here at 1949 and such was the importance attached to this major airfield that three B-52D cells ('Maple', 'Gold' and 'Green') were committed to the attack. Six minutes later, at 1955, Phuc Yen air base also began to reel under the weight of bombs deposited by 'Purple' and 'Walnut' cells. Thus far, all appeared to have gone more or less according to plan and the way was now open for the Guam-based aircraft to swing into action.

The 27 'Buffs' that comprised Andersen's contribution to Wave 1 were spearheaded by three cells of B-52Ds. 'Rose' was in the lead and began offloading its ordnance on the Kinh No complex at 2001. Two more B-52D cells ('Lilac' and 'White') followed suit at two-minute intervals before three B-52G cells ('Rust', 'Black' and the most appropriately named 'Buff') added their contribution between 2007 and 2011. Finally, bringing up the rear, three more B-52G cells hit the Yen Vien railway yards. 'Charcoal' cell was first in, with a planned TOT (time over target) of 2014, with 'Ivory' and 'Ebony' cells planned to follow up by 2018.

In fact, it appears that the element tasked with striking the Yen Vien yards was running a couple of minutes late, since the leading bomber (B-52G 58-0201 'Charcoal 1') was hit by a SAM at 2017, during the final stages of its run-in to the weapons release point. At that precise moment, it became the first US victim of the *Linebacker II* campaign. Aircraft commander Lt Col Donald Rissi and gunner MSgt Walt Ferguson are understood to have sustained fatal injuries at missile impact, while co-pilot Lt Bob Thomas was subsequently listed as missing in action. The remaining three members of the crew fared rather better and were able to escape the doomed bomber, with navigator Capt Bob Certain, radar navigator Maj. Dick Johnson and electronic warfare officer Capt Dick Simpson all surviving the ordeal of being shot down and having to endure a short period of captivity before being freed in early 1973.

Even as 'Charcoal 1' went down, the second wave of bombers from Guam was winging its way towards North Vietnam. Running about four hours behind the opening assault, this group of 33 aircraft was also destined to lose one of its number, with B-52G 'Peach 2' (58-0246) suffering a SAM proximity detonation just seconds after releasing its ordnance on the Kinh No complex. Despite being severely damaged, the bomber remained flyable and was able to get clear of the high-threat area surrounding Hanoi.

At least two members of the seven-man crew had been injured by shrapnel, one of whom was Lt Col Hendsley Conner who occupied the instructor pilot's seat as Deputy Airborne Mission Commander for this wave. Happily, neither he nor the gunner was seriously wounded, although it was starkly apparent that their aircraft was in a bad way. For the moment, though, it remained airworthy and crew members began to contemplate the possibility of making an emergency landing at U-Tapao. Assessment of the damage revealed that a substantial chunk of the port wing-tip was missing along with the port outer pair of engines.

By itself, that would not have prevented a safe recovery but the situation was complicated by the fact that the B-52G was burning. Worse still was the discovery that leaking fuel was feeding the blaze as the crippled machine limped towards Thailand in company with a pair of Phantom fighter escorts. It was this which eventually left the seven occupants with no option but to abandon the doomed bomber, Conner jumping through the hole left by the navigator's ejection. Shortly after that, while Conner was still floating down beneath his parachute, the B-52G crashed, but by then everyone had got out safely and within 20 minutes, all seven had been picked up by Marine Corps helicopters and flown to the nearby base at Nam Phong.

Five hours later, a third Stratofortress fell victim to the North Vietnamese defences when B-52D 56-0608 'Rose 1' from U Tapao was hit by a missile while bombing the Hanoi radio station. In general, though, mission objectives were certainly achieved on day one. As for day two, if anything, this was even more satisfactory in so far as 93 sorties were scheduled against several targets – Kinh No was hit again and so was Yen Vien, but one new objective was the Thai Nguyen thermal power plant which received the attentions of nine cells of aircraft.

During this evening, the previously hard-line rule about no manoeuvring during the run-in from the initial point to the target was relaxed, subject to the proviso that cell integrity was maintained and that aircraft were flying straight and level immediately before dropping their bombs. The reason for this change of heart was that analysis of radar camera film from day one confirmed that weapon aiming points stood out exactly as predicted and it was determined that sufficient time existed for crew members responsible for weapons release to identify those aiming points and make adjustments during the final stages of the run-in to target. In addition, gyroscopes associated with the bombing system had sufficient time to settle, thus guaranteeing a stable and accurate bombing platform.

This change was implemented after the first wave of the second night had been in action and was first used by wave two, which actually took a bit of stick from the Hanoi defences, resulting in a B-52D and a B-52G sustaining battle damage. The former aircraft ('Ivory 1') was in fact quite badly knocked about and seems to have been fortunate to make a satisfactory emergency landing at Nam Phong – the latter ('Hazel 3') was able to finish its mission and make it home to Andersen. By some quirk of good fortune, 'Hazel 3' was the only B-52G to survive the experience of being damaged by a SAM.

By the start of day three, over 200 sorties had been scheduled against targets in the North for the loss of just three aircraft, although several more had been quite badly damaged. In essence, though, that equated to a loss rate of less than two per cent, a rate that was unwelcome – but not unacceptable, in view of estimations which predicted attrition levels of from three to five per cent. Coupled with the fact that all raiders came through more or less unscathed on day two, the low rate thus far may have lulled the mission planners and tacticians into a false sense of security.

Whatever the reason, apart from minor refinements, it was determined that day three would be very much a case of the 'mixture as before', with a total of 99 sorties scheduled for the three waves that were due to go north. As on the previous two days, the effort would be shared by the bases at Andersen and U Tapao, with a mixed force of B-52Ds and B-52Gs in action. Targets for the night's activity included the Yen Vien railway yards, the Ai Mo storage area which lay nearby, the Thai Nguyen thermal power plant, the Bac Giang transhipment area, the Kinh No complex, the railway repair facility at Gia Lam and the Hanoi POL products storage dump. It would also witness the most determined defensive effort – and the most successful one.

MiG-21 fighters were seen by a number of bomber crews that night and it seems that some interceptions were attempted, albeit without success. While they may not have been effective in that way, the fighter pilots did apparently relay data on the bomber stream altitude, heading and speed to missile crews and the consensus of the US airmen was that the SAMs were rather more accurate than on previous nights. That contention is supported by the fact that no less than six 'Buffs' failed to survive their exposure to Hanoi's defences – however, since well over 200 SAMs were launched, it was easily the busiest night missile-wise.

For the bomber force, the bad news began almost immediately the attack opened, with Wave 1 suffering three losses in a little over 20 minutes. The first victim was a B-52G which was hit over Yen Vien. The cell identification of the aircraft concerned seems to confirm that the planners had run out of colours to use. As for the bomber itself, 'Quilt 3' ran out of luck at 2010 hours local time on 20 December, when it received a direct hit while in the post-target turn manoeuvre. Such was the extent of the damage inflicted that the aircraft (57-6496) went down in flames almost immediately, although four crew members were able to eject before it crashed.

Just 12 minutes later, it was the turn of 'Brass 2'. Again, this was a B-52G (57-6481) and again it was struck while in the post-target turn after bombing the railway yards at Yen Vien. This time, the damage was not immediately terminal and the 42nd BW crew from Loring AFB, Maine managed to coax the 'Buff' as far as Thailand before leaving it to its own devices. All six were soon recovered, but good fortune deserted four members of the crew of the third aircraft to fall foul of the defences at Yen Vien that night.

This time, the unlucky machine was a B-52D from U-Tapao (56 0622 'Orange 3') which was bracketed by two missiles at 2032 hours, while flying straight and level in readiness for weapons release. Despite exploding almost instantaneously, two of the crew somehow managed to survive and ended up in a PoW camp. They weren't the first and nor would they be the last.

Having suffered what was undoubtedly a catastrophic opening to the events of that night, SAC commanders now faced a quandary. Should they carry on, in the almost certain knowledge that more losses would follow? Should they call a halt, admit defeat,

ABOVE A B-52D (56-0587) gets a tow, apparently at U-Tapao, during *Arc Light* bombing efforts over South Vietnam. The bomb pylons located inboard of the engines are empty now. This view shows the flight deck windscreens in good detail. The 'Buff's' crosswind landing gear worked so effectively that pilots actually looked out the side window, at times, to line up on the runway for landing *(USAF)*

and, in so doing, shatter an Air Force tradition of never having been turned back as a result of enemy action? Just how close-run the decision was is something only CinCSAC Gen John C Meyer could say for certain, since the choice of whether or not to continue ultimately fell to him – in the end, he directed the bombers of Wave 2 to carry on.

As it transpired, the second wave was scheduled to operate against targets situated a reasonable distance from Hanoi, where the defences could reasonably be expected to be lighter and less likely to take a toll of the incoming bombers. Nonetheless, two cells of Andersen-based B-52Gs were recalled, for there was now plenty of evidence to indicate this model was more vulnerable than the B-52D. In fact, the ECM capability of the B-52G varied and two different suites of equipment were fitted to the aircraft that had deployed to

Guam in support of the war effort. Study of the losses thus far revealed that it was the unmodified examples that were taking the greatest punishment by virtue of being unable to properly defend themselves. Ordering the six B-52Gs that were airborne as part of Wave 2 to return to base was not exactly the most desirable course of action, but it was deemed to be the right one. In the event, the remaining elements of the second wave pressed home their attack and came through the ordeal quite unscathed.

Wave 3 was another story, for this included four B-52G cells, made up of a mixture of modified and unmodified machines, which would be operating against the fiercely defended Kinh No complex. In this instance, despite the fact that the mission planners were well aware of the risks to be faced by the bombers, the recall order was not given, since it was felt that the weapon shortfall was likely to seriously compromise the effectiveness of the mission. So, they pressed on towards the Kinh No complex, with the attack going in as dawn was breaking, some nine hours after wave one.

The first aircraft in action were actually three B-52D cells from Andersen. These bombed the Gia Lam railway repair shops and an alert missile crew added another victim to the night's work when it scored a hit on 'Straw 2' as it was in the post-target turn manoeuvre. Damage was extensive, but not so severe as to prevent the B-52D (56-0669) from being flown out of North Vietnamese airspace to the slightly friendlier skies of northern Laos. Once there, the crew parted company with the crippled bomber. Five were subsequently picked up by rescue helicopters, with only the radar navigator being posted as missing in action.

Next came the four B-52G cells that had been tasked against Kinh No. In addition to the normal six crew members, the leading aircraft ('Olive 1') was also carrying the Deputy Airborne Mission Commander, Lt Col Keith Heggen. The final stages of the run-in to weapons release were safely negotiated but this bomber was hit moments later and went down almost immediately. Three of those aboard are known to have survived, but Heggen was to die in captivity from wounds received during the shoot-down, leaving only pilot Lt Col James Nagahiro and navigator Capt Lynn Beens to be repatriated after a short spell as prisoners-of-war.

Another aircraft was also destroyed during the attack on Kinh No, this being B-52G 58-0169 'Tan 3'. However, there appears to be some confusion in the circumstances surrounding this loss. Both of the main sources used in determining *Linebacker II* attrition agree that 'Tan 3' was hit by a SAM, with the excellent account by Brig Gen James McCarthy and Lt Col George Allison reporting this occurred when it became separated from the other two members of 'Tan' cell. If that account is accurate, 'Tan 3' clearly went down after 'Olive 1'. However, an official listing of USAF fixed-wing combat losses alludes to an aircraft with a 'Tan' call-sign as being lost before one with an 'Olive' call sign. Times quoted for the respective incidents are 2200 and 2211, which equates to 0500 and 0511 Hanoi time.

Leaving aside such fine details, it seems that 'Tan 3' was badly damaged by a proximity detonation beneath the aircraft and that pilot Capt Randall Craddock succeeded in regaining a measure of control, whereupon a second missile scored a direct hit and administered the coup de grace. At this point, Craddock ordered the crew to abandon 'Tan 3', but only one member survived to become a PoW, this being gunner SSgt James Lollar.

The night's excitement wasn't quite over, since a number of bombers were also scheduled to attack POL storage facilities in the Hanoi neighbourhood and one of these came uncomfortably close to being the seventh victim of that night. The B-52Ds that comprised 'Brick' cell were in fact the final bombers in action and drew heavy fire from the massed Hanoi defences, with 'Brick 2' being severely damaged by a proximity detonation immediately after letting go its bomb-load. This time, the damage was not terminal and the B-52D was safely recovered at U-Tapao.

That was, however, one of the few causes for optimism on a disastrous night in which six bombers had gone down, 17 airmen had died and nine more faced incarceration as 'guests' of the notorious 'Hanoi Hilton'. It was starkly evident that major changes to tactics were imperative if the campaign was to continue - and it had already been decreed that it would.

LINEBACKER II
KEEPING UP THE PRESSURE

When it comes to reviewing the contribution made by the B-52 force to *Linebacker II*, it could fairly be described as being a campaign of three phases. The first, spanning the period 18-20 December, was one of intense pressure, with three waves being in action on each and every night. The second, which began on 21 December and ran until Christmas Eve, was more concerned with keeping up the pressure, while the final phase, which opened on 26 December and continued until the 29th, could be likened to 'turning the screw'.

As mentioned, phase two fundamentally involved keeping the North Vietnamese under pressure and yet, paradoxically, for the bomber crews who were involved in the effort, the pressure may well have eased somewhat once it got under way. It certainly did as far as the Andersen-based force was concerned, for this actually enjoyed a fairly quiet spell during 21-25 December, when only 12 dedicated *Linebacker II* sorties were staged from Guam. It would, however, be wrong to infer that the airmen at Guam were able to spend all of that time on the beach, for 'Arc Light' missions continued apace – and cells of three bombers regularly roared off of Andersen's switch-back runway and set course for the war zone throughout this spell.

U-Tapao's much smaller fleet of B-52Ds drew the short straw on this occasion and more or less carried the war into North Vietnam single-handedly over the four days that immediately preceded the Christmas break. During that interval, 30 sorties were scheduled for each day, with all but the dozen mentioned a few moments ago being flown from U-Tapao.

Phase two opened with an attack on three fresh targets within the neighbourhood of Hanoi, specifically the storage depots at Bac Mai and Van Dien and the airfield at Quang Te. Although all three objectives were hit hard, it was not what could be described as a good night for the Thai-based B-52Ds, since two of them fell victim to Hanoi's formidable defences.

First to go down was 'Scarlet 1' (55-0061) which was hit while attempting to hand-over responsibility for the cell lead to another aircraft after its bombing radar became inoperative. In making this move, mutual ECM protection broke down, resulting in the B-52D becoming dangerously exposed. For the crew of 'Scarlet 1', the consequences were disastrous and they were promptly shot out of the sky, while their colleagues in 'Scarlet 2' also had to endure some anxious moments, when a marauding MiG attempted to engage them. Luckily, his aim was poor.

The night's other loss was B-52D 55-0050 'Blue 1'. This was also tasked against Bac Mai, with a TOT of 0347 local, just four minutes later than that of 'Scarlet' cell. Heavy SAM activity was visible as this 'Buff' approached the weapons release point, with this reaching a peak when no fewer than 10 missiles were salvoed in the direction of the bomber cell. 'Blue 1' just about managed to get its bombs away before being sandwiched by a brace of SAMs. These inflicted terminal damage on the aircraft and shrapnel wounds were suffered by four of the six crew, but all of them managed to get clear safely and survived a period of incarceration as prisoners-of-war before eventually being returned to the USA after the ceasefire came into effect.

After operating against Hanoi throughout the previous four days, the next three nights witnessed a switch to targets that lay some distance from the capital. The major port city of Haiphong was first to get a taste of what Hanoi had been going through and came under attack on the night of 22-23 December when 30 bombers from U-Tapao were tasked against railway yards and petroleum storage sites.

Careful selection of approach paths and particularly effective suppression of the SAM threat resulted in the defences being rendered more or less powerless to intervene. This was obviously welcomed by the bomber crews, for Haiphong possessed a formidable array of defensive firepower. Light, medium and heavy anti-aircraft artillery – missiles – small arms, you name it and Haiphong had it. In terms of reputation, then, it was right up there alongside Hanoi as a place that was generally to be avoided like the proverbial plague.

On this specific night, those defences were definitely perplexed by the bomber tactics, for they let fly with less than 50 missiles. No hits were scored, although the crews of the B-52Ds of 'Walnut' and 'Red' cells almost certainly experienced a few nerve-racking moments as they passed through the lethal zone, since a considerable number of SAMs were fired at them.

The next raid (on 23 December) also made use of a new tactic, even though elements of the support forces failed to meet their obligations which meant that the 30 bombers – composed of 12 from Andersen and 18 from U-Tapao – were effectively on their own. For a time, it seemed as if a recall was on the cards, but after careful consideration, the commanders opted to let the attack go ahead, a decision that was wholly vindicated by subsequent events.

The main target was the Lang Dang railway centre to the north of Haiphong. This was hit by 24 aircraft, but the night's work actually began with two B-52D cells from Andersen engaging three SAM sites in the vicinity of Kep Ha and Son Dong. At the time, there was some puzzlement as to why these particular sites had been chosen, but the logic came clear just a couple of days later. However, rather than despatch a whole cell against each site, the planners instead directed the two cells involved to break formation and operate as individual aircraft – in this way, each of the three missile sites was struck by two bombers.

Part of the reason for this was that it would be necessary for the 'Buffs' to actually overfly the sites in order to bomb them. This meant that the benefits of mutual ECM protection were bound to be negated, due to the fact that the ground radars were sufficiently powerful to overcome jamming once an aircraft encroached within a certain radius of the site. This phenomenon was known as 'burn-through'.

Secondly, since it looked as if some of the North Vietnamese missile crews were using Cell leaders to refine their aim, it was hoped that the radar operators far below would be deceived into thinking the approaching aircraft were actually just the lead elements of cells – and would hold their fire until it was

ABOVE *Big Belly* B-52D 55-0100 letting loose a string of M117 750-lb (340-kg) iron bombs from high altitude on an Arc Light incursion into a Viet Cong-held sector of South Vietnam. Critics questioned the efficiency of using a strategic bomber for high-altitude drops on mobile guerrilla forces, but captured Viet Cong documents confirm that B-52 missions did harm the insurgents *(USAF)*

too late. That, in effect, appears to have been the outcome and for the second night in a row no damage was suffered by any of the aircraft involved.

On Christmas Eve, Andersen despatched 30 *Arc Light* sorties while U-Tapao contributed a like number of B-52Ds against the north. This time, the targets were the railway yards at Kep and Thai Nguyen, which both lay approximately 40 miles from Hanoi. However, instead of approaching up the Tonkin Gulf as had been the case on the previous couple of days, the bombers routed overland, crossing Laos and then heading north-east across enemy territory before swinging around to approach their targets from a northerly direction.

Good intelligence and careful planning allowed a route to be selected that lay outside the SAM threat envelope until the final stages. This was successful in as

much as no bomber suffered damage from a SAM, but one B-52D did sustain minor flak damage, this actually being the only such instance during the entire 11 days of *Linebacker II* operations. Moreover, the generally unsatisfactory performance of the North Vietnamese defenders was compounded by the loss of a second MiG-21 to a B-52D tail gunner. On this occasion, A1C Albert Moore was the successful individual and 'Ruby 3' was no doubt very quickly adorned with a red star to signify its rare status as a 'MiG-killer'.

That success and the fact that three days had gone by since the last B-52 shoot-down must have buoyed the spirits of the airmen involved in operations against the north. It is also likely that they would have been cheered by the 24-hour pause called for Christmas Day, partly to observe seasonal festivities and partly as a gesture towards North Vietnam. As had happened so many times before, the gesture was ignored, leaving the US with little option but to implement the final phase of *Linebacker II* with effect from 26 December. In some ways, this was to prove the most impressive phase of all.

It began with a raid that became a classic, in as much as it involved no fewer than 40 cells (ie, 120 aircraft). That made it far and away the biggest single raid of all, and it therefore required ingenious planning. More importantly, it was executed almost flawlessly, despite involving significantly revised tactics and a glitch that came close to forcing the whole exercise to be scrubbed. If the previously established practice of cycling the bomber cells through in fairly strict rotation had been adhered to, it would probably have required somewhere in the region of 80-90 minutes for the entire force to deposit its ordnance and several aircraft might well have been shot down.

Instead, the planners chose to break the force up into seven distinct waves, each of which had the same initial TOT. In this way, they succeeded in introducing an element of raid compression which meant that 10 separate targets would be struck within the space of just 15 minutes. Essentially, the objective was to overwhelm the defences with sheer weight of numbers and, in so doing, to reduce the risks faced by the bomber crews. That objective was achieved, for just two bombers were claimed by the defences. A factor in reducing the hazardous nature of the night's work was the earlier attack on the three SAM sites that lay close to ingress and egress routes to be flown by a dozen bomber cells on 26 December.

Turning to consider the targets, seven of them were in and around Hanoi, two were within the environs of Haiphong and the last was close to Thai Nguyen – with the combined effect of all the ingress and egress tracks to be flown by the bombers making it look as if someone had dumped a mess of spaghetti all over the map of North Vietnam.

Four waves were composed entirely of B-52Ds and these, not surprisingly, were aimed at the most heavily defended objectives, namely those that were concentrated around Hanoi. Wave one would consist of six cells, which would be equally split between the railway yards and POL storage facilities in 'downtown' Hanoi. Wave three would provide one cell to take on the much-feared SAM site known as 'VN549', while the following five cells pounded the nearby Van Dien vehicle park. Wave four had the Giap Nhi railway yard as its target and consisted of six cells, while the final clutch of 18 B-52Ds made up wave five which was tasked against the Kinh No complex and Duc Noi railway yard.

As for the B-52G, this version was certainly not omitted from the action, for it made up 15 cells in three equal-sized waves. In deference to the greater vulnerability of the B-52G, it was used against targets that lay outside the Hanoi perimeter, since these were deemed to be marginally less hazardous. Wave two was despatched to hit the Thai Nguyen rail yards and

RIGHT Post-strike reconnaissance imagery provides a graphic appreciation of the kind of damage that could be inflicted by the B-52 force during *Linebacker II* operations against targets deep inside North Vietnam. Haiphong's railway network has come under attack here and appears to have been particularly hard hit, with tracks uprooted, buildings destroyed and items of rolling stock damaged beyond repair *(USAF)*

would be augmented by a solitary B-52D cell. Finally, waves six and seven would be busy in the vicinity of Haiphong, with the former hitting the rail network and the latter attempting to knock out electrical supplies by bombing the transformer station.

Irrespective of bomber model, the TOT of each wave was 2230 hours local time. If all went according to plan, the entire force of 120 bombers should have completed the attack and be on their way out of the area by 2245. It was an ambitious undertaking and it should come as no surprise to learn that it posed a number of interesting problems as well as some awkward moments. One such problem cropped up at Andersen when it was discovered that there was no room with sufficient capacity in which to brief all of the primary and back-up crews involved in launching 78 bombers. In the end, those responsible for the briefing were left with no option but to tackle the task by bomber model in separate locations – a novel solution, but one that worked.

Even more demanding was the physical problem of actually putting that mass of bombers into the air (the launch from Andersen eventually took just under two-and-a-half hours to complete), since even a minor snafu had the potential to develop into a major setback. In fact, the departure went just about perfectly, but events elsewhere held the seeds of failure. They involved a Military Airlift Command C-141 Starlifter which was forced to make an emergency landing at Kadena at about the same time as a group of KC-135s was due to launch to refuel the B-52Ds of wave three. In the event, the tankers were about 15 minutes behind schedule, putting a serious kink in the entire game plan.

By replanning the rendezvous and shifting it much closer to the delayed tanker task force, it looked as if some of the lost time could be recouped, but it would still be necessary for the bombers of wave three to fly a much revised route at an increased speed if they were to stand any chance of making the specified TOT. Even then, there was no guarantee – and such a seemingly minor factor as a shift in wind direction or speed could still compromise the entire mission. Somehow, though, it all came together; the tanker rendezvous was successfully accomplished; the desired fuel was transferred; and, by dint of some judicious throttle-bending and corner-cutting, wave three made it to the target area in time and got their bombs off exactly on schedule.

As already noted, two of the force were unfortunate enough to take hits from SAMs. Both were B-52Ds from U-Tapao, with 'Ebony 2' (56-0674) being struck while attacking Giap Nhi. In this case, it went down almost at once, but four crew members managed to get out alive. 'Ash 1' (56-0584) was the other victim of that night and came agonisingly close to making it back to U Tapao, only to crash near the airfield with fatal consequences for four of the crew. Co-pilot Lt Bob Hymel and gunner TSgt. Spencer Grippin were the only survivors.

That raid was undoubtedly the high point of the *Linebacker* campaign, but there were still three more days to go – and two more Buffs to be lost – before it ran its course. On each of those three days, 60 sorties were planned, with the bombing effort being split equally between Andersen and Guam. Throughout this phase, as on the 26th, the B-52D force operated against the most fiercely defended targets, while the B-52Gs stayed well outside the Hanoi area. In fact, all of the 48 B-52G sorties scheduled during the final three days were tasked against the marshalling yards at Lang Dang, way up in the north-east of the country and barely 20 miles from the border with China.

Other targets that were struck during this period included missile support and storage facilities in Hanoi as well as the usual railway yards and a small number of SAM sites. Notable amongst the latter was 'VN549', which was struck for the second night in succession. It had already won a reputation for accuracy during the previous few days and the planners eventually decided that it merited the attentions of a B-52D cell on the night of the 27th at the same time as two other missile sites were hit.

'Lemon' cell was given responsibility for the attack on VN549, but unfortunately failed to achieve the desired result, since the site was able to launch a missile within seconds of being bombed. Worse still, that missile succeeded in inflicting mortal damage on 'Ash 2' (B-52D 56-0599) which was itself engaged in bombing SAM site VN243. 'Ash 2' did, however, remain flyable for long enough to reach the safety of Thailand, where it was eventually abandoned close to the US base at Nakhon Phanom. In the process, it became the last *Linebacker II* victim but all six crew members were recovered in good shape.

Another bomber was also claimed by the defences that night, with 'Cobalt 1' (B-52D 56-0605) coming under fire as it pressed home its attack on the rail yards at Trung Quan. That fire was indeed accurate and at least one missile found its mark, with 'Cobalt 1' actually being hit shortly after 'Ash 1', at about 2305 hours local time. Unlike 'Ash 1', however, this bomber went down almost straight away, crashing in the immediate vicinity of the target with the loss of two members of the crew.

Two more days of operations against the North remained and it was evident from accounts provided by those who flew on those final nights that the defences were almost spent. No aircraft were hit and on the very last night of the campaign few missiles were even fired, although a feeble attempt at interception was made by a MiG. For the bombers and their crews, *Linebacker II* effectively ended at 2343 hours local time on 29 December when Thailand-based B-52D 'Gray 3' deposited its ordnance on the Trai Ca missile storage site near Thai Nguyen.

In attempting to review the achievements of the *Linebacker II* campaign, it would perhaps be simplest to limit one's attentions to purely statistical aspects. Thus, one could report that a total of 729 sorties was logged; that 34 targets were hit; that some 15,287 tons of ordnance were dropped; that somewhere in the region of 900 SAMs were fired; and that 15 B-52s were shot down at a cost of 33 crew members either missing in action or killed in action – and leave it at that. As to the effect, contemporary bomb damage assessment indicated that 1600 military structures had been damaged or destroyed; 372 items of rolling stock had suffered similarly; three million gallons of petroleum based products had been lost and about 80 per cent of North Vietnam's electricity generating capacity had been knocked out. Turning to casualties, North Vietnam admitted 1318 civilians had died, but at least some were probably victims of SAM and AAA debris falling back to earth after missing its target.

That, however, is only a narrow, numerical view of the story which reveals little of the circumstances and the outcome. If the wider context is considered, it would not be unreasonable to observe that the B-52 was the weapon that won the war – or, at least, that allowed Nixon to secure the peace he was looking for so desperately. This perception is held by many, but is perhaps an over-simplification.

It's undeniable that the mighty 'Buff' was influential in bringing about a peaceful solution to the war in Vietnam, albeit a short-lived one, but I doubt that even its most ardent supporters would claim that it achieved this single-handedly. To do that would be to deny other equally courageous airmen their fair share of the credit, for it should not be forgotten that the B-52 was just one of several types that were committed to combat action in *Linebacker* and *Linebacker II*.

When all is said and done, of course, it carried the greatest weight of bombs and drew the heaviest criticism from those who were opposed to the USA's involvement in South-East Asia. That hostility is perhaps best epitomised by referring to an incident that occurred during a briefing of the House Armed Services Committee (HASC) in the aftermath of *Linebacker II*, when a photograph showing damage to a residential area of Hanoi was projected. Enraged by what she perceived as erratic bombing, a member of the HASC challenged the briefing officer to explain the circumstances and was informed that the damage was attributed to a bomber that crashed with fatal consequences for all six crew members. Not content with that explanation, the irate member of Congress screamed, 'Dammit, General. Can't you teach your pilots to crash somewhere else?'

It is to be hoped that the physical remains of the airmen who lost their lives over North Vietnam were treated with greater respect than this.

FROM *CHROMEDOME* TO *LINEBACKER II*

THE STRATEGIC AIR COMMAND's emblem included a mailed fist, poised to smash any enemy (but clutching an olive branch in addition to flashes of lightning). In real life, the mailed fist was the strategic nuclear mission.

Until 1991 when the practice of 24-hour alert came to an end, SAC was poised to disperse its bombers, retaliate for missile strikes on North America, and carry a lethal load of atomic warheads deep into the Soviet Union. Before 1968, B-52 bombers actually stayed in the air with live Mk 28 hydrogen bombs and North American AGM-28 Hound Dog stand-off missiles – in the manner of a loaded pistol, cocked and ready to go. Before 1960 (when the surface-to-air missile, or SAM, entered the picture in a stylish debut by knocking down Francis Gary Powers' U-2 reconnaissance aircraft on 1 May), real and rehearsed atomic bomb missions were carried out at high altitude where

the B-52 was deemed, at the time, to have its best chance of evading interceptors.

'Suddenly', with the SA-2 *Guideline* missile on the scene, 'high altitude was a bad word', remembers Lt Col Lawrence Nilssen, who eventually became tactics officer for the 7th Bombardment Wing at Carswell AFB, Texas. But as late as 1964, when Nilssen was

BELOW Normal landing and departure methods weren't applicable to the 'Buff' because of the novel undercarriage arrangement, which precluded rotation on lift-off. In an ideal world, the main members would all touch down simultaneously but it didn't always work out like that. When taking-off, the wings began to 'fly' before the fuselage, but the main gear trucks almost always left concrete at the same instant. At Kadena AB, Okinawa, during *Arc Light* combat operations, this B-52D (56-0663) demonstrates the proper relationship between bomber and ground *(US Navy)*

learning how to fly the B-52 at Castle AFB, California, no one dreamed that the mighty bomber might be used to drop ordinary bombs, using ordinary explosives, upon ordinary men in the rain jungles of South-East Asia. Of the many transitions in the Stratofortress's career, none was more difficult.

Remembers Nilssen, 'SAC had become ossified in its doctrine. They believed that the response to everything was just to go lower, lower, lower. Now, as we determined, the PK (probability of kill) of the ground is 1.0, meaning it's 100 per cent, if you hit the ground you're dead.

'You have to fly where the PK of the threat equals the PK of the ground. Obviously, when you're above the ground the PK is less and less. When you're going at 50 ft (15.48 m) your PK is 0.5. When you're flying at 100 ft (31 m), you have a PK of 0.25. I'm just throwing out arbitrary numbers. If you have a missile and the PK is .2, you'd better be flying where the PK of the missile equals the PK of your ability to avoid the ground. That's the optimum place to fly.

'If you're up against an I-HAWK (a US-designed surface-to-air missile) on a clear day, over water, without defenses, your PK is about 1.0. You'd better be almost hitting the ground. That's where you want to be. You've got nothing to lose. You want to be where the PKs are equal.

'But', continues Nilssen, 'we discovered that being low wasn't enough. If you take a look at a Dash One (pilot's manual), a B-52 has 11 different radar sets and emitters, the tail gun radar, the height radar altimeter, forward-looking ground mapping radars, all these things. To go into a hostile environment with all that stuff turned on is like holding a lot of flashlights at night: it says to everybody, "Here we are!" Fighters up there can look down and see you. You're an easy target. When we realised we were going into the conventional-bombing business, we also felt we had to re-think a lot of this stuff.'

Lt Col Patrick A Briggs was one B-52 pilot who saw it all – *Chromedome* aerial alert with ticking Mark 28s, and *Arc Light* missions in Vietnam. Briggs learned to fly in Class 61-C, graduated with wings in the fall of 1960, and flew B-47 Stratojets until July 1964 when he was assigned to the 465th Bomb Wing at Robins AFB, Georgia. The 465th was one of the first bomber wings to fly the B-52G model. At the time, Briggs recalls, no one thought of the 'Buff' as anything but a nuclear weapon.

NEW PILOT

'I did a year in this B-52G outfit (after training in D and F-models). Then, in 1965, I went to Squadron Officer School and wrote a thesis about using the B-52 for conventional bombing. They laughed me out of the place. I returned to flying B-52s.'

Briggs found the Air Force's leadership by 'bomber generals' a little stultified. He also found the G-model the most difficult Stratofortress to fly.

'They went to the chopped-off tail because the tall tail (found on all models through the B-52F) caused induced turbulence close to the ground. However, the short tail reduced stability at high altitude. When they introduced the G-model, they also moved the generators out to the wing, took the ailerons off, and went to spoilers. All of this contributed to a less stable and somewhat easier-to-manoeuvre aeroplane. The G-model was SAC's answer to, 'Let's go low level'.

'Every time you turned the plane the spoilers would come up. So they initially reduced drag (before dumping lift) which caused the aircraft to go nose up and yaw horizontally. You had to learn to push opposite rudder to keep nose on a point.

'As for delivering nuclear bombs, in the B-47 we had had techniques called 'Short Look' and 'Long Look', depending on the explosive force of weapon. With Short Look, we lobbed a parachute-retarded nuclear weapon.

'All of this was dropped with the B-52. The B-52 mission called for a straight flyover at high speed, and a gravity drop of parachute-retarded weapons. The B-52 could not do LABS (low altitude bombing system), a method of tossing the bomb during an Immelmann turn. In the B-52 to drop the early weapons, you attacked at low level to defeat SAMs, then popped up to 17,000 ft (5263 m).'

It was a time when the world was on the brink. Stanley Kubrick's film *Dr Strangelove, Or How I Learned to Stop Worrying and Love the Bomb* was a farce about how a wayward Stratofortress crew brought about the end of the world. *Fail Safe*, the film based on a novel by Eugene Burdick and William Lederer, was a more serious tale about how an error on a B-52 mission could accidentally start an atomic war. Both stories reflected the nuclear fears of the era far better than lesser-known adventure tales like *Bombers B-52* with Karl Malden, which earned little notice and no Academy Awards.

In SAC, pilots and crew members were rigidly monitored as part of the Human Reliability Program. They wanted to know, remembers Pat Briggs, 'if you drank too much or fought with your wife'. Gen Curtis LeMay could get spot promotions for bomber crews – bitterly resented elsewhere in the Air Force – but anybody who screwed up was yanked off flight status. The programme was, in a sense, the predecessor of the US military's no-notice drug testing programme of the 1990s, except that it restricted civil liberties even more.

It was a reliability, not a loyalty, test. 'Everyone was committed', remembers Briggs. 'No one ever expressed doubts.'

NUCLEAR RISK

Pilot Briggs was flying bombers – B-47s, not B-52s – when the world came closest to atomic Armageddon. He emphasises that his own experience was shared by men who flew Stratofortresses at the time. The Cuban Missile Crisis of October 1962 brought 'a pretty high level of panic the whole time', he says.

'We'd all seen films of bomb tests. We'd seen pictures of shock waves knocking houses down. We knew fallout was bad. During the Cuban Missile Crisis, the US went on heightened civil defense warning. The balloon was halfway up. My dream – my nightmare – was, the horn blows and I can't get to my airplane in time. Nuclear weapons are coming inbound from Russia. I'm running in slow motion, the airplanes are getting ready to go. We're starting the war. And I can't get to my bomber.

'That month, we deployed with nuclear weapons all over the US. We were ready to go to war. The idea was to disperse the bomber force.' As the world now knows, the crisis ended without conflict. But it was a difficult time for SAC crews.

In normal times, life in SAC was demanding. There was not just the Human Reliability Program. An entire B-52 crew could be fired on the spot for a trivial infraction of the rules. Officers were not merely hounded about their reliability, but had to show top flying skills and leadership ability. Pat Briggs remembered going on nuclear alert – which, before 1968, meant 24 hours in the air on a *Chromedome* mission carrying the 'real thing'.

'Before going on alert, you studied your primary set of targets and were quizzed on them by the wing CO (commanding officer). You studied your route of flight,

timing, the types of weapons, where the refuelling was, where your post-strike recovery airfield was. This was our portion of the SIOP (Single Integrated Operations Plan), the targeting scenario for the first hours of nuclear conflict, and we were expected to know it, inside and out.

'Our standard weapon was the Mk 28 (thermonuclear bomb). The warhead was common to the two Hound Dog missiles hanging under pylons on the wings and the four bombs in the bay. We were to launch the Hound Dogs at high altitude *first*, and then go down to low altitude for our run-in to the target.

'Typically, we'd take off and fly to a "go, no go" line arbitrarily laid out. We couldn't pass that line without a strike order' – meaning, confirmation that the National Command Authority (NCA) had authorised an assault with atomic weapons. At the time, the NCA ran from the President to the Secretary of Defense to the CINCs, or commanders in chief, of the major US warfighting commands.

In the mid-1980s, the Chairman of the Joint Chiefs of Staff was added between the Secretary and the CINCs – the first time any general in the Pentagon was given a role in commanding American forces in combat.

The strike order 'could, under some circumstances, be given to us before we launched. Or it could come by radio, UHF (ultra high frequency) or single sideband or even from rockets designed for broadcasting the "go code". Once you crossed the line and started to war, you programmed your Hound Dogs and launched them at altitude, then flew to your low-level entry point and made a low-level approach to four targets for your four bombs.

CREW JOBS

'Major workload fell on the RN (radar navigator, the term for the bombardier) and nav (navigator). One improvement the B-52 gave you over B-47 was that you had two navs. They'd get you there on time. En route they program the Hound Dog missiles. You have to remember, the bomb/nav system on those B-52s gave you only 15 hours on average between failures, so you used every possible source of information to continuously upgrade yourself as you pressed your attack. The RN and nav were extremely busy during the whole damned flight.

'As for us pilots, our workload was heavy at take-off,

at air refuelling, and once we'd started descent for low-level. The pilot was also the aircraft commander, or AC, responsible for everything in the aircraft. The co-pilot was your quarterback – he'd keep track of fuel and work with the two navs to coordinate checklists and navigation. All through this time the electronic warfare officer was listening to the entire electronic environment. He had capability to discern the difference between various airborne and ground radars. He co-ordinated with the gunner.'

While flying *Chromedome* alert missions and other, more routine sorties at the height of the Cold War, Stratofortress pilot Briggs encountered the usual glitches. He once had a situation where fuel tanks were not feeding. He once had to shut down an engine on fire. None of these events, in his view, were serious.

'The B-52 was the finest, most capable airplane for the mission. They had a chance to see the mistakes made with the B-47, in reliability and efficiency, and they produced a great airplane.'

As the Vietnam war unfolded, nuclear missions became only one of SAC's duties. The prelude to *Arc Light* operations in Vietnam began in February 1965 when personnel from Barksdale AFB, Louisiana, and Mather AFB, California, deployed to Guam with B-52Fs equipped to carry 51 750-lb (340-kg) bombs, 27 internally and 24 externally.

On 18 June 1965, 30 aircraft were launched from Guam to hit Viet Cong bases in Binh Duong province north of Saigon. As the aircraft were on their way in on their first air refueling, two B-52s collided and broke apart in flames, killing eight of twelve crew members on board. One of the men killed was 27-year-old Capt Charles Blankenship, high school classmate of an author of this volume.

Stuck with 'two wars', nuclear and conventional, SAC suddenly didn't have enough of anything. A first lieutenant at the time, Patrick A Briggs was advanced quickly through the ranks. 'They needed people. They had training problems. In my case they waived 250 hours to become make me an AC (they required 2000 hours total, which I didn't have, including 1000 in B-52s which I had).

'By the spring of 1966 I was an AC. In spring of 1967, they waived 500 flying hours to make me an instructor pilot, or IP (they required 2500 hours, including 1500 in B-52s). By this time, Air Force policy was you'd do one tour in South-East Asia followed by a tour on nuclear alert, and then back to Vietnam.'

ATOMIC ACCIDENT

The *Chromedome* airborne alert flights, which assured survival of some B-52s in the event of nuclear attack, were ended after the 1968 Greenland incident which saw a B-52 carrying four hydrogen bombs crash land and burn out on the ice near the USAF base at Thule.

Keeping a meaningful number of B-52s armed and in the air around the clock for an extended period of time was also deemed impractical because it seriously curtailed training of new crews and other essential programs while the demands on maintenance and support services were greatly multiplied. After 1968 when *Chromedome* was ended, a 24-hour airborne alert could have been resumed at any time – but never was. Instead, facing as little as 20 minutes' warning time of incoming Soviet missiles, SAC concentrated on its *Quick Start* programme which allowed all B-52s on runway alert at all bases to be started simultaneously.

But 1st Lt Patrick Briggs was already leaving the world of nuclear warfare. 'My wing CO at Robins, Coll (later Brig Gen) James M Keck, a West Point graduate, got some of us together and said, "Vietnam is cranking up . . ." He had a heart to heart talk with B-52 crews. "When your country goes to war and a combat situation comes up, you should give consideration to getting yourself involved in it. It's an experience you'll grow with."'

Briggs continues, 'I volunteered for *anything* in Vietnam – C-123s, A-ls, anything. I kept calling SAC headquarters over six to eight months and didn't hear anything. I found out I really wasn't in the Air Force. I was in SAC. SAC was giving up people to go to 'Nam but not its good people: it was getting rid of the ash and trash.

'Finally, I was able to transfer to B-52Ds in the 99th Bomb Wing at Westover AFB, Massachusetts, as an instructor pilot in preparation for South-East Asia. I went there in July 1967. I turned in my flight records to the Standardisation Group to introduce myself and they said, "Where you from?" I said Robins. I said I'm an IP. They saw my slick wings – for I didn't yet have the combination of 2000 hours and seven years' service to qualify as a senior pilot, with a star on my wings – and they didn't believe I was an instructor. They decided they'd test me, show me a thing or two. What they didn't know was the tall-tail B-52D was far easier to fly than the G-model.

'We went for checkouts in the B-52D. On refu-

ABOVE Vietnam-era camouflage on B-52D 56-0684 *(USAF)*

elling, they figured they'd really test me. They said, "Okay, we're gonna refuel with the autopilot off." They thought this was a big challenge. Remember, the airplane was heavy, we had a yoke, and if you were going to manoeuvre it, you needed a lot of pressure on the yoke. When you refuelled it was very fatiguing to refuel with one hand on the yoke and one on the throttle, and the autopilot reduced this load. When they put me to the test, they were surprised I flew the aircraft better than the guy who was watching me.'

Many pilots, like Briggs, made the transition from the new (but more difficult) B-52G to the B-52D. 'The D had a higher tail, ailerons, no spoilers. Air refuelling with the autopilot off was easier than air refuelling with autopilot on in the G-model. Once you got up behind the tanker, went through the bow wave, and worked into position, the requirement for control inputs to stay there was very little, much less than the G-model.

'As a measure of how much confidence the guys had, there was a time when the gunner had to take a crap. In the D-model, he was in the tail and it was against procedure for him to be off the headset, unstrapped, parachute off. The gunner had enough confidence in me to take his chute off, slip his flight suit off, and use the porto-potty under his seat.'

Speaking of bathroom functions, the Stratofortress, says Briggs, 'had a urinal like a hollow telephone pole. Pilots had to go downstairs because it was on the nav's table down below. When you used it, more or less by nature, you used one hand to steady yourself on a vertical bar which ran up from the nav's table. I did so much flying that I found that even on the ground, for it to "feel" right, I had to hold onto something to take a leak!'

SOUTH-EAST ASIA

Briggs went to war with the 99th Bomb Wing from Westover. The wing deployed together to become part of the 3d Air Division. It was known as the 'cadre' unit – a function which rotated – because all other crews assigned to Guam, Okinawa, and later U-Tapao, were an adjunct to the cadre bomb wing. Westover's wing commander, operations officer, and senior staff, all came over together. Crews from other units came individually, most after flying B-52Gs and B-52Hs. Although the B-52F had begun the Vietnam fighting, all bombers on Guam now were *Big Belly* mod B-52Ds able to carry 108 bombs inside and outside.

On Guam, Briggs began with a check-ride by an experienced crew (IP, instructor RN). It was an 'over the shoulder' ride ('you fly, they watch'). Jump seats are located behind the AC and, down below, the RN.

A bombing mission to Vietnam from Guam meant a 20-hour day, Pat Briggs remembers, 'You get up, get dressed, get fed, do the pre-takeoff briefings, preflight the airplane, start engines on time, hit your taxi time, hit your take-off time, hit your air refuelling time. The mission would last 12 hours.

'It was a different life. Being a nuclear pilot in SAC was a very structured life – a week on alert, four days off, flying for ten days, then back on alert. You knew days ahead of time where you'd go and what you'd do. Most people were unaware of the mind set you developed. There were no surprises. Everything was done in a measured fashion.

'When we got to South-East Asia, everything was *still* done in a measured fashion but as the war progressed fewer and fewer of the checkpoints were there and, more and more, the skill and professionalism of the crew members came into play.

'If you were on a plane trying to make the mission and you rolled out on the runway and your engines didn't check out, or your bomb/nav (system) was out and you had to abort, aborting didn't mean you wouldn't go. It meant you went through a very hectic baggage drill. You went back, parked the airplane, unstrapped the parachute, stuck your helmet in a helmet bag, grabbed your briefcase, ran down the stairs, threw all your gear in the truck, went to another B-52, which already had its engines running because the crew chief had started them. You threw all your gear on, climbed in, strapped in, and took off as fast as you could. This was very unsettling to someone who, for years, lived in a system where everything was structured, and paced, and measured. For the old heads, by the end of your six-month combat tour, you came to the realisation that the airplane would fly *without* two days of preparation.'

Another pilot reflects on flying the B-52D to war. 'The mission: you fly high. You take-off high, refuel, and don't go low unless you absolutely have to. You have a lot of time to think. The thinking part isn't healthy. In the northern neck of South Vietnam, and in the southern part of North Vietnam, there was the beginning of a serious SAM threat. They didn't shoot down any B-52s in the 1960s, but at the time we didn't know it would be that way . . .'

ARC LIGHT

Patrick Briggs flew his first *Arc Light* mission in September 1967. 'We flew in cells of three, named by colour – 'Red', 'Blue' and 'Orange'. A typical mission was two, sometimes three, cells but during the Tet Offensive (January-February 1968), we flew up to 12-ship missions. During Tet I was bombing over South Vietnam down near Saigon and counted the number of callsigns I could hear on radio. We had 60 B-52s in the air at one time. During Tet, (Gen William) Westmoreland regarded B-52s as a sort of roving infantry division: We went where the bad guys were and tried to knock them off guard and hurt them. Tet came as a big surprise. They'd massed a lot of people and weapons for an all-out push. I remember dropping bombs and breaking off the target and thinking (as we looked back at secondary explosions), I hope to God that we're doing the right thing.' By this, Briggs means he hoped they were hitting the right target at the right time, because Americans on the ground were under heavy assault.

'Each crew tape-recorded its conversations (from the beginning of a flight) up to "bombs away". So if there were bad bombs they'd play back every crew's tapes to see what went wrong – and maybe hang your ass. Once you knew the bombs were on target, you could put on musical tapes. *The Man of La Mancha* was playing then – the impossible dream, the unbeatable foe. It misted my eyes. I hoped to God we were doing the right thing here because we were getting clobbered by VC.

'There was a frustration level at flying so many missions and doing so much bombing. We got positive feedback from bombing missions along the DMZ (the misnamed Demilitarised Zone) at Con Tien, an outpost on a hilltop where they were monitoring infiltration. We used to get letters from Marines stationed at Con Tien telling us how much they appreciated the bombing we were doing. One Marine said, "Second only to a letter from home is an *Arc Light* strike." Con Tien looked like the back side of the Moon with bomb craters lip to lip, sometimes overlapping.

'During the battle of Khe Sanh in early 1968, where a Marine garrison was surrounded by North Vietnamese regular forces, we did some special things with the B-52. Normally we bombed from 30,000 to 33,000 ft (9288 to 10,216 m). We went down to the low twenties, maybe 24,000 ft (7430 m) and we slowed down – which we normally did not do. This improves accuracy and gets better dispersion of bombs. Down at lower altitude you have less wind to contend with. We were told, "No bombing within 1000 metres (3230 ft) of Khe Sanh" because with an *Arc Light* strike the concussion of the bombs is awesome.'

Another rule placed constraints on bombing in a straight line near the Khe Sanh garrison. 'If you're close to the side of a bomb track, you can get hurt. Some bombs as they dropped off rack would hit slipstream and get so nose-up that the tail fins couldn't bring the surface back down so it was predictable that bomb would fall 4000 metres (12,920 ft) short of the box. There was no way to predict this, so we never bombed in a straight line going in or out of Khe San. Instead, our bomb runs were done tangentially.

'Twenty years later a Marine told me, "you guys bombed within 500 metres (1615 ft) of the camp". I said, "No that's not possible. We came in with your guidance, with great care. We slowed down to put our bombs where we were told." The Marine looked at me and said, "Yeah, but *we lied to you*. We brought you in to 500 metres and *didn't tell you*, because the VC (Viet Cong; in fact, the enemy forces at Khe Sanh were North Vietnamese) figured out that you were supposed to come no closer than 1000 metres."

B-52D BOMBING

On most of his missions, pilot Pat Briggs flew higher as was the norm in the Stratofortress. 'But a fully loaded B-52D, because of the weight of the aircraft and the drag of the bombs, couldn't get much higher than 36,000 ft (11,145 m). We'd bomb at 450 kts true in the low thirties with the cell stacked up, The second ship in the cell was 500 ft (155 m) higher than the first, the third ship 500 ft higher than the second. This enabled you to drop bombs on Lead's call if your bomb/nav system was out. If I was cell leader and my system went out, I'd trade places and go to the back of the stack and we'd drop visually off the lead bomber. We talked to each other (between aircraft) very little.

'Whenever an *Arc Light* strike was inbound, our side would broadcast on Guard (the emergency warning frequency), "Heavy artillery on the 150 radial of the Da Nang VOR at 40 miles." It didn't take a rocket scientist to figure out *that* meant our B-52 strikes. We assume the Viet Cong could easily figure out where it was coming.'

Pat Briggs flew 62 combat missions on his first tour, which concluded in March 1968. 'It's a mistake to think we didn't have a SAM threat. Eight of my first 15 missions were over North Vietnam in the southern portion of the country (which was as far north as B-52s went at the time). We were bombing SAM sites. When we did this, we had a lot of support ahead of us – F-105s flew *Iron Hand* to get them to put their heads down, EB-66s flew ECM (electronic countermeasures) suppression and jammed their radars and missile acquisition systems, and above us F-4s flew MiGCAP (MiG combat air patrol). We did all this mostly on radio silence.

'In 1967-68, when the book said the target was the "extreme west DMZ", that meant Laos.' As late as 1969, President Nixon personally denied that American forces were bombing Laos, but they were doing so regularly. Later in the war, clandestine – and still later, public – combat missions were also flown over Cambodia.

'My first tour ended and we went back to the 99th BW at Westover. Our wing was replaced on Guam by another B-52D bomb wing (the cadre job was rotated around). We reconstituted the nuclear alert force. We decompressed, stood alert, and got ready to go back over again. We were home for six months. Three to four months after coming home, we started training to go back and do it all over again for the second time.'

When Briggs' bomb wing returned to Guam in September 1968 to re-assume its role as cadre for the *Arc Light* B-52 force, the US was beginning to operate from U-Tapao naval base in Thailand, which became the Stratofortress base closest to the war zone. 'In my second tour there was more bombing out of U-Tapao. We were at Guam but went TDY to Okinawa and U-Tapao. We would fly a mission to Vietnam, drop bombs, and recover in Thailand. Guam was a 12-hour mission and a 20-hour day. Okinawa was an 8-hour mission, and a 16-hour day. Guam to U-Tapao was probably a seven- to eight-hour mission. A mission to and from U-Tapao three to four hours.

'Another thing that changed on my second tour: we were doing more and more *Sky Spot* bombing. This is high-altitude bombing directed by ground controllers at a radar site on the ground who provide vectors to the target.

'You took off and went to an entry point on the coast of Vietnam without all of the intense pre-briefing and regimentation which had been so typical of my

first tour. The ground folks said, "Show up with a bomb load and we'll tell you where to bomb". On my first tour, we were bombing with information that was 24 hours old. This new concept brought a three-ship cell close to Vietnam, only after that the pilot was told whom to call at a certain site, and then, based on the latest intel from the ground, they'd vector you to a bomb release point. You gave them your altitude, air speed, and wind velocity at altitude. They would do a 'reverse bombing equation' and guide you to a release point in the air. You never knew what the target was. They could bomb a site they'd only found an hour earlier. With this new method, you possibly sacrificed accuracy in bombing but you took away from the enemy any prospect of advance warning that you were coming.

'I came back in March 1969 and my B-52 experience ends in June 1969. My rank at that time was captain. I had 3200 hours of B-52 time, 1200 hours of combat, 148 missions, including 15 up north, a year in South-East Asia, and an average of 100 flying hours per month. Got a DFC (Distinguished Flying Cross) plus eight Air Medals and change. This was fairly typ-

ical. After that I went to SAC Headquarters and worked in the underground command post, there, on the SIOP, war games, and other issues.'

NEW CAMPAIGN

In 1972, the US resumed bombing North Vietnam after a three-year bombing halt in Operation *Linebacker* which began on 8 May. During this campaign, the B-52 force on Guam and the 307th Strategic Wing at U-Tapao were built up by increased deployments in Operation *Bullet Shot*, which was to eventually put more than 12,000 airmen in temporary bed-down facilities at Guam's Andersen Air Force Base. *Linebacker* ended in October when it looked like a settlement was at hand. When Hanoi balked, President Nixon authorised *Linebacker II* – the Eleven Day War, 18-29 December 1972. As chronicled elsewhere in this

ABOVE Routine maintenance was often undertaken out of doors during the *Arc Light* era, as demonstrated here by a technician attending to some of the B-52D's many black boxes *(USAF)*

narrative, *Linebacker II* marked the first time the B-52 was unleashed against hard targets deep inside North Vietnam, and on the opening night no fewer than 129 B-52s were sent 'downtown' to Hanoi. The B-52Ds already committed to South-East Asia were joined by some B-52G models.

Lt Col Hendsley R Conner, who commanded one of the provisional squadrons on Guam, remembered the first massive attack against North Vietnam on 18 December 1972. 'Each squadron was given responsibility for one wave of each raid', Conner recalls, 'My staff and I worked almost around the clock getting things ready for the first raid. The schedule was prepared, crews were notified, transportation ordered, flying equipment prepared, meals ordered, and all the myriad things done to prepare 33 crews and airplanes for a combat mission.

'Each wave would have a senior officer along as Airborne Mission Commander (ABC). The wing commander would be the ABC on the lead wave and I was assigned as deputy ABC to the second wave. I would not fly in a crew position but would go along in the instructor pilot's seat as the seventh man on the aircraft. By not having any crew duties, I could concentrate on how the mission was progressing and be aware of any problems the wave might encounter.'

Lt Col Conner talks through his *Linebacker II* strike from beginning to end. He is, however, modest about the tension which gripped Stratofortress crews at this time. In the midst of a surge of force without any precedent, crews were uptight about what they perceived as unimaginative tactics and, with very good reason, worried about Hanoi's missiles and MiGs. Conner makes it all sound very prosaic.

'The planning was complete, the briefings were finally over, and we arrived at the aircraft to preflight the bombs and equipment. Wave II was scheduled to begin taking off at 1900 (7.00 pm). Every 90 seconds after the first take-off another fully loaded B-52 would roll down the runway.

'After we levelled off, I tried to get some sleep. I had gotten very little rest the night before because of the many problems that had come up during mission planning. I slept about three hours before the co-pilot woke me up for our inflight refuelling. When the refuelling was over, I tuned in the radio to hear how the lead wave was doing. They should then be in the target area and we should be able to hear how the enemy was reacting.

The first report I heard was when Col Rew (Col Thomas F Rew, commander of the 72nd Strategic Wing (Provisional) on Guam) made his call-in after they exited the target area. They had had a tough experience. One airplane was known to be shot down by SAMs, two were presently not accounted for, and one had received heavy battle damage. He initially estimated that the North Vietnamese had fired over 200 SAMs at them. There were no reports of MiG fighter attacks. The anti-aircraft artillery was heavy, but well below their flight level. For us, the worst part was now they knew we were coming, and things probably would be even worse when we got there.

MET BY MISSILES

'I saw the SAMs as we came in closer to the target area. They made white streaks of light as they climbed into the night sky. As they left the ground, they would move slowly, pick up speed as they climbed, and end their flight, finally, in a cascade of sparkles. There were

ABOVE Almost hidden from view, the B-52D in the background will shortly be groaning under the weight of the 84 Mk 82 500 lb bombs that stand adjacent to it. Facilities for pre-loading the 'clip-in' assemblies were supposed to make life easier for munitions teams, although in practice it seems bombs were often loaded individually, using a device known as a 'stuffer' *(USAF)*

so many of them it reminded me of a Fourth of July fireworks display. A beautiful sight to watch if I hadn't known how lethal they could be. I had flown over 200 missions in B-57s (Martin B-57 Canberra) and I thought I knew what was in store for us, but I had never seen so many SAMs. I did not feel nearly as secure in the big, lumbering bomber as I had in my B-57 Canberra that could manoeuvre much better.

'Just before we started our bomb run, we checked our emergency gear to make sure everything was all right in case we were hit. We would be most vulnerable on the bomb run, since we would be within lethal range of the SAMs and would be flying straight and level. We had been briefed not to make any evasive manoeuvres on the bomb run so that the radar navigator would be positive he was aiming at the right target. If he was not absolutely sure he had the right target, we were to withhold our bombs and then jettison them into the ocean on our way back to Guam. We did not want to hit anything but military targets. Precision bombing was the object of our mission. The

crews were briefed this way and they followed their instructions.

'About half way down the bomb run, the electronic warfare officer on our crew began to call over the interphone that SAMs had been fired at us. One, two, three, now four missiles had been fired. We flew straight and level.

'"How far out from the target are we, Radar?"

'"We're ten seconds out. Five. Four. Three. Two. One. Bombs away! Start your . . . turn, Pilot."

'We began a right turn to exit the target area.

'"Kaboom!" We were hit. I felt like we had been in the centre of a clap of thunder. The noise was deafening. Everything went really bright for an instant, then dark again. I could smell ozone from burnt powder, and had felt a slight jerk on my right shoulder. I quickly checked the flight instruments and over the interphone said, "Pilot, we're still flying. Are you okay?"

'"Yes, I'm fine, but the aircraft is in bad shape, Let's check it over and see if we can keep it airborne. Everybody check in and let me know how they are."

'"Navigator and Radar are okay. We don't have any equipment operating, but I'll give you a heading for Thailand any time you want it."

'"EW is okay, but Guns has been hit. We have about two more minutes in lethal SAM range, so continue to make evasive manoeuvres if you can."

'"Guns is okay. I have some shrapnel in my right

arm, but nothing bad. The left side of the airplane is full of holes.”

ONBOARD CRISIS

Conner, the high-ranking extra man in this Stratofortress, continues his tale with a recollection that he was very busy. 'I called the lead aircraft to let them know we had been hit. He said he could tell we had been hit because our left wing was on fire and we were slowing down. I asked him to call some escort fighters for us.

'The airplane continued to fly all right, so the pilot resumed making evasive manoeuvres. We flew out of the range of the missiles, finally, and began to take stock of the airplane. The SAM had exploded off our left wing. The fuel tank on that wing was missing along with part of the wing tip. We had lost No 1 and No 2 engines. Fire was streaming out of the wreckage they had left. Fuel was coming out of holes all throughout the left wing.

'Most of our flight instruments were not working. We had lost cabin pressurisation. We were at 30,000 ft (9288 m) altitude. Our oxygen supply must have been hit, because the quantity gauge was slowly decreasing. I took out two walk-around bottles for the pilot and co-pilot. If we ran out, they, at least, would have enough emergency oxygen to get us down to an altitude where we could breathe.

'We turned to a heading that would take us to U-Tapao. I called again for the fighter escort to take us toward friendly territory.

'"We're here, buddy."

'Two F-4s joined us and would stay with us as long as they were needed. One stayed high, and the other stayed on our wing, as we descended to a lower altitude and to oxygen. They called to alert rescue service in case we had to abandon the aircraft. Our first concern was to get out of North Vietnam and Laos. We did not want to end up as POWs (prisoners of war). We knew they did not take many prisoners in Laos.

'Thailand looked beautiful when we finally crossed the border. Since Thailand was not subject to bombing attacks, they still had their lights on at night. We flew for about 30 minutes after we had descended to a lower altitude and began to think we would be able to get the airplane on the ground safely. The first in the left pod was still burning, but it didn't seem to be getting any worse. One F-4 left us. The other one said he

would take one more close look at us before he, too, would have to leave. He flew down and joined on our left wing.

'"I'd better stay with you, friend. The first is getting worse and I don't think you'll make it."

'I unfastened my lap belt and leaned over between the pilot and co-pilot to take another look at the fire. It had now spread to the fuel leaking out of the wing and the whole left wing was burning. It was a wall of red flame starting just outside the cockpit and as high as I could see.

'I said, "I think I'll head downstairs."

'"Good idea", said the pilot.

TIME TO GO

'The six crew members in the B-52G have ejection seats that they could fire to abandon the aircraft. Anyone else on board has to go down to the lower compartment and manually bail out of the hole the navigator or radar navigator leaves when their seat is ejected. I quickly climbed down the ladder and started to plug in my interphone cord to see what our situation was.

'The red "Abandon" light came on.

'"Bam!" The navigator fired his ejection seat and was gone. The radar navigator turned toward me and pointed to the hole the navigator had left and motioned for me to jump. I climbed over some debris and stood on the edge of the hole. I looked at the ground far below. Did I want to jump? The airplane began to shudder and shake, and I heard other explosions as the other crew members ejected. I heard another louder blast. The wing was exploding. Yes, I wanted to jump! I rolled through the opening and as soon as I thought I was free of the airplane, I pulled the ripcord on my parachute.

'I felt a sharp jerk and looked to see the parachute canopy open above me. The opening shock felt good even though it had hurt more than I had expected. Everything was quiet and eerie. There was a full moon, the weather was clear, and I could see things very well. I looked for other parachutes. One, two, three, that's all I saw. Then I saw the airplane. It was flying in a descending turn to the left and the whole fuselage was now burning and parts of the left wing had left the airplane. It was exploding as it hit the ground.

'I saw I was getting close to the ground, so I got

ready to land. I was floating backwards, but I could see I was going to land in a little village. I raised my legs to keep from going into a hootch (house). I certainly did not want to land in someone's bedroom. I got my feet down, hit the ground, and rolled over on my backside. I got up on one knee and began to feel around to see if I was all right. Everything seemed to be fine. There was a little blood on my right shoulder from where a piece of shrapnel had hit, but otherwise, just bruises. It felt good to be alive.

'About 20 or 25 Thai villagers came out of their homes and stood watching me. They were very quiet and friendly and brought water for me to drink. None of them spoke English, so we spent our time waiting for rescue, trying to communicate with sign language. They kept pointing to the sky and showing what must have been an airplane crashing and burning. I tried to describe a helicopter to let them know one would be coming soon to pick me up, I hoped.

'In about 20 minutes a Marine helicopter did come, and I was picked up. We had bailed out near the Marine base at Nam Phong. All six of the crew had already been rescued, and none had serious injuries. We were flown to U-Tapao, and then on back to Guam the next day. One particular ordeal in the bombing raids was over. The crew had performed well. I was proud of them. The reason I had decided to fly with them on the mission was because I thought they were one of my most professional crews. They were from the 2nd Bomb Wing, Barksdale AFB, Louisiana. The aircraft commander was Maj Cliff Ashley. His co-pilot was Capt Gary Vickers. The radar navigator was Maj Archie Myers, navigator 1st Lt Forrest Stegelin, electronic warfare officer Capt Jim Trammel, and gunner Mst Sgt Ken Connor. The outstanding way they handled our emergency showed how competent and courageous they were.

'The crew I had flown with, along with survivors from other aircraft, were flown back to the States for rest and leave. They were short of squadron commanders on Guam, so I had to stay and help prepare other raids that were continuing each night.

ELEVEN DAY WAR

Linebacker II grew and its tempo quickened. Among a few crews there were emotions which ranged from serious concern to outright disgust as SAC refused to modify tactics, and the B-52s continued to pour into

North Vietnam in three-plane cells using predictable headings, courses, and altitudes. 'I pictured the North Vietnamese aircraft gunner at his station', says Lt Col Michael P Curphey. 'The way I saw him, he'd take another sip of tea, yawn, look at his watch, glance at his fingernails. "No problem", he'd say to a comrade. "The Americans won't be here for another 13 minutes."'

The sheer predictability of American tactics may have contributed to the furious resistance encountered by B-52 crews on 20 December 1972, the third day of *Linebacker II*. Capt Rolland A Scott, who was TDY (temporary duty) from Barksdale had the unpleasant experience of sampling everything the North Vietnamese could throw at him, but survived.

'I flew in "Gold 2" with another crew as a substitute pilot. The time, track, and target location were nearly the same as my mission on (December) the 18th. Shortly after take-off, we lost one engine and flew the mission on seven. That wasn't too serious a problem in the G-model, but I would have felt better if it hadn't happened. On the northbound leg over NVN (North Vietnam) we heard a good deal of fighter activity and numerous sightings were made of aircraft with lights on, presumably friendly fighters. There appeared to be no SAM activity.

'On the south-east leg approaching the IP (initial point), my co-pilot stated he saw a MiG-21 on the right wing of our aircraft. In mild disbelief, I stretched to see out his window and sure enough, a MiG-21 with lights off was flying tight formation with us. I believe we could actually see the pilot. The approach of the fighter had not been detected by onboard systems. Shortly, two or three minutes later, the co-pilot reported the MiG had departed. Almost immediately I saw the same, or another, enemy aircraft flying formation on the left side of us. After a brief period, less than a minute, it departed.

'Our sighs of relief were short-lived, and we quickly learned what the MiGs had been up to. We visually detected missiles approaching from our eleven and one o'clock positions. Several pairs of missiles were simultaneously launched from these directions. I was extremely worried that missiles were also approaching from our rear that we could not see. The EW reported no Uplink or Downlink signals with the missiles on this mission as were reported on the night of the 18th. However, these missiles appeared to be a lot more accurate than on the 18th. They seemed to readjust

ABOVE Boeing's facility at Wichita was also the location for the unveiling of the first camouflaged B-52G. This jet made its debut in the latter half of the 1960s, although the identity of this example remains unknown *(Boeing)*

their track as I made small turns. I waited for each to get as close as I dared, and then would make a hard, although relatively small, manoeuvre in the hope of avoiding them.

'They arrived in pairs, just a few seconds apart. Some, as they passed, would explode – a few close enough to shake my aircraft. In fact, one exploded so close and caused such a loud noise and violent shock that I stated to the crew that I thought we had been hit. In a very few seconds, after assessing engine instruments and control responses, and having received an okay from downstairs, I determined we had not been hit, or were at least under normal control, and we continued the bomb run. Apparently the MiG-21 we saw was flying with us to report heading, altitude and air speed to the missile sites.

'The missiles were no longer directed toward us in the latter half of the bomb run; however, I could see SAM activity ahead in the vicinity of the target. In fact, while on the run we saw a large ball of fire erupt some few miles ahead of us and slowly turn to the right and descend. I thought it was a Buff and was sure no

one would survive what was apparently a direct hit. I later learned what I saw was "Quilt 3" going down in flames. Amazingly, four crew members successfully ejected.

OVER THE TARGET

'We completed our bomb run and were in the middle of our post target right turn when we again became an item of interest to the missiles. From our left and below were at least three missiles, perhaps four, approaching rapidly. I felt I had no chance to avoid them by either maintaining or rolling out of the right turn, so I increased the planned bank angle drastically and lowered the nose. The SAMs passed above us from our left. I lost some altitude in the manoeuvre, and in the attempt to climb and accelerate on seven engines I lagged behind lead and somewhat out of position. There were no further SAMs directed at our aircraft; however, there was apparently a lot of enemy fighter activity on our withdrawal, according to radio transmissions. We could see numerous fighters with lights on, and the gunner reported numerous targets on radar, one of which appeared to follow us, but not in the cone of fire. We saw no aircraft which appeared to be hostile, nor any hostile manoeuvres.

'As we passed east of NKP (Nakhon Phanom, Thailand) on a southerly heading, we heard what was apparently a B-52 crew abandoning their aircraft over friendly territory. In the distance toward NKP, we soon saw a fireball which we assumed to be a Buff impacting the ground. It must have been "Brass 2" and Capt John Ellinger and his crew were mighty lucky.'

That night, two B-52Gs and one B-52D were shot down and three of nine cells had experienced losses. After many years of seemingly being impervious in Vietnam's skies, Stratofortresses were suffering losses which everyone considered too high. To some crews, it was grounds for near mutiny – at least if tactics weren't changed, and changed quickly.

A US Air Force history of *Linebacker II* operations uses capital letters to refer to this Darkest Hour for the embattled Stratofortress crews. Gen John C. Meyer, SAC commander, who was following events from SAC headquarters in Omaha, wanted a detailed report. Brig Gen Harry N Cordes and other staff officers went over with Meyer 'every aspect of the situation', according to Cordes, including:

- Damage inflicted on the enemy
- Aircraft loss rates, damage rates
- Apparent causes of losses and damage
- Enemy defence status – running low on SAMs?
- Current tactics, new tactics, ECM
- Support packages and tactics
- Possible new targets outside high threat areas
- Crew morale and discipline
- Penetration analysis loss predictions
- Air Force doctrine and history, examing the specific areas of no defence against a determined air attack, and never turning back due to enemy action.

Exactly what Meyer was told about 'crew morale' has never been revealed. In the quarter-century since *Linebacker II*, the US Air Force has never acknowledged that a significant number of B-52 crew members were on the verge of a sit-down strike.

These men were not war protestors, not cowards, indeed not lacking in courage. They were simply exasperated about the way SAC was going to war in so predictable a fashion, using unweildy tactics that gave away advantages to an enemy who was not being forced to work hard enough. But it's clear that Meyer was, in fact, reminded that no crew had ever turned back and, despite the American bomber disgruntlement, it was not going to happen now.

As the US Air Force relates the situation, 'Gen

Meyer experienced first-hand the "loneliness of command". He and he alone must make the decision. He listened judge to all the evidence. He polled every single man in the room – general, colonel, captain, lieutenant – go or no-go? He polled Jerry Johnson (Lt Gen Gerald W Johnson, Eighth Air Force commander and, like Meyer, a World War II fighter ace) – "Can the crews take it?" Johnson's answer is not on record. 'Then he made his decision, probably the most difficult of his career – "Press on!"'

By the end of day four, 11 B-52s had been lost. Eight had gone down in the near vicinity of Hanoi and three had held up long enough to get their crews back to friendly territory. Of the eleven, six were B-52Gs from Andersen. Of the remaining five B-52Ds, four were from U-Tapao, with the one Andersen D being flown out of hostile territory before bail-out.

ONGOING CONFLICT

On the crews' minds was an unplanned but cruel irony. a B-52D crew could risk its life to deliver 100 bombs to Hanoi, but a B-52G crew – in an aircraft deemed more difficult to fly, and less effective in a dense ECM environment – risked their lives on the same mission, under the same circumstances, to deliver just 27. Only about half of the B-52Gs on Guam had an update to their ECM systems which reduced their vulnerability to Hanoi's defenses. The men were facing possible death, yet their ability to inflict harm on the enemy was unequal.

Minor changes in tactics were introduced on the eighth day of the Eleven Day War – 26 December 1972 – when launches from Andersen were clustered more closely together and some ingress routes were changed. Col James R McCarthy (who commanded the B-52Ds of the 43rd Strategic Wing on Guam while Rew commanded the B-52Gs of the 72nd) recorded some of his impressions as North Vietnamese defenses continued to exact a lethal toll and morale among Stratofortress crews went through ups and downs.

McCarthy's recollection, 'As we headed north over the Gulf of Tonkin, I heard (pilot) Tom Lebar call in that his wave was at the join-up point on time and that his wave was compressed. They had done one hell of a fine job.

'When we crossed the 17th parallel, we were committed. That was the last point at which I or higher headquarters could recall the forces. From here until the target area we would be using radio silence procedures. The only radio call allowed would be if you got jumped by a MiG and you needed MiGCAP support.

'As Haiphong passed off our left wing, we could see that the Navy support forces were really working over the SAM and AAA (antiaircraft artillery) sites. The whole area was lit up like a Christmas tree. We could hear Red Crown (a Navy early-warning vessel offshore) issuing SAM and MiG warnings to the friendly aircraft over Haiphong. We hoped that this activity would divert their attention from our G-model bombers, who would soon be arriving. Even though they weren't going to downtown Hanoi anymore, they were headed for the port city. As we all knew, that was plenty tough duty. We coasted in north-east of Haiphong and headed for our IP, where we would turn south-west toward Hanoi. The IP turned out to be in the same area that Marty Fulcher had led the 'Buffs' on (December) 23rd against SAM sites that had a reputation of being lousy shots.

'The flak started coming up when we made our first landfall. Once again, we were most vividly aware of the heavy, black, ugly explosions which characterized the 100 mm (gun). Even at night, the black smoke from these explosions is visible. Since we were at a lower altitude than we had flown before, our wave would be more vulnerable to this AAA than on most previous missions. Close to the IP the flak became more intense and the explosions were closer to the aircraft.

'As we turned over the IP we picked up the first SAM signals. We could see them lift off, but their guidance seemed erratic. The SAMs exploded far above us and at a considerable distance from the formation. It appeared that "F Troop" (slang for an incompetent group of boy scouts) was still in business and their aim was as bad as it had always been.

SAM WARNINGS

'However, inbound to the target the SAM signals became stronger. Capt Don Redmon, the EW, reported three very strong signals tracking the aircraft. Bill Stocker ordered the cell to start their SAM threat manoeuvre (introduced because of the near-mutiny by some crews). The navigator, Maj Bill Francis, reported that we had picked up the predicted 100-kt headwinds.

'Then the SAMs really started coming. It was apparent that this was no "F Troop" doing the aiming. The missiles lifted off and headed for the aircraft. As we had long ago learned to do, we fixed our attention on those which maintained the same relative position even as we manoeuvred. All six SAMs fired appeared to maintain their same relative position in the windshield. Then AlC Ken Schell reported from the tail that he had three more at six o'clock heading for us. The next few minutes were going to be interesting.

'Now that the whole force was committed and we were on the bomb run, I had nothing to do until after bombs away, so I decided to count the SAMs launched against us. Out the co-pilot's window, 1st Lt Ron Thomas reported four more coming up on the right side and two at his one o'clock position. Bill reported three more on the left side as the first six started exploding. Some were close – too close for comfort.

'Listening to the navigation team on the interphone downstairs, you would have thought they were making a practice bomb run back in the States. The checklist was unhurried. Capt Joe Gangwish, the RN, calmly discussed the identification of the aiming point that they were using for this bomb run with his teammate, Maj Francis.

'About 100 seconds prior to bombs away, the cockpit lit up like it was daylight. The light came from the rocket exhaust of a SAM that had come up, right under the nose. The EW had reported an extremely strong signal, and he was right. It's hard to judge miss distance at night, but that one looked like it missed us by less than 50 ft (15 m). The proximity fuse should have detonated the warhead, but it didn't. Somebody upstairs was looking after us that night.

'After 26 SAMs, I quit counting. They were coming up too fast to count. It appeared in the cockpit as if they were now barraging SAMs in order to make the lead element of the wave turn from its intended course.

'Just prior to bombs away, the formation stopped manoeuvring to provide the required gyro-stabilisation to the bombing computers. Regardless of how close the SAMs appeared, the bomber had to remain straight and level.

'At bombs away, it looked like we were right in the middle of a fireworks factory that was in the process of blowing up. The radio was completely saturated with SAM calls and MiG warnings. As the bomb doors closed, several SAMs exploded nearby. Others could be seen arcing over and starting a descent, then detonating. If the proximity fuse didn't find a target, SA-2s were set to self-destruct at the end of a predetermined time interval.'

OUT OF HANOI

Col McCarthy's account goes on to explain that his Stratofortress's bombs were dropped exactly on time, on target. 'Minutes afterwards, as we were departing the immediate Hanoi area, there was a brilliant explosion off to our left rear that lit up the whole sky for miles around. A B-52D ("Ebony 2") had been hit and had exploded in mid-air. Momentarily, the radios went silent. Everyone was listening for the emergency beepers that are automatically activated when a parachute opens. We could make out two, or possibly three, different beepers going off. Miraculously, four of the Kincheloe Air Force Base, Michigan, crew escaped the aircraft, becoming POWs. Then there was a call from another aircraft, "Ash 1", stating that he had been hit and was heading for the water. The pilot reported that he was losing altitude and he was having difficulty controlling the aircraft. Red Crown started vectoring F-4s to escort the crippled bomber to safety.'

McCarthy's wave was surrounded by more SAMs rushing upward in the night as they withdrew from the target area. 'Suddenly, one of the cells in our wave reported MiGs closing in and requested fighter support. Red Crown, who had been working with "Ash 1", started vectoring other F-4s to the 'Buff' under possible attack. I gave the command for all upper rotating beacons and tail lights to be turned off – a courageous decision which increased the danger of collision to crews in the crowded sky – 'and as the F-4s approached, the MiG apparently broke off his attack, because our fighters couldn't locate him and the target disappeared from the gunners' radars.'

Unfortunately, as McCarthy relates, the pilot of "Ash 1", Capt Jim Turner, didn't bring his crew home. Turner 'reported that his aircraft seemed to be flyable and he was going to try to make it to U-Tapao. There were probably a couple thousand guys who were listening that were praying he would make it. He almost did. He crashed just beyond the runway at "U-T", a tragic loss after so heroic an effort.

'Only the gunner and co-pilot survived the crash, and the co-pilot would not have made it without the bravery of Capt Brent Diefenbach, who had himself landed only moments earlier. His quick thinking and ingenuity enabled him to reach the crash site, where he pulled 1st Lt Bob Hymel from the wreckage. TSgt Spencer Grippin escaped the burning wreck when the tail section broke free on impact.'

On day nine of *Linebacker II*, 27 December, the strike force consisted of 60 bombers, 21 B-52Gs and 39 B-52Ds, a somewhat reduced number perhaps in part because more flexible ingress routes were being tried. There is some evidence that morale improved. Waves of bomber cells were made appreciably smaller and given new directions of attack. The crews apparently felt, finally, that their concerns were being addressed.

HURTING HANOI

North Vietnam's infrastructure was being badly battered. Most in the B-52 force were certain their raids were doing what Washington wanted – forcing Hanoi towards a settlement which would enable the US to withdraw from the only war it never won. Capt John Mize and his B-52D crew from Ellsworth AFB, South Dakota, flew out of U-Tapao on 27 December using the callsign "Ash 2".

Their target was a SAM site. According to eyewitnesses in "Paint" cell, just behind "ASH", the latter's bombs destroyed at least one SA-2 in the lift-off stage and sent several others on completely erratic flight paths. But their egress route took them past another SAM site known to the Americans as Killer 549.

A missile made what seemed to be a highly successful near miss and a detonation shook the B-52D and wounded every member of its crew. Despite his wounds and severe damage to the aircraft, Capt Mize flew his B-52 for 48 more minutes into Laos, where he finally gave the order to bail out.

All were rescued. John Mize was awarded the Air Force Cross, making him the highest-decorated B-52 crewman ever.

The *Linebacker II* attacks for day ten, 28 December 1972, called for 60 B-52s – equal numbers of Ds and Gs from Andersen and 30 B-52Ds from U-Tapao. They formed into six waves attacking five targets. Four waves and their targets were in the immediate Hanoi area, while the other two waves attacked the Lang Dang railroad yards. Those yards, a key choke point in the supply routes from China, got heavier attention during the last days of the campaign than any other target.

The next day – the last of the Eleven Day War – Lang Dang was at the top of the target list. Sixty B-52s were assigned to the mission again, 30 from U-Tapao. In addition to contributing 18 B-52Ds and 12 B-52Gs,

Andersen AFB despatched a further 30 B-52G models on *Arc Light* strikes to South Vietnam.

In 11 days, B-52 Stratofortresses flew 729 sorties against 34 targets in North Vietnam above the 20th parallel. They expended over 15,000 tons of ordnance. Bomb damage assessments revealed 1600 military structures destroyed or damaged, 500 rail interdictions, 372 pieces of rolling stock destroyed or damaged, three million gallons of petroleum products destroyed (estimated to be one-fourth of North Vietnam's reserves), ten interdictions of airfield runways and ramps, an estimated 80 per cent of electrical power production capability destroyed, and numerous instances of specialised damage, such as to open stockpiles, missile launchers and so forth. All areas of the nation's livelihood and productivity were severely affected.

The best estimate is that 884 SAMs were fired at the B-52s and 24 achieved hits for a 2.7 per cent success rate. Of the 24, 15 resulted in downed aircraft. There were 92 crewmembers aboard the 15 aircraft which fell victim to the defences. Sixty-one of these went down over North Vietnam, roughly half killed and half taken prisoner.

As for pushing the enemy to the conference table, North Vietnam's deadline in December gave way to meaningful negotiations beginning on 8 January 1973, and the agreement ending the American role in the war took effect on 23 January 1973.

In Hanoi, Col John P Flynn, commander of American prisoners of war, told his people when he heard B-52 bombs going off that it was time, figuratively, to pack their bags. 'I don't know when we're going home, but we're going home.' The POWs were released in March.

COLD WAR AGAIN

The B-52 Stratofortress returned to its intended purpose as part of a nation's nuclear deterrent. During an alert in the October 1973 Middle East war, the B-52 force reached its highest point of readiness since the Cuban Missile Crisis.

Ahead lay a period of change and innovation in the nuclear bombing role. But in the early 1970s, it did not seem likely that the B-52 would ever drop a conventional bomb again. After recovering from one of the last Stratofortress missions of the Vietnam war – still, at that time, less than half-way through the service career of the longest-serving warplane in history – one crew member is reported to have said, 'Thank goodness we won't have to do that again'.

Nearly two decades later, he was proved wrong in that belief.

DESERT STORM
THE 'BUFF'S' LAST WAR?

DESPITE THE FACT that it was no longer in the first flush of youth, responsibility for carrying the Strategic Air Command contribution to the war against Iraq was entrusted to the mighty Stratofortress. Thus it was that almost 20 years after last being called upon to drop bombs in anger, the long-serving 'Buff' was once again given the chance to go to war. On this occasion, following the retirement of the B-52D almost a decade earlier, it was the B-52G model which fulfilled conventional bombing tasks.

While it may not have possessed the almost legendary bomb carrying abilities of the *Big Belly*-configured B-52D, the B-52G had been increasingly concerned with non-nuclear attack missions in the interval that had elapsed since the end of the Vietnam War and a considerable amount of attention had been directed towards boosting capability in this area. One

notable benefit arising from this process concerned the B-52G's conventional weapons payload, which had almost doubled as a result of the external pylons being adapted to each carry a maximum of 12 M117 750-lb bombs or other similar weapons.

In concert with the internal weapons bay, this increased munitions capacity to a maximum of 51 such weapons and there was no other aircraft in the Gulf War capable of delivering anything like that number of bombs in a single sortie. As will be seen, however, the Stratofortress certainly wasn't employed

BELOW The rain-swept and windy expanse of Fairford during February 1991, when bombers from this former SAC base made the long haul to and from Iraq on an almost daily basis. Fairford was the last of four bases to support B-52s engaged in carrying the war to Iraqi forces *(API/J Flack)*

LEFT Flat-bed trucks laden with M117 750 lb bombs were particularly commonplace at Fairford during January and February 1991. These examples have still to be prepared and adorned with graffiti *(API/J Flack)*

purely as a bomb-carrier during the six weeks that the conflict lasted and it did get the chance to utilise other weapons systems, most notably and tellingly during the opening phase of the aerial onslaught that was known as *Desert Storm*.

That onslaught did not, in fact, get under way until January 1991, some several months after the crisis blew up with the subjugation of Kuwait in early August 1990. Diplomacy formed the first line of attack in the effort to secure the liberation of Kuwait but the possibility that force might one day have to be used to eject the invaders was apparent from the very start and was certainly not ignored. Nor, for that matter, was the possibility that the territorial designs of Iraq and Saddam Hussein might not end with Kuwait. In fact, it was the fear that Saudi Arabia might also be attacked that prompted such a vigorous response from the various members of the US-led Allied coalition.

In the case of the USA, operation *Desert Shield* was launched within hours of the invasion, so as to ensure that Saudi Arabia would not also fall victim to further Iraqi aggression. Tactical Air Command (TAC) assets such as McDonnell Douglas F-15 Eagle fighters of the 1st Tactical Fighter Wing at Langley AFB, Virginia provided by far the most visible evidence of US reinforcement of the Gulf region in the immediate aftermath of the Iraqi invasion. Other forces didn't lag far behind, with Navy aircraft carriers setting course for Gulf waters even as US Army troops embarked on transport aircraft bound for the Middle East.

Apart from its tanker fleet, which was in the very thick of things from the outset, SAC resources were by no means as prominent – but nor were they omitted. Political considerations were almost certainly a factor in the somewhat lower profile taken by SAC when it came to assigning bombers to the theatre as part of *Desert Shield*. That's quite understandable, for there's

no doubt that the appearance of 20 or so B-52s at a Saudi Arabian air base could well have been interpreted by Iraq as an unwelcome upping of the ante and it might well have prompted a sudden and drastic escalation. Nevertheless, deployment of B-52s was not long delayed. However, these *Desert Shield* reinforcements were actually sited quite a long way from the main area of interest, ending up at Diego Garcia in the Indian Ocean.

This base was sufficiently far from the scene to not precipitate hasty action on the part of Hussein and yet sufficiently close to allow the Stratofortresses to intervene effectively with conventional munitions in the event of Iraq instigating further military action before enough Allied reinforcements had arrived to negate that possibility. Sticking the 'Buff' force on Diego Garcia placed the bombers far enough away to be out of sight, if not exactly out of mind.

That was clearly politically desirable, especially for the government of Saudi Arabia. Unfortunately, in the early stages of the crisis at least, the down-side of that argument had regrettable consequences for the bomber crews, since it could well have seriously affected their ability to perform the missions allocated to them. This had its origins in a lack of training opportunities, for Saudi Arabia initially refused to allow SAC bomber crews to use its airspace. Eventually, the Saudis relaxed their previously hard-line attitude and the B-52 crews wasted no time in familiarising themselves with the different demands of night low-level sorties over desert terrain. This was undoubtedly of great value when the time eventually arrived to go to war in mid-January of 1991.

That likelihood may well have seemed remote when movement of a force of B-52Gs to Diego Garcia began on around 8 August. The initial cadre evidently numbered about 20 aircraft and these were all in place by 16 August, at which time they had been loaded with an assortment of conventional munitions and placed on alert status, ready to launch in the event of further acts of aggression. At this time, it should be recalled that a gradual phase-out had begun of the B-52G model in May 1989, with about 20 redundant bombers having already been despatched to the storage facility at Davis-Monthan AFB, Arizona when the Iraqi forces crossed into Kuwait.

In fact, this process didn't come to a halt with the crisis in the Middle East, for at least a dozen more examples were retired between August and the outbreak of hostilities in January 1991. Fortunately for all concerned, that didn't materially affect the outcome, since there were still plenty of B-52Gs around and the force which assembled at Diego Garcia was actually made up of aircraft from several US-based units. Most came from the conventionally-tasked outfits, specifically the 42nd Bomb Wing at Loring and one squadron (the 62nd BS) of the 2nd Bomb Wing at Barksdale, but some were also obtained from the 93rd Bomb Wing at Castle and the 416th Bomb Wing at Griffiss.

Once in place at Diego Garcia, these aircraft were assigned to the 4300th Bomb Wing (Provisional), a hastily formed organisation that also controlled the activities of a number of KC-135 Stratotankers and KC-10 Extenders which operated from this island base. Subsequently, when the prospect of war became imminent, another temporary bomber unit was created at Jeddah's King Abdul Aziz International Airport in Saudi Arabia.

Given the designation 1708th Bomb Wing (Provisional), this was positioned about as near to the front line as it was possible to be and missions from Jeddah were of relatively short duration. In fact, the Jeddah-based organisation was established in the week immediately before the outbreak of war and provides perhaps the clearest evidence of just how far the Saudi attitude had changed since August 1990. Within hours of the war starting, a fleet of 20 B-52Gs obtained from units at Barksdale, Castle, Griffiss, Loring and Wurtsmith had been committed to combat from Jeddah and this number may well have risen to as many as 30 with effect from day two of the conflict.

Two other temporary units were also formed with B-52s. Like the 4300th, these were both situated at a considerable distance from the seat of the action, with missions routinely lasting more than 12 hours from take-off to touch-down. The first of them was located at Moron, Spain and appears to have been involved in combat virtually from the outset, with command of the 801st Bomb Wing (Provisional) being given to Colonel Ronald Marcotte. Personnel resources were mainly obtained from Barksdale, unlike the 16 or so bombers on charge which were apparently drawn from a variety of B-52G units.

The final temporary bomber unit also proved to be

RIGHT A 'Sonic Blast' for Iraq is positioned with the assistance of a hydraulic loader prior to being attached to the weapons rack beneath a Fairford-based B-52G in February 1991. As far as is known, the 806th Bomb Wing (Provisional) only used M117 bombs, unlike other bases which also expended cluster bomb units and Mk 83 thousand-pounders *(API/J Flack)*

the smallest and shortest-lived, making its debut quite some time after diplomacy had been replaced by force of arms in the effort to free Kuwait. Set up at RAF Fairford, England in early February 1991, this was the 806th Bomb Wing (Provisional) and it drew upon Eaker's 97th Bomb Wing for its core of personnel as well as its commanding officer, Col George I Conlan. In the event, the 806th existed for almost exactly a month. During that interval, it completed a number of combat missions and there's no doubt that it made a worthwhile contribution even though the number of aircraft on strength at Fairford never exceeded eight. It is perhaps also ironic to note that none of the 10 aircraft that were observed here during the period in question actually came from the 97th Bomb Wing. Most were drawn from the units at Griffiss and Wurtsmith, but single examples from Barksdale and Castle were also seen.

There appears to be an element of doubt as to exactly how many B-52Gs were committed to combat action during the course of *Desert Storm*. Some sources talk of 74, while others refer to a figure of 86. The truth probably lies somewhere between the two extremes, but what cannot be doubted is that the Stratofortress was worked pretty hard during the conflict and that it was responsible for delivering almost a third of the

BELOW In addition to a dozen weapons on each external rack, the 'Buffs' based at Fairford could also accommodate a total of 27 750 lb bombs internally. Here, groundcrew members go about the laborious task of fitting those weapons in place *(API/J Flack)*

total tonnage of bombs dropped by US aircraft in six weeks of war.

For a long time it was thought that the B-52 force employed only gravity munitions in *Desert Storm* operations and it wasn't until a year afterwards that the USA revealed the part played by the 'Buff' in the opening night's activities. World headlines at the time were understandably dominated by images coming from Iraq and Saudi Arabia and concentrated on far more exciting warplanes such as the F-117 'stealth fighter' and Tornado fighter-bomber.

As a consequence, nobody appears to have paid too much attention to the role of the B-52, which evidently went about its business with little or no fuss. The fact that most of the heavy bombers were operating from bases that were situated at a considerable distance from their targets was obviously a major factor in minimising the amount of publicity but the type of ordnance employed was probably also influential. After all, the B-52 force was predominantly operating with 'dumb' bombs' and was therefore less well equipped to match some of the spectacularly telegenic imagery associated with 'smart' weapons' such as those used by the F-117. In some ways, though, that may have been to the advantage of the bomber crews, for it allowed them to concentrate on the task on hand.

Even though it may not have gained too much credit at the time, there's absolutely no doubt at all that the B-52 did complete its fair share of spectacular missions in the short conflict. Few were more spectacular than the 35-hour epic undertaken by elements of the 2nd Bomb Wing from Barksdale AFB, although a full year was to elapse before this operation received any publicity.

The 'Buff' had demonstrated the potential of its global reach on numerous occasions, especially during the early part of its service career, when it made several record-breaking flights. However, it had never actually been utilised for a 'round-robin' combat operation from the continental USA, something that was to change dramatically on day one of *Desert Storm* when seven aircraft flew all the way from Barksdale to Saudi Arabia and back again to complete the longest successful combat mission ever carried out by any air arm. The objective of this marathon 14,000-mile round trip was the desire to engage a number of key target complexes deep inside Iraq with a weapon that was to remain on the secret list for another 12 months. It was, in almost every way, a stunningly successful mission and a remarkable demonstration of the Cruise Missile's capabilities.

The missile used was actually a conventional warfare version of the nuclear-tipped AGM-86B. Given the designation AGM-86C and initially known as *Senior Surprise*, it had been in the inventory for about two years at the time of the Iraqi invasion and was developed to provide a conventional stand-off capability. In fact, the driving force behind development of this version of the Cruise Missile was the US experience in operation *Eldorado Canyon*, when Navy and Air Force warplanes bombed several targets in Libya. That complex April 1986 mission was successful, in as much as it put a stop to Libyan terrorism, but it was not accomplished without cost, since an F-111 was lost with its crew. In addition, planning, co-ordinating and executing the attacks proved particularly time consuming and the end results did not offer quite the precise degree of accuracy required.

Senior personnel in the Pentagon then began casting around for other options whereby they could instigate so called 'surgical strikes'. It soon became apparent that the cruise missile offered the best chance of satisfying accuracy criteria. Additionally, as far as speed of response was concerned, only the Air Force was in a position to offer the potential to strike virtually anywhere in the world with little more than 24 hours notice to execute an attack.

So it was that the AGM-86B was selected to be modified from a nuclear weapon to a conventional one. Boeing engineers were responsible for this task, the process of reconfiguration involving removal of the W80 warhead and its replacement with a 1000-lb blast fragmentation device that apparently offered an explosive effect comparable to a 2000-lb 'iron' bomb. At the same time, the original TERCOM (Terrain Contour Matching) guidance system was also deleted, with Global Positioning System satellite receiver equipment being installed in its place.

Trials with the resulting Conventional Air Launched Cruise Missile (CALCM) got under way in the summer of 1987 and an operational capability was attained about a year later with the 2nd Bomb Wing at Barksdale. Somewhere in the region of 40 weapons were adapted to form a stockpile, although the existence of the AGM-86C variant of this weapon continued to remain a closely guarded secret.

In the summer of 1990, though, it began to appear as if this weapon's moment was at last at hand. Almost as soon as the scale of the invasion of Kuwait became known, a number of Barksdale based B-52Gs were placed on alert with the AGM-86C. At the same time, the national command authorities were informed that some SAC bombers possessed the capability to strike at high-value targets inside Iraq. That was true, although in the immediate aftermath of the Iraqi incursion, it was perhaps a slight exaggeration, since only one crew had any experience of actually using the weapon – and even that crew could have been excused for being 'rusty', since it had been involved with the trials project some three years earlier.

Within a very short space of time, however, an intense training effort resulted in remaining members of the 596th Bomb Squadron getting to grips with the intricacies of *Senior Surprise* or *Secret Squirrel* as it became informally known so as not to betray the project's real code name. In the event, these crews were soon committed to the alert operation, although after about a week or so the urgency of the situation lessened as the risk of Iraqi forces moving on into Saudi Arabia diminished.

For the personnel of the 596th BS, that eased the pressure slightly, but it should be recalled that this outfit was also required to undertake nuclear alert duty, while remaining ready to perform a conventional strike with the CALCM if the national command authorities deemed it necessary. Latterly, as the time for the deadline's expiry drew ever nearer, personnel resources became even more scarce as crews were detached to join the bomber task forces being established at selected overseas locations.

Against that background, planning for the initial stages of what became *Desert Storm* was pressing ahead, even though there was as yet no guarantee that force of arms would become necessary. As we now know, Hussein pushed the UN coalition up to and beyond the point of no return, with the first offensive strikes against targets in Iraq taking place in the early morning of 17 January 1991, little more than 24 hours after the expiry of the deadline. The CALCM-armed bombers from Barksdale didn't figure in the first waves, but those whose job it was to prepare for the aerial campaign were determined to sustain the pressure on Iraq for as long as possible during the opening phase.

In this regard, it became evident that a lull in the attack intensity might well occur in about mid-morning. It was to deny this respite that seven B-52Gs

(colourfully known as 'Doom' flight) set off from Barksdale at about first light on 16 February. Between them, the B-52Gs were armed with 39 CALCMs. In addition to the normal crew of six, each B-52G carried an extra pilot and radar navigator so as to allow other crew members the chance to take a rest during what was always going to be a long mission. Finally, determined not to be left behind when his troops went about their business, the 596th Bomb Squadron's commanding officer, Lt Col Jay Beard, was on board the lead aircraft ('Doom 31').

Departure from Barksdale took place at about 4 pm in the afternoon, Baghdad-time, and there was still about eight or nine hours to go before the first Saudi-based warplanes would take-off and turn north towards their targets in Iraq. By then, the gaggle of bombers would be well into their mission and have completed the first of four in-flight refuellings.

They would also be nearing Mediterranean waters and a second refuelling with KC-10s from Moron, but mission timing was such that the bombers would not pass Libya until after the first wave of F-117s had struck Baghdad. This was to eliminate any possibility of the imminent breaking of *Desert Storm* leaking out before the first bombs started dropping.

Although all seven aircraft had made it this far, not

ABOVE By the time of the Gulf War, many SAC aircraft displayed imposing nose art. B-52G 58-0195 *Eternal Guardian* of the Loring-based 42nd Bomb Wing was typical, and also carries the unit badge as well as a fairly imposing tally of mission symbols. Despite sterling service in the liberation of Kuwait, the B-52G was soon retired, a victim of post-Cold War defence cuts

everything had gone smoothly, for at least one member of the formation ('Doom 34') had experienced a spot of bother on departure from the Louisiana base. Faced with fluctuating oil pressure on one engine, aircraft commander Capt Bernie Morgan opted to conform to the very finest 'press on' traditions of SAC, by shutting down the troublesome J57 and keeping quiet until such time as he and his crew passed the point of no return. While the loss of an engine was not exactly desirable, it had already been established that the B-52G would be perfectly able to carry out the mission with just six engines – on that basis, Morgan quite clearly still had something in reserve.

Transit of the Mediterranean was accomplished without lights and in strict radio silence and the bombers then continued across the Red Sea and on towards the designated missile launch area which was in western Saudi Arabia approximately 100 miles south of the border with Iraq. At this time, other problems began to become apparent in that four of the CALCMs weren't fully functional. Since the 'rules of engagement' for this mission forbade the launch of any weapon that wasn't working entirely as advertised, it was evident that the defective quartet could not be fired. Fortunately, the other 35 were in much better shape and all of these missiles were duly despatched on their respective routings during a fairly hectic 10-minute interval.

Few details have emerged as to the precise location of the targets that were struck by the CALCMs, but it is known that there were eight. Most were situated in central and southern Iraq and they included a power station at Mosul; a telephone exchange in Basra; and other electrical generating facilities. Routes taken by the CALCMs were planned to allow all the missiles to reach their disparate targets virtually simultaneously. So, some proceeded more or less directly to their objectives, while others flew much more devious tracks.

Subsequent post-strike reconnaissance revealed that this mission surpassed expectations in terms of achievement, with all but two of the 35 missiles evidently reaching their appointed targets. As far as the

failures were concerned, one fell to earth in the launch area, where it was later found and destroyed. The fate of the other was never determined but it may have been a victim of the Iraqi defences. In terms of accuracy, quite a number of missiles scored direct hits on their targets and one actually snapped its telephone pole aiming-point in half.

Matters such as mission analysis were probably far from the minds of the crewmen aboard 'Doom' Flight in the immediate aftermath of missile launch. The objective may have been achieved, but there was still a heck of a long way to go before the end of the mission. It was now, after close to 15 hours aloft, that things started to turn nastier, with the weather being particularly uncooperative when the time came for the first of two scheduled post-attack aerial refuellings.

For a while, visibility dropped below the normally permitted minima and it was touch and go as to whether the bombers would get their fuel before

BELOW Another B-52G of the 42nd Bomb Wing stands with its radome hinged upwards and its antenna and LV6 sensors exposed as it receives attention from technicians. Once again, mission markings and nose art are much in evidence

reaching 'bingo' state and being forced to land at a diversionary field in Spain. Eventually, with just 30 minutes fuel remaining, things picked up a bit and the B-52s managed to get their fuel. By this time, though, two of the formation were flying with engines shut down and two others were monitoring their instruments very carefully indeed, since oil pressure readings were giving rise for concern.

Matters weren't helped by the fact that four aircraft had 'hung' missiles which increased drag and fuel burn. In time, as the force continued westwards, what was expected to be a routine Atlantic crossing turned into something that was more akin to an endurance test as the weather again showed its nastier side. This mainly manifested itself in the form of stronger than anticipated headwinds, which hovered around 130-140 kts as opposed to the 90 kts 'worst-case' situation that was allowed for when planning the mission. Efforts to escape the wind proved unavailing and matters certainly weren't helped by the news that severe weather had prevented the KC-135 tankers at Lajes from getting airborne for the fourth and last refuelling rendezvous.

Word was passed to the tanker cell at Moron and some KC-10s were very quickly sent to provide assistance. Even then, the amount of fuel transferred wasn't sufficient to see the bombers safely home again, although it certainly put them well on the way. However, having come so far, Lt Col Beard was even more determined than ever to get back to Barksdale, if only to avoid the potential embarrassment of pitching up unannounced at an air base on the eastern seaboard with a bunch of aircraft carrying what at first glance looked like unused nuclear missiles.

It was already more than evident that the wind was showing little sign of relenting and it was equally apparent that more fuel would be essential if Beard was to get all of his bombers home in one piece. So, further communication ensued, with a view to setting up another tanker rendezvous. This time, Beard made contact with the Eighth Air Force command post and once again he was successful, with two 'strip alert' KC-135R Stratotankers of the 19th Air Refueling Wing being scrambled from Robins AFB, Georgia, to meet the returning bombers as they went 'feet dry' (ie crossed the coast).

Fate wasn't quite content to leave it there and had still one more jolt awaiting. This manifested itself in the form of a communications breakdown which pre-

vented one of the B-52s that was in dire need of fuel from establishing direct contact with a tanker. Luckily, a back-up communication system permitted Beard to talk to the respective pilots of the B-52 and KC-135 and by dint of relaying messages between the two he was able to make sure that all elements of his force got the fuel they needed to make it back to Barksdale, where they landed in near darkness almost exactly 35 hours after setting off.

By then, almost 24 hours had elapsed since the first bombs began detonating in Baghdad and it was fast becoming evident that Allied air power had achieved near total surprise and was well on the way to attaining total air supremacy. Iraq had already been on the receiving end of some quite shattering blows and many more lay in store.

The near-exhausted crews of 'Doom' Flight had been responsible for delivering some of those blows, although they could perhaps be excused for thinking it seemed like a remote way to make war, since they were denied the opportunity of seeing their weapons detonate. Other crews on other B-52Gs fought their war at much closer quarters and some of those aircraft were evidently committed to action in the very earliest stages of *Desert Storm*. However, instead of using stand-off weapons, they carried the fight right into Iraq, utilising conventional 'iron' bombs and cluster bomb units against a number of targets.

Barely an hour after the initial F-117 attacks on Baghdad, a dozen B-52Gs from Diego Garcia were cruising across Iraq as they neared their objectives. Several hours earlier, some 18 bombers and 13 supporting tankers had launched from the base in the Indian Ocean and set course for Iraq. Five of the B-52Gs were actually designated as 'spares' and these eventually broke away from the main formation so as to return to base with their munitions unused.

The rest bored on through the night, with the uneventful transit involving two air refuelling hook-ups from accompanying KC-10s at normal operating altitudes before the bombers dropped down to low level as they moved ever closer to the border with Iraq. Nearly 40 years after it first entered service and more than 30 years after the decision was taken to shift from high to low-level, the Stratofortress was on the brink of making its very first low-level combat mission. In the various cockpits of the bombers, pilot and co-pilot used night vision goggles and other high tech equipment to maintain a height that probably hovered

ABOVE Another view of B-52G 58-0182 *What's Up Doc* all bombed-up and ready to go visiting. The blended wing-fuselage fairing indicates that this was one of the 98 B-52Gs adapted to operate with the AGM-86B ALCM, and it also displays the badge of the 379th Bomb Wing, from which it came and to which it returned after the successful conclusion of operation *Desert Storm (API/J Flack)*

around the 300-ft mark. Behind and below them, the navigator and radar navigator would have been monitoring their instruments closely and paying particular attention to the radar altimeter which provided the most accurate indication of height above ground at any given moment.

Elsewhere, the electronic countermeasures officer and the gunner would be alert for any indication of hostile action as they closed on the target for tonight. Tonight, perhaps surprisingly, all seemed quiet as the bomber formation separated to allow each distinct section to head for a target.

There were in fact five objectives, consisting of four major air bases and a highway strip. Ordnance to be expended was a mixture of 1000-lb iron bombs and CBU-89/B sub-munitions dispensers, with the latter containing 72 BLU-91 anti-personnel and 24 BLU-92 anti-armour mines. Aircraft involved in these attacks carried one or other of these weapons but not both, although it appears that both types were almost certainly used against each target. As far as specific objectives were concerned, the bombs were principally intended to inflict heavy damage on the paved surfaces that linked hardened aircraft shelter complexes to runways, while the sub-munitions were scattered haphazardly to disrupt the work of repair teams by denying access for a certain period of time.

In conjunction with other attacks on the air base network, such as those made by British Tornados, it was hoped to prevent the Iraqi Air Force (IAF) from

getting airborne in anything like the strength it possessed. This desire was in fact accomplished in handsome style and apart from a few ineffectual sorties in the first few days, the IAF played virtually no part in the conflict, other than to provide a number of fortunate Coalition fighter pilots with opportunities for target practice.

On day one of the war, sweeping in at low level during the final stages of the approach to the target, the bomber crews actually had to climb slightly before ordnance release. This was done to allow the heavier weapons time to nose over and penetrate the surface before detonating, rather than have them strike tangentially and perhaps richochet harmlessly into the desert. Popping up in this fashion increased the risk of taking hits from anti-aircraft artillery fire but good co-ordination and the use of different approach and egress paths allowed all of the B-52s involved in the opening night to return home safely.

Similar fortune also attended the force when it returned at low level on the next two nights but despite often intense gunfire, there were few instances of dam-

ABOVE Badges of the 806th Bomb Wing (Provisional) adorn this study of a Fairford-based 'Buff' spewing out the traditional cloud of smoke as it struggles to gain altitude after yet another heavyweight take-off bound for the distant Gulf. Oddly, it appears that engine numbers three, four, seven and eight are doing most of the work, although it's possible they were just heavy smokers!

age and no losses were sustained. Not everyone made it through unscathed, of course, and there were occasions when elements of the bomber force had to endure some moments of anxiety.

For the most part, though, such moments were few and far between, although one B-52G had to be nursed home with care after being hit by an unknown type of missile which caused damage to the tail section. Another lost a couple of engines as a result of a near miss by an SA-3 missile which also rendered the port outrigger inoperative and removed several ECM antennae, while still another received shrapnel damage from a near miss by heavy calibre AAA.

Those episodes were obviously unwelcome, but could be ascribed to being part and parcel of the fortunes of war. Much more embarrassing was the 'blue-on-blue' (friendly fire) incident in which a B-52G operating in the area of Baghdad was struck by a US missile. Disaster was averted, but it could so very easily have ended with tragic consequences.

In this particular encounter, the B-52G took a direct hit from an AGM-88A HARM (High-Speed Anti-Radiation Missile) fired by another US aircraft that was providing defence suppression support for the bomber force. It appears that the missile was aimed at a ground-based radar that was tracking the B-52s, but that it subsequently broke lock, went 'ballistic' and then found a fresh radar emission to home on. Unfortunately, the source of that emission was the tail-mounted, gun-laying radar of the B-52G and the HARM continued to home unerringly on the allied bomber. It eventually impacted upon the starboard tailplane, promptly obliterating the tail turret and also removing a sizeable chunk of the Buff's aft fuselage section. Luckily for the crew, who had received no warning of the impending missile strike and who had no real idea of just what it was that had hit them, the aircraft remained flyable and pilot Capt Linwood Mason was able to land safely at Jeddah.

After the first three days, when the dual threats of the IAF and surface-to-air missiles had been all but eliminated, the B-52 force only ever operated from altitudes that put them well above the reach of small calibre weapons. Typically flying at around 35,000 ft in cells of three aircraft, the B-52s were now mostly used as a form of airborne artillery, undertaking BAI (battlefield air interdiction) missions against concentrations of Iraqi troops, guns and armour in the desert. This fundamentally involved the use of irresistible force rather than finesse, but there's little doubt that it was awesomely effective – and Iraqi prisoners-of-war repeatedly testified to the demoralising effect of being exposed to unexpected bombing attacks.

While they may not have been able to attain levels of accuracy achieved by precision munitions, that was more than compensated for by sheer firepower, for it should be recalled that a cell of three B-52s could deposit no fewer than 153 bombs in a fairly confined target box within seconds. This kind of 'carpet-bombing' was perfectly suited to the destruction of large area targets and there were certainly plenty of those available for the B-52s.

As mentioned a few moments ago, Iraqi ground forces were frequently on the receiving end, but they were by no means the only targets. For instance, in the early stages, three B-52 cells were employed to conduct simultaneous CBU attacks on three major Iraqi radar facilities near Baghdad. It may have lacked the style of the 'Wild Weasel' and the near surgical precision of an anti-radar missile but dumping the best part of 90,000 bomblets across the respective sites was no less effective and certainly succeeded in silencing each facility.

Later, half-a-dozen aircraft teamed up to deposit almost 100 tons of iron bombs on an ammunition factory, initiating secondary explosions that apparently left it completely flattened and quite unable to contribute further to the Iraqi war machine. However, the most sustained effort and arguably the greatest success was achieved in missions against the Iraqi Army, with repeated B-52 attacks having a devastating impact on the effectiveness of this force. Ordnance employed in these strikes varied according to target, but included bombs and cluster bomb units.

The principal 'iron' bomb used against the targets alluded to above as well as armour and artillery was the Korean War vintage M117. Described as a 750-lb weapon, once the fins and fusing device were attached, it actually weighed about 820 lb in the most commonly used configuration. Since the B-52G was physically only capable of carrying a maximum of 51 bombs of this type (and some could only take 45), it follows that payload varied from 37,000 lb to approximately 41,800 lb.

In the case of those aircraft that were configured for the maximum number of bombs, the internal weapons bay accommodated 27, with 12 more carried on each of the underwing racks. B-52Gs that could only take 45 bombs also housed 27 internally, but were fitted with Heavy Stores Adapter Beams (HSABs) that were limited to nine, for a total of 18 externally. Mk 82 500lb bombs were also extensively utilised in the BAI role against the so-called 'hard' targets such as tanks and armoured personnel carriers.

In addition, at least three types of cluster bomb unit were expended. Tanks, APCs and artillery pieces again provided many targets, with the CBU-87 being the preferred option, since its sub-munitions were particularly nasty, being perfectly capable of penetrating armour. The same type of CBU was also utilised in the

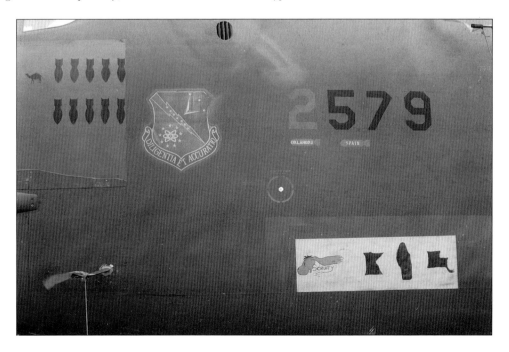

RIGHT Artwork on the forward fuselage of B-52G 59-2579 at Fairford just after the conclusion of *Desert Storm*. Aircraft ownership is confirmed by the presence of a low-visibility 379th Bomb Wing badge, and the ten bomb mission symbols seem to confirm that this 'Buff' completed its fair share of raids. However, the significance of the camel motif is less apparent *(API/J Flack)*

'Great Iraqi Scud Hunt' in which B-52s teamed up with F-15E Strike Eagles to locate and destroy the elusive missile launchers before they could wreak further havoc. For strikes on what were euphemistically known as 'soft' targets - ie, troop concentrations, POL (petrol, oil, lubricant) storage centres and vehicles other than tanks and armoured personnel carriers – the CBU-52 and CBU-58 came into their own and contributed greatly to rendering a significant proportion of the Iraqi Army virtually non-effective as a fighting force.

Perhaps the easiest way to sum up the contribution made by the B-52 to *Desert Storm* is to quote some statistics. 'Buffs' operating from all locations evidently completed approximately 1620 sorties; released just over 72,012 weapons and delivered about 25,700 tons of ordnance. That equates to almost a third of the entire tonnage of bombs dropped by US aircraft. That's a fairly remarkable achievement by itself, but it perhaps comes into sharper focus when one realises that the number of B-52s committed to action actually accounted for less than ten per cent of the number of combat aircraft deployed by the USA.

As far as individual contributions are concerned, the Jeddah-based bombers understandably claimed top honours, delivering just over half the bombs dropped by B-52s in the process of completing 846 sorties. The great productivity of the 1708th BW(P) obviously had a lot to do with its proximity to the battlefield, for this meant that missions were relatively short and that aircraft could often log two sorties per day. That was clearly not possible from Diego Garcia, Moron and Fairford, since missions staged from these locations routinely exceeded 12 hours in duration. But, they certainly weighed in with varying contributions to the grand total.

As for the achievements of individual aircraft, several are known to have completed more than 40 sorties, but the most prolific 'Buff' of all may well have been 58-0203 from the 93rd Bomb Wing. This was attached to the 1708th BW(P) at Jeddah and it is understood to have finished the war with no fewer than 57 mission symbols adorning the forward fuselage section. Assuming that it was configured to tote a full complement of 51 bombs and that all of these missions were successfully completed, this one aircraft could conceivably have delivered 2907 bombs by itself, which equates to more than 1000 tons of ordnance.

As already noted, no examples of the B-52 fell foul of enemy action. Tragically, though, the B-52 fleet did not escape entirely unscathed, with one example (59-2593 of the 42nd BW) being lost on 3 February when it was forced to ditch in the Indian Ocean after experiencing a catastrophic electrical system failure while returning to Diego Garcia.

Ironically, having survived the hazards of a successful mission, the aircraft went down virtually within sight of home base. By a stroke of good fortune, three members of the crew of six were recovered alive, along with the body of a fourth, but no trace was found of the remaining two.

LEFT *What's Up Doc* again, but this time in close-up, showing artwork detail as well as the badge of the parent 379th Bomb Wing at Wurtsmith AFB, Michigan. Interestingly, this aircraft features a different method of presentation of bomb mission symbols *(API/J Flack)*

ABOVE Pictured on the storage line at Davis-Monthan AFB in November 1969, the sole NB-52A (52-0003) had only recently been retired. The special pylon attachment used to carry the X-15 is still present beneath the wing (*L Peacock*)

RIGHT NB-52B 52-0008 prepares to make yet another drop from high altitude in the vicinity of Edwards AFB. At this time, it still carried the badge of the Air Force Flight Test Center (*USAF*)

RIGHT In immaculate condition and fresh from the paint shop in a shiny new coat of Vietnam-era battledress, B-52D 56-0684 was one of the first 'Buffs' to wear this scheme. Having survived numerous Vietnam tours, and a further decade of peacetime flying, this jet was finally retired to Davis-Monthan in May 1983 (*Boeing*)

LEFT Most of the early Stratofortresses that found their way to Davis-Monthan featured the original natural metal finish of the 1950s and early 1960s, as seen here on B-52E 57-0028, which was retired in 1967 when its fatigue life ran out *(L Peacock)*

LEFT Although the B-52Bs were retired in 1965-66, large-scale withdrawal didn't really get under way until 1969 when many B-52E and B-52F models were retired from use. B-52F 57-0053 was typical of these aircraft *(L Peacock)*

BELOW The massive flap area of the 'Buff' is readily apparent in this view of a B-52G soon after lift-off *(L Peacock)*

ABOVE B-52G 59-2584 is caught with everything down and out on final approach. The scheme of this EVS-fitted 'Buff' is typical of that which was worn throughout the 1970s and on into the next decade. Eventually, however, wrap-around camouflage was universally applied. This jet is currently preserved at Snohomish, Washington state – a further six G-models have been put on display across the USA *(via USAF)*

BELOW B-52H 61-0026 is the most recent example of the 'Buff' to crash, being destroyed in a tragic accident while rehearsing for a farewell airshow for the 92nd Bomb WIng and the Stratofortress at Fairchild in June 1994. It is seen here in happier days when with the 319th Bomb Wing at Grand Forks AFB, North Dakota, at the start of the 1980s *(L Peacock)*

LEFT The 'triangle-K' device on the fin of B-52G 58-0189 confirms that it was assigned to the 379th Bomb Wing when it visited RAF Marham in England to take part in an RAF bombing competition. Later, 'Buffs' of the 379th adopted a 'low-viz' version of this distinctive marking *(L Peacock)*

LEFT B-52G 59-2596 of the 2nd Bomb Wing at Barksdale AFB, Louisiana, was one of a small number of aircraft that deployed to RAF Brize Norton, England, for a NATO exercise in September 1983 *(L Peacock)*

LEFT Responsibility for training bomber crews to fly and service the Stratofortress was entrusted to the 93rd Bomb Wing at Castle AFB for many years. Here, B-52G 57-6486 returns to the roost at the end of a training mission in 1984. This jet was retired to Davis-Monthan in September 1991

ABOVE Pictured far above the mountainous terrain of the eastern Sierras in May 1984, B-52G 58-0190 of the 93rd BW replenishes its fuel stocks from a KC-135. This particular 'Buff' was destroyed by fire during depot-level maintenance at Kelly AFB, Texas, on 20 July 1989 – it was assigned to the 2nd BW at the time

RIGHT Although any one of the main undercarriage units can be lowered individually, it is rare for this to be caught on film. 93rd BW B-52G (58-0206) was photographed with the port forward unit deployed while 'circuit-bashing' at Castle AFB in October 1984 (L Peacock)

LEFT With its underwing weapons racks fully laden, B-52G 58-0182 strikes a menacing pose at Fairford when operating with the 806th Bomb Wing (Provisional) in the closing stages of the war against Iraq (API/J Flack)

BELOW LEFT A clutch of fully assembled M117 750 lb bombs is visible in the right foreground of this study of 2nd Bomb Wing B-52G 58-0245 at Fairford. All that appears to be required is the muscle-power to suspend them from the racks and Equipoise II will be ready again to face the long haul across the Mediterranean to the distant Gulf region (API/J Flack)

BELOW Endearing and insulting inscriptions adorn the M117 bombs visible on the underwing stores station of B-52G 58-0182 What's Up Doc. All of the 'Buffs' that flew from Fairford were able to carry 12 bombs under each wing, plus 27 internally (API/J Flack)

BELOW Fairford's Gulf War aircraft resources came from several SAC units, although since most had special fin markings deleted for the duration it was necessary to get close to determine their origins. This 'Buff' was from the 93rd BW at Castle AFB (L Peacock)

ABOVE February 1995 saw a quartet of B-52Hs from the 2nd BW at Barksdale, Louisiana, deploy to RAF Fairford for NATO exercise *Strong Resolve 95*. Wearing the very latest ACC overall mid-grey scheme, plus 'LA' fin codes, the four jets were flown daily to the exercise area off the Norwegian coast by crews from the 20th BS. Three of the four 'Buffs' deployed lacked the M61 cannon fitment *(L Peacock)*

BELOW A total of 98 B-52Gs was adapted to serve as launch platforms for the Boeing AGM-86B Air-Launched Cruise Missile, all of which were given a blended wing root/fuselage fairing to allow identification by reconnaissance satellites. In this instance, no such aid to recognition is needed, for the aircraft is quite clearly carrying a clutch of ALCMs under each wing *(USAF)*

ABOVE Toting a full load of
ALCMs beneath each wing,
and plugged into the
boom, a B-52G takes on
more fuel from a KC-135
for its thirsty J57 turbojets
(USAF)

LEFT External pylons
permit up to 12 AGM-86B
missiles to be carried on
B-52 wing stations. Here,
munitions specialists
perform a loading drill
(USAF)

ABOVE An early production example of the B-52H during the course of trials with the ill-fated GAM-87 Skybolt air-launched ballistic missile system (USAF)

RIGHT Conventionally-tasked B-52Ds often visited Britain for NATO exercises. Here, 22nd BW B-52D 56-0617 whistles in to land at RAF Brize Norton in 1980. This jet was one of the last D-models retired to Davis-Monthan, arriving for storage in Arizona in September 1983 (L Peacock)

RIGHT Adorned with an assortment of non-standard markings, B-52H 60-0057 of the 410th BW was one of several 'Buffs' that took part in the 1981 RAF bombing competition (L Peacock)

ABOVE Illustrated on the previous page, B-52H 60-0057 had moved on to the 28th BW by September 1983, when it was photographed after an air-to-air refuelling somewhere over Utah *(L Peacock)*

RIGHT The many bumps, blisters and bulges associated with the electro-optical viewing system and enhanced avionics suite are shown to advantage in this close up of the nose section of 7th BW B-52H 60-0016 at Carswell in 1991. It is also noteworthy in having overall camouflage *(Robert F Dorr)*

LEFT The lull after the storm! B-52G 58-0168 of the 379th BW leaves Fairford in early March 1991 after the Gulf War ceasefire came into effect. Weapons racks are still in place, but now they are empty *(L Peacock)*

RIGHT Turbofan engines provide the only visual clue that the 'Buff' hanging on the boom is a B-52H. Today, this is the only model still in USAF service, equipping Bomb Wings at Barksdale and Minot

BELOW The 1981 RAF bombing competition brought five distinctively marked 'Buffs' to Marham, England. All were B-52Hs, comprising 60-0057 (410th BW), 60-0026 (319th BW), 61-0028 (410th BW), 60-0046 (5th BW) and 61-0022 (319th BW) from front to rear, As mentioned earlier, 60-0026 was written-off in 1994 whilst serving with the 92nd BW (L Peacock)

RIGHT Recalling the days when the 'Buff' was adorned in colourful unit insignia, this shot shows the 93rd Bomb Wing badge as applied to B-52F 57-0039 in March 1967 (via L Peacock)

BELOW Close-up detail of the *Looney Toons*-inspired fin marking carried by 60-0046 and 60-00026 of the 319th BW at Marham, England, in July 1981 (L Peacock)

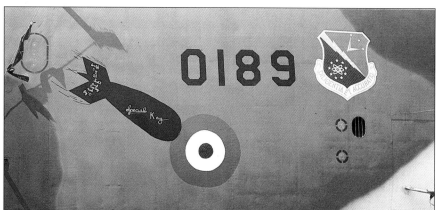

ABOVE The intent to beat the RAF is confirmed by nose artwork applied to 379th BW B-52G 58-0189 in July 1980 (L Peacock)

LEFT An outline map of Michigan was combined with a rainbow motif to form a colourful nose marking on 410th BW B-52H 60-0057 in July 1981 (L Peacock)

LEFT SAC's shield was often displayed to port on B-52s in the early 1960s, as on 60-0008 of the 19th BW. It was commonplace, but not inevitable, for the Wing badge to appear in a similar location on the starboard side *(via L Peacock)*

BELOW Now preserved at the USAF Academy in Colorado Springs, the nose of B-52D 55-0083 displays an impressive mission tally that brings to mind its past exploits

No fewer than 478 examples of the Stratofortress were sent for storage at Davis-Monthan AFB, Arizona, between May 1965, when the first B-52B flew in, and May 1994, when the last B-52G reached the Aircraft Maintenance and Regeneration Center. This small collection of photographs gives an idea of the imposing spectacle of the mass of redundant bombers on the storage lines, and also portrays the fate that awaits them, since the chances are that most will be broken up in due course. In time, it is likely that the majority of the B-52Hs will also arrive for scrapping, but for now the 'Cadillac' still has a mission to fulfil, and may go on to celebrate the 'Buff's' half-century of service with the USAF *(all photos by Mark Wagner)*

LEFT The familiar, but spartan, cockpit of the B-52 has been 'home' to generations of pilots and co-pilots of the Strategic Air Command and Air Combat Command since the 'Buff' entered service way back in 1955 *(USAF)*

BELOW Sunset for this particular aircraft, but not, it seems, for the 'Buff' itself, since the B-52H is evidently due to remain in regular service for quite some time yet *(USAF)*

Low-level Mission

On 22-25 February 1991, one of the authors travelled to Carswell Air Force Base at Fort Worth, Texas, to fly a nine-hour, low-level simulated nuclear bombing mission in a B-52.

The flight will be made with a crew of the 9th Bombardment Squadron commanded by Lt Col Gerald J Venteicher. The squadron is one of the oldest in the US Air Force: its men flew the first long-range reconnaissance missions in Salmson 2A2 biplanes, the wind strumming the wires of their fabric-covered crates near Gondreville-sur-Moselle in 1918.

As for the squadron's parent 7th Bombardment Wing, its pilots fought in B-17E Flying Fortresses and LB-30 Liberators, engulfed amid Japanese Zeros, during the hopeless rout on Java in 1942, and later slogged through the China-Burma-Indian Theatre in B-24 Liberators. Today, we fly Boeing B-52H Stratofortress 60-0016, radio call sign 'Lazer 64', painted in today's *de rigeur* 36081 monochrome gray – sometimes called charcoal, a bit incorrectly and wearing gaudy nose art and the nickname *Junk Yard Dog*. Pilot of the bomber for the upcoming mission is Capt Pat Wathen.

Pat Wathen is 27. He looks younger. He looks very young, indeed, to be an aircraft commander and instructor in this hunk of metal overcast which weighs 505,000 lb (229,062 kg), which spreads its shroud-like drooping wings out to a span of 185 ft (56.39 m) and which could, on any day of the week, become the bearer of atomic Armageddon. Throughout much of the Cold War, SAC pilots were mostly in their forties and mostly lieutenant colonels. Today, they're *all* young, mostly captains, and one or two of them are the grandsons of that earlier breed.

When Wathen was introduced to the brooding, droop-winged 'Buff' in training, he was told the bomber's engines had as much power as four railroad freight locomotives. Beneath the rumpled skin of the B-52, they told Wathen, was enough electrical wire to light up a city the size of Colorado Springs, Colorado.

BELOW Once seen, never forgotten. In terms of visual and aural splendour, a heavyweight take-off by the B-52G was a shattering experience, and a stirring one, though it is doubtful if ecology freaks would agree. It could only be bettered by a MITO departure of a cell of two or three bombers

In building fuselage, wings, and empennage, they said to Wathen, they'd used enough metal to manufacture 10,000 tin cans. 'And that's exactly how this thing flies', a grizzled instructor told him. 'Like a bunch of railroad locomotives straining uphill while dragging all of that metal behind it'. Pilots seeking to praise an aircraft often point out that it's a 'stable platform'. The Stratofortress, they told Wathen, is as stable as an anvil.

None of the crew men aboard *Junk Yard Dog* was born when this B-52H made its first flight. None of the creased faces of the old SAC crowd are around any longer – retired, all of them, their spurs hung on the wall, the glory days with LeMay, the spot promotions, the *Chromedome* airborne nuclear alert missions, all part of a past which unfolded before Pat Wathen was a boy.

But today, too, will become the past. Sooner than any of us can guess. Our combat rehearsal takes place while the Soviet Union threatens the United States with nuclear annihilation, while B-52 bombers stand on 24-hour runway alert with atomic weapons in their bellies, while Carswell is one of the great bastions of the Strategic Air Command and SAC is the bulwark for the defense of the free world. The world is changing and there's no greater sense of it than the way

everyone's mind is focused, today, on a single subject. Today's date is five weeks into Operation *Desert Storm*.

GETTING THERE

You get to Carswell by arriving at Dallas-Fort Worth International Airport and piloting your rental car along Highway I-30, which cuts like a knife through the twin cities of this Texas metroplex. You drive bumper-to-bumper part of the way, through congested Dallas-Fort Worth. Here, thousands of military people, aerospace workers and journalists scour newspapers, stare down TV sets, and strive laboriously to pick up news from the Persian Gulf.

Dallas-Fort Worth is home to General Dynamics, which sees F-16 Fighting Falcon production as uncertain beyond 1994, and suffered cancellation of the US Navy A-12 Avenger medium attack aircraft. A headline in the 8 January 1991 Fort Worth *Star-Telegram* told of local reaction to the demise of the Avenger: 'A-12 Program Dies As Cheney's Ax Falls'. President Bush's defense secretary, Dick Cheney, is a 'hawk' in many respects, but here in Texas they see him as a ruthless, cost-slashing 'dove' who wants to cut the armed forces to the bone. 'We have finally have hit bottom now', Cheney said this week, speaking of the drawdowns, the cancellations, the unemployment lines. The men and women who work the wiring harnesses and drill presses, those ordinary mainstream Americans who create the forgings, castings, tubing, wiring, and other widgetry of aerospace, don't believe it. Nor do those at Carswell who work on, maintain, and support the B-52 Stratofortress.

BELOW The upper surface camouflage pattern is clearly visible in this view of a B-52 complete with EVS and Phase VI ECM fit, cruising at altitude somewhere above the USA. In later years, the traditional white anti-flash undersides so long associated with the 'Buff' were finally abandoned in favour of a far less attractive wrap-around camouflage scheme

The Dallas-Fort Worth metroplex is also headquarters for LTV, which has ended its quest for sales of its upgraded Vought YA-7F Corsair II, but hopes to build the Argentine-designed FMA IA-63 Pampa 2000 as the US Air Force and Navy JPATS (Joint Primary Aircraft Trainer System). Here, too, is Bell, whose V-22 Osprey tilt-rotor aircraft Cheney cancelled, but Congress is still pushing it. As the new decade of the 1990s unfolds, LTV will be re-named Vought, the decision on JPATS will still be pending after this selection of a primary trainer has consumed more time than World War II, and Cheney's decision on the V-22 will be reversed.

General Dynamics, LTV and Bell still receive defence dollars, but among the hardy, struggling Texans who labour on the production lines, the talk is of lay-offs, downsizing, unemployment compensation, and fears for loved ones pitted in battle against Iraq. In February 1991, it looks as if the war against Saddam Hussein may last several years. B-52 crews at Carswell expect to be pressed into the fight.

Near Carswell, B-52 pilot Pat Wathen, wife Paula, and two toddlers live in a straightforward wooden bungalow which would qualify for the slum section of a civilian community but is typical for underpaid Americans in uniform. 'In the military we all share one thing', observes squadron commander Venteicher. 'Money isn't our thing. None of us is very rich or very poor'. The house is pristine, the flag on display. Over lasagna and Diet Coke in the squeaky-clean social setting of Americans under arms in the 1990s – no alcohol, no obscene jokes, no risque flying songs – our banter is interrupted by the telephone. 'Jim just called', Pat Wathen tells everybody, referring to another B-52 pilot. 'He's got his TV on. The land war started an hour ago.'

The frustration seethes beneath the surface here, like those childhood monsters which lurk beneath the bed and come out only at night. Most who don't actually fly the Stratofortress – especially Paula, who is pregnant – are sick with worry. But in the 9th Bombardment Squadron, to a man, everyone wishes he was not here in the heart of Texas but over there, in the fight. Although it will go out of vogue in a Brave New World which lies just around the corner from 1991, a motto is posted on signs and bumper stickers all over Carswell – *The mission of the United States Air Force is to fly and fight, and don't you ever forget it*. Says Leslie Little, wife of B-52 navigator 1st Lt Jerry Little, 'I tried to

bribe a personnel officer to get Jerry sent'. Squadron commander Lt Col Venteicher is even more dispirited than Leslie: 'I've been doing this, flying B-52s, for 17 years and have never had a chance to make a real difference'. Incredible as it seems, here in this Texas doldrum – 18 years have passed since B-52s were over Hanoi.

So our evening at B-52H pilot Wathen's home is low-key, with more than a little unspoken anxiety. In the old Air Force we'd be drinking, smoking, swearing. Now Little utters, 'Doggone it!' There is talk of Maj Brian C 'Buck' Rogers, B-52H pilot, a friend and former member of the 9th Squadron, who is flying combat missions in the 'Buff' while we follow up dinner with Paula's strawberry dessert.

BOMBING MISSION

Inside the metal cocoon of the B-52H being brought to life for today's mission, the author will occupy the jump seat – it folds down, and in truth it's merely two-thirds of a seat, not enough to take the weight off the feet – on the port side immediately behind pilot Pat Wathen and co-pilot Capt Robert C Thomson. 'Jump' is the most uncomfortable slot aboard an unspeakably uncomfortable aircraft. The 'Buff' looks big on the outside but has no arm or leg room inside: cramped confines make it impossible ever to fully sit, stand, or lie, but always to be crouched bearing the weight of all the gear.

Dress for this occasion is flight coveralls, Nomex gloves (required during take-off and landing, because of fire risk), flight jacket, HGU-55P lightweight helmet, tinted helmet visor, intercom cord and oxygen mask. The author believed he was being issued a parachute. After scrutinising the label, he learned it was a 'Personnel Lowering Device', Model PCU-10P. It feels like a ton of bricks. Nine hours later, he'll feel like he's walked for nine hours bearing a back-pack filled with rocks. At the Green Oaks Inn across from the main gate, where each room comes with a poster calling the place a 'bird watcher's paradise' ('the F-16, F-111, KC-135, B-52. As long as we hear our planes overhead, we won't be hearing any enemy's'), they'll spend the next 24 hours chasing down liniment and ice bags for this aviation writer. Legs and knees will take weeks to mend.

In the air, an abrupt mishap can fling this Stratofortress down and smash everybody in it. Flying involves some danger. Flying at low-level involves more danger. Flying a low-level, terrain-hugging simulated combat mission gives the pilot and everyone on board the smallest amount of time – seconds, at most – for decision making in an emergency.

This is a matter of special interest to the sod in the jump seat. What if something goes wrong and this eight-engine monstrosity plummets the short distance of 800 ft (or 248 metres) which will separate it from the ground, perhaps in flames? It doesn't happen often. But you always brief for an emergency.

In an emergency, pilot and co-pilot eject upward, navigator and radar navigator can eject downward, and 'E-Dub' (the intercom call sign for EW, electronic warfare officer) and 'Guns' (the gunner) can eject upward or climb out. Pilot, CO, E-Dub and Guns all occupy Weber ejection seats 'designed a thousand years before today's (Douglas-licensed, Weber-built) ACES II', as one of them describes the seat – 'the old kind with gas-pressure cartridge and shotgun shell'. Because the EWO and gunner face backward, their seats are equipped with a 'hatch lifter' which transforms the hatch above them into a speed brake, and holds it out of the way as they depart.

As for the author – while the Stratofortress falls from the sky – he is briefed to disconnect oxygen and intercom, undo seat belt, take several steps to the rear, clasp the fire pole, climb down the ladder, crouch over the windblasted empty space left by 'Nav's' departed ejection seat, lean forward – and jump. They might as well tell you to bend over and kiss your ass goodbye.

At least, from the jump seat, you can see out. Nav, Radar, E-Dub and Guns have no windows. The electronic warfare officer and gunner are farthest back in the aircraft. For the gunner, it's a big improvement over all models up to the B-52G, where the gunner sat in the tail-gun position and was severely battered when the aircraft moved around in the sky. To get out in an emergency, the gunner was obliged to jettison the entire turret and make an unassisted bailout. The task became difficult if the jet assumed a nose-down attitude of ten degrees or more, and the B-52 had a tendency to pitch down when the turret was discarded.

In the B-52G, and in our B-52H, the gunner is much more comfortably situated in the forward compartment, away from the shake, rattle and roll of the tail compartment. It's a lot more comfortable to be up front and to have another crew member to draw moral support from.

Down below where the navigator and radar-navigator reside, their cramped dungeon is illuminated only by their instruments. Navigator Jerry Little insists that he likes no job better than being confined in this 'Black Hole of Calcutta'. One dare not make the metaphor that these crewmen inhabit the bowels of the ship, for aboard the B-52 there is no facility for, hence no need to discuss, bowels. To heist a question from James Michener's *The Bridges at Toko-ri*, 'Where do we get such men?'

PLANNING AHEAD

It's worth pointing out that the planning of mission 'Lazer 64', flown by the 9th Bomb Squadron, 7th Bomb Wing, began 24 hours before 'stepping' – slipping on flying gear, testing oxygen masks, and preparing to fly – and took a full working day to accomplish. A mission planning day starts with general information, followed by task assignments, target and route studies for each cell of aircraft, and spin-off briefings in which the crews coordinate their efforts. The final briefing is a walk-through by each crew member to ensure proper co-ordination. Areas covered include weather, routes, the target, training requirements to be covered for each crew member, noise complaints along the routes, and environmentally sensitive areas to be avoided.

Today, we'll simulate a long-range, low-level nuclear attack on a strategic target deep in the Soviet Union. Actually, we're going to bomb Melrose, New Mexico, not with B61 hydrogen bombs but with BDU-38 training shapes which replicate characteristics of the B61. The exact profile of the sortie is never fully shared by the crew, but it's a hi-medium-lo-lo bombing mission in which we'll launch, climb to altitude for a brief period perhaps reaching 33,000 ft (10,215 m), then we'll descend somewhat to hit the tanker, and then we'll ingress and egress the target at low altitude.

Most elements of our sortie will be identical to those of a conventional mission with iron bombs. But before we go up, refuel at medium altitude, then begin our hours-long treetop run-in on the target at low-level, we'll first depart Carswell as if caught up in the frenzied, hectic early moments of a fast-unfolding nuclear exchange with the Soviet Union.

We go aloft in a MITO (Minimum Interval Take-Off), accompanied by another Buff, 'Lazer 94' (B-52H 60-0018). The idea is simple. Buff crews know they can

breach Soviet air defences and rip out the heart of the world's other superpower. But it won't do a bit of good if they can't get off the ground in time to elude an incoming submarine-launched ballistic missile (SLBM) or intercontinental ballistic missile (ICBM). If we're lucky and the warning bells go off as planned, the Strategic Air Command may get as much as 15 minutes' notice that Soviet warheads are arriving. In real life, Buff crews expect 15 minutes. Hence, MITO. Wathen, 'You simply have to get the B-52 off the ground before your airfield is vaporised'.

Before we reached the bomber, the day began at 4:30 am when buses delivered crews to the flight line for the latest weather briefing and a check with maintenance control for the status of their aircraft. Once crew members reach the Stratofortress, the maintenance log is checked, each crew member completes his portion of the walk-around inspection, and the pre-flight check list is started.

Strapped in, cleared to go, pilot Wathen engages co-pilot Thomson in a verbal odyssey through cockpit checklists which is misleading, for in the earphones it is calm and businesslike. It's misleading because these men know the stakes. Their aircraft is worth something like $100 million and spreads across 185 ft (56.39 m). In a few moments they'll try to ease it out of its 'spot' (parking slot) able to see ahead but almost blind on both sides. Behind them, visibility from the 'Buff' is about the same as from a coffin.

In a C-5 Galaxy, you post a loadmaster to serve as scanner to clear you on the intercom, so you won't dig out the second floor of a building with your wingtip. In a B-52, the ability to scan is down close to zero, and the aircraft is moved in much the way you'd drive a car

ABOVE The aerial link-up between tanker and 'Buff' was one of the most ubiquitous events of Vietnam fighting and of the Cold War. This KC-135A has latched onto a B-52H in July 1979 during Exercise *Global Shield*, which was billed as the largest and most comprehensive SAC war game in more than two decades (*USAF*)

with no side windows and no rear-view mirrors. Wathen is also talking, via an umbilical, to an enlisted ground crew member. 'What's our spot number?' he asks. He's also filling out a form.

E-Dub has a problem. Capt Tony Maderspach, the EW officer, interrupts the start-up ritual. 'I'm on the interphone', he says. 'I need the pubs'.

A pause. Wathen says nothing. 'I forgot 'em', Maderspach adds.

'Don't worry. I'm flogging him.' Wathen communicates the problem to the ground and it's quickly rectified. 'Everybody should be on gloves for engine start, please.' The rules say, slip on flight gloves for take-off and landing because that's when the risk of fire is at its greatest.

Wathen continues working his checklist with Thomson and the ground. Brakes. Doors. Psi. 'Guns', he asks, 'are our radios too hot?'

'Pilot, this is Guns', says Sgt Ken 'Obie' Oberman, the gunner, uttering Wathen's intercom callsign and his own. 'Obie' has 1500 hours in the 'Buff'. A generation ago, 'Obie' would have been called an FCO (fire control operator). The term lapsed into disuse and today he's called a gunner. 'Say again about radios?'

'Guns, I was asking if our radios are too hot?'

'I'm not complaining, sir.'

'Okay. Offence. Defence. Ready for engine start?'

'Ready CO', says the co-pilot.

'E-Dub's ready', says Maderspach.

'Nav?'

'Radar's okay', says 1st Lt Dennis Utsler, the radar navigator, which is what we call the 'Buff' crew member who drops the bombs.

ENGINE START

Wathen checks with the ground to clear right and left, gets a verbal okay, and begins the methodical business of starting engines. The APU (auxiliary power unit), or 'dash-60' air cart, is hooked up to the number two pod, where engines Three and Four.

'Starting Three', the pilot intones. The B-52H model has a three-position switch with 'on' and 'off' as on other 'Buff' models, plus a continuous ignition feature not found on the others. Wathen goes to continuous ignite; number Three gives him a solid engine light and comes up. Carefully, the pilot watches for an 'overtemp'. When Three comes up to 15 per cent rpm (revolutions per minute), Wathen brings his throttle over its hump to the 'idle' position. Now, he must idle this engine for two minutes to let the generator oil warm up.

'There are two different ways to start number Four, which is in the same pod', he explains later. 'Either you get it from the air cart, or you hit the starter switch for Four followed quickly by 90 per cent rpm on Three. You let Four sit for two minutes, then start the others.'

Now, Wathen ignites the six remaining engines all at once. It's his job as pilot to monitor the gauges for One and Two, while co-pilot Thomson fixes his eyes on the remainder. From the jump seat, you have a clear view of the pilots' gloved hands shoving the throttles forward. All eight throttles protrude from a thick console between Wathen's right foot and Thomson's left. They're big. They take some muscle. From the jump seat, however, while all bundled up, you really do not sense the enormous power of eight engines running.

It's really uncomfortable in Jump. There's no place to stand erect, no extra room for helmet, oxygen, gloves, parachute. As the TF33 engines start up, the aircraft trembles some inches from side to side. Wathen, 'You can disconnect the air cart there, Ground.'

Thomson, 'Eight turning.'

Pilot and co-pilot run through a series of flight surface checks, no easy task in a huge bomber with the full repertoire of flaps, spoilers, elevators, and rudder (but no ailerons). 'Okay, the cart's disconnected. He's waving us out.'

'Good day, sir', says the airman on the ground, disconnecting. The B-52 shudders and strains against its brakes.

'IP, Guns. When we start to taxy, put on your seatbelts, please.' Wathen's first callsign is the abbreviation for instructor pilot. Today, he's using IP to refer to the author. Also known as 'Jump'.

'Guns is strapped in.'

'IP's in', the author confirms.

With engine start complete and systems checked, aircraft 60-0016 is cleared to the runway. Wathen and Thomson continue their big-crew banter during the crisp moments when, all but blind, Wathen eases *Junk Yard Dog* out of its spot and turns on the taxyway. The two men talk about emergency procedures, including brake energy limits, the drag chute envelope (70-120 knots), the 'commit' speed in the take-off run (120 kts) and other details. There's a brief moment when Wathen has time for frivolous chatter, so he points out that the faded black paint on his control yoke surrounds a knob of bare metal. The manufacturer's name plate, reading 'B-52H', installed at the factory before Wathen was born, is not there. 'Most of them are missing,' he explains. The implication is that hundreds of Buff control yoke consoles are displayed behind the cocktail bar in the 'Go to hell room' that every pilot has in his house. Right next to the fireplace and lounge chair, right there with the plaque from flight school, the odd photo, the model airplane, the letter of commendation from some general. The author knows where one is located, in a basement in Arlington, Virginia, heisted from one of these bombers while Wathen was in grammar school.

'Pilots are notorious vandals', says Guns from back in the depths of the taxying bomber.

'They're all like that', E-Dub confirms. It's not clear whether he means that all 'Buff' yokes are bereft of their name plates, or that all pilots are vandalous. Pilot Wathen and co-pilot Thomson follow a yellow stripe on the taxyway. Wathen turns toward runway's end. He is back to checklists with Thomson again. Pilot and CO will do most of the chattering back and forth throughout the flight. If this were a DEFCON 1 (Defense Condition 1 means war has begun), we'd be rushing toward the take-off point at top speed. Since this is only practice, we'll follow MITO procedure only for the actual take-off. Pilots, incidentally, acknowledge that on long missions the control yoke can be very tiring but few complain because, in the words of 1 Lt Jim Casey, who is flying companion 'Lazer 94', 'You don't come up with a lot of lip when you're flying a legend.'

From the jump seat, with only a partial view around the two pilots and through the narrow wind screen, taxying in the 'Buff' is more an auditory than a visual experience. Although the 157-ft 7-in fuselage of a fully loaded B-52H rides in a slightly nose-down attitude when rolling on concrete, the jump seat is a couple of inches lower than the pilots', hindering the view on the ground. You can see flat runway ahead as Wathen turns to take off. But most of what you know comes through the ears. You hear 'Viper' doing a go-around – that's the callsign for acceptance flights from General Dynamics' F-16 plant on the far side of the airfield. You hear 'Cowpoke' straightening out Wathen on some aspect of pre-departure planning. Who's 'Cowpoke'? 'That's the CP at Carswell', says Wathen, meaning the command post. 'They're not experts on anything. They handle communications. Their job is to keep us hooked up with SAC headquarters.'

At the hammerhead facing into the runway, 'Fox-trot', alias the SOF (Supervisor of Flight) performs a visual inspection of *Junk Yard Dog*, looking for a stray panel hanging down, a serious oil leak – anything Wathen might have overlooked or not seen. He gives the go-ahead. Carswell clears Wathen for takeoff. Wathen turns our B-52H turns into the runway. Pilot Wathen and co-pilot Thomson line the aircraft on the runway centreline, and bring eight engines to takeoff thrust. The *Junk Yard Dog*, aka 'Lazer 64', doesn't exactly bolt forward the way fighters do. Remarkably, the start of the take-off roll is much like an airliner. Wathen is obviously working to hold the huge bomber on the centre strip, and all eight engine needles are in the black 'take-off power' zone on the dial. 'Lazer 64' – that's us – heads down the runway. Companion ship 'Lazer 94' turns on the hammerhead behind us, rolls, and begins its take-off run.

MITO LIFT-OFF

Getting B-52s off the ground quickly can make the Kremlin's targeting job vexingly difficult. How close is minimum interval? Distances aren't publicized but time intervals of twelve seconds have been announced. Judging on the voice traffic in the earphones, it sounds like 'Lazer 94' is getting off no more than twelve seconds behind us, and possibly less. It's not 100 per cent

RIGHT A B-52G rehearses the new bombing technique of the missile age – down in the weeds where interception by fighters or surface-to-air missiles is deemed most difficult. This Stratofortress (59-2580) is helping out the fighter guys near Tyndall AFB, Florida, in 1980 during Exercise *William Tell*, a real-life war game for the USAF's interceptor force. The 'Arkansas razorback on the fin identifies this jet as a member of the 97th BW (USAF/TSgt William Franqui)

comforting to know that 505,000 lb (229,063 kg) of full-bore warplane is accelerating rapidly *behind* you. In wartime, this MITO launch might involve dozens of bombers and tankers, one following another at incredibly short gaps. The result is a furball of churning jet exhaust and careening aircraft – all choreographed, but giving the impression of chaos as well as profound danger.

Capt Pat Wathen pulls 'Lazer 64' off the pavement and into the sky. The complex, four-way bicycle gear comes up. In the B-52G and H models, flap retraction time has been increased from 40 seconds to one minute to permit use of smaller, lighter electrical drive motors than on previous Stratofortress models. There's a brief, distinct nudge when the gear doors close and the flaps complete their trip upward.

The B-52H, of course, is the high-power version of the 'Buff'. Its 17,000-lb (7,711-kg) thrust flat-rated Pratt & Whitney TF33-P-3 turbofan engines, also used on improved versions of the 707 and KC-135, give a 30 per cent power increase over the B-52G using water injection. As Wathen indicated in our conversation, the turbofans are exceedingly responsive to input on the throttle. This is not always a blessing. Too rapid movement of the throttle in certain situations can cause the bomber to pitch up at a rate beyond the pilot's ability to control with elevator authority. The culprit here, in part at least, is fuel slosh – in the B-52H's wet wing, fuel flows slowly back during acceleration, changing the center of gravity. In an extreme occurrence, the pilot could lose control.

In most big aircraft, you reach your cruising level, then relax – the job mostly boredom, albeit with the potential for abrupt crisis at any instant. 'There is never', says Wathen, 'never *ever* a time when you're bored flying the Buff'. Since we're coming and going to our target mostly at low level, there will be little time for pilot or co-pilot to relax. Like the rest of the crew, Wathen and Thomson will be working very hard all day.

We won't see them as this flight progresses, but more of the hardest-working people in the Air Force are at 'Cowpoke'. The communicators at the Carswell CP – every B-52 base has an equivalent location – are plugged into every plane their airfield has aloft and to SAC headquarters. Those monitoring the mission constantly are not experienced pilots or experts (as Wathen noted) but part of their job is to find the experts on near-zero notice if help is needed in over-

seeing the mission. Suffering lower lumbar agony from the survival pack, helmet, and other gear, the author is only partly heeding the exchange when 'Cowpoke' authorizes 'Lazer 64' – that's Wathen – to begin mission activities. Pat Wathen swaps intercom banter with E-Dub. We are still gathering altitude, still heading out toward lesser populated regions of the country, but E-Dub alias Captain Tony Maderspach is already working magic with his black boxes.

We take a long look at America at low altitude. Even in the 1990s, there are expanses of desert and mountains where you can fly for long periods and see only an occasional road or farmhouse. During this flight, there is frequent radio chatter with 'Cowpoke', the Command Post at Carswell, with various FAA Centers, with 'Thumper 73' (KC-135A Stratotanker 62-3529 from the 71st Air Refueling Squadron at Barksdale AFB, Louisiana), and absolutely not a word exchanged with nearby 'Pyote 31', one of those spanking-crisp B-1B bombers replete with hotplate, coffee pot, and a little space to stretch the arms and legs – held in utter disdain by Buff crews. 'Goddamn thing even has a chemical toilet,' one of them remarks as 'Pyote 31's' voice booms in our earphones. No self-respecting 'Buff' crewman would think of going aloft with such a luxury.

We're beginning as a two-ship cell, to be joined by a third Buff well into the mission. Wathen and Thomson have a responsive aircraft in their hands. The B-52G and H models replaced fuel bladder cells with an integral fuel tank, a 'wet wing', and an initial weight saving of 5847 lbs (2652 kg). The fin was chopped from 48 ft (14.86 m) to 40 ft (12.38 m) a step which, together with elimination of the aileron system – spoilers are used instead – shaved another 12,000 pounds (5,443 kg). But, because of structural beefing up and other changes, the B-52G and H are actually heavier than earlier Stratofortresses. Constant improvements to the bomber, aimed at enhancing its low-level function and easing the electronic warfare officer's job, have added further flab so that a typical B-52H now grosses just slightly less than 500,000 pounds (226,780 kg). 'Lazer 64', as we've noted, started at a gross weight which is slightly higher than typical.

Elimination of the spoilers changed the lateral response. When Wathen initiates a turn, raising the spoilers can sometimes induce a very slight buffet. The spoilers also induce a slight nose pitch-up with little real effect (though it further inhibits visibility from the

already unsatisfactory jump seat). Minor changes have been introduced to the flight control system over time but most pilots still find it fatiguing.

After hours of jerking, vibrating, and trembling, we're joined by latecomer 'Lazer 91' (B-52H 61-0038). Our three-ship cell now takes up a formation in triangle shape with two trailing B-52s 1000 ft behind our lead. Our next task, before heading back to the deck, is to refuel from 'Thumper 73'.

You may need an air sickness bag, sir', warns Guns over the intercom. The author turns around and looks back toward the gunner's location, though it can't be seen from the jump seat. 'This', replies the author, 'is not the time to call me "sir."'

At the 'schoolhouse' where they teach men to fly the B-52, air refuelling (AR, for short) is not part of the deal. AR is an 'on the job' syllabus for upgrade to aircraft commander. There is no requirement for the co-pilot, sitting in the right seat, to be qualified in AR although of course many, like Thomson, are.

AR is considered especially difficult in an aircraft this size. Pat Wathen is perhaps aware of this as our bomber comes to the air refuelling IP (initial point).

ABOVE B-52G 59-2601 with everything hanging out, on approach to RAF Greenham Common for an International Air Tattoo open day in 1983. From this angle, the well doors for the outrigger wheels are shown to good advantage, as are the main landing gear trucks. Flaps and spoilers on the wing trailing edge were larger than the entire wings on some aircraft, and could grab a considerable amount of air when deployed at the 45-degree position. The 'Buff' afforded excellent visibility to the two pilots during approaches and landings *(John Dunnell)*

'Thumper 73', that all-important KC-135, is observed in a left-hand orbit. We're at 29,000 ft (8980 m) now and he is a thousand feet lower. By synchronising our efforts – in a wartime situation, we'd do this based on a pre-arranged plan, with no communication between the two planes – he'll roll out in front of us at the twelve o'clock position. We descend below him, close to within a mile, and begin a gentle climb to close in to refuelling position, right under the tanker.

For Pat Wathen and other pilots who fly the 'Buff', refuelling is a chore to be learned and a skill in need of constant practice if it's to be maintained. Many B-52 missions call for two refuellings, one after take-off and climbout, and one in the middle of the flight (though we'll only plug in once during 'Lazer' cell's mission. A handful of pilots never master the task of refuelling, especially at night and in bad weather. Under good conditions it requires 15 to 20 minutes to take on 100,000 lbs (45,345 kg) of fuel. A proficient pilot is expected to remain on the boom, without temporary disconnects, while taking on the gas. From the standpoint of the boom operator peering down at us from a prone position in the tanker above, the B-52 – because of the length of time a refuelling consumes – is the second most difficult customer to handle. Worst of all for boomers is the C-141 Starlifter which has its receptacle in an awkward location and also must loiter on the boom for up to 20 minutes.

The author peers over Wathen's shoulder as we seemingly drive up into the boom. Pilot's job is not easy. He must keep the aircraft stable in a somewhat box-shaped area so that the boom operator can keep the end of the boom in our receptacle, just aft of the flight cabin. If the pilot deviates from the box, or envelope, the boom is supposed to recoil, retract, and disconnect. If it malfunctions, it can snap off.

GOING DOWN

Once refuelled, Wathen eases off on the throttles, breaks away, and takes us down. It takes about twenty minutes to get down to low level where the bulk of our flying will take place. In wartime, we'd go even lower. This is one reason why the *Junk Yard Dog* has a navigation system called EVS, which helps us to hug the earth and avoid surface-to-air missiles.

Radar alone is not enough for a successful attack while rushing along almost brushing the terrain. When operating in a nuclear environment (though not on today's training version), heavy curtains shutter the B-52 crew making the pilots all but blind. The answer is EVS (Electro-Optical Viewing System), an innovative use of television which evolved by accident when a Boeing engineer tested a Sony TV camera on the tail of a B-52 for a totally different purpose. SAC learned of this and issued a 1965 requirement on the feasibility of using visual sensors, including infrared, in the B-52G/H fleet to complement the radar terrain avoidance system and enhance strike capability. Five years of testing preceded the award of a production contract for the Westinghouse/Hughes AN/ASQ-151

EVS – this device is what gives a modern B-52 its curmudgeonly jowls, or 'double cheeks.'

The system consists of a Westinghouse steerable TV sensor, capable of operating by starlight, a Hughes FLIR (forward-looking infrared), and lash-up equipment which enables the two sensors to work together. A radar scan converter links EVS and the terrain avoidance radar so that the radar video presentation can be displayed on EVS monitors.

Wathen and Thomson, up front in 'Lazer 64', have EVS displays which show the terrain avoidance profile trace and a 'select' toggle which gives them a choice between TV and infrared, both of which make similar images on the screen, thanks to the computer. The navigator and radar navigator have a screen display the same as the pilots' except theirs lacks an artificial horizon. All four of these crew members use, and like, EVS, which greatly improves safety during a low-level penetration. Some obstacles, such as tall, thin antenna towers, do not show up on terrain avoidance radar but can be picked out instantly by the FLIR.

So both pilots, and both navs, are busy as the *Junk Yard Dog* rushes across America at low-level.

On a real mission, we would be penetrating the Soviets' integrated air defense network about now. Tony Maderspach, aka E-Dub, is busy foiling their search-and-track radar and keeping on the alert for indicators that they've scrambled fighters against us. The Russians still use a ground control intercept (GCI) system which relies heavily on radar, voice radio, encrypted radio, and other gadgetry which emits electrons – meaning that E-Dub can clue into what they're doing. 'Obie' Oberman, alias Guns, is ready to shoot if their Sukhoi or MiG fighters become a serious threat. Most, however, believe that Russians can't get down low enough, or use their speed advantage effectively enough, to have a realistic chance of shooting down a B-52 when it's coming at them, as Maderspach says, 'balls to the wall'.

The geometry seems to indicate that the Sukhoi or MiG pilot has a near impossible challenge. In exercises, it's repeatedly demonstrated that there's no effective way to detect, launch, intercept, and engage an onrushing B-52 while still enjoying the leisure of attacking head-on or from a 90-degree angle. Most fighters lack the terrain-hugging, bad-weather capability of the Buff and are likely to be caught 'on the wrong end of the power curve', in Maderspach's words – if they don't crash into a mountain or a microwave tower. Every realistic version of intercept geometry says that the fighter must attack from behind, possibly even from all the way behind in the six o'clock position where his advantages are fewest.

'He can't get in front of us and he can't get *below* us', says Maderspach, 'because there's going to be just a hair's breadth between our belly and the ground. So he's behind, with a look-down, shoot-down radar that is questionable. Is he going to use a radar missile against us? How? We'll foil the radar. Is he going to use a heat-seeking infrared missile like the American Sidewinder? Hey, our engine exhausts are shielded from above by the biggest, widest *wing* you ever saw in your life. We simply do not emit heat in any location that's convenient to this stressed-up, flustered fighter pilot who's trying to fight down on the deck where we call the plays. So is he going to guns? Down where we fly, we can out-think and outmanoeuvre him. We can use his bullet fly-out time to manoeuvre away from his firing path.'

When the Stratofortress entered service, there was scepticism whether its tail gun served any purpose. Just as fighters were thought not to need guns any longer (a temporary view of the late 1950s and early 1960s), it was thought that long-range combat dispensed with any need for a gun aboard a B-52. The six-barrel 20 mm GE Aerospace (later, Martin Marietta) M61A1 Vulcan, or 'Gatling' gun with of Mk 56 ammunition was, in the view of some, dead weight. The gun is tied into the AN/ASG-71 fire control system and gives a choice of two rates of fire, 3000 or 6000 rounds per minute. Curiously, a few months after today's mission, SAC will dispense with the gun, not for tactical but for financial reasons. Meanwhile, Oberman claims he can kill any MiG that gets within the 'cone' of his cannon's fly-out capability. Allegedly, the gun is good at distances up to a thousand yards.

Today, we're not attacking the Tu-16 *Badger* base at Anadyr or the anti-missile radar facility at Krasnoyarsk. Hour upon hour of low-level flying – simulating the profile of a real mission – and we'll end up across only one state line from where we began in Texas.

TO THE TARGET

Melrose is the bombing range a few miles from Melrose, New Mexico, which, given the passage of hours, we seem to have reached by way of Peru and the Yukon. For those interested in callsigns, Carswell's 9th squadron routinely uses Lazer while the base's other Buff squadron, the 20th, uses Luger. Each man believes his squadron is the best. But it's not true, as those guys in the 9th assert, that men in the 20th Squadron require smaller helmets.

When Radar tells Pilot that we have reached the IP (initial point), we're two-thirds into the mission and the unbearable weight of that goddamned 'Personnel Lowering Device' has become the only concern on the author's mind. Guns was wrong about heaving up, however, and there is time to reflect that (unlike crowded Dallas-Fort Worth), the American West still has expanses where you can fly at 380 kts, at 800 ft, and see only an occasional road, cattle trail, or farm house. You must *be* an American to understand the joy of looking down at Wild West expanses from the Buff. Once, cattle were herded here, *bandidos* hid out from the sheriff, and a culture of rugged, heavily-armed individualism was strengthened.

Coming in, Melrose is a giant bulls-eye laid out on this land, a rude wooden structure in its center. None of this 'Bombs away!' stuff. Radar merely counts down, 'Five, four, three, two, one. Release.' We are dropping BDU-38 inert bombs which simulate the B61 armed bomb. There *is* a distinct shudder as the bomb is dropped and the bay doors closed. Crews pride themselves on accuracy and a bomb hit within 50 ft of center is termed a 'shack' because, if real explosives were used, that wooden shack would be pulverized. 'Lazer 64's' crew, followed by the two other 'Buffs', makes the bomb run on Melrose three times, drops three BDU-38s, and scores three 'shacks.'

Obviously, the Air Force prefers standoff weapons when they can be used. A variety of weapons including the AGM-129 ACM (Advanced Cruise Missile) and the recently cancelled AGM-137 TSSAM (Tri-Service Stand-off Missile) were expected to give the USAF ways of attacking targets without having to fly over the sites themselves. Both are modern-day improvements over the GAM-77 Hound Dog which served with SAC for so many years.

Other options are the Boeing AGM-86 ALCM and AGM-69 SRAM (Short-Range Attack Missile). Discarded in the early 1960s was another option, the Skybolt, which ran into cost and developmental problems. But the old-fashioned method of flying over a target and dropping a bomb on it is still one arrow in SAC's quiver.

TEXAS

Our return flight is much the same as the outgoing segment – almost all of it at low level.

While we're landing at Carswell, others in the area search for news of the war and practice the trade, wishing they were shoulder to shoulder with comrades in the Gulf.

In Dallas-Fort Worth, the twin-city bastion for Buffs and Tomcats, builder of Ospreys, Corsairs and Vipers, a nation's gluttonous overdose of patriotism manifests itself in American flags flapping in the wind everywhere, painted on walls, inscribed on bumper stickers, often with the motto the world has heard from Yorktown to Ia Drang: *These Colors Don't Run*. On the B-52 flight line at Carswell, several of the huffers, or APU carts, are adorned with variations on this allegiant theme.

Physically, *Junk Yard Dog* is warm and clammy after its flight. For those other crew members who occupy normal seats, the cushions no longer cushion after these hours, and there's a tension inside the plane now that everybody is ready to shut down and debrief. There'll be plenty of paperwork while the inside of the 'Buff' is airing out.

Nothing is more exasperating or offers greater drudgery for an exhausted crew than the post-flight maintenance briefing. After a very long day, the aircraft commander and usually the other crew members must gather around a table with the maintenance staff to fill out a mountain of paperwork and face an oral grilling. If they do not remember every hiccough which occurred during the mission – a persistently low hydraulic pressure reading, an unexplained vibration

ABOVE Parachute brake deployed and spoilers raised, a B-52G (57-6512) decelerates on the runway after touching down. The combination of camouflage and a white underside became commonplace at the end of the Vietnam era. Unlike the B-47, which unfurled a drogue chute to achieve stability while still airborne in the pattern, the B-52 follows the more tradiitional practice of popping the chute only after touching ground *(USAF)*

when engaging autopilot, an unexplained pitch problem – the B-52 may not be ready for its next mission. In the end, Wathen bears responsibility for passing along a bomber in good working order.

The purpose of our flight in 'Lazer 64', of course, is to get some feeling for how it feels to fly a 'Buff' in combat and to drop nukes on the Russians or iron bombs on Iraq's Republican Guards. The glimpses in Dallas-Fort Worth – of insecure aerospace workers, of other warplanes howling overhead, of patriotic symbols everywhere – are a stark reminder that our aerospace industry is in decline at the very time a shooting war is at the forefront of Texans' minds. On the day of my B-52 flight, Defense Secretary Dick Cheney appears on a Dallas TV station to report a news blackout on the newly-begun land war. A youngster sees his face and cries: 'Hey, Dad, here's the guy who cancelled the A-12!' Cheney may know of another popular local slogan: *Don't mess with Texas*.

Such is this report from one spot in America. For readers who ask how it feels to fly in a B-52, try this: Get a back pack, fill it with bricks, throw on any sort of helmet, climb on a roller-coaster, and spend nine hours in the crouching position. And take care of necessary functions first.

Postscript: As readers, know, the Allies defeated Iraq in 100 hours of land warfare, following weeks of aerial combat. The preceding text was written while the battle was still joined, the outcome not known. Rarely has such a turning point in history exploded upon us with such swiftness. The B-52H crews of the 7th Bomb Wing at Carswell wanted nothing more in their lives than to get into this fight – but it ended before they could and, in fact, no B-52Hs were employed in the war. Their inability to play a part will always burden these men. As for the G-models which *did* participate, a Pentagon report spoke well of them:

'The role of the large conventional bomber was revalidated in the Gulf war. B-52s flew 1624 missions, dropped over 72,000 weapons, and delivered over 25,700 tons of munitions on area targets in the KTO (Kuwaiti Theatre of Operations), and on airfields, industrial targets, troop concentrations and storage areas in Iraq. Despite being over 30 years old, the B-52 had a mission capable rate of over 81 per cent – 2 per cent higher than its peacetime rate. B-52s dropped 29 per cent of all US bombs and 30 per cent of all Air Force bombs during the war. Through effective modification of the B-52, it remains a useful platform. As Iraqi prisoners report, B-52 raids had devastating effects on enemy morale. Estimates show that from 20 to 40 per cent of troop strength had deserted their units prior to the G-Day (the beginning of the ground phase of the conflict). While fighters employed precision guided munitions to destroy pinpoint targets, the B-52's successes demonstrated the need to preserve the large conventional bombers' ability to destroy large target areas.'

Eight months after our B-52H mission, on 26 September 1991, President Bush announced an end to the nuclear alert function – maintained by SAC bomber crews for more than 40 years – so that for the first time Stratofortresses no longer sit at runway's end, hydrogen bombs on board, cocked and ready to go. On 1 October 1991, the Air Force put Sgt Ken (Obie) Oberman and all other 'Buff' gunners out of a job, continuing to fly the big bombers with the guns installed but no gunner manning the weapons – and by late 1994 the guns began to disappear from the B-52s too, ending any prospect of a reversal of this decision. A year later, the 7th Bomb Wing at Carswell stood down. Fort Worth is no longer home to the B-52 Stratofortress but the situation in the city is little changed – a depressed aerospace industry, a troubled mood, the manufacturer of the F-16 undergoing its third name change to Lockheed Martin.

The 7th Wing designation has been shifted to Dyess AFB, Texas, an operator of the Rockwell B-1B Lancer and strategic nuclear bombing missions receive less emphasis, today than conventional bombing – but in other bomb wings and other squadrons, the 'Buff' soldiers on. Of the courageous Allied troops who fought in *Desert Storm*, and the B-52 crews and others who backed them up from places as distant as Dallas, one might quote Lord Howard of Effingham: 'God, send me to see such a company together again when need is.'

RIGHT EVS fairings and blisters associated with the Phase VI ECM suite mar the otherwise clean contours of the noses of this neat line of 28th Bomb Wing B-52Hs at Ellsworth AFB, South Dakota. One of the first outfits to acquire the enduring and endearing 'Buff', the 28th has since progressed to the B-1B Lancer, although there are some who would vehemently deny that that is progress! *(USAF)*

THREE DECADES OF DECLINE

HAVING ASSEMBLED WHAT was undeniably the most powerful fleet of bomber aircraft ever seen, the USA - and, to be more specific, SAC – wasn't destined to hang on to that fleet for very long. Retirement of the B-47 Stratojet had been well advanced even as the final examples of the Stratofortress joined the arsenal, and was accelerated during the first half of the 1960s as more and more missiles became available and were positioned in silos across the mid-western states.

Nevertheless, SAC possessed close to 650 B-52s at peak strength, with this type representing a most formidable force in its own right. As described elsewhere, dispersal of the B-52 fleet had resulted in it being distributed amongst a total of 42 squadrons at 38 different air bases by the close of 1963. As it transpired, this level was to be short-lived, for the first actions to reduce the size of the heavy bomber component occurred as early as March 1965. By coincidence, the removal of the first B-52 from the operational inventory took place just a few weeks after the deployment of 30 B-52Fs from two Bomb Wings situated in the USA to Andersen AFB, Guam.

At the time, that deployment was viewed as a contingency response to the latest aggressive act by the North Vietnamese. Later, it was to be acknowledged as having far-reaching import for SAC's heavyweight, for barely three months would pass between retirement of the first B-52 and staging of the first *Arc Light* mission over South Vietnam. The two events weren't connected of course, but involvement in eight years of conventional warfare did eventually exert some influence on the pace of the B-52 retirement programme, in so far as the planned withdrawal of the B-52D derivative was delayed by more than a decade, in the wake of specialised modification for conventional bombing duties.

LEFT The sixth B-52H on an early trials flight. Retaining the shortened vertical tail of the G-model, the B-52H differed in introducing 17,000-lb (7,711-kg) Pratt & Whitney TF-33-P-3 turbofan engines. These engines were more powerful and, more importantly, did not disgorge the massive clouds of noxious black smoke associated with the J57 *(Boeing)*

RIGHT Seen in August 1977, this B-52G (59-2565), wearing typical post-Vietnam camouflage, is on a mission near Fairchild AFB, Washington (USAF/Yuen-Ge Yee)

Other versions were much less fortunate, but the process of decline has been fitful, with flurries of activity being interspersed with long periods of stability. Today, although less than 100 examples of the B-52H still feature in the frontline inventory, and there is good reason to believe that they are likely to survive for a few more years. However, many others have been withdrawn not for reasons of choice or obsolescence, but simply to satisfy tighter controls on the beleaguered defence budget. Thirty years ago, when the first examples of the B-52 family were retired, the rationale behind their disposition was far more logical, for the aircraft involved had pretty much come to the end of their fatigue lives.

The very first Stratofortress to leave the operational force was B-52B 52-8714 which was withdrawn by the 22nd BW at March AFB, California on 8 March 1965. Unlike most later machines, however, it was not fated to end up in the so-called 'boneyard' at Davis-Monthan AFB, Arizona. Instead, this particular aircraft found a new, non-flying, lease of life as an instructional aid with Air Training Command at Chanute AFB, Illinois. Within little more than a year, it had been followed into retirement by virtually all the other B-52Bs – of the two operational Wings that had been equipped with this version, the 22nd BW was fortunate enough to be re-equipped with the B-52D, but the 95th BW fared much less well and was inactivated.

Perhaps surprisingly, the 95th was not the first B-52 wing to disappear from the scene, for that dubious honour had been claimed a year earlier by the 39th BW. This Eglin-based outfit had been responsible for carrying out many operational trials with the B-52G

model but by June 1965 its work was considered to be at an end and it was therefore inactivated after reassigning its solitary squadron (the 62nd BS) to the 2nd BW at Barksdale AFB. That change actually had little effect on overall bomber resources, but retirement of the B-52B did result in the number on hand dropping to about 590 by the close of 1966.

Of far greater import for the future of SAC's bomber force was the announcement by Secretary of Defense Robert S McNamara on 8 December 1965 of a long-term phase-out programme involving several versions of the Stratofortress as well as Convair's B-58 Hustler and replacement of both types by the General Dynamics FB-111A. As will be seen, implementation didn't quite go wholly to plan, but the original intention was to dispose of all remaining B-52C, B-52D, B-52E and B-52F aircraft by the middle of 1971.

More immediately, 1966 witnessed the departure of four SAC Bomb Wings, of which the 95th was one. Three others faded from view as a direct result of the desire to retain units that were deemed to be of historical significance, although their demise didn't always result in a straightforward transfer of the assets previously assigned. Nevertheless, the 340th BW, 462nd SAW and 494th BW all fell by the wayside in 1966, with some of the B-52Ds that had been allocated being used to replace B-52Bs with the 22nd BW and others passing directly to the 509th BW which had previously operated the B-47E. Another former Stratojet unit that acquired the 'Buff' in 1966 was the 380th SAW, although in this instance it picked up B-52Gs made surplus by the inactivation of one of the two squadrons that had been assigned to the 42nd BW at Loring.

A somewhat more ambitious series of inactivations occurred during 1967-68, when a total of eight Bomb Wings disappeared from the scene for good. In reality, this actually had little effect on force size, for most of the resources were redistributed amongst other units and only some two dozen time-expired B-52Es and B-52Fs were despatched to the Military Aircraft Storage and Disposition Center (MASDC) at this time. Units that ceased B-52 operations in 1967 were the 6th SAW and 484th BW.

Turning to 1968, the half-a-dozen casualties were the 11th SAW, 91st BW, 397th BW, 450th BW, 461st BW and 465th BW. In most cases, constituent Bomb Squadrons were inactivated, but this wasn't true of the 397th BW. In this instance, control of the subordinate 596th BS and its complement of B-52Gs passed to the 2nd BW, which henceforth enjoyed the rare status of being a two-squadron 'superwing'. In addition, two of the units experienced what was tantamount to redesignation, with the resources of the 450th BW forming the basis of a rejuvenated 5th BW at Minot, while the 465th BW was supplanted at Robins by the 19th BW.

Serious reductions in bomber strength began to become apparent during 1969-71 when parts of the plan announced by McNamara a few years earlier

ABOVE 'Hey guys. Run out there and remove those air intake covers so Linn can get a clean shot!' B-52D 55-0095 of the 7th BW based at Carswell AFB, Texas, seen during a visit to McGuire AFB, New Jersey, on 30 May 1982. The Vietnam-era paint scheme and tall tail were soon to become history. 55-0085 was rapidly approaching the end of its flying career at this juncture, being sent to Chanute AFB, Illinois, to act as an instructional airframe just weeks after this shot was taken *(Don Linn)*

were implemented. This, in effect, brought a sudden halt to the B-58's operational career after barely a decade of service and also saw the end of the B-52C and B-52E with SAC, while the B-52F was henceforth relegated to training tasks with the 93rd BW at Castle AFB. Retirement of these models resulted in the number of Stratofortresses on hand falling sharply, from 579 at the end of 1968 to 412 exactly three years later and almost all the aircraft removed from SAC's line up at this time found their way into long-term storage at MASDC.

Reductions in numerical strength weren't actually matched by comparable reductions in unit numbers, for only five Wings lost the B-52 during this period. Two of them (the 380th SAW and the 509th BW) were

LEFT B-52D 55-0674 of the 7th BW based at Carswell AFB, Texas, drops in for a visit at McGuire AFB, New Jersey, on 24 May 1981. This jet made history on 4 October 1983 when it arrived at Davis-Monthan AFB, as it was the last D-model retired by the USAF *(Don Linn)*

re-equipped with 'McNamara's Folly' (the FB-111A), but the other three (the 70th, 72nd and 454th BWs) were all victims of inactivation.

After the flurry of aircraft retirements, a long period of stability ensued, with the number of B-52s on strength generally hovering at around the 410-420 mark until the end of 1977. The same good fortune wasn't exactly shared by operating units, for a handful of Bomb Wings did disappear from the line-up during this period. First to go were the 99th and 306th BWs, which both inactivated in 1974, even though the 99th had actually been non-operational since April 1972 and the 306th since November 1973.

They were followed at the end of September 1975 by the 456th BW at Beale, although this was actually one of those confusing actions designed to ensure the continued survival of a historically significant unit. In view of that, B-52G operations from this California base continued, with aircraft and personnel resources simply passing from the 456th BW to the 17th BW. As it turned out, Beale's reprieve as a bomber base was not a long one, for the 17th BW was itself stood down exactly one year later.

The final unit to disappear during the 1970s was the 449th BW at Kincheloe AFB, Michigan. This was inactivated at the end of September 1977, but its disappearance had virtually no impact on the B-52 fleet - nor on the number of active squadrons, since the 28th BW at Ellsworth picked up 'superwing' status at the start of July, when it gained a second squadron using

most of the B-52Hs made redundant by the impending closure of Kincheloe.

Even though there were no more cuts in unit numbers until the latter half of 1982, the same cannot be said of bomber quantities, for 1978 was notable in seeing a short-lived but nevertheless intense resumption of the retirement programme. By the close of that year, the number on hand had plunged by more than 70, with the latest crop of 'retirees' to reach MASDC comprising two dozen or so B-52Fs that had been used for crew training from Castle and a sizeable intake of B-52Ds.

This latest batch of withdrawals basically left SAC with a manned bomber force that consisted of about 410 aircraft. As had been the case for more than a decade, the mainstay of that force was the Stratofortress. Some 344 examples were still on charge, made up of about 79 B-52Ds, 169 B-52Gs and 96 B-52Hs, distributed between 18 Bomb Wings. Most of those units controlled the activities of just one Bomb Squadron and a tanker element but there were three 'superwings' with two Bomb Squadrons. In addition, there were 66 FB-111As at two bases.

Structural modification of the remaining B-52Ds in the latter half of the 1970s allowed them an extended lease of life, but by the early part of the new decade even the most youthful of these machines were 26 years old and well into their dotage in so far as flying hours and fatigue lives were concerned. So it was that the last of the 'tall-tailed birds' began to head towards

LEFT Seen weeks before it was sent for storage, B-52E 57-0026 of the 92nd SAW draws interested admirers at Fairchild's open house in May 1969. The conventional 'iron' bombs beneath the wing were for display purposes only *(Arnold Swanberg)*

LEFT The final B-52G to be procured with FY 1958 funds, 58-0258 is in typical landing attitude as it settles towards the runway. Featuring EVS and Phase VI ECM equipment, it was assigned to the 416th BW at the time

the storage lines at Davis-Monthan during 1982. In fact, of the 80 or so aircraft that were withdrawn at this time, only just over 50 ended up in MASDC. Of the remainder, some were scrapped where they stood, some were reassigned to ground instructional tasks at technical training centres – and a lucky few found their way to hard-earned retirement as artifacts in museum collections.

Retirement of the final B-52Ds coincided with another crop of inactivations as further inroads were made into the size of the manned bomber fleet, although not all of these involved B-52D units. Of the four Wings that had continued operating the B-52D until the bitter end, one (the 22nd BW) disposed of its aircraft and became a specialist tanker outfit; one (the 43rd SW) obtained B-52Gs and two (the 7th and 96th BWs) re-equipped with B-52Hs.

Bombers involved in these re-equipment programmes were drawn from a number of other units and SAC indulged in a mild orgy of aircraft-trading as it carried out a strategic force realignment project which resulted in the remaining resources being distributed in a very different way. Units that gave up B-52Gs altogether as part of this rationalisation comprised the 19th BW and the 68th BW, although

both remained in existence as tanker only elements. The former unit lost its Stratofortresses in 1983, passing most of them to the 43rd SW at Andersen, while the 68th BW B-52Gs were ferried north-east in 1982 to join the 319th BW at Grand Forks as replacements for the B-52H.

Moving on to the latter model, aircraft previously flown by the 319th BW were handed on to the 96th BW at Dyess, Texas, and the Ellsworth-based 28th BW's elevated 'superwing' status was abruptly terminated when it reassigned some B-52Hs to the 7th BW's 9th Bomb Squadron in 1982. Subsequently, in 1983, the 7th BW's second squadron also converted from the B-52D to the B-52H, although in this case it drew its new aircraft from various sources, including some that had been used for crew training.

At the close of 1983, therefore, only two versions of the Stratofortress remained active with SAC and the 260-odd examples on charge were spread between 15 Wings at as many air bases. For the record, those equipped with the more numerous B-52G model comprised the 2nd BW (62nd and 596th BS), 42nd BW (69th BS), 43rd SW (60th BS), 92nd BW (325th BS), 93rd BW (328th BS), 97th BW (340th BS), 319th BW (46th BS), 320th BW (441st BS), 379th BW (524th BS) and 416th BW (668th BS), while the B-52H served with the 5th BW (23rd BS), 7th BW (9th and 20th BS), 28th BW (77th BS), 96th BW (337th BS) and 410th BW (644th BS).

No further significant cuts in the size of the force would occur for a few more years, even though SAC did at last succeed in getting its hands on a long over-due new bomber in the form of the Rockwell B-1B Lancer during that interlude. In fact, it was the advent of this new hardware that precipitated the next round of cuts in unit disposition, for three B-52 Wings figured among the four outfits that equipped with about 100 B-1Bs in 1986-88. Transition to the new type was not, however, accompanied by force level reductions, for the B-52s made available by this programme were sim-ply redistributed to other bases.

Initial deliveries of the B-1B were made to the 96th BW which disposed of the B-52H in the autumn and winter of 1984-85. Next to convert was the 28th BW, which started running down its B-52H operations in October 1985, before accepting its first B-1B in 1986. Some of the redundant 'Buffs' were used to convert the 92nd BW to the B-52H, with the ALCM-configured B-52Gs made available by this move being handed on to the 2nd BW's 596th BS at Barksdale AFB. Finally, in 1986, the 319th BW lost its B-52Gs, with the last example leaving Grand Forks in December, clearing the way for the arrival of the first B-1B in early 1987.

Not long afterwards, the missions assigned to some of the outfits that were still equipped with the Strato-fortress began to take radically different paths. As is evident from the long period of involvement in South-East Asia, conventional warfare had certainly not been neglected in the years prior to 1988 but it had always been undertaken as an adjunct to the nuclear role, rather than as the sole prerogative. In consequence, all bomber units had pulled their fair share of nuclear alert duty as part of the Single Integrated Operational Plan (SIOP), irrespective of the model of B-52 assigned. In 1988, however, this policy was abandoned in favour of a new concept which affected a handful of units that operated the B-52G. Henceforth, these Bomb Wings would abandon the nuclear mission entirely and specialise in purely conventional strike roles.

The best part of 30 years of attrition had inevitably taken its toll of the B-52G fleet, which had diminished in size from its original level of 193 to a force that was 166-strong at the close of 1988. Apart from a couple of aircraft assigned to the Air Force Flight Test Center at Edwards AFB, they were wholly allocated to SAC. The greater proportion were still nuclear capable machines, for almost all of the 90 B-52Gs that had been adapted to operate with the AGM-86B ALCM remained on charge. Units which were still SIOP-ded-icated comprised the 97th BW at Blytheville; the 379th BW at Wurtsmith and the 416th BW at Griffiss, plus the 2nd BW's 596th BS at Barksdale. These operated the bulk of the ALCM-configured B-52Gs, but some were also utilised for crew training tasks by the 93rd BW at Castle.

Turning to aircraft which would in future be con-

RIGHT Another view of one of the first B-52Gs to be repainted in drab tactical battledress at Boeing's Wichita facility, which was clearly quite busy with the Stratofortress at the time. The contrast between this unidentified machine and the basically silver 'Buffs' visible in the background is quite striking. and illustrates well just how dramatic the switch in colour schemes was
(Boeing)

ventionally tasked, approximately 66 B-52Gs had previously been adapted to carry such weapons as the Harpoon air-to-surface anti-ship attack missile and it was these machines which equipped the units that relinquished the SIOP mission at this time. For the record, they consisted of the 42nd BW at Loring, the 43rd SW at Andersen, the 320th BW at Mather, plus the 2nd BW's 62nd BS at Barksdale. As with the ALCM-configured machines, a limited number of the non-nuclear aircraft were allocated to the 93rd BW for training.

The change of mission was in fact destined to be short-lived for two of the outfits involved, since the time was fast approaching for the B-52G to leave the front-line force. Retirement began shortly before the end of the 1980s, but proved to be a fairly long and drawn-out process, spanning almost exactly five years before the final example was removed from the inventory. This period was interrupted by the Gulf War of 1991, but that conflict doesn't seem to have materially affected the rate at which the withdrawal process was accomplished.

Mather's 320th BW was the first B-52G unit to be inactivated and ceased operations in July 1989, standing down not long after. The same year also saw the first B-52Gs being processed inwards at Davis-Monthan, but only five examples had actually arrived by

the end of 1989. Next to go was the 43rd SW at Andersen, with formal inactivation taking place on 15 June 1990, following disposal of the dozen or so B-52Gs that had been flown. Several of them were also destined for storage and the Aerospace Maintenance and Regeneration Center (AMARC, as MASDC had become in October 1985) welcomed 10 more B-52Gs in the first four months of the year.

Although no more units were stood down until 1992, the intervening period did witness a further influx of B-52Gs at Davis-Monthan. Indeed, some 50-odd examples recorded their final flights between July 1990 and the end of 1991, with the inexorable process of withdrawal causing the number of B-52Gs in service to fall to about 90, a level that allowed the B-52H to enjoy numerically superior status for the first time in its long career. Many of the B-52Gs retired at this time came from the 97th and 379th BWs which were both inactivated in 1992.

Further inroads were made in the size of the fleet during the last six months of 1992, with about half the remaining B-52Gs being withdrawn from service. In this case, retirement was driven by the re-equipment of the 2nd and 416th BWs with the B-52H. Most of the 'Cadillacs' involved in this realignment came from the 7th BW which was itself stood down. For once, though, it wasn't all a tale of despondency, in so far as a new recruit to the long list of Stratofortress operators made its debut in 1992, when the first of the so-called 'composite' intervention Wings included a B-52G squadron in its line-up. The unit concerned was the 366th Wing with headquarters at Mountain Home AFB, Idaho but the eight-strong contingent of 'Buffs' actually resided at Castle AFB.

That was good news, but it certainly didn't stave off the inevitable, with continuing reductions in defence spending clearly signposting the end of the road for the B-52G model. Yet more cuts in 1993 were allied to the

BELOW A B-52H (60-0016) in the wraparound charcoal grey paint scheme which became standard in the early 1990s. This bomber, nicknamed the *Spirit Of Texas*, belongs to the 9th BS/7th BW at Carswell AFB, Texas. The 7th is one of the oldest USAF establishments, tracing its origins to the 1st Army Observation Group founded in September 1918. It flew B-17s, B-24s and LB-30s in Java and India, and later waged the Cold War in B-36s and 'Buffs'. Today, the 7th Wing has been re-located at Dyess AFB, Texas, and flies the B-1B Lancer *(USAF)*

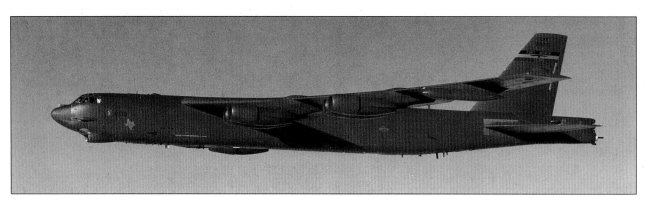

final phase-out and resulted in barely two dozen examples remaining in the inventory when 1994 dawned. By then, Loring's 42nd BW had virtually disposed of all its aircraft and both of the Castle-based elements were beginning to ferry their B-52Gs to the storage centre in Arizona.

That process continued at a fairly brisk pace throughout the early part of the year and finally came to a close in the late spring when the last B-52G sortie was flown. For the 366th Wing, new equipment in the form of the B-1B was in prospect, but the 42nd BW and the 93rd BW are both expected to be inactivated once they have completed the depressing task of closing the bases from which they served with distinction for so many years.

The only vestige that now remains of the once-mighty Stratofortress fleet is the B-52H, and the chances of the 94 examples that are still part of the inventory surviving for the immediate future appear quite resonable. So while there's life, there's hope – and as far as is known, no example of the 'Cadillac' has yet been despatched to storage.

Indeed, the ultimate model of the 'Buff' has recently been deployed for the first time with a second-line element of the Air Force Reserve, with the 917th Wing at Barksdale accepting the first of about eight B-52Hs during December 1993. How long it will be permitted to operate Boeing's finest bomber has yet to be determined, but it may well turn out to be one of the final units, since current USAF intentions are that three of the five remaining first-line B-52H units will be inactivated in the latter half of 1994.

For the record, these are the 92nd, 410th and 416th BWs, but their demise hasn't signalled wide-scale retirement of aircraft, since the redundant B-52Hs have been reassigned to the 2nd and 5th BWs, which both established additional squadrons to cope with the extra bombers. In the case of the 2nd BW, this has culminated in a return of the three-squadron Wing organisation that existed during the early period of the B-52's long career, a situation that seemed highly unlikely ever to arise again.

At the time of writing, then, the future of the 'Buff' is assured, for there are no plans to withdraw any B-52Hs in the near-term, although ACC has stated that only 65 of the 94 survivors are to be considered as combat-ready, with the residue forming a kind of 'reserve' to permit aircraft utilisation to be spread evenly throughout the fleet.

ABOVE B-52s undergo dismantling at the Military Storage & Disposition Center (MASDC) at Davis-Monthan AFB in the early 1980s. B-52C, D-, E- and F-models were retired in some cases for budgetary reasons, even though the aircraft could have been upgraded and kept operational longer. For the benefit of Soviet reconnaissance satellites policing the Strategic Arms Limitation Treaty (SALT), B-52s were broken apart in such a way that the scrapping could be easily confirmed from aloft. MASDC, the Soviet Union and SALT are all history now, but at the re-named AMARC boneyard, the process of visibly dismantling B-52s is set to continue throughout the 1990s *(USAF)*

APPENDIX 1

Comparative Specification Data

(Aircraft as originally built)

B-52B

Powerplants: eight Pratt & Whitney J57-P-1WA turbojet engines, each rated at 11,400 lb st with water injection
Dimensions: length 156 ft 6.9 ins; span 185 ft 0 ins; height 48 ft 3.6 ins; wing area 4000 sq ft
Weights: empty 164,081 lbs; combat 272,000 lbs; maximum take-off 420,000 lbs
Defensive armament: two 20 mm M24A1 cannon, with 400 rounds each or four 0.50 calibre M-3 machine guns, with 600 rounds each
Offensive payload: circa 43,000 lbs
Performance: maximum speed at optimum altitude 546 kts at 19,800 ft; service ceiling at combat weight 47,300 ft; combat radius 3110 nautical miles; take-off ground run 8200 ft

B-52D

Powerplants: eight Pratt & Whitney J57-P-19W turbojet engines, each rated at 12,100 lb st with water injection
Dimensions: length 156 ft 6.9 ins; span 185ft 0 ins; height 48 ft 3.6 ins; wing area 4000 sq ft
Weights: empty 177,816 lbs; combat 293,100 lbs; maximum take-off 450,000 lbs
Defensive armament: four 0.50 calibre M-3 machine guns, with 600 rounds each
Offensive payload: circa 60,000 lbs

Performance: maximum speed at optimum altitude of 551 kts at 20,200 ft: service ceiling at the combat weight 46,200 ft; combat radius of 3012 nautical miles; take-off ground run 8000 ft

B-52G

Powerplants: eight Pratt & Whitney J57-P-43WB turbojet engines, each rated at 13,750 lb st with water injection
Dimensions: length 160 ft 10.9 in; span 185 ft 0 in; height 40 ft 8 ins; wing area 4000 sq ft
Weights: empty 168,445 lbs; combat 302,634 lbs; maximum take-off 488,000 lbs
Defensive armament: four 0.50 calibre M-3 machine guns, with 600 rounds each
Offensive payload: exceeds 50,000 lbs
Performance: maximum speed at optimum altitude 551 kts at 20,800 ft; service ceiling at combat weight 47,000 ft; combat radius 3550 nautical miles; take-off ground run 8150 ft

B-52H

Powerplants: eight Pratt & Whitney TF33-P-3 turbofan engines, each rated at 17,000 lb st
Dimensions: length 156 ft 0 ins; span 185 ft 0 ins; height 40 ft 8 ins; wing area 4000 sq ft
Weights: empty 172,740 lbs; combat 306,358 lbs; maximum take-off 488,000 lbs
Defensive armament: one 20 mm Vulcan M61 cannon with 1242 rounds
Offensive payload: exceeds 50,000 lbs
Performance: maximum speed at optimum altitude 547 kts at 23,800 ft; service ceiling at combat weight 47,700 ft; combat radius 4176 nautical miles; take-off ground run 7420 ft

LEFT AND LOWER LEFT Starboard and port-side views of Edwards-based NB-52A 52-0003 when it served as a 'mother-ship' for the North American X-15. The pylon from which the X-15 was suspended is visible beneath the starboard wing, but the rocket-powered research craft is not being carried. Nicknamed *The High and Mighty One*, the NB-52A was eventually placed in storage shortly before the end of the 1960s. Today, it can still be seen in the Pima County museum at Tucson, Arizona

APPENDIX 2

B-52 Production Details

BOEING (SEATTLE)

Variant	Serial Number(s)	Construction Number(s)	Quantity
XB-52-BO	49-0230	16248	1
YB-52-BO	49-0231	16249	1
B-52A-1-BO	52-0001/0003	16491/493	3
RB-52B-5-BO	52-0004/0006	16494/496	3
RB-52B-10-BO	52-0007/0013	16497/503	7
RB-52B-15-BO	52-8710/8715	16838/843	6
RB-52B-20-BO	52-8716	16844	1
RB-52B-25-BO	53-0366/0372	16845/851	7
B-52B-25-BO	53-0373/0376	16852/855	4
RB-52B-30-BO	53-0377/0379	16856/858	3
B-52B-30-BO	53-0380/0387	16859/866	8
B-52B-35-BO	53-0388/0398	16867/877	11
B-52C-40-BO	53-0399/0408	16878/887	10
B-52C-45-BO	54-2664/2675	17159/170	12
B-52C-50-BO	54-2676/2688	17171/183	13
B-52D-55-BO	55-0068/0088	17184/204	21
B-52D-60-BO	55-0089/0104	17205/220	16
B-52D-65-BO	55-0105/0117	17221/233	13
B-52D-70-BO	56-0580/0590	17263/273	11
B-52D-75-BO	56-0591/0610	17274/293	20
B-52D-80-BO	56-0611/0630	17294/313	20
B-52E-85-BO	56-0631/0649	17314/332	19
B-52E-90-BO	56-0650/0656	17333/339	7
B-52E-90-BO	57-0014/0022	17408/416	9
B-52E-95-BO	57-0023/0029	17417/423	7
B-52F-100-BO	57-0030/0037	17424/431	8
B-52F-105-BO	57-0038/0052	17432/446	15
B-52F-110-BO	57-0053/0073	17447/467	21

BOEING (WICHITA)

Variant	Serial Number(s)	Construction Number(s)	Quantity
B-52D-1-BW	55-0049/0051	464001/003	3
B-52D-5-BW	55-0052/0054	464004/006	3
B-52D-10-BW	55-0055/0060	464007/012	6
B-52D-15-BW	55-0061/0064	464013/016	4
B-52D-20-BW	55-0065/0067	464017/019	3
B-52D-20-BW	55-0673/0675	464020/022	3
B-52D-25-BW	55-0676/0680	464023/027	5
B-52D-30-BW	56-0657/0668	464028/039	12
B-52D-35-BW	56-0669/0680	464040/051	12
B-52D-40-BW	56-0681/0698	464052/069	18
B-52E-45-BW	56-0699/0712	464070/083	14
B-52E-50-BW	57-0095/0109	464084/098	15
B-52E-55-BW	57-0110/0130	464099/119	21
B-52E-60-BW	57-0131/0138	464120/127	8
B-52F-65-BW	57-0139/0154	464128/143	16
B-52F-70-BW	57-0155/0183	464144/172	29
B-52G-75-BW	57-6468/6475	464173/180	8
B-52G-80-BW	57-6476/6485	464181/190	10
B-52G-85-BW	57-6486/6499	464191/204	14
B-52G-90-BW	57-6500/6520	464205/225	21
B-52G-95-BW	58-0158/0187	464226/255	30
B-52G-100-BW	58-0188/0211	464256/279	24
B-52G-105-BW	58-0212/0232	464280/300	21
B-52G-110-BW	58-0233/0246	464301/314	14
B-52G-115-BW	58-0247/0258	464315/326	12
B-52G-120-BW	59-2564/2575	464327/338	12
B-52G-125-BW	59-2576/2587	464339/350	12
B-52G-130-BW	59-2588/2602	464351/365	15
B-52H-135-BW	60-0001/0013	464366/378	13
B-52H-140-BW	60-0014/0021	464379/386	8
B-52H-145-BW	60-0022/0033	464387/398	12
B-52H-150-BW	60-0034/0045	464399/410	12
B-52H-155-BW	60-0046/0057	464411/422	12
B-52H-160-BW	60-0058/0062	464423/427	5
B-52H-165-BW	61-0001/0013	464428/440	13
B-52H-170-BW	61-0014/0026	464441/453	13
B-52H-175-BW	61-0027/0040	464454/467	14

PRODUCTION BREAKDOWN BY VARIANT

Variant	Serial Numbers	Batch Total	Type/ Cumulative Total
XB-52	49-0230	1	1/1
YB-52	49-0231	1	1/2
B-52A	52-0001/0003	3	3/5
B-52B	53-0373/0376	4	
	53-0380/0398	19	23/28
RB-52B	52-0004/0013	10	
	52-8710/8716	7	
	53-0366/0372	7	
	53-0377/0379	3	27/55
B-52C	53-0399/0408	10	
	54-2664/2688	25	35/90
B-52D	55-0049/0117	69	
	55-0673/0680	8	
	56-0580/0630	51	
	56-0657/0698	42	170/260
B-52E	56-0631/0656	26	
	56-0699/0712	14	
	57-0014/0029	16	
	57-0095/0138	44	100/360
B-52F	57-0030/0073	44	
	57-0139/0183	45	89/449
B-52G	57-6468/6520	53	
	58-0158/0258	101	
	59-2564/2602	39	193/642
B-52H	60-0001/0062	62	
	61-0001/0040	40	102/744

B-52 VARIANTS

XB-52	New-build	1 produced
YB-52	New-build	1 produced
B-52A	New-build	3 produced
B-52B	New-build	23 produced
RB-52B	New-build	27 produced
B-52C	New-build	35 produced
B-52D	New-build	170 produced
B-52E	New-build	100 produced
B-52F	New-build	89 produced
B-52G	New-build	193 produced
B-52H	New-build	102 produced

NB-52

B-52A 52-0003 was modified in the late 1950s for use as a 'mother-ship' for the North American X-15 rocket-powered experimental research craft. It subsequently adopted the NB-52A designation and eventually carried the X-15 aloft on 59 of the powered flights conducted by that machine between 1959 and 1968, after which it was retired. It now belongs to the Pima County Museum Collection in Tucson.

GB-52B

Some redundant B/RB-52Bs were allocated to Air Force Training Command for ground instructional duties, adopting a 'G' prefix to indicate that they were permanently grounded airframes. Aircraft 52-0005 was certainly one such airframe, and 52-8714 may well have been another.

NB-52B

RB-52B 52-0008 received similar modifications to the sole NB-52A and was used for identical tasks in connection with the X-15 project, as well as serving as a launch platform for lifting bodies and remotely-piloted research vehicles. It still serves with NASA's Dryden facility as '008'.

JB-52C

This designation was allocated to two examples of the B-52C, both of which spent almost all of their flying careers on test duties. Use of the JB-52C designation by aircraft 53-0399 apparently related to a period of time when this machine was based at Wright-Patterson for ECM development. The other aircraft was 54-2676, which was destroyed in March 1957 while in use with Boeing's facility at Wichita.

RB-52C

Applicable to B-52Cs configured for reconnaissance with the weapons bay capsules first employed by the RB-52Bs. This designation was seldom used officially.

GB-52D

A few aircraft were reassigned for instructional duties at technical training centres, with the 'G' prefix indicating that these were permanently grounded. Examples include 55-0095, 55-0679, 56-0589, 56-0603 and 56-0664.

JB-52D

This designation may have been allocated to B-52D 56-0620, which is known to have undertaken tests of an unspecified nature with the Air Force's Special Weapons Center at Kirtland AFB, New Mexico (see also NB-52D)

NB-52D

At least one B-52D (56-0620) was apparently assigned to permanent test duties with Air Force Systems Command and the Air Force's Special Weapons Center. It was retired from service in November 1971, and may also have operated with the JB-52D designation at some point in its life.

GB-52E

At least one redundant B-52E (56-0708) was assigned to the Air Training Command on ground instructional duties as a GB-52E at the end of its flying career. In addition, 56-0637 may also have adopted this designation while serving as a ground instructional airframe at Andersen in the early 1970s.

NB-52E

One aircraft (56-0632) was allocated for test duties from the outset, and evaluated a number of features during the course of its career. These included nose-mounted winglet devices as well as electronic and electrical actuation of flight control surfaces. Apart from a basically red and white colour scheme, the most visible evidence of special purpose modification was a long nose probe which was still fitted when the jet was retired in June 1974. A second machine (57-0119) also used the NB-52E designation, but this was assigned to General Electric and spent much of its test career as a seven-engined aircraft, with a single XTF39 turbofan replacing the starboard inner pair of J57 turbojets.

GB-52F

A few aircraft were reassigned for instructional duties at technical training centres, with the 'G' prefix indicating these were permanently grounded. Aircraft that used this designation included 57-0042, 57-0048 and 57-0071.

GB-52G

A few aircraft were reassigned for instructional duties at technical training centres, with the 'G' prefix indicating these were permanently grounded. Examples noted to date comprise 57-6469, 58-0200 and 59-2578.

JB-52G

A temporary test designation that was allocated to a limited number of B-52G aircraft that were used for special research, development, test and evaluation duties. Known examples comprise 57-6470, 57-6471, 57-6473, 57-6477, 58-0159 and 58-0182.

XB-52G

This designation was reportedly applied to the first production B-52A (52-0001) which was used for tests of B-52G features such as the short fin in the mid to late 1950s.

JB-52H

A temporary test designation that was allocated to a limited number of B-52H aircraft that were used for special research, development, test and evaluation duties. Known examples comprise 60-0002, 60-0003, 60-0004, 60-0005 and 60-0006.

YB-52H

This designation was reportedly applied to one B-52G (57-6471 – see also JB-52G) which flew for a period with Pratt & Whitney TF33 turbofan engines as fitted to the definitive B-52H model. It subsequently reverted to standard B-52G configuration and saw service with several SAC units.

APPENDIX 3

VARIANTS IN DETAIL

XB/YB-52

Two aircraft were completed by Boeing's Seattle factory to serve as Stratofortress prototypes. Both were initially ordered as XB-52s, although the second example was redesignated as the YB-52 in the wake of a 1949 Boeing proposal which recommended installing some tactical equipment in order that it might serve as a production prototype. This idea was endorsed by the US Air Force, but apparently fell by the wayside, since there were no appreciable differences between the two when they were eventually completed and flown in 1952. Official USAF acceptance occurred in March 1953 (YB-52) and April 1953 (XB-52), but both machines were bailed to Boeing until 1957-58. At that time, the XB-52 went to the Wright Air Development Center at Wright-Patterson AFB, Ohio, with which it later flew as a six-engined aircraft with four J57s inboard and two J75s outboard.

PROCUREMENT CONTRACT

W-33-03A-ac-15065 - Signed on 28 June 1946, this letter contract was approved on 2 September 1947 and was later amended several times as the design was refined and as development progressed towards the hardware stage. It was eventually expanded to include the pair of XB-52 prototypes, which were given the serial numbers 49-0230 and 49-0231 (c/n 16248-16249). However, as already noted, the second example (49-0231) was actually completed as the YB-52.

BLOCK NUMBERS

Not applicable - these aircraft were known simply as the XB-52-BO (49-0230) and YB-52-BO (49-0231).

OPERATIONAL USAGE

Nil - Both were employed for test-orientated duties throughout their flying careers.

DISPOSITION

Both aircraft ended their days at Wright-Patterson AFB, Ohio. The XB-52 was involved in flight test duties for some time, which included the period of use as a six-engined aircraft, before it was scrapped in the mid-1960s. The YB-52 had been donated to the USAF Museum collection as early as 27 January 1958 after logging 738 flying hours in 345 sorties. Like the XB-52, it was also scrapped in the mid-1960s, both aircraft evidently falling foul of a drive to clean-up the nation of surplus military hardware which had been inaugurated by President Lyndon B Johnson's wife.

B-52A

Although it looked at one time as if as many as 13 B-52A aircraft would be built, changes to procurement planning meant that production of this model totalled just three aircraft. All were built by Boeing at Seattle, with the trio being formally accepted by the USAF between June and September 1954.

PROCUREMENT CONTRACT

AF33(038)-21096 - Officially signed on 14 February 1951, this contract originally called for 13 aircraft but was amended on 9 June 1952 to cover just three, with the remainder earmarked for completion as B-52Bs. Serial numbers were 52-0001 to 52-0003 (c/n 16491-16493).

BLOCK NUMBERS

B-52A-1-BO – 52-0001 to 52-0003 (three in total)

OPERATIONAL USAGE

Nil - All three served on test-orientated tasks throughout their flying careers.

DISPOSITION

After several years of test-dedicated taskings, two of the three aircraft were retired from flying duty at the beginning of the 1960s. One subsequently found further use as a ground instruction aid, while another was broken up, with the third playing a major part in the X-15 project until it was also retired shortly before the end of the decade.

Ground Instruction: 20001 (Chanute Technical Training Centre)

Scrapped in 1961: 20002 (Reclamation authorised 4/61; at Tinker AFB, Ok)

Modified to NB-52A: 20003 (retired to Davis-Monthan AFB, Az, on 15 October 1969 and later passed on to the Pima County Air Museum at Tucson, Az)

B-52B

Production of this version of the Stratofortress totalled 50, with deliveries to the USAF starting in August 1954 and continuing until August 1956. All of them were manufactured at Seattle, with 27 being completed as RB-52Bs.

PROCUREMENT CONTRACTS

AF33(038)-21096 - This contract originally specified 13 B-52As but was changed on 9 June 1952, when the number of B-52As was cut back to three. In its amended form, it was decided that the other 10 machines covered by this contract would be produced as B-52Bs, along with another seven aircraft added at this time. As it transpired, all 17 were actually completed as RB-52Bs. Serial numbers were 52-0004 to 52-0013 (c/n 16494-16503) and 52-8710 to 52-8716 (c/n 16838-16844).

AF33(600)-22119 - As initially drawn up in September 1952 and formally signed on 15 April 1953, this contract covered a total of 43 RB-52Bs. Subsequently, in May 1954, it was amended and the number of RB-52Bs fell to 33, with the remaining 10 machines due for completion as RB-52Cs. In fact, only 10 of these aircraft were actually built as RB-52Bs, with the rest emerging from the factory as B-52Bs. Airframe serial numbers were 53-0366 to 53-0398 (c/n 16845-16877).

BLOCK NUMBERS

RB-52B-5-BO	52-0004 to 52-0006	(3)
RB-52B-10-BO	52-0007 to 52-0013	(7)
RB-52B-15-BO	52-8710 to 52-8715	(6)
RB-52B-20-BO	52-8716	(1)
RB-52B-25-BO	53-0366 to 53-0372	(7)
B-52B-25-BO	53-0373 to 53-0376	(4)
RB-52B-30-BO	53-0377 to 53-0379	(3)
B-52B-30-BO	53-0380 to 53-0387	(8)
B-52B-35-BO	53-0388 to 53-0398	(11)

OPERATIONAL USAGE

22 BW	1963-66	(2 BS)
93 BW	1955-65?	(328 BS)
	1955-65?	(329 BS)
	1955-63	(330 BS)
95 BW	1959-66	(334 BS)
99 BW	1958-59	(346 BS)
	1958-59	(347 BS)
	1958-59	(348 BS)

DISPOSITION

Most surviving examples were retired during 1965-66, with 52-8714 being the very first B-52 to be retired by a SAC outfit when it was transferred to Chanute AFB, Illinois, on 8 March 1965. As is usual, most ended up at Davis-Monthan AFB, Arizona, but a few examples went straight to museum collections - these included 52-8711, which had been the first Stratofortress to be handed over to SAC a decade earlier. Remarkably, in view of its age, one early production example still flies with NASA.

Currently active:
 20008 (as NB-52B '008' with NASA at Dryden Research Facility, Edwards AFB, Ca)

Retired to MASDC 5/65 to 2/67:
 20004, 20005, 20006, 20007, 20010, 20011, 20012, 28710, 28712, 28713, 28715, 30366, 30367, 30368, 30369, 30370, 30372, 30373, 30374, 30375, 30376, 30378, 30381, 30383, 30385, 30386, 30387, 30388, 30389, 30391, 30392, 30395, 30396, 30397, 30398

To AFFTC in 1965:
 30379 (deleted from inventory in 1970)

Tested to destruction 6/66:
 20007, 20010 (both via store at MASDC between 2/66-5/66 - destroyed at Holloman)

Retired/preserved:
 20013 (Atomic Museum, Kirtland AFB, NM)
 28711 (SAC Museum, Offutt AFB, Ne)
 30394 (USAF Museum, Wright-Patterson AFB, Oh)

Attrition:
 20009, 28716, 30371, 30380, 30382, 30384, 30390, 30393

Ground Instruction:
 20005 (To Lowry TTC, via MASDC)
 28714 (To Chanute TTC)
 30377 (Andersen AFB, Guam - scrapped there?)

B-52C

Only 35 examples of the B-52C were completed, and these were all handed over to the USAF between February and December 1956. The B-52C was also noteworthy in being the last model to be built solely at Seattle.

PROCUREMENT CONTRACTS

AF33(600)-22119 - In its original form, this contract covered 43 RB-52Bs but a May 1954 amendment resulted in the last 10 being ordered as RB-52Cs. At the same time, 25 more RB-52Cs were added. In the event, these emerged as B-52Cs, featuring dual bomber and reconnaissance capability. Serial numbers were 53-0399 to 53-0408 (c/n 16878-16887) and 54-2664 to 54-2688 (c/n 17159-17183).

BLOCK NUMBERS

B-52C-40-BO	53-0399 to 53-0408	(10)
B-52C-45-BO	54-2664 to 54-2675	(12)
B-52C-50-BO	54-2676 to 54-2688	(13)

OPERATIONAL USAGE

42 BW	1956-57 (69 BS)
	1956-57 (70 BS)
	1956-57 (75 BS)
99 BW	1956-66 (346 BS)
	1956-61 (347 BS - to 4047 SW with B-52D)
	1956-66 (348 BS)

During 1957-61, the 99th BW also operated the B-52D model, although it seems that these aircraft were consolidated and departed with the 347th BS when that squadron was reassigned to the 4047th SW. After 1966, B-52Cs that had been assigned to the 99th BW were used as 'trainers' by a number of Wings until 1971. Units known to have employed the B-52C in this fashion comprised the 22nd BW; 28th BW; 70th BW; 91st BW; 92nd SAW; 96th SAW; 99th BW; 306th BW; 454th BW; 461st BW and 509th BW.

DISPOSITION

Apart from a few aircraft that were destroyed while in service, the B-52C remained active until 1971, when 29 examples were sent for long term storage at Davis-Monthan AFB. The last aircraft to be withdrawn ended its flying career with the Air Force Flight Test Center at Edwards AFB in July 1975.

Retired to MASDC 3/71-9/71:
 30400, 30401, 30402, 30403, 30404, 30405, 30407, 30408, 42664, 42665, 42668, 42669, 42670, 42671, 42672, 42673, 42674, 42675, 42677, 42678, 42679, 42680, 42681, 42683, 42684, 42685, 42686, 42687, 42688

Retired to MASDC 7/75:
 30399

Attrition:
 30406, 42666, 42667, 42676, 42682

B-52D

Production of this version totalled 170, all of which were accepted by the USAF between June 1956 and November 1957. As well as being the second most numerous derivative, it was also the first to be manufactured at two locations. Boeing's parent factory at Seattle was responsible for the completion of 101 aircraft, with the second-source centre at Wichita accounting for the balance of 69. In fact, it was a Wichita-built aircraft which was the first B-52D to fly, on 4 June 1956.

PROCUREMENT CONTRACTS

AF33(600)-26235 - Concluded on 29 November 1954, this was the first contract for Wichita-built aircraft and covered 27 B-52Ds. Two batches of serial numbers were assigned to these aircraft, comprising 55-0049 to 55-0067 (c/n 464001-464019) plus 55-0673 to 55-0680 (c/n 464020-464027).

AF33(600)-28223 - Finalised on 31 August 1954, this covered the procurement of an initial batch of 50 aircraft from Boeing's factory at Seattle. Serial numbers allocated to these aircraft were 55-0068 to 55-0117 (c/n 17184-17233).

AF33(600)-31155 - Signed on 10 August 1955 but not finalised until 31 January 1956, this was the second contract for Wichita-built aircraft and consisted of 42 examples of the B-52D plus 14 of the B-52E sub-types. Serial numbers of the B-52Ds were 56-0657 to 56-0698 (c/n 464028-464069).

AF33(600)-31267 - Signed on 26 October 1955, this was also drawn up to cover procurement of both the B-52D and B-52E from the factory at Seattle. It comprised 51 examples of the B-52D, as well as 26 B-52Es. Serial numbers of the B-52Ds were 56-0580 to 56-0630 (c/n 17263-17313).

BLOCK NUMBERS

B-52D-1-BW	55-0049 to 55-0051	(3)
B-52D-5-BW	55-0052 to 55-0054	(3)
B-52D-10-BW	55-0055 to 55-0060	(6)
B-52D-15-BW	55-0061 to 55-0064	(4)
B-52D-20-BW	55-0065 to 55-0067	(3)
	55-0673 to 55-0675	(3)
B-52D-25-BW	55-0676 to 55-0680	(5)
B-52D-30-BW	56-0657 to 56-0668	(12)
B-52D-35-BW	56-0669 to 56-0680	(12)
B-52D-40-BW	56-0681 to 56-0698	(18)
B-52D-55-BO	55-0068 to 55-0088	(21)
B-52D-60-BO	55-0089 to 55-0104	(16)
B-52D-65-BO	55-0105 to 55-0117	(13)
B-52D-70-BO	56-0580 to 56-0590	(11)
B-52D-75-BO	56-0591 to 56-0610	(20)
B-52D-80-BO	56-0611 to 56-0630	(20)

OPERATIONAL USAGE

7 BW	1971-82 (9 BS)
	1969-83 (20 BS)
22 BW	1966-82 (2 BS)
	1966-71 (486 BS - from 340 BW)
28 BW	1957-71 (77 BS)
	1957-60 (717 BS - to 4245 SW)
	1957-60 (718 BS - to 4128 SW)
42 BW	1957-59 (69 BS)
	1957-59 (70 BS)
	1957-59 (75 BS - to 4039 SW with B-52G)
43 SW	1972-83 (60 BS)
	1972-73 (63 BS(P))
70 BW	1968-69 (6 BS)
91 BW	1963-68 (322 BS - replaced 326 BS/4141 SW)
92 BW/SAW	1957-71 (325 BS)
	1957-61 (326 BS - to 4141 SW)
	1957-60 (327 BS - to 4170 SW)
93 BW	1956-58; 1965-74 (328 BS)
	1956-58; 1965-71 (329 BS)
	1956-58 (330 BS)
96 SAW/BW	1969-82 (337 BS)
99 BW	1957-61; 1966-72 (346 BS)
	1957-61 (347 BS - to 4047 SW)
	1957-61; 1966-72 (348 BS)
306 BW	1963-73 (367 BS - replaced 347 BS/4047 SW)
307 SW	1970-73 (direct Wing control - replaced 4258 SW)
	1973-75 (364 BS(P))
	1973-74 (365 BS(P))
340 BW	1963-66 (486 BS - replaced 335 BS/4130 SW; to 22 BW)
376 SW	1970 (direct Wing control - replaced 4252 SW)
454 BW	1966-69 (736 BS)
461 BW	1963-68 (764 BS - replaced 718 BS/4128 SW)
462 SAW	1963-66 (768 BS - replaced 327 BS/4170 SW)
484 BW	1963-67 (824 BS - replaced 336 BS/4138 SW)
494 BW	1963-66 (864 BS - replaced 717 BS/4245 SW)
509 BW	1966-69 (393 BS)
4047 BW	1961-63 (917 BS - assets to 367 BS/306 BW)
4128 SW	1960-63 (718 BS - assets to 764 BS/461 BW)
4130 SW	1959-63 (335 BS - assets to 486 BS/340 BW)
4138 SW	1959-63 (336 BS - assets to 824 BS/484 BW)
4141 SW	1961-63 (326 BS - assets to 322 BS/91 BW)
4170 SW	1960-63 (327 BS - assets to 768 BS/462 SAW)
4245 SW	1960-63 (717 BS - assets to 864 BS/494 BW)
4252 SW	1968-70 (direct Wing control - replaced by 376 SW)
4258 SW	1967-70 (direct Wing control - replaced by 307 SW)

Other units using B-52Ds as 'trainers' in the late 1970s were the 2nd BW; 28th BW; 92nd BW; 93rd BW; 97th BW; 319th BW; 379th BW; 410th BW and 416th BW. The number assigned was typically two or three, although one unit had as many as five. They were among the 37 B-52Ds withdrawn in August-December 1978. Since they were not the primary model in use, they are not listed under operational useage heading.

DISPOSITION

Apart from attrition losses and isolated withdrawals, the B-52D fleet remained virtually intact until 37 examples were retired and consigned to storage at Davis-Monthan AFB between August and December 1978. The final phase-out took place in 1982/83, when over 50 B-52Ds were despatched to the Arizona storage facility over a 12-month period, with many others joining museum collections across America.

Retired to MASDC 11/71-6/77: 50076, 60598, 60620.

Retired to MASDC 8-12/78:
50049, 50051, 50052, 50053, 50054, 50055, 50064, 50072, 50081, 50096, 50106, 50109, 50117, 50678, 50680, 60581, 60582, 60583, 60590, 60592, 60603, 60604, 60609, 60611, 60613, 60615, 60618, 60619, 60623, 60624, 60626, 60673, 60675, 60678, 60682, 60691, 60693

Retired to MASDC 1982-83:

50059, 50066, 50067, 50069, 50070, 50073, 50074, 50075, 50077, 50079, 50080, 50084, 50086, 50087, 50088, 50090, 50091, 50092, 50101, 50104, 50105, 50107, 50111, 50113, 50673, 50674, 50675, 60580, 60587, 60588, 60596, 60600, 60602, 60606, 60614, 60617, 60621, 60658, 60659, 60660, 60663, 60666, 60667, 60668, 60670, 60671, 60672, 60679, 60684, 60686, 60690, 60694, 60697, 60698

Possibly retired in 1983:

50071 (removed from store and to Mobile)

Attrition losses:

50050, 50056, 50058, 50060, 50061, 50065, 50078, 50082, 50089, 50093, 50097, 50098, 50102, 50103, 50108, 50110, 50114, 50115, 50116, 50676, 60584, 60591, 60593, 60594, 60595, 60597, 60599, 60601, 60605, 60607, 60608, 60610, 60622, 60625, 60627, 60630, 60661, 60669, 60674, 60677, 60681

Tested to destruction:

50112 (at Wichita in 1973)
60616 (at Wichita in 1971)

Blown-up:

60662, 60680, 60688 (at Carswell, Tx 4/84)

Ground Instruction:

50095 (Chanute, Il)
50099 (Andersen, Guam - scrapped post-1986?)
60586 (Andersen, Guam - scrapped post-1986?)
60589 (Sheppard, Tx)
60603 (Lowry, Co - removed from storage)
60628 (Dyess, Tx - scrapped early 1980s)
60664 (Andersen, Guam - scrapped post-1986?)

Preserved aircraft:

50057 (Maxwell, Al)
50062 (K I Sawyer, Mi)
50063 (Pate Museum, Cresson, Tx)
50067 (Pima County, Tucson, Az - ex store)
50068 (Lackland, Tx)
50071 (Mobile, Al - ex-store)
50083 (AF Academy, Colorado Springs, Co)
50085 (Robins, Ga)
50094 (McConnell, Ks)
50100 (Andersen, Guam)
50105 (Seoul, Korea - ex-store)
50677 (Willow Run, Mi)
50679 (March, Ca)
60585 (Edwards, Ca)
60612 (Castle, Ca)
60629 (Barksdale, La)
60657 (Ellsworth, SD)
60676 (Fairchild, Wa)
60683 (Pease, NH, then to Whiteman, Mo)
60685 (Dyess, Tx)
60687 (Orlando Fl)
60689 (Duxford, England)
60692 (Kelly, Tx)
60695 (Tinker, Ok)
60696 (Travis, Ca)

Unaccounted for:

60665 (note - scrapped circa 1980 due to life expired?)

B-52E

Production of this model eventually totalled 100, all of which were accepted by the USAF between October 1957 and June 1958. Like the B-52D, manufacture was undertaken at two locations, with Seattle completing 42 aircraft while Wichita contributed the remaining 58.

PROCUREMENT CONTRACTS

AF33(600)-31155 - Signed on 10 August 1955, this covered 14 B-52E model aircraft, all to be built at Wichita. Serial numbers were 56-0699 to 56-0712 (c/n 464070-464083).

AF33(600)-31267 - Concluded on 26 October 1955, this was essentially a B-52D contract to which 26 B-52Es were added. Serial numbers allotted to these aircraft were 56-0631 to 56-0656 (c/n 17314-17339) and they came from the Seattle line.

AF33(600)-32863 - Signed on 2 July 1956, this covered a further 16 B-52Es as well as 44 B-52Fs, all to be built in Seattle. Serial numbers were 57-0014 to 57-0029 (c/n 17408-17423).

AF33(600)-32864 - Signed on 2 July 1956, this was the last of the four contracts that included B-52E model procurement and was also the largest, adding a further 44 aircraft. Serial numbers were 57-0095 to 57-0138 (c/n 464084-464127) and they were all built in Wichita.

BLOCK NUMBERS

B-52E-45-BW	56-0699 to 56-0712	(14)
B-52E-50-BW	57-0095 to 57-0109	(15)
B-52E-60-BW	57-0131 to 57-0138	(8)
B-52E-85-BO	56-0631 to 56-0649	(19)
B-52E-90-BO	56-0650 to 56-0656	(7)
	57-0014 to 57-0022	(9)
B-52E-95-BO	57-0023 to 57-0029	(7)

OPERATIONAL USAGE

6 BW/SAW	1957-67 (24 BS)
	1957-63 (39 BS)
	1957-67 (40 BS)
11 BW/SAW	1958-68 (26 BS)
	1958-60 (42 BS - to 4043 SW)
17 BW	1963-68 (34 BS - replaced 42 BS/4043 SW)
70 BW	1963-68 (6 BS - replaced 98 BS/4123 SW)
93 BW	1957-58; 1967-70 (328 BS)
	1957-58; 1967-70 (329 BS)
	1957-58 (330 BS)
96 SAW	1963-70 (337 BS)
4043 SW	1960-63 (42 BS - assets to 34 BS/17 BW)
4123 SW	1959-63 (98 BS - assets to 6 BS/70 BW)

A few B-52Es are known to have been assigned to the 22nd BW as 'trainers' in 1968-70.

DISPOSITION

A small number of life-expired airframes were retired for storage at Davis-Monthan AFB, Arizona during the course of 1967, with the bulk of the fleet following suit between May 1969 and March 1970 when no fewer than 82 examples were withdrawn from the inventory for long-term storage. Of the other 10 aircraft, two passed to ground instructional tasks; three were assigned to test duties; two were almost certainly reclaimed and scrapped and three were destroyed in accidents.

Retired to MASDC 1/67-6/67:

70014, 70028, 70029, 70111, 70113, 70114, 70117, 70137

Retired to MASDC 5/69-3/70:

60632, 60634, 60635, 60638, 60639, 60640, 60641, 60642, 60643, 60644, 60645, 60646, 60647, 60648, 60649, 60650, 60651, 60652, 60653, 60654, 60656, 60699, 60700, 60701, 60702, 60703, 60704, 60705, 60706, 60707, 60709, 60710, 60711, 60712, 70015, 70016, 70017, 70020, 70021, 70022, 70023, 70024, 70025, 70026, 70027, 70095, 70096, 70097, 70098, 70099, 70100, 70101, 70102, 70103, 70104, 70105, 70106, 70107, 70108, 70109, 70110, 70112, 70115, 70116, 70118, 70120, 70121, 70122, 70123, 70124, 70125, 70126, 70127, 70128, 70129, 70130, 70131, 70132, 70133, 70135, 70136, 70138

Test airframes:

60632 (Retired by AFFTC on 26/6/74)
60636 (Retired by Pratt & Whitney on 30/7/81)
70119 (General Electric - preserved?)

Attrition:

60633, 60655, 70018

Scrapped:

70019 (Possibly reclaimed and cannibalised at Tulsa in late 1965 after service with 70 BW)
70134 (In inactive status at Tinker AFB, Ok in 3/66 for storage/reclamation after service with 96 SAW)

Ground Instruction:

60637 (Andersen AFB, Guam - scrapped there?)
60708 (Chanute Technical Training Center)

B-52F

Production of this model totalled 89, all of which were handed over to the USAF between June 1958 and February 1959. Manufacture was undertaken at two locations, with Seattle closing out its contribution to the Stratofortress production programme by completing 44 aircraft, while Wichita was responsible for the remaining 45 airframes that made up the USAF order.

PROCUREMENT CONTRACTS

AF33(600)-32863 - Signed on 2 July 1956, this contract covered a small batch of B-52Es, but was predominantly for the B-52Fs that were built in Seattle. Serial numbers of the B-52Fs were 57-0030 to 57-0073 (c/n 17424-17467).

AF33(600)-32864 - Also signed on 2 July 1956, this too was a mixed-model contract, covering the procurement of 44 B-52Es and 45 B-52Fs, all of which were built at Wichita. Serial numbers of the B-52Fs were 57-0139 to 57-0183 (c/n 464128-464172).

BLOCK NUMBERS

B-52F-65-BW	57-0139 to 57-0154	(16)
B-52F-70-BW	57-0155 to 57-0183	(29)
B-52F-100-BO	57-0030 to 57-0037	(8)
B-52F-105-BO	57-0038 to 57-0052	(15)
B-52F-110-BO	57-0053 to 57-0073	(21)

OPERATIONAL USAGE

2 BW	1963-65 (20 BS - replaced 436 BS/4238 SW; to 7 BW)
7 BW	1958-68 (9 BS)
	1965-69 (20 BS - from 2 BW)
93 BW	1958-78 (328 BS)
	1958-71 (329 BS)
	1958-63 (330 BS)
320 BW	1963-68 (441 BS - replaced 72 BS/4134 SW)
454 BW	1963-66 (736 BS - replaced 492 BS/4228 SW)
4134 SW	1958-63 (72 BS - assets to 441 BS/320 BW)
4228 SW	1959-63 (492 BS - assets to 736 BS/454 BW)
4238 SW	1958-63 (436 BS - assets to 20 BS/2 BW)

Other units that evidently employed examples of the B-52F model as 'trainers' in the late 1970s include the 2nd, 28th, 42nd, 92nd, 97th and 416th BWs. It appears that no more than two aircraft were assigned to any of these units and these machines were among the 22 B-52Fs that were withdrawn from service during the course of 1978. Since they were not the primary model in use with these Wings at the time, they do not appear under the operational useage heading.

DISPOSITION

Some 15 life-expired airframes were retired for storage at Davis-Monthan AFB during the 1967-68 timeframe, with 37 more following suit between June 1969 and May 1973, before a last batch of 23 aircraft was withdrawn for storage between August and December 1978. Of the remaining aircraft, at least one was preserved and two passed directly to ground instructional training tasks at the end of their flying careers.

Retired to MASDC 1/67-8/68:

70030, 70040, 70044, 70049, 70068, 70070, 70141, 70144, 70146, 70156, 70157, 70158, 70164, 70167, 70181

Retired to MASDC 6/69-12/78:

70031, 70032, 70033, 70034, 70035, 70037, 70039, 70045, 70046, 70048, 70051, 70052, 70053, 70054, 70055, 70056, 70057, 70058, 70059, 70060, 70061, 70062, 70063, 70064, 70065, 70066, 70067, 70069, 70072, 70139, 70140, 70142, 70143, 70145, 70147, 70148, 70150, 70151, 70152, 70153, 70154, 70155, 70159, 70160, 70161, 70162, 70163, 70165, 70168, 70169, 70170, 70171, 70174, 70175, 70176, 70177, 70178, 70180, 70182, 70183

Preserved airframe:

70038 (Oklahoma City State Fairground)

Attrition losses:

70036, 70041, 70043, 70047, 70149, 70166, 70172, 70173, 70179

Ground Instruction:

70042 (Chanute Technical Training Center)
70048 (Lowry Technical Training Center - ex-storage at Davis-Monthan)
70071 (Sheppard Technical Training Center)

Unaccounted for:

70050 (last reported as 93 BW in 1969 but may have suffered a ground accident or undergone abnormal deterioration between 6-9/70. Could well have been scrapped at Castle AFB, Ca)

70073 (with Boeing at Seattle until at least July 1962. Subsequent fate unknown)

B-52G

This eventually became the most numerous sub-type of the Stratofortress family, with 193 examples being delivered to the USAF between October 1958 and February 1961. It was also the first derivative to be manufactured only at the Wichita factory.

PROCUREMENT CONTRACTS

AF33(600)-35992 - Finalised on 15 May 1958, this was the initial contract for the B-52G model and covered 53 aircraft purchased with FY 57 funding appropriations. Serial numbers were 57-6468 to 57-6520 (c/n 464173-464225)

AF33(600)-36470 - Also finalised on 15 May 1958, the second B-52G contract at one time also looked like being the last, since this completed procurement of the 603 aircraft target that had been set in December 1956. It covered a total of 101 jets, obtained with FY 58 funds. Serials were 58-0158 to 58-0258 (c/n 464226-464326).

AF33(600)-37481 - The third and last B-52G contract was formally finalised on 28 April 1959 and was the first of three 'add-ons' which raised total procurement of all models to 744. It covered 39 aircraft, obtained with FY 59 funds. Serial numbers allocated were 59-2564 to 59-2602 (c/n 464327-464365).

BLOCK NUMBERS

B-52G-75-BW	57-6468 to 57-6475	(8)
B-52G-80-BW	57-6476 to 57-6485	(10)
B-52G-85-BW	57-6486 to 57-6499	(14)
B-52G-90-BW	57-6500 to 57-6520	(21)
B-52G-95-BW	58-0158 to 58-0187	(30)
B-52G-100-BW	58-0188 to 58-0211	(24)
B-52G-105-BW	58-0212 to 58-0232	(21)
B-52G-110-BW	58-0233 to 58-0246	(14)
B-52G-115-BW	58-0247 to 58-0258	(12)
B-52G-120-BW	59-2564 to 59-2575	(12)
B-52G-125-BW	59-2576 to 59-2587	(12)
B-52G-130-BW	59-2588 to 59-2602	(15)

OPERATIONAL USAGE

2 BW	1965-92 (62 BS - ex 39 BW 25/6/65)
	1968-92 (596 BS - ex 397 BW 15/4/68)
5 BW	1959-68 (23 BS)
	1959-60 (31 BS - to 4126 SW 1/60)
17 BW	1975-76 (34 BS)
19 BW	1968-83 (28 BS)
28 BW	1971-77 (77 BS)
39 BW	1963-65 (62 BS - replaced 301 BS/4135 SW; to 2 BW)
42 BW	1959-94 (69 BS)
	1959-66 (70 BS)
43 SW/BW	1983-90 (60 BS)
68 BW	1963-82 (51 BS - replaced 73 BS/4241 SW)
72 BW	1959-71 (60 BS)
92 SAW/BW	1970-86 (325 BS)
93 BW	1966-67, 1974-94 (328 BS)
	1966-67 (329 BS)
97 BW	1960-92 (340 BS)

319 BW	1982-87 (46 BS)
320 BW	1968-89 (441 BS)
366 Wing	1992-94 (34 BS)
379 BW	1977-92 (524 BS)
380 SAW	1966-71 (528 BS)
397 BW	1963-68 (596 BS - replaced 341 BS/4038 SW; to 2 BW)
416 BW	1963-92 (668 BS - replaced 75 BS/4039 SW)
456 SAW/BW	1963-75 (744 BS - replaced 31 BS/4126 SW)
465 BW	1963-68 (781 BS - replaced 342 BS/4137 SW)
4038 SW	1960-63 (341 BS - assets to 596 BS/397 BW)
4039 SW	1960-63 (75 BS - assets to 668 BS/416 BW)
4126 SW	1960-63 (31 BS - ex 5 BW 1/60; assets to 744 BS/456 SAW)
4135 SW	1959-63 (301 BS - assets to 62 BS/39 BW)
4137 SW	1960-63 (342 BS - assets to 781 BS/465 BW)
4241 SW	1959-63 (73 BS - assets to 51 BS/68 BW)

DISPOSITION

Apart from attrition losses, no example of the B-52G was deleted from the operational inventory until just before the end of the 1980s. The process of retirement finally ended in the spring of 1994 when the last active B-52Gs went to Davis-Monthan AFB. A few examples were passed to museum collections in the United States.

Retired to AMARC 5/94:

76470, 76471, 76472, 76473, 76474, 76475, 76476, 76477, 76478, 76480, 76483, 76484, 76485, 76486, 76487, 76488, 76489, 76490, 76491, 76492, 76495, 76497, 76498, 76499, 76500, 76501, 76502, 76503, 76504, 76505, 76506, 76508, 76510, 76511, 76512, 76513, 76514, 76515, 76516, 76517, 76518, 76519, 76520, 80159, 80160, 80162, 80163, 80164, 80165, 80166, 80167, 80168, 80170, 80171, 80172, 80173, 80175, 80176, 80177, 80178, 80179, 80181, 80182, 80183, 80184, 80186, 80189, 80192, 80193, 80194, 80195, 80197, 80199, 80202, 80203, 80204, 80205, 80206, 80207, 80210, 80211, 80212, 80213, 80214, 80216, 80217, 80218, 80220, 80221, 80222, 80223, 80224, 80226, 80227, 80229, 80230, 80231, 80232, 80233, 80235, 80236, 80237, 80238, 80239, 80240, 80241, 80242, 80243, 80244, 80245, 80247, 80248, 80249, 80250, 80251, 80252, 80253, 80254, 80255, 80257, 80258, 92564, 92565, 92566, 92567, 92568, 92569, 92570, 92571, 92572, 92573, 92575, 92579, 92580, 92581, 92582, 92583, 92585, 92586, 92587, 92588, 92589, 92590, 92591, 92592, 92594, 92595, 92598, 92599, 92602

Retired by 12/93 (location unknown):

80158, 80234, 92577

Preserved aircraft:

76468 (SAC Museum, Offutt AFB, Ne)
76509 (Eighth AF Museum, Barksdale AFB, La)
80183 (Pima County Museum - ex-AMARC store)
80195 (Eglin AFB, Fl)
80191 (Hill AFB, Ut)
80225 (Griffiss AFB, NY)
92584 (Snohomish, Wa?)
92596 (Darwin, Australia)
92601 (Langley AFB, Va)

Attrition losses:

76479, 76481, 76482, 76493, 76494, 76496, 76507, 80161, 80169, 80174, 80180, 80187, 80188, 80190, 80196, 80198,

80201, 80208, 80209, 80215, 80219, 80228, 80246, 80256, 92574, 92576, 92593, 92597, 92600

Ground instruction:

76469 (Sheppard Technical Training Center)
80200 (Sheppard Technical Training Center)
92578 (Sheppard Technical Training Center)

B-52H

Production of the Stratofortress family terminated with a total of 102 turbofan-powered B-52Hs, all of which were accepted by the USAF between March 1961 and October 1962. As with the B-52G, manufacture was undertaken solely at Wichita.

PROCUREMENT CONTRACTS

AF33(600)-38778 - The first contract for the B-52H was finalised on 6 May 1960 and covered 62 aircraft with FY 60 funding. Serial numbers were 60-0001 to 60-0062 (c/n 464366-464427).

AF33(600)-41961 - Procurement of the Stratofortress terminated with this contract, for 40 B-52Hs. It was initiated by letter on 28 July 1960 but was not finalised until late 1962. Serial numbers were 61-0001 to 61-0040 (c/n 464428-464467).

BLOCK NUMBERS

B-52H-135-BW	60-0001 to 60-0013	(13)
B-52H-140-BW	60-0014 to 60-0021	(8)
B-52H-145-BW	60-0022 to 60-0033	(12)
B-52H-150-BW	60-0034 to 60-0045	(12)
B-52H-155-BW	60-0046 to 60-0057	(12)
B-52H-160-BW	60-0058 to 60-0062	(5)
B-52H-165-BW	61-0001 to 61-0013	(13)
B-52H-170-BW	61-0014 to 61-0026	(13)
B-52H-175-BW	61-0027 to 61-0040	(14)

OPERATIONAL USAGE

2 Wing/BW	1994-current (11 BS)
	1992-current (20 BS - from 7 BW)
	1993-current (96 BS - assets from 596 BS)
	1992-93 (596 BS - assets to 96 BS)
5 BW	1968-current (23 BS - replaced 720 BS/450 BW)
	1995-current (72 BS)
7 BW	1982-92 (9 BS)
	1983-92 (20 BS - to 2 Wing)
17 BW	1968-75 (34 BS)
19 BW	1962-68 (28 BS)
28 BW	1977-86 (37 BS)
	1977-82 (77 BS)
92 BW	1986-94 (325 BS)
93 BW	1974-83 (328 BS)
96 BW	1982-85 (337 BS)
319 BW	1963-82 (46 BS - replaced 30 BS/4133 SW)
379 BW	1961-77 (524 BS)
410 BW	1963-94 (644 BS - replaced 526 BS/4042 SW)
416 BW	1992-94 (668 BS)
449 BW	1963-77 (716 BS - replaced 93 BS/4239 SW)
450 BW	1963-68 (720 BS - replaced 525 BS/4136 SW; replaced by 23 BS/5 BW)
917 Wg/AFRes	1993-current (93 BS)

4042 SW	1961-63 (526 BS - assets to 644 BS/410 BW)
4133 SW	1962-63 (30 BS - assets to 46 BS/319 BW)
4136 SW	1961-63 (525 BS - assets to 720 BS/450 BW)
4239 SW	1961-63 (93 BS - assets to 716 BS/449 BW)

DISPOSITION

No B-52Hs have been retired, and virtually all of the original 102 jets are still active with frontline, second-line and test units.

Attrition losses:

00006, 00027, 00039, 00040, 10026, 10030, 10033, 10037

ABOVE AND BELOW Two more views of the NB-52A show it carrying the X-15 and moments after launching the research craft on another foray into the fringes of the earth's atmosphere. Just under 200 powered flights were made before the project ended, with NB-52B 52-0008 also being used as a 'mothe-ship'

APPENDIX 4

B-52 Wing Organisations

2ND BW

Operated B-47 from Hunter AFB, Georgia, as 2 BW(M) until 1/4/63. On that date, it was redesignated 2 BW(H) and moved to Barksdale AFB, Louisiana, taking over aircraft and personnel previously assigned to the 4238 SW. Redesignated 2 Wing on 1/10/91 and 2 BW on 1/10/93. Currently active with B-52.

11th BS
Activated on 1/7/94 as part of consolidation process that has concentrated the B-52H fleet at two bases. Assigned to 2 BW with immediate effect to fulfil crew training duties. Currently active with B-52H as part of 2 BW

20th BS
Acquired B-52Fs previously used by the 436 BS/4238 SW on 1/4/63 and operated these as part of the 2 BW until reassigned to the 7 BW on 25/6/65. Reassigned to 2 Wing on 17/12/92 and currently active with B-52H as part of 2 BW.

62nd BS
Equipped with B-52G when reassigned from the 39 BW on 25/6/65. Utilised this model with 2 BW/Wg until 17/12/92, when inactivated and replaced by 20 BS.

96th BS
Activated on 1/10/93 to replace the 596 BS with 2 BW. Currently active with B-52H as part of this Wing.

596th BS
Equipped with B-52G when reassigned from the 397 BW on 15/4/68. Utilised this model with 2 BW/Wg until 1992, when re-equipped with B-52H. Inactivated 1/10/93 and replaced by 96 BS.

5TH BW

Disposed of RB/B-36 in 1958 as 5 BW(H) and acquired the B-52 in 1959 at Travis AFB, California. Subsequently moved to Minot AFB, North Dakota, on 25/7/68, taking over aircraft and personnel formerly with the 450 BW. Currently operating B-52.

23rd BS
Equipped with B-52G from 2/59 and utilised this model until 1968. Transferred to Minot AFB, North Dakota, on 25/7/68 and acquired B-52H aircraft previously flown by the 720 BS/450 BW. Currently active with B-52H as part of 5 BW.

31st BS
Equipped with B-52G in 1959, before being transferred to the 4126 SW. Remained assigned to 5 BW until 1/10/59 and was attached to 5 BW from 2/10/59 to 18/1/60, while moving from Travis to Beale. Full control passed to the 4126 SW on 18/1/60.

72nd BS
Activated at Minot on 6/1/95 as part of consolidation process that has concentrated the B-52H at two bases. Assigned to 5 BW with immediate effect, and currently active with B-52Hs as part of this Wing.

6TH BW

Converted from B-36 to B-52 during 1957 as 6 BW(H) at Walker AFB, New Mexico. Redesignated as 6 SAW 1/5/62. Ceased B-52 operations in early 1967 and then redesignated 6 SW at time of transfer to Eielson AFB, Alaska on 25/3/67.

24th BS
Equipped with B-52E from 12/57 and used this version until 1967. Inactivated on 25/1/67.

39th BS
Equipped with B-52E from 12/57 and used this version until 1963. Inactivated on 15/9/63.

40th BS
Equipped with B-52E from 12/57 and used this version until 1967. Inactivated on 25/1/67.

4129th CCTS
Established within 6 BW on 1/8/59 as part of expanded crew training force. Used B-52E until inactivated on 15/9/63.

7TH BW

Converted from B-36 to B-52 during 1958 as 7 BW(H) at Carswell AFB, Texas. Moved to Dyess AFB, Tx, 1/10/93, replacing 96 BW.

9th BS
Equipped with B-52F from 6/58 until inactivated on 25/6/68. Reactivated on 31/12/71 and equipped with B-52D which it utilised until 1982 when it converted to the B-52H. Passed aircraft to 2 Wing prior to inactivating on 15/8/92.

20th BS
Equipped with B-52F when transferred from the 2 BW on 25/6/65. Subsequently converted to B-52D in 1969 which it used until 1983 when it received the B-52H. Unit identity transferred to 2 Wing at Barksdale on 17/12/92.

98th BS
Attached to 7 BW between 1-10/12/57, when reassigned to the 4123 SW at Carswell. May possibly have begun to equip with the B-52E while on attachment.

492nd BS
Equipped with B-52F from 6/58 until 15/6/59 when moved to Columbus AFB, Mississippi, and reassigned to the 4228 SW.

4018th CCTS
Established within 7 BW on 1/4/74 as part of expanded crew training organisation. Used B-52D from 4/74 until inactivated on an unknown date.

11TH BW

Disposed of B-36 at Carswell AFB, Texas, in 1957 as 11 BW(H) and moved to Altus AFB, Oklahoma, on 13/12/57. Was equipped with B-52 in 1958. Redesignated 11 SAW 1/4/63. Ceased flying B-52 in 1968 and redesignated 11 ARW 2/7/68.

26th BS
Equipped with B-52E from 1/58 until 1968, operating initially from Clinton-Sherman AFB, Oklahoma, while construction work was carried out at Altus. Inactivated on 2/7/68.

42nd BS

Equipped with B-52E from 1/58 until 1/6/60, when reassigned to the 4043 SW at Wright-Patterson AFB, Ohio. Operated initially from Clinton-Sherman AFB, Oklahoma, while construction work was carried out at Altus.

17TH BW

Redesignated from 17 BW(T) to 17 BW(H) and activated on 15/11/62. Organised at Wright-Patterson AFB, Ohio, on 1/2/63 and took over aircraft and personnel previously assigned to the 4043 SW. Moved to Beale AFB, California, on 30/9/75, where it took over aircraft and personnel previously assigned to the 456 BW. Inactivated 30/9/76.

34th BS

Acquired B-52Es previously used by the 42 BS/4043 SW on 1/2/63 and used these until 1968, when re-equipped with B-52H. Disposed of last B-52H in 7/75 and moved to Beale AFB, California, on 30/9/75, taking over B-52Gs and personnel previously assigned to the 744 BS/456 BW. Inactivated 30/9/76.

19TH BW

Operated B-47 until 1961 as 19 BW(M) from Homestead AFB, Florida. Redesignated as 19 BW(H) on 1/7/61 and equipped with B-52 during 1962. Moved to Robins AFB, Georgia, on 25/7/68, where it took over aircraft and personnel previously assigned to the 465 BW. Ceased B-52 operations in 1983 and then redesignated as 19 ARW on 1/10/83.

28th BS

Equipped with B-52H from 2/62 and utilised this model until 1968. Transferred to Robins AFB, Georgia, on 25/7/68 and acquired B-52G aircraft previously flown by the 781 BS/465 BW. Inactivated on 1/10/83.

22ND BW

Operated B-47 until 1963 as 22 BW(M) from March AFB, California. Redesignated as 22 BW(H) on 15/3/63 and equipped with B-52. Ceased B-52 operations during 1982 and then redesignated 22 ARW on 1/10/82.

2nd BS

Equipped with B-52B from 9/63 until 1966 when it converted to B-52D which it retained until 1982. Also used some B-52Cs in 1967-71 and B-52Es in 1968-70. Inactivated 1/10/82.

486th BS

Equipped with B-52D when reassigned from the 340 BW on 2/10/66. Flew this model until 1971, as well as some B-52Cs in 1967-71 and B-52Es in 1968-70. Inactivated 1/7/71.

28TH BW

Converted from RB-36 to B-52 during 1957 as 28 BW(H) at Ellsworth AFB, South Dakota. Converted to B-1B in 1986.

37th BS

Equipped with B-52H on activation 1/7/77 and operated this model until inactivated on 1/10/82.

77th BS

Equipped with B-52D in 6/57 and operated this type until 1971,

plus some B-52Cs during 1967-71. Converted to B-52G in 1971 and B-52H in 1977. Converted to B-1B in 1986.

717th BS

Equipped with B-52D from 6/57 until 1/2/60, when reassigned to the 4245 SW at Sheppard AFB, Texas.

718th BS

Equipped with B-52D from 6/57 until 20/2/60, when reassigned to the 4128 SW at Amarillo AFB, Texas.

39TH BW

Established as 39 BW(H) and activated on 15/11/62. Was organised at Eglin AFB, Florida, on 1/2/63 and took over aircraft and personnel formerly assigned to the 4135 SW. Was discontinued and inactivated on 25/6/65.

62nd BS

Acquired B-52Gs previously used by the 301 BS/4135 SW on 1/2/63. Utilised this model as part of the 39 BW until 1965, being reassigned to the 2 BW at Barksdale AFB, Louisiana, on 25/6/65.

42ND BW

Converted from B-36 to B-52 during 1956 as 42 BW(H) at Loring AFB, Maine. Disposed of B-52 during 1993-94 and inactivated on 30/9/94.

69th BS

Equipped with B-52C in 6/56, but disposed of these in 1957 when it received the B-52D model. Converted again in 1959 to the B-52G. Disposed of B-52G during 1993-94, with last aircraft departing on 8/3/94. Since inactivated.

70th BS

Equipped with B-52C in 6/56, but disposed of these in 1957 when it received the B-52D model. Converted again in 1959 to the B-52G, which it operated until inactivated on 25/6/66.

75th BS

Equipped with B-52C in 6/56, but disposed of these in 1957 when it received the B-52D model. Used B-52D until 15/10/59, when reassigned to the 4039 SW at Griffiss AFB, New York.

43RD SW

Redesignated from 43 BW(M) to 43 SW on 4/2/70 and then activated at Andersen AFB, Guam, on 1/4/70. Replaced the 3960 SW. Wing organisation evidently gained direct responsibility for managing B-52D operations from the 4133 BW(P) in 7/70 and did not relinquish this until circa 3/72, when the 60 BS took over. Was redesignated as 43 BW on 4/11/86 and inactivated 30/9/90.

60th BS

Assigned with effect from 1/7/71 but remained in non operational status until ca 3/72, when assumed responsibility for B-52D operations from parent 43 SW. Used B-52D until 1983, when converted to B-52G, which it retained until 1990, being inactivated on 30/4/90.

63rd BS(P)

Established and attached to the 43 SW on 15/6/72. Operated B-52D from 6/72 until ca 11/73, thereafter remaining attached to the 43 SW until disestablished on 30/6/75.

68TH BW

Operated the B-47 from Chennault AFB, Louisiana, as 68 BW(M) until 15/4/63. On that date, it was redesignated as 68 BW(H) and moved to Seymour Johnson AFB, North Carolina, where it took over jets and personnel previously assigned to the 4241 SW. Ceased B-52 operations during 1982 and was officially inactivated on 30/9/82.

51st BS

Acquired B-52Gs previously used by the 736 BS/4241 SW on 15/4/63. Operated B-52G model until 1982. Inactivated 30/9/82.

70TH BW

Redesignated from 70 BW(M) to 70 BW(H) and activated on 15/11/62. Organised at Clinton-Sherman AFB, Oklahoma, on 1/2/63 and took over aircraft and personnel previously assigned to the 4123 SW. Inactivated 31/12/69.

6th BS

Acquired B-52Es previously used by the 98 BS/4123 SW on 1/2/63. Operated B-52E until 1968 when re-equipped with B-52D, which it flew until 1969. Some B-52Cs also assigned in 1968-69. Inactivated 31/12/69.

72ND BW

Disposed of RB-36 in 1958 as 72 BW(H) and acquired B-52 in 1959 at Ramey AFB, Puerto Rico. Inactivated 30/6/71.

60th BS

Equipped with B-52G from 8/59 and utilised this model until 1971. With inactivation of the 72 BW on 30/6/71, squadron transferred to the control of the 43 SW with effect from 1/7/71.

91ST BW

Redesignated from 91 SRW(M) to 91 BW(H) and activated on 15/11/62. Organised at Glasgow AFB, Montana, on 1/2/63 and took over aircraft and personnel previously assigned to the 4141 SW. Ceased flying B-52 in 1968 and then redesignated as 91 SMW on 25/6/68, when moved to Minot AFB, North Dakota.

322nd BS

Acquired B-52Ds previously used by the 326 BS/4141 SW on 1/2/63. Also used some B-52Cs in 1967-68. Inactivated 25/6/68.

92ND BW

Converted from B-36 to B-52 during 1957 as 92 BW(H) at Fairchild AFB, Washington. Redesignated 92 SAW 15/2/62 and 92 BW(H) 31/3/72. Operated B-52 until 1994, when redesignated as an Air Refueling Wing with effect from 1/7/94.

325th BS

Equipped with B-52D from 3/57 and used this until 1971, plus some B-52Cs during 1967-71. Received B-52G in 1970-71 and B-52H in 1985. Disposed of B-52H during 1994. Inactivated 1/7/94.

326th BS

Equipped with B-52D from 3/57 until 1/4/61, when reassigned to the 4141 SW at Glasgow AFB, Montana. (Note: Unit was detached from 92 BW between 1/3-1/4/61 - at Glasgow?)

327th BS

Equipped with B-52D from 3/57 until 1/6/60, when reassigned to 4170 SW at Larson AFB, Washington.

93RD BW

Redesignated from 93 BW(M) to 93 BW(H) at Castle AFB on 1/2/55 even though it retained some B-47s until 1956. Received first B-52 in 6/55 and continued to operate this type until it disposed of its last B-52G in 5/94. Was declared non-operational with effect from 7/2/94, but still in existence at start of 2/95 to supervise closure of Castle AFB.

328th BS

Equipped with B-52B from 6/55 and used this until 1965, as well as the B-52D (6/56 to 1958 and 1965-74); B-52E (1957-58 and 1967-70); B-52F (1958-74), B-52G (1966-67 and 1974-94) and B-52H (1974-83). Inactivated 15/6/94.

329th BS

Equipped with B-52B from 6/55 until 1965, as well as the B-52D (6/56-1958 and 1965-71); B-52E (1957-58 and 1967-70), B-52F (1958-71) and B-52G (1966-67). Inactivated on 30/9/71.

330th BS

Equipped with B-52B from 6/55 and used this until 1963, as well as B-52D (6/56-1958), B-52E (1957-58) and B-52F (1958-63). Inactivated on 15/9/63.

329th CCTS

Assigned from an unknown date to an unknown date. Probably replaced 4017 CCTS. Ground training only?

4017th CCTS

Established 8/1/55 and operated B-52B from 6/55 until 1956, when assumed ground training role. Replaced by 329 CCTS?

95TH BW

Converted from B-36 to B-52 during 1959 as 95 BW(H) at Biggs AFB, Texas. Discontinued and inactivated 25/6/66.

334th BS

Equipped with B-52B in 1959 and used this version until early 1966, being inactivated on 25/6/66.

96TH BW

Converted from B-47 to B-52 during 1963 as 96 SAW at Dyess AFB, Texas. Redesignated as 96 BW(H) on 31/3/72. Converted to B-1B in 1985.

337th BS

Activated on 15/9/63 and equipped with B-52E from 12/63. Used this version until 1970. Began converting to B-52D in 1969, retaining these until 1982 and also using some B-52Cs in 1969-71. Re-equipped with B-52H in 1982 and B-1B in 1985.

97TH BW

Operated B-47 until 1959 as 97 BW(M) from Biggs AFB, Texas. Moved to Blytheville AFB, Arkansas, on 1/7/59 and was redesignated as 97 BW(H) on 1/10/59, being equipped with B-52 during 1960. Inactivated 1/4/92.

340th BS
Equipped with B-52G from 1/60 and utilised this model until 1992, being inactivated on an unknown date.

99TH BW

Operated RB-36 until 1956 as 99 BW(H) from Fairchild AFB, Washington. Moved to Westover AFB, Massachusetts, on 4/9/56 and equipped with B-52. Inactivated 31/3/74.

346th BS
Equipped with B-52C from 12/56 and flew this model in varying quantities until 1971. Also operated B-52D during 1957-61 and 1966-72 as well as some B-52Bs in 1958-59. Non-operational from circa 30/4/72 until inactivated on 31/3/74.

347th BS
Equipped with B-52C from 12/56 and flew this until 1961. Also used some B-52Bs in 1958-59 as well as the B-52D from 1957 until 1/9/61, when reassigned to the 4047 SW at McCoy AFB, Florida.

348th BS
Equipped with B-52C from 12/56 and flew this model in varying quantities until 1971. Also operated B-52D during 1957-61 and 1966-72 as well as some B-52Bs in 1958-59. Non-operational from ca 30/4/72 until inactivated on 30/9/73.

306TH BW

Operated B-47 until 1963 as 306 BW(M) from MacDill AFB, Florida. Redesignated 306 BW(H) on 1/4/63 and moved on the same date to McCoy AFB, Florida, equipping with resources previously assigned to the 4047 SW. Inactivated 1/7/74.

367th BS
Acquired B-52Ds previously used by the 347 BS/4047 SW on 1/4/63 and operated these until Autumn 1973, along with some B-52Cs in 1967-71. Non-operational from circa 1/11/73 until inactivated on 1/7/74.

307TH SW

Redesignated from 307 BW(M) to 307 SW on 21/1/70 and activated at U-Tapao AB, Thailand on 1/4/70. Replaced the 4258 SW. Inactivated 30/9/75. Wing organisation evidently had direct responsibility for managing B-52D operations at various times between 4/70 and 6/75

364th BS(P)
Established and attached to the 307 SW on 1/7/72. In non-operational status from 1/7/72 until ca 29/1/73 and again from 9-30/6/75. Directed B-52D operations from 1/73 until 6/75.

365th BS(P)
Established and attached to the 307 SW on 1/7/72. In non-operational status from 1/7/72 until circa 29/1/73. Thereafter directed B-52D operations until disestablished on 1/7/74.

319TH BW

Redesignated from 319 FBW to 319 BW(H) and activated on 15/11/62. Organised at Grand Forks AFB, North Dakota, on 1/2/63 and took over aircraft and personnel previously assigned to the 4133 SW. Converted to B-1B in 1987.

46th BS
Acquired B-52Hs previously used by the 30 BS/4133 SW on 1/2/63 and operated this model until 1982 when re-equipped with the B-52G. Disposed of B-52G in 1986 and subsequently gained the B-1B in 1987.

320TH BW

Redesignated from 320 BW(M) to 320 BW(H) on 15/11/62. Organised at Mather AFB, California, on 1/2/63 and took over aircraft and personnel previously assigned to the 4134 SW. Inactivated 30/9/89.

441st BS
Acquired B-52Fs previously used by the 72 BS/4134 SW on 1/2/63 and operated this model until 1968. It converted to the B-52G in 1968 and flew this version until 1989, before being inactivated on 30/9/89.

340TH BW

Operated B-47 till 1963 as 340 BW(M) from Whiteman AFB, Missouri. Redesignated as 340 BW(H) on 1/9/63 and moved simultaneously to Bergstrom AFB, Texas, taking over aircraft and personnel previously assigned to the 4130 SW. Discontinued and inactivated 2/10/66.

486th BS
Acquired B-52Ds previously used by the 335 BS/4130 SW on 1/9/63 and operated this model until 2/10/66, when moved to March AFB, California, and assigned to the 22 BW.

366TH WING

One of the first multi-mission organisations to be set up in the early 1990s, this has its headquarters at Mountain Home AFB, Idaho. Resources included one B-52 squadron during 1992-94.

34th BS
Activated on 29/6/92 and subsequently equipped with the B-52G, although stationed at Castle AFB, California, away from Wing headquarters. Disposed of B-52G in 1993-94, moved to Ellsworth on 4/4/94 and equipped with B-1B, still as part of 366 Wing.

376TH SW

Redesignated from 376 BW(M) to 376 SW on 23/1/70 and activated at Kadena AB, Okinawa on 1/4/70. Replaced the 4252 SW. B-52Ds deployed to Kadena were evidently under direct operational control of the Wing organisation from 1/4/70 until 9/70, when Arc Light missions from this base were terminated.

379TH BW

Operated B-47 until 1960 as 379 BW(M) from Homestead AFB, Florida. Redesignated as 379 BW(H) on 9/1/61 and simultaneously moved to Wurtsmith AFB, Michigan, where it was subsequently equipped with the B-52. Ceased flying the B-52 in 1992 and inactivated 2/12/92.

524th BS
Equipped with B-52H from 5/61 and utilised this model until 1977 when converted to the B-52G which was retained until 1992. Inactivated 15/6/93.

380TH SAW

Operated B-47 until 1965 as 380 SAW from Plattsburgh AFB, New York. Received B-52 during 1966 and operated until 1971, when re-equipped with FB-111A. Redesignated as 380 BW(M) on 1/7/72.

528th BS

Equipped with B-52G from 6/66 until 1/71, acquiring aircraft from the 70 BS/42 BW at Loring AFB, Maine. Assumed non operational status with effect from 6/1/71, while awaiting the FB-111A.

397TH BW

Established as 397 BW(H) and activated on 15/11/62. Was organised at Dow AFB, Maine, on 1/2/63 and took over aircraft and personnel formerly assigned to the 4038 SW. Was discontinued and inactivated on 25/4/68.

596th BS

Acquired B-52Gs previously used by the 341 BS/4038 SW on 1/2/63 and used these as part of the 397 BW until 1/4/68 when detached to 2 BW control. Moved to Barksdale AFB, Louisiana, on 15/4/68 and officially reassigned to 2 BW on 25/4/68.

410TH BW

Established as 410 BW(H) and activated on 15/11/62. Was organised at K I Sawyer AFB, Michigan, on 1/2/63 and took over aircraft and personnel formerly assigned to the 4042 SW. Disposed of aircraft during second half of 1994. Still in existence at end of 1994, but scheduled to inactivate shortly.

644th BS

Acquired B-52Hs previously used by the 526 BS/4042 SW on 1/2/63. Transferred final B-52H to 5 BW at Minot on 21/11/94 in preparation for imminent inactivation.

416TH BW

Established as 416 BW(H) and activated on 15/11/62. Was organised at Griffiss AFB, New York on 1/2/63 and took over aircraft and personnel formerly assigned to the 4039 SW. Disposed of aircraft during second half of 1994. Still in existence at end of 1994, but scheduled to inactivate shortly.

668th BS

Acquired B-52Gs previously used by the 75 BS/4039 SW on 1/2/63 and operated this model until converted to the B-52H in 1992. Transferred last two B-52Hs to 5 BW at Minot on 15/11/94 in preparation for imminent inactivation.

449TH BW

Redesignated from 449 FBW to 449 BW(H) and activated on 15/11/62. Was organised at Kincheloe AFB, Michigan on 1/2/63 and took over aircraft and personnel previously assigned to the 4239 SW. Inactivated on 30/9/77.

716th BS

Acquired B-52Hs previously used by the 93 BS/4239 SW on 1/2/63 and flew this model until 1977. Inactivated 30/9/77.

450TH BW

Redesignated from 450 TFW to 450 BW(H) and activated on 15/11/62. Organised at Minot AFB, North Dakota, on 1/2/63 and took over jets and personnel assigned to the 4136 SW. Discontinued and inactivated on 25/7/68, when replaced at Minot by the 5 BW.

720th BS

Acquired B-52Hs previously used by the 525 BS/4136 SW on 1/2/63 and flew this model until inactivated on 25/7/68, when aircraft and personnel resources were passed to the 23 BS/5 BW.

454TH BW

Redesignated from 454 TCW(M) to 454 BW(H) and activated on 15/11/62. Was organised at Columbus AFB, Mississippi, on 1/2/63 and took over aircraft and personnel previously assigned to the 4228 SW. Inactivated on 2/7/69.

736th BS

Acquired B-52Fs previously used by the 492 BS/4228 SW on 1/2/63 and flew this model until 1966 when converted to B-52D which remained in use until 6/69. Some B-52Cs were also assigned during 1968-69. Inactivated on 2/7/69.

456TH BW

Redesignated from 456 TCW(M) to 456 SAW and activated on 15/11/62. Was organised at Beale AFB, California, on 1/2/63 and took over aircraft and personnel previously assigned to the 4126 SW. Redesignated as 456 BW(H) on 1/7/72. Inactivated on 30/9/75, when replaced at Beale by the 17 BW.

744th BS

Acquired B-52Gs previously used by the 31 BS/4126 SW on 1/2/63 and flew these until inactivation on 30/9/75, when aircraft and personnel passed to the 34 BS/17 BW.

461ST BW

Redesignated from 461 BW(T) to 461 BW(H) and activated on 15/11/62. Was organised at Amarillo AFB, Texas, on 1/2/63 and took over aircraft and personnel previously assigned to the 4128 SW. Discontinued and inactivated on 25/3/68.

764th BS

Acquired B-52Ds previously used by the 718 BS/4128 SW on 1/2/63 and flew these until 1/68. Some B-52Cs also assigned during 1967-68. Inactivated 25/3/68.

462ND SAW

Established as 462 SAW and activated on 15/11/62. Was organised at Larson AFB, Washington, on 1/2/63 and took over aircraft and personnel previously assigned to the 4170 SW. Was discontinued and inactivated on 25/6/66.

768th BS

Acquired B-52Ds previously used by the 327 BS/4170 SW on 1/2/63 and used these until 1966. Inactivated on 2/4/66.

465TH BW

Redesignated from 465 TCW(M) to 465 BW(H) and activated on 15/11/62. Was organised at Robins AFB, Georgia, on 1/2/63 and took over aircraft and personnel previously assigned to the 4137 SW. Was discontinued and inactivated on 25/7/68, when replaced at Robins by the 19 BW.

781st BS

Acquired B-52Gs previously used by the 342 BS/4137 SW on 1/2/63 and used these until inactivated on 25/7/68, when aircraft and personnel passed to the 28 BS/19 BW.

484TH BW

Established as 484 BW(H) and activated on 15/11/62. Was organised at Turner AFB, Georgia, on 1/2/63 and took over aircraft and personnel previously assigned to the 4138 SW. Was discontinued and inactivated on 25/3/67.

824th BS

Acquired B-52Ds previously used by the 336 BS/4138 SW on 1/2/63 and used these until 1967. Inactivated on 25/1/67.

494TH BW

Established as 494 BW(H) and activated on 15/11/62. Was organised at Sheppard AFB, Texas, on 1/2/63 and took over aircraft and personnel previously assigned to the 4245 SW. Was discontinued and inactivated on 2/4/66.

864th BS

Acquired B-52Ds previously used by the 717 BS/4245 SW on 1/2/63 and used these until 1966. Inactivated on 2/4/66.

509TH BW

Operated B-47 until 1965 as 509 BW(M) from Pease AFB, New Hampshire. Was redesignated 509 BW(H) on 2/4/66 and equipped with B-52 which it operated until shortly before being redesignated as 509 BW(M) on 1/12/69. To FB-111A in 1970.

393rd BS

Equipped with B-52D from ca 3/66 and used these until 11/69, plus some B-52Cs in 1968-69. Subsequently to FB-111A.

917TH WING

Acquired responsibility for bombing operations with effect from 1/10/93 at Barksdale AFB, Louisiana, having previously been a Fighter Wing. In the process, it became the first Reserve force unit to operate the B-52.

93rd BS

Activated on 1/10/93 and assigned to the control of the 917 Wg (AFRes). Received first B-52H on 7/12/93. Currently active.

3960TH SW

Activated at Andersen AFB, Guam on 1/4/55. Inactivated on 31/3/70 and replaced by 43 SW on 1/4/70. Also known as 3960 ABW and 3960 CSG for brief periods. Possible this organisation played a role in control of B-52s deployed to Andersen between April 1964 and February 1966, when the 4133 BW(P) was established. Precise details of variants deployed during that period are vague, but it is known that B-52Fs from four ConUS based Bomb Wings were here at different times between 2/65 and 2/66 - these were the 2 BW (20 BS circa 12/2-circa 5/5/65); 7 BW (9 BS circa 6/5-1/12/65 and 20 BS circa 1/8-1/12/65); 320 BW (441 BS 11/2-circa 1/7/65 and 1/12/65-circa 21/3/66) and 454 BW (736 BS 16/11/65-31/3/66). Jets from the 9 BS/7 BW and 441 BS/320 BW took part in the first *Arc Light* bombing mission to Vietnam on 18/6/65.

4038TH SW

Activated at Dow AFB, Maine on 1/8/58. Inactivated on 1/2/63 when aircraft and personnel resources passed to the 397 BW at the same base.

341st BS

Reassigned from 97 BW to 4038 SW on 15/2/60 and equipped with B-52G from 5/60 until 1/2/63, when discontinued and inactivated. Resources passed to the 596 BS/397 BW.

4039TH SW

Activated at Griffiss AFB, New York, on 1/8/58. Inactivated on 1/2/63 when aircraft and personnel resources passed to the 416 BW at the same base.

75th BS

Reassigned from 42 BW to 4039 SW on 15/10/59 and equipped with B-52G from 1/60 until 1/2/63, when discontinued and inactivated. Resources passed to the 668 BS/416 BW.

4042ND SW

Activated at K I Sawyer AFB, Michigan, on 1/8/58. Inactivated on 1/2/63 when aircraft and personnel resources passed to the 410 BW at the same base.

526th BS

Reassigned from 19 BW to 4042 SW on 1/6/61 and equipped with B-52H from 7/61 until 1/2/63, when discontinued and inactivated. Resources passed to the 644 BS/410 BW.

4043RD SW

Activated at Wright-Patterson AFB, Ohio on 1/4/59. Inactivated on 1/2/63 when aircraft and personnel resources passed to the 17 BW at the same base.

42nd BS

Reassigned from 11 BW to 4043 SW on 1/6/60 and equipped with B-52E from 6/60 until 1/2/63, when discontinued and inactivated. Resources passed to the 34 BS/17 BW.

4047TH SW

Activated at McCoy AFB, Florida in 1958-59. Inactivated on 1/4/63 when aircraft and personnel resources passed to the 306 BW at the same base.

347th BS

Reassigned from 99 BW to 4047 SW on 1/9/61 and equipped with B-52D from 9/61 until 1/4/63, when discontinued and inactivated. Resources passed to the 367 BS/306 BW.

4123RD SW

Activated at Carswell AFB, Texas, on 10/12/57. Moved to Clinton-Sherman AFB, Oklahoma, on 25/2/59. Inactivated 1/2/63 when aircraft and personnel assets passed to 70 BW at the same base.

98th BS

Relieved from attachment to 7 BW and reassigned from 11 BW to 4123 SW on 10/12/57. Equipped with B-52E from 1958 until 1/2/63, when discontinued and inactivated. Resources were passed to the 6 BS/70 BW. Initially operated from Carswell AFB, Texas, but then were moved to Clinton-Sherman AFB, Oklahoma, on 1/3/59.

4126TH SW

Activated at Beale AFB, California on 8/2/59. Inactivated on 1/2/63 when aircraft and personnel resources passed to the 456 SAW at the same base.

31st BS

Reassigned from 5 BW to 4126 SW on 1/10/59 but remained attached to 5 BW from 2/10/59 until 18/1/60. Moved from Travis to Beale between 11/59-1/60. Operated B-52G until 1/2/63, when discontinued and inactivated, with unit resources being passed to the 744 BS/456 SAW.

4128TH SW

Activated at Amarillo AFB, Texas in 1958-59. Inactivated on 1/2/63 when aircraft and personnel resources passed to the 461 BW at the same base.

718th BS

Reassigned from 28 BW to 4128 SW on 20/2/60 and equipped with B-52D from 2/60 until 1/2/63 when discontinued and inactivated. Resources passed to the 764 BS/461 BW.

4130TH SW

Activated at Bergstrom AFB, Texas, on 1/10/58. Inactivated on 1/9/63 when aircraft and personnel resources passed to the 340 BW at the same base.

335th BS

Reassigned from 95 BW to 4130 SW on 15/1/59 and equipped with B-52D from 1/59 until 1/9/63 when discontinued and inactivated. Resources passed to the 486 BS/340 BW.

4133RD SW

Activated at Grand Forks AFB, North Dakota, on 1/9/58. Inactivated on 1/2/63 when aircraft and personnel resources passed to the 319 BW at the same base.

30th BS

Reassigned from 19 BW to 4133 SW on 1/1/62 and equipped with B-52H from 4/62 until 1/2/63 when discontinued and inactivated. Resources passed to the 46 BS/319 BW.

4134TH SW

Activated at Mather AFB, Ca, on 1/5/58. Inactivated on 1/2/63 when both jets and personnel resources passed to 320 BW at same base.

72nd BS

Reassigned from 5 BW to 4134 SW on 1/7/58 and equipped with B-52F from 10/58 until 1/2/63 when discontinued and inactivated. Resources passed to the 441 BS/320 BW.

4135TH SW

Activated at Eglin AFB, Florida, on 1/12/58. Inactivated on 1/2/63 when aircraft and personnel resources passed to the 39 BW at the same base.

301st BS

Reassigned from 72 BW to 4135 SW on 17/6/59 and equipped with B-52G from 7/59 until 1/2/63 when discontinued and inactivated. Resources passed to the 62 BS/39 BW.

4136TH SW

Activated at Minot AFB, North Dakota, on 1/9/58. Inactivated on 1/2/63 when aircraft and personnel resources passed to the 450 BW at the same base.

525th BS

Reassigned from 19 BW to 4136 SW on 15/3/61 and equipped with B-52H from 7/61 until 1/2/63 when discontinued and inactivated. Resources passed to the 720 BS/450 BW.

4137TH SW

Activated at Robins AFB, Georgia, on 1/2/59. Inactivated on 1/2/63 when aircraft and personnel resources passed to the 465 BW at the same base.

342nd BS

Reassigned from 97 BW to 4137 SW on 1/5/60 and equipped with B-52G from 8/60 until 1/2/63 when discontinued and inactivated. Resources passed to the 781 BS/465 BW.

4138TH SW

Activated at Turner AFB, Georgia, in 1958-59. Inactivated on 1/2/63 when aircraft and personnel resources passed to the 484 BW at the same base.

336th BS

Reassigned from 95 BW to 4138 SW on 1/7/59 and equipped with B-52D from 7/59 until 1/2/63 when discontinued and inactivated. Resources passed to the 824 BS/484 BW.

4141ST SW

Activated at Glasgow AFB, Montana, in 1958-59. Inactivated on 1/2/63, aircraft/personnel resources passed to 91 BW at same base.

326th BS

Reassigned from 92 BW to 4141 SW on 1/4/61 and equipped with B-52D from 4/61 until 1/2/63 when discontinued and inactivated. Resources passed to the 322 BS/91 BW.

4170TH SW

Activated at Larson AFB, Washington, in 1958-59. Inactivated on 1/2/63 when aircraft and personnel resources passed to the 462 SAW at the same base.

327th BS

Reassigned from 92 BW to 4170 SW on 1/6/60 and equipped with B-52D from 6/60 until 1/2/63 when discontinued and inactivated. Resources passed to the 768 BS/462 SAW.

4228TH SW

Activated at Columbus AFB, Mi, on 1/7/58. Inactivated on 1/2/63 when jets and personnel resources passed to 454 BW at same base.

492nd BS

Reassigned from 7 BW to 4228 SW on 15/6/59 and equipped with

B-52F from 6/59 until 1/2/63 when discontinued and inactivated. Resources passed to the 736 BS/454 BW.

4238TH SW

Activated at Barksdale AFB, Louisiana, on 1/3/58. Inactivated on 1/4/63 when aircraft and personnel resources passed to the 2 BW at the same base.

436th BS

Reassigned from 7 BW to 4238 SW on 1/8/58 and equipped with B-52F from 8/58 until 1/4/63 when discontinued and inactivated. Resources passed to the 20 BS/2 BW.

4239TH SW

Activated at Kincheloe AFB, Michigan, on 1/2/59. Inactivated on 1/2/63 when aircraft and personnel resources passed to the 449 BW at the same base.

93rd BS

Reassigned from 19 BW to 4239 SW on 1/8/61 and equipped with B-52H from 11/61 until 1/2/63 when discontinued and inactivated. Resources passed to the 716 BS/449 BW.

4241ST SW

Activated at Seymour Johnson AFB, North Carolina, on 1/10/58. Inactivated on 15/4/63 when aircraft and personnel resources passed to the 68 BW at the same base.

73rd BS

Reassigned from 72 BW to 4241 SW on 5/1/59 and equipped with B-52G from 7/59 until 15/4/63 when discontinued and inactivated. Resources passed to the 51 BS/68 BW.

4245TH SW

Activated at Sheppard AFB, Texas on 5/1/59. Inactivated on 1/2/63 when aircraft and personnel resources passed to the 494 BW at the same base.

717th BS

Reassigned from 28 BW to 4245 SW on 1/2/60 and equipped with B-52D from 2/60 until 1/2/63 when discontinued and inactivated. Resources passed to the 864 BS/494 BW.

4252ND SW

Activated at Kadena AB, Okinawa, on 12/1/65, initially as an air refuelling outfit. Inactivated on 1/4/70 and replaced by the 376 SW. Possible that the 4252 SW exercised operational control over the B-52Ds at Kadena from 2/68, although subordinate MajCom units may have been established to facilitate control.

4258TH SW

Activated at U-Tapao AB, Thailand, on 2/6/66, initially as an air refuelling outfit. Inactivated on 1/4/70 and replaced by the 307 SW. Possible that the 4258 SW exercised operational control over the B-52Ds stationed at U-Tapao from 4/67, although subordinate MajCom units may have been established to facilitate control.

PROVISIONAL UNITS

Note – All were temporary organisations created specifically for combat in either South-east Asia during 1966-70 and 1972-73 or the Arabian Gulf in 1990-91. Designations are therefore suffixed with the letter 'P' for Provisional, viz 72 SW(P) and 801 BW(P).

72ND SW(P)

Activated at Andersen AFB, Guam, on 1/6/72. Inactivated on 15/11/73.

64th BS(P)

Activated at Andersen AFB, Guam, on 1/6/72 and attached to 72 SW until inactivated on 15/11/73. Operated B-52Gs detached from ConUS from 6/72 until 1973

65th BS(P)

Activated at Andersen AFB, Guam, on 1/6/72 and attached to 72 SW until inactivated on 15/11/73. Operated B-52Gs detached from ConUS from 6/72 until 1973.

329th BS(P)

Activated at Andersen AFB, Guam, on 1/6/72 and attached to 72 SW until inactivated on 15/11/73. Operated B-52Gs detached from ConUS from 6/72 until 1973.

486th BS(P)

Activated at Andersen AFB, Guam, on 1/6/72 and attached to 72 SW until inactivated on 15/11/73. Operated B-52Gs detached from ConUS from 6/72 until 1973.

801ST BW(P)

Activated at Moron AB, Spain, in 1/91. Inactivated 3/91. Operated B-52Gs detached from ConUS during that period and may have had a subordinate provisional Bomb Squadron to serve as an intermediate link in the chain of command.

806TH BW(P)

Activated at RAF Fairford, England on 5/2/91. Inactivated on 9/3/91. Operated B-52Gs detached from ConUS during that period and may have had a subordinate provisional Bomb Squadron to serve as an intermediate link in the chain of command.

1708TH BW(P)

Activated at Jeddah/King Abdul Aziz International Airport, Saudi Arabia, in 1/91. Inactivated 3/91. Operated B-52Gs detached from ConUS during that period and may have had provisional Bomb Squadrons to serve as intermediate links in the chain of command.

4133RD BW(P)

Activated 1/2/66 at Andersen AFB, Guam. Inactivated on 1/7/70. Directed operations of US-based units deployed here on a rotational basis for combat duty from 2/66 until 7/70, when responsibility passed to the 43 SW. Two versions were employed, specifically the B-52F (from 2/66 until 3/66) and the B-52D (from 3/66 until 7/70). It is possible that one or two provisional Bomb Squadrons were organised to facilitate control.

4300TH BW(P)

Activated at Diego Garcia in 8/90. Inactivated 3/91. Operated B-52Gs detached from ConUS during that period and may have one or two provisional Bomb Squadrons to serve as intermediate links in the chain of command.

APPENDIX 5

B-52 STRATOFORTRESS BOMB SQUADRONS

Number	Wing	Base	Period Assigned	Remarks	Variants and periods of operation
2 BS	22 BW	March	15/9/63-1/10/82	Got B-52D from 768 BS/462 SAW in 1966	B-52B (9/63-66), B-52D (66-82). Note that some B-52C (67-71) and B-52E (68-70) were also assigned.
6 BS	70 BW	Clinton-Sherman	1/2/63-31/12/69	Resources from 98 BS/4123 SW	B-52E (2/63-68), B-52D (68-69). - B-52C (68-69) were also assigned
9 BS	7 BW	Carswell	6/6/52-25/6/68		B-52F (6/58-68)
	7 BW	Carswell	31/12/71-15/8/92		B-52D (71-82), B-52H (82-92)
11 BS	2 BW	Barksdale	1/7/94-current	Crew training unit	B-52H (7/94-current)
20 BS	2 BW	Barksdale	16/6/52-25/6/65	Resources from 436 BS/4238 SW	B-52F (4/63-6/65)
	7 BW	Carswell	25/6/65-17/12/92	Reassigned to 2 Wg at Barksdale.	B-52F (65-69), B-52D (69-83), B-52H (83-92)
	2 Wing	Barksdale	17/12/92-1/10/93		B-52H (12/92-10/93)
	2 BW	Barksdale	1/10/93-current		B-52H (10/93-current)
23 BS	5 BW	Travis	16/6/52-25/7/68		B-52G (2/59-68)
	5 BW	Minot	25/7/68-current	Resources from 720 BS/450 BW	B-52H (7/68-current)
24 BS	6 BW	Walker	16/6/52-1/5/62		B-52E (12/57-62)
	6 SAW	Walker	1/5/62-25/1/67		B-52E (62-67)
26 BS	11 BW	Altus	13/12/57-1/4/62	Initial B-52 operations from Clinton-Sherman AFB due to runway work at Altus	B-52E (1/58-62)
	11 SAW	Altus	1/4/62-2/7/68		B-52E (62-68)
28 BS	19 BW	Homestead	1/6/53-25/7/68		B-52H (2/62-68)
	19 BW	Robins	25/7/68-1/10/83	Resources from 781 BS/465 BW	B-52G (68-83)
30 BS	4133 SW	Grand Forks	1/1/62-1/2/63	Resources to 46 BS/319 BW	B-52H (4/62-63)
31 BS	5 BW	Travis	16/6/52-1/10/59		B-52G (59)
	5 BW	Travis	2/10/59-18/1/60*	Assigned 4126 SW. Transferred to Beale 11/59-1/60	B-52G (59-60)
	4126 SW	Beale	18/1/60-1/2/63	Resources to 744 BS/456 SAW	B-52G (60-63)
34 BS	17 BW	Wright-Patterson	1/2/63-30/9/75	Resources from 42 BS/4043 SW	B-52E (2/63-68), B-52H (68-75)
	17 BW	Beale	30/9/75-30/9/76	Resources from 744 BS/456 BW	B-52G (75-76)
	366 Wing	Castle	29/6/92-4/4/94	Parent Unit at Mountain Home. Received - B-1B at Ellsworth	B-52G (92-94)
37 BS	28 BW	Ellsworth	1/7/77-1/10/82	Received B-52H from 716 BS/449 BW and 524 BS/379 BW	B-52H (77-82)
39 BS	6 BW	Walker	16/6/52-1/5/62		B-52E (12/57-62)
	6 SAW	Walker	1/5/62-15/9/63		B-52E (62-63)
40 BS	6 BW	Walker	16/6/52-1/5/62		B-52E (12/57-62)
	6 SAW	Walker	1/5/62-25/1/67		B-52E (62-67)
42 BS	11 BW	Altus	13/12/57-1/6/60	Initial B-52 operations from Clinton-Sherman AFB due to runway work at Altus	B-52E (1/58-60)
	4043 SW	Wright-Patterson	1/6/60-1/2/63	Resources to 34 BS/17 BW	B-52E (60-63)
46 BS	319 BW	Grand Forks	1/2/63-4/12/86	Resources from 30 BS/4133 SW. Received B-1B in 1987-88	B-52H (2/63-82), B-52G (82-86)
51 BS	68 BW	Seymour Johnson	16/6/52-30/9/82	Resources from 73 BS/4241 SW	B-52G (4/63-82)
60 BS	72 BW	Ramey	16/6/52-30/6/71	Aircraft to 77 BS/28 BW	B-52G (8/59-71)
	43 SW	Andersen	1/7/71-4/11/86	Not operational until circa 2/72. Received a/c from 486 BS/22 BW	B-52D (7/71-83), B-52G (83-86)
	43 BW	Andersen	4/11/86-30/4/90		B-52G (86-90)
62 BS	39 BW	Eglin	1/2/63-25/6/65	Resources from 301 BS/4135 SW	B-52G (2/63-65)
	2 BW	Barksdale	25/6/65-1/10/91		B-52G (65-91)
	2 Wing	Barksdale	1/10/91-17/12/92	Replaced by 20 BS from 7 BW on this date	B-52G (91-92)
63 BS(P)	43 SW	Andersen	15/6/72-30/6/75*	Temporary unit to control B-52D element engaged in combat in 1972-73. Non-operational circa 11/73 onwards	B-52D (6/72-73)
64 BS(P)	72 SW(P)	Andersen	1/6/72-15/11/73*	Temporary unit to control B-52G element engaged in combat	B-52G (6/72-73)

Number	Wing	Base	Period Assigned	Remarks	Variants and periods of operation
65 BS(P)	72 SW(P)	Andersen	1/6/72-15/11/73*	Temporary unit to control B-52G element engaged in combat	B-52G (6/72-73)
69 BS	42 BW	Loring	25/2/53-?/94	Disposed of a/c in 1994. Inactivated on unknown date	B-52C (6/56-57), B-52D (57-59), B-52G (59-94)
70 BS	42 BW	Loring	25/2/53-25/6/66	Aircraft to 528 BS/380 SAW	B-52C (6/56-57), B-52D (57-59), B-52G (59-66)
72 BS	4134 SW	Mather	1/7/58-1/2/63	Resources to 441 BS/320 BW	B-52F (10/58-63)
(72 BS)	5 BW	Minot	6/1/95-current		B-52H (1/95-current)
73 BS	4241 SW	Seymour Johnson	5/1/59-15/4/63	Resources to 51 BS/68 BW	B-52G (7/59-63)
75 BS	42 BW	Loring	25/2/53-15/10/59		B-52C (6/56-57), B-52D (57-59)
	4039 SW	Griffiss	15/10/59-1/2/63	Resources to 668 BS/416 BW	B-52G (1/60-63)
77 BS	28 BW	Ellsworth	16/6/52-?/86	Gained B-52G from 60 BS/72 BW in 1971 and B-52H from 716 BS/449 BW and 524 BS/379 BW in 1977. To B-1B	B-52D (6/57-71), B-52G (71-77), B-52H (77-86). Note that some B-52C (67-71) were also assigned
93 BS	4239 SW	Kincheloe	1/8/61-1/2/63	Resources to 716 BS/449 BW	B-52H (11/61-63)
	917 Wing	Barksdale	1/10/93-current	AFRes unit. First Reserve outfit with B-52s	B-52H (12/93-current)
96 BS	2 BW	Barksdale	1/10/93-current	Resources from 596 BS/2 Wing	B-52H (10/93-current).
98 BS	7 BW	Carswell	1/12/57-10/12/57*	Not equipped. Assigned to 11 BW	(not equipped at this time)
	4123 SW	Carswell	10/12/57-25/2/59		B-52E (58-59)
	4123 SW	Clinton-Sherman	25/2/59-1/2/63	Resources to 6 BS/70 BW	B-52E (59-63)
301 BS	4135 SW	Eglin	17/6/59-1/2/63	Resources to 62 BS/39 BW	B-52G (7/59-63)
322 BS	91 BW	Glasgow	1/2/63-25/6/68	Not op circa 1/5/68 onwards. Resources from 326 BS/4141 SW	B-52D (63-68). Note that some B-52C (67-68) were also assigned.
325 BS	92 BW	Fairchild	16/6/52-15/2/62		B-52D (3/57-62)
	92 SAW	Fairchild	15/2/62-31/3/72		B-52D (62-71), B-52G (70-72). Note that some B-52C (67-71) were also assigned
	92 BW	Fairchild	31/3/72-1/7/94		B-52G (72-85), B-52H (85-94)
326 BS	92 BW	Fairchild	16/6/52-1/4/61	Detached 1/3/61 onwards	B-52D (3/57-61)
	4141 SW	Glasgow	1/4/61-1/2/63	Almost certainly arrived 1/3/61 on det from 92 BW. Resources to 322 BS/91 BW	B-52D (61-63)
327 BS	92 BW	Fairchild	16/6/52-1/6/60		B-52D (3/57-60)
	4170 SW	Larson	1/6/60-1/2/63	Resources to 768 BS/462 SAW	B-52D (60-63)
328 BS	93 BW	Castle	16/6/52-15/6/94	Disposed of a/c 1993-94.	B-52B (6/55-65), B-52D (6/56-58; 65-74), B-52E (57-58; 67-78), B-52F (58-74), B-52G (66-67; 74-94), B-52H (74-83)
329 BS	93 BW	Castle	16/6/52-30/9/71	Later reformed as CCTS, replacing 4017 CCTS (which see)	B-52B (6/55-65), B-52D (6/56-58; 65-71), B-52E (57-58; 67-71), B-52F (58-71), B-52G (66-67)
329 BS(P)	72 SW(P)	Andersen	1/6/72-15/11/73*	Temporary unit to control B-52G element engaged in combat	B-52G (6/72-73)
330 BS	93 BW	Castle	16/6/52-15/9/63		B-52B (6/55-63), B-52D (6/56-58), B-52E (57-58), B-52F (58-63)
334 BS	95 BW	Biggs	16/6/52-25/6/66		B-52B (59-66)
335 BS	4130 SW	Bergstrom	15/1/59-1/9/63	Resources to 486 BS/340 BW	B-52D (1/59-63)
336 BS	4138 SW	Turner	1/7/59-1/2/63	Resources to 824 BS/484 BW	B-52D (7/59-63)
337 BS	96 SAW	Dyess	15/9/63-31/3/72		B-52E (12/63-70), B-52D (69-72). Note that some B-52Cs (69-71) were also assigned
	96 BW	Dyess	31/3/72-22/1/85	Subsequently to B-1B	B-52D (72-82), B-52H (82-85)
340 BS	97 BW	Blytheville	16/6/52-1/4/92		B-52G (1/60-92)
341 BS	4038 SW	Dow	15/2/60-1/2/63	Resources to 596 BS/397 BW	B-52G (5/60-63)
342 BS	4137 SW	Robins	1/5/60-1/2/63	Resources to 781 BS/465 BW	B-52G (8/60-63)
346 BS	99 BW	Westover	1/1/53-31/3/74	Not operational circa 30/4/72 onwards	B-52C (12/56-71), B-52D (57-61; 66-72). Note that some B-52B (58-59) were also assigned
347 BS	99 BW	Westover	1/1/53-1/9/61		B-52C (12/56-61), B-52D (57-61). Note that some B-52B (58-59) were also assigned
	4047 SW	McCoy	1/9/61-1/4/63	Resources to 367 BS/306 BW	B-52D (9/61-63)
348 BS	99 BW	Westover	1/1/53-30/9/73	Not operational circa 30/4/72 onwards	B-52C (12/56-71), B-52D (57-61; 66-72). Note that some B-52B (58-59) were also assigned

Number	Wing	Base	Period Assigned	Remarks	Variants and periods of operation
364 BS(P)	307 SW	U-Tapao	1/7/72-30/6/75*	Not operational 1/7/72-circa 29/1/73 and 9-30/6/75	B-52D (1/73-75)
365 BS(P)	307 SW	U-Tapao	1/7/72-1/7/74*	Not operational 1/7/72-circa 29/1/73	B-52D (1/73-74)
367 BS	306 BW	McCoy	16/6/52-1/7/74	Not op circa 1/11/73 on. Resources from 347 BS/4047 SW	B-52D (63-73). Note that some B-52C (67-71) were also assigned
393 BS	509 BW	Pease	6/6/52-19/11/69	Still had B-52 crews early 1970 but no aircraft. Gained aircraft from 864 BS/494 BW. Now has B-2A	B-52D (66-69). Note that some B-52C (68-69) were also assigned
436 BS	4238 SW	Barksdale	1/8/58-1/4/63	Resources to 20 BS/2 BW	B-52F (8/58-63)
441 BS	320 BW	Mather	1/2/63-30/9/89	Resources from 72 BS/4134 SW	B-52F (63-68), B-52G (68-89)
486 BS	340 BW	Bergstrom	20/10/52-2/10/66	Resources from 335 BS/4130 SW	B-52D (63-66)
	22 BW	March	2/10/66-1/7/71	Aircraft transferred to 60 BS/43 SW?	B-52D (66-71). Note that some B-52C (67-71) and B-52E (68-70) were also assigned
486 BS(P)	72 SW(P)	Andersen	1/6/72-15/11/73*	Temporary unit to control B-52G element engaged in combat	B-52G (6/72-73)
492 BS	7 BW	Carswell	16/6/52-15/6/59		B-52F (6/58-59)
	4228 SW	Columbus	15/6/59-1/2/63	Resources to 736 BS/454 BW	B-52F (59-63).
524 BS	379 BW	Wurtsmith	1/11/55-2/12/92	Began B-52 operations in 5/61	B-52H (5/61-77), B-52G (77-92)
525 BS	4136 SW	Minot	15/3/61-1/2/63	Assigned to 19 BW 9/1-15/3/61, but moved to Minot 8/3/61. Resources to 720 BS/450 BW	B-52H (7/61-63)
526 BS	4042 SW	K I Sawyer	1/6/61-1/2/63	Resources to 644 BS/410 BW	B-52H (8/61-63)
528 BS	380 SAW	Plattsburgh	11/7/55-5/1/71	Not operational 6/1/71 onwards, due FB-111 transition. Gained aircraft from 70 BS/42 BW	B-52G (66-71)
596 BS	397 BW	Dow	1/2/63-25/4/68	Detached 1-25/4/68. Resources from 341 BS/4038 SW	B-52G (63-68)
	2 BW	Barksdale	15/4/68-1/10/91	(Confusion over transfer dates)	B-52G (68-91)
	2 Wing	Barksdale	1/10/91-1/10/93	Resources to 96 BS/2 BW	B-52G (91-92), B-52H (92-93)
644 BS	410 BW	K I Sawyer	1/2/63-current	Resources from 526 BS/4042 SW. To inactivate 1995	B-52H (63-94)
668 BS	416 BW	Griffiss	1/2/63-current	Resources from 75 BS/4039 SW. To inactivate 1995	B-52G (63-92), B-52H (92-94)
716 BS	449 BW	Kincheloe	1/2/63-30/9/77	Resources from 93 BS/4239 SW. Aircraft to 28 BW	B-52H (63-77)
717 BS	28 BW	Ellsworth	16/6/52-1/2/60		B-52D (6/57-60)
	4245 SW	Sheppard	1/2/60-1/2/63	Resources to 864 BS/494 BW	B-52D (60-63)
718 BS	28 BW	Ellsworth	16/6/52-20/2/60		B-52D (6/57-60)
	4128 SW	Amarillo	20/2/60-1/2/63	Resources to 764 BS/461 BW	B-52D (60-63)
720 BS	450 BW	Minot	1/2/63-25/7/68	Resources from 525 BS/4136 SW. Resources to 23 BS/5 BW	B-52H (63-68)
736 BS	454 BW	Columbus	1/2/63-2/7/69	Resources from 492 BS/4228 SW	B-52F (63-66), B-52D (66-69). Note that some B-52C (68-69) were also assigned
744 BS	456 SAW	Beale	1/2/63-1/7/72	Resources from 31 BS/4126 SW	B-52G (63-72)
	456 BW	Beale	1/7/72-30/9/75	Resources to 34 BS/17 BW	B-52G (72-75)
764 BS	461 BW	Amarillo	1/2/63-25/3/68	Resources from 718 BS/4128 SW	B-52D (63-68). Note that some B-52C (67-68) were also assigned
768 BS	462 SAW	Larson	1/2/63-2/4/66	Parent not inactivated until 25/6/66. Resources from 327 BS/4170 SW. Aircraft to 2 BS/22 BW	B-52D (63-66)
781 BS	465 BW	Robins	1/2/63-25/7/68	Resources from 342 BS/4137 SW. Resources to 28 BS/19 BW	B-52G (63-68)
824 BS	484 BW	Turner	1/2/63-25/1/67	Parent not inactivated until 25/3/67. Resources from 336 BS/4138 SW	B-52D (63-67)
864 BS	494 BW	Sheppard	1/2/63-2/4/66	Resources from 717 BS/4245 SW. Aircraft to 393 BS/509 BW	B-52D (63-66)

B-52 STRATOFORTRESS COMBAT CREW TRAINING UNITS

Number	Wing	Base	Period Assigned	Remarks	Variants and periods of operation
329 CCTS	93 BW	Castle	?-?	Replaced 4017 CCTS on unknown date	Probably no aircraft assigned, since thought to be more concerned with ground instructional tasks
4017 CCTS	93 BW	Castle	8/1/55-?	Replaced by 329 CCTS on unknown date	B-52B (6/55-56). Subsequently assumed responsibility for ground instruction and may not have been assigned B-52s again
4018 CCTS	7 BW	Carswell	1/4/74-?		B-52D (4/74-?)
4129 CCTS	6 BW	Walker	1/8/59-1/5/62		B-52E (8/59-62).
	6 SAW	Walker	1/5/62-15/9/63		B-52E (62-63)

OTHER SAC USERS

43 SW	Andersen	1/4/70-30/4/90	Gained combat mission with B-52 from 4133 BW(P) on 1/7/70. B-52s under direct Wing control until 1/7/71		B-52D (7/70-7/71). Note that this unit parented the 60 BS (B-52D/G) with effect from 1/7/71
307 SW	U-Tapao	1/4/70-30/9/75	B-52s under direct Wing control during some of this time		B-52D (at various dates when resident bombers under direct Wing control).
376 SW	Kadena	1/4/70-	B-52s under direct Wing control 1/4/70-19/9/70		B-52D (4/70-9/70)
801 BW(P)	Moron	1/91-3/91	Temporary unit for *Desert Storm*		B-52G (1/91-3/91)
806 BW(P)	Fairford	5/2/91-9/3/91	Temporary unit for *Desert Storm*		B-52G (2/91-3/91)
1708 BW(P)	Jeddah	1/91- 3/91	Temporary unit for *Desert Storm*		B-52G (1/91-3/91)
3960 SW	Andersen	(4/64)-1/4/70	Probably responsible for management of B-52 alert force with effect from 4/64 and combat operations with B-52F from 18/6/65 until 1/2/66		Various models on rotational duty (4/64-2/66) plus B-52F on combat operations (6/65-2/66)
4133 BW(P)	Andersen	1/2/66-1/7/70	Established to control B-52 combat operations from Guam and probably assumed this task from 3960 SW. B-52s under Wing control throughout, until 43 SW took over in 7/70		B-52F (2/66-4/66), B-52D (4/66-7/70)
4252 SW	Kadena	12/1/65-1/4/70	Directed B-52 operations 2/68-1/4/70		B-52D (2/68-4/70)
4258 SW	U-Tapao	2/6/66-1/4/70	Directed B-52 operations 11/4/67-1/4/70		B-52D (4/67-4/70)
4300 BW(P)	Diego Garcia	8/90-3/91	Temporary unit for *Desert Shield/Storm*		B-52G (8/90-3/91)

* Signifies attached, rather than assigned. Where known, unit of assignment is shown in the remarks column.

Footnote:
The 5th, 7th, 42nd, 92nd, 93rd, 97th, 379th, 410th and 416th BWs were all redesignated as Wings on 1/9/91, only to regain Bomb Wing status on 1/6/92, with the single exception of the 97th Wing which was inactivated in the intervening period.

APPENDIX 6

B-52 BASES - CONTINENTAL USA

Location	Resident units/periods
Altus AFB, Ok	11 BW/SAW (1/58-2/7/68)
Amarillo AFB, Tx	4128 SW (20/2/60-1/2/63) 461 BW (1/2/63-25/3/68)
Barksdale AFB, La	4238 SW (8/58-1/4/63) 2 BW/Wg/BW (1/4/63-current) 917 Wg (12/93-current)
Beale AFB, Ca	4126 SW (1/60-1/2/63) 456 SAW/BW (1/2/63-30/9/75) 17 BW (30/9/75-30/9/76)
Bergstrom AFB, Tx	4130 SW (1/59-1/9/63) 340 BW (1/9/63-2/10/66)
Biggs AFB, Tx	95 BW (1959-25/6/66)
Blytheville AFB, Ar	97 BW (1/60-1/4/92)
Carswell AFB, Tx	7 BW (6/58-late 1992) 4123 SW (58-25/2/59)
Castle AFB, Ca	93 BW (6/55-4/94) 366 Wg (detached basis 6/92-5/94)
Clinton-Sherman AFB, Ok	4123 SW (25/2/59-1/2/63) 70 BW (1/2/63-31/12/69)
Columbus AFB, Ms	4228 SW (6/59-1/2/63) 454 BW (1/2/63-2/7/69)
Dow AFB, Me	4038 SW (5/60-1/2/63) 397 BW (1/2/63-25/4/68)
Dyess AFB, Tx	96 SAW/BW (9/63-1985)
Eaker AFB, Ar	(ex-Blytheville AFB, see above)
Eglin AFB, Fl	4135 SW (7/59-1/2/63) 39 BW (1/2/63-25/6/65)
Ellsworth AFB, SD	28 BW (6/57-1986)
Fairchild AFB, Wa	92 BW/SAW/BW (3/57-6/94)
Glasgow AFB, Mt	4141 SW (1/4/61-1/2/63) 91 BW (1/2/63-25/6/68)
Grand Forks AFB, ND	4133 SW (4/62-1/2/63) 319 BW (1/2/63-1987)
Griffiss AFB, NY	4039 SW (1/60-1/2/63) 416 BW (1/2/63-11/94)
Homestead AFB, Fl	19 BW (2/62-25/7/68)
Kincheloe AFB, Mi	4239 SW (11/61-1/2/63) 449 BW (1/2/63-30/9/77)
Larson AFB, Wa	4170 SW (1/6/60-1/2/63) 462 SAW (1/2/63-25/6/66)
Loring AFB, Me	42 BW (6/56-3/94)
March AFB, Ca	22 BW (9/63-1/10/82)
Mather AFB, Ca	4134 SW (10/58-1/2/63) 320 BW (1/2/63-7/89)
McCoy AFB, Fl	4047 SW (1/9/61-1/4/63) 306 BW (1/4/63-1/7/74)
Minot AFB, ND	4136 SW (7/61-1/2/63) 450 BW (1/2/63-25/7/68) 5 BW (25/7/68-current)
Pease AFB, NH	509 BW (3/66-11/69)
Plattsburgh AFB, NY	380 SAW (6/66-1/71)
Robins AFB, Ga	4137 SW (8/60-1/2/63) 465 BW (1/2/63-25/7/68) 19 BW (25/7/68-1983)
K I Sawyer AFB, Mi	4042 SW (8/61-1/2/63) 410 BW (1/2/63-11/94)
Seymour Johnson AFB, NC	4241 SW (7/59-15/4/63) 68 BW (15/4/63-1/10/82)
Sheppard AFB, Tx	4245 SW (1/2/60-1/2/63) 494 BW (1/2/63-2/4/66)
Travis AFB, Ca	5 BW (2/59-25/7/68)
Turner AFB, Ga	4138 SW (7/59-1/2/63) 484 BW (1/2/63-25/3/67)
Walker AFB, NM	6 BW/SAW (12/57-25/3/67)
Westover AFB, Ma	99 BW (12/56-31/3/74)
Wright-Patterson AFB, Oh	4043 SW (1/6/60-1/2/63) 17 BW (1/2/63-30/9/75)
Wurtsmith AFB, Mi	379 BW (5/61-2/12/92)

B-52 BASES - OVERSEAS

General notes: These are the only locations known to have hosted resident B-52s for any extended period of time. B-52s have routinely visited other airfields for many years. For example, they frequently called at the four SAC 'clutch' bases in England on training flights during the early 1960s, and have often deployed to European airfields in order to participate in major NATO exercises since then. However, such visits are generally of short duration and must be viewed as temporary in nature – as a result, no details are presented here.

Location	Resident units/periods
Andersen AFB, Guam	3960 SW (4/64-2/66) 4133 BW(P) (1/2/66-1/7/70) 43 SW (1/7/70-30/9/90) 72 SW(P) (1/6/72-15/11/73)
Diego Garcia	4300 BW(P) (8/90-3/91)
RAF Fairford, England	806 BW(P) (5/2/91-9/3/91)
Jeddah, Saudi Arabia	1708 BW(P) (1/91-3/91)
Kadena AB, Okinawa	4252 SW (2/68-1/4/70) 376 SW (1/4/70-9/70)
Moron AB, Spain	801 BW(P) (1/91-3/91)
Ramey AFB, Puerto Rico	72 BW (8/59-30/6/71)
U-Tapao AB, Thailand	4258 SW (4/67-1/4/70) 307 SW (1/4/70-30/9/75)

B-52 'Tails'

A.
B-52A to B-52F with tail gunner's compartment

B.
B-52D with the addition of radar warning aerials

C.
B-52G introduced cropped fin and remotely controlled tail guns and chaff/flare launchers

D.
B-52G later modified aircraft (test configuration), featuring a variety of EW aerials and jamming equipment in tail fairings

E.
B-52H tail fairing housing M61A Vulcan cannon in place of the four .50 cal guns of all other models

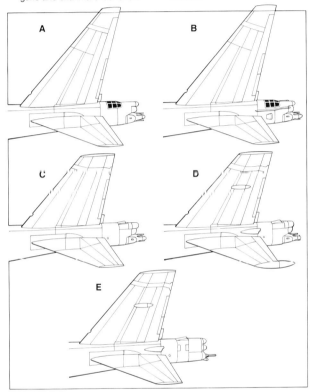

B-52 'Noses'

A.
YB-52 prototype with tandem cockpit for pilot and co-pilot

B.
B-52A to B-52F with airliner type cockpit

C.
B-52G early production aircraft had revised crew accommodation, rear gunner moved to nose section from tail barbette and generator fairings on engine cowlings

D.
B-52G with enhanced vision system (EVS) electro-optical turrets beneath nose and extensive EW aerials. Aircraft which were modified to carry cruise missiles on wing pylons had distinctive curved fairings to wing root

E.
B-52H initial production aircraft with TF-33 engines

F.
B-52H later fitted with EVS equipment. Jet capable of carrying cruise missiles on rotary launcher in internal bomb bay, hence wing root 'strakelets'

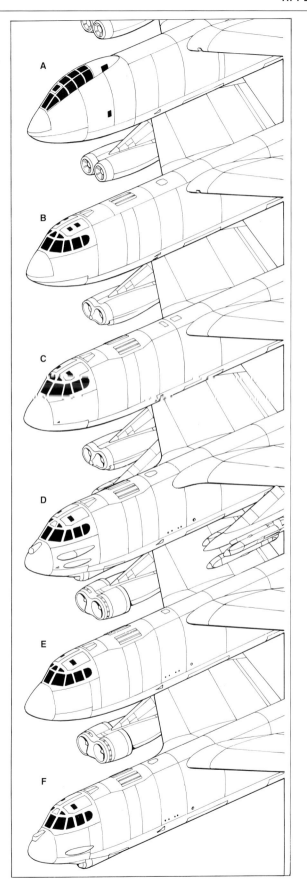

Boeing B-52G Stratofortress cutaway drawing key

1 Nose radome
2 ALT-28 ECM antenna
3 Electronic Countermeasures (ECM) equipment bay
4 Front pressure bulkhead
5 Electronic cooling intake
6 Bombing radar
7 Low-light television scanner turret (EVS system), infrared on starboard side
8 Television camera unit
9 ALQ-117 radar warning antenna
10 Underfloor control runs
11 Control column
12 Rudder pedals
13 Windscreen wipers
14 Instrument panel shroud
15 Windscreen panels
16 Cockpit eyebrow windows
17 Cockpit roof escape/ejection hatches
18 Co-pilot's ejector seats
19 Drogue chute container
20 Pilot's ejection seat
21 Flightdeck floor level

22 Navigator's instrument console
23 Ventral escape/ejection hatch, port and starboard
24 Radar navigator's downward firing ejection seat, navigator to starboard
25 Access ladder and hatch to flightdeck
26 EWO instructor's folding seat
27 Electronics equipment rack
28 In-flight refuelling receptacle, open
29 Refuelling delivery line
30 Electronic Warfare Officer's (EWO) ejection seat
31 Rear crew members' escape/ejection hatches
32 EWO's instrument panel
33 Gunner's remote control panel
34 Gunner's ejection seat
35 Navigation instructor's folding seat

36 Radio and electronics racks
37 Ventral entry hatch and ladder
38 Lower deck rear pressure bulkhead
39 ECM aerials
40 ECM equipment bay
41 Cooling air ducting
42 Upper deck rear pressure bulkhead
43 Water injection tank, capacity 1200 US gal (4542 litres)
44 Fuselage upper longeron
45 Astro navigation antenna
46 Tank access hatches
47 Leading edge 'strakelets' fitted to identify cruise missile carriers
48 Forward fuselage fuel tank
49 Airconditioning plant
50 Forward starboard main undercarriage bogie
51 Landing lamp
52 Forward port main under carriage landing bogie
53 Torque scissor links
54 Steering jacks
55 Main undercarriage door
56 Main undercarriage leg strut
57 Wing/front spar/fuselage /main undercarriage attachment frame
58 Main undercarriage wheel bay
59 Doppler aerial

60 Central electronic equipment bay
61 Airconditioning intake duct
62 Front spar attachment joint
63 Wing root rib
64 Wing panel bolted attachment joint
65 Centre section fuel tank bay
66 Wing centre section carry-through
67 Starboard wing attachment joint
68 Vortex generators
69 Starboard wing integral fuel tank bays: total fuel tank system capacity (includes external tanks), 48,030 US gal (181813 litres)
70 Engine ignition control unit
71 Bleed air ducting
72 Starboard engine nacelles
73 Nacelle pylons
74 Fixed external fuel tank capacity 700 US gal (2650 litres)
75 Tank pylon
76 Fuel venting channels
77 Tip surge tanks
78 Starboard navigation light
79 Wing tip fairing
80 Fixed portion of trailing edge

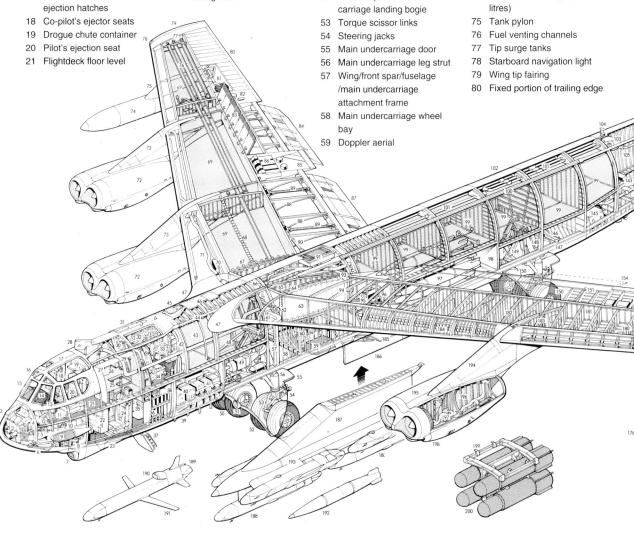

81 Starboard outrigger wheel, stowed position
82 Hydraulic equipment bay
83 Roll control spoiler panels, open
84 Outboard single-slotted, Fowler-type flap, down position
85 Inboard fixed trailing edge segment
86 Chaff dispensers and flare launchers
87 Inboard single slotted flap, down position
88 Flap guide rails
89 Flap screw jacks
90 Flap drive torque shaft
91 Life raft stowage
92 Wing centre/longeron ties
93 Central flap drive motor
94 Rear spar attachment joint
95 AGM-69 missile environmental control unit
96 Bomb bay rotary missile launcher
97 AGM-69 SRAM, air to ground missiles
98 Bomb bay rear bulkhead
99 Rear fuselage bag-type fuel tanks
100 Rear fuselage longeron
101 Fuel delivery and transfer piping
102 Fuselage skin panelling
103 Fuselage fuel system surge tank
104 Data link antenna
105 Rear fuselage frame construction
106 Rear equipment bay air conditioning plant
107 Ram air intake
108 Starboard tailplane
109 Vortex generators
110 Starboard elevator
111 Fin spar attachment joint: fin folds to starboard

112 Tailfin rib construction
113 VOR aerial
114 Lightning isolator
115 Fin tip aerial fairing
116 Rudder
117 Rudder tab
118 Hydraulic rudder control jack
119 Rudder aerodynamic balance
120 Rear ECM and fire control electronics pack

121 ECM aerial fairing
122 Brake parachute stowage
123 Parachute and door release mechanism
124 ALQ-117 retractable aerial fairing
125 AN/ASG-15 search radome
126 ALQ-117 and APR-25 ECM radome
127 Four 0.5-in (12.7mm) machine-guns
128 AN/ASG-15 tracking radome
129 Remote control gun turret
130 Ammunition feed chutes
131 Ammunition tanks, 600 rounds per gun
132 Elevator tab
133 Port elevator
134 ALQ-153 tail warning radar
135 All-moving tailplane construction
136 Tailplane carry-through box section spar
137 Elevator aerodynamic balance
138 Centre section sealing plate
139 Tailplane trimming screw jack
140 Air conditioning ducting
141 Fuel system venting pipes
142 Ventral access hatch
143 Rear fuselage ECM equipment bay
144 ECM aerials
145 Strike camera compartment
146 Rear main undercarriage wheel bay
147 Bomb/wheel bay box section longeron
148 Main undercarriage mounting frame
149 Hydraulic retraction jack
150 Rear main undercarriage bogie units
151 Flap shroud units

152 ECM dispensers
153 Fixed portion of trailing edge
154 Port flaps, down position
155 Outboard single slotted flap
156 Port roll control spoiler panels
157 Hydraulic reservoir
158 Outrigger wheel bay
159 Fixed portion of trailing edge
160 Glass-fibre wing tip fairing

161 Port navigation light
162 Outer wing panel integral fuel tank
163 Port outrigger wheel
164 Fixed external fuel tank
165 Fuel tank pylon
166 Outrigger wheel retraction strut
167 Outer wing panel attachment joint
168 Engine pylon mounting rib
169 Pylon rear attachment strut
170 Engine pylon construction
171 Pratt & Whitney J57-P-43WB turbojet engine
172 Engine oil tank, capacity 8.5US gal (32 litres)
173 Accessory equipment gearbox
174 Generator cooling air duct
175 Oil cooler ram air intakes
176 Engine air intakes
177 Detachable cowling panels
178 Leading edge rib construction
179 Front spar
180 Wing rib construction
181 Rear spar
182 Port wing integral fuel tank bays
183 Inboard pylon mounting rib
184 Leading edge bleed air and engine control runs
185 Weapons bay doors, open (loading) position
186 Bomb doors, open
187 Wing mounted cruise missile pylon
188 Boeing AGM-86B Air Launched Cruise Missiles (ACLM), six perwing pylon, stowed configuration
189 AGM-86B missile in flight configuration
190 Retractable engine air intake
191 Folding wings
192 AGM-69 SRAM, alternative load
193 Missile adapters
194 Nacelle pylon
195 Port inboard engine nacelles
196 Central engine mounting bulkhead/firewall
197 Bleed air ducting
198 Generator cooling air ducting
199 Fuselage bomb mounting cradle
200 Free-fall 25-megaton nuclear weapons (four)

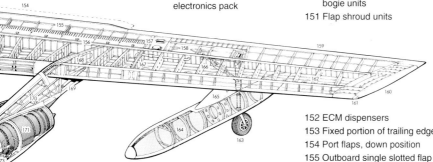

APPENDIX 7

B-52 Unit Disposition Over Three Decades

B-52 UNIT DISPOSITION AS AT DECEMBER 1957

Second Air Force, Barksdale AFB, La

- 11th BW, Altus AFB, Ok.
  (26th BS/42nd BS - nil a/c, B-52E due)
- 4123rd SW, Carswell AFB, Tx.
  (98th BS - nil a/c, B-52E due)

Eighth Air Force, Westover AFB, Ma

- 45th Air Division (Loring)
  - 42nd BW, Loring AFB, Me
    (69th BS/70th BS/75th BS - B 52D)
- 57th Air Division (Westover)
  - 99th BW, Westover AFB, Ma
    (346th BS/347th BS/348th BS-B 52C/D)

Fifteenth Air Force, March AFB, Ca

- 47th Air Division (Walker)
  - 6th BW, Walker AFB, NM
    (24th BS/39th BS/40th BS - nil a/c, B-52E due)
- 28th BW, Ellsworth AFB, SD
  (77th BS/717th BS/718th BS - B-52D)
- 92nd BW, Fairchild AFB, Wa
  (325th BS/326th BS/327th BS - B-52D)
- 93rd BW, Castle AFB, Ca
  (328th BS/329th BS/330th BS - B-52B/D)

B-52 UNIT DISPOSITION AS AT DECEMBER 1963

Second Air Force, Barksdale AFB, La

- 4th Air Division (Barksdale)
  - 2nd BW, Barksdale AFB, La
    (20th BS - B-52F)
  - 340th BW, Bergstrom AFB, Tx
    (486th BS - B-52D)
  - 494th BW, Sheppard AFB, Tx
    (864th BS - B-52D)
- 19th Air Division (Carswell)
  - 7th BW, Carswell AFB, Tx
    (9th BS - B-52F)

- 40th Air Division (Wurtsmith)
  - 379th BW, Wurtsmith AFB, Mi
    (524th BS - B-52H)
  - 410th BW, K I Sawyer AFB, Mi
    (644th BS - B-52H)
  - 449th BW, Kincheloe AFB, Mi
    (716th BS - B-52H)
- 42nd Air Division (Blytheville)
  - 97th BW, Blytheville AFB, Ar
    (340th BS - B-52G)
  - 454th BW, Columbus AFB, Ms
    (736th BS - B-52F)
- 810th Strategic Aerospace Division (Minot)
  - 319th BW, Grand Forks AFB, ND
    (46th BS - B-52H)
  - 450th BW, Minot AFB, ND
    (720th BS - B-52H)
- 816th Strategic Aerospace Division (Altus)
  - 11th SAW, Altus AFB, Ok
    (26th BS - B-52E)
  - 70th BW, Clinton-Sherman AFB, Ok
    (6th BS - B-52E)

Eighth Air Force, Westover AFB, Ma

- 6th Air Division (Dow)
  - 17th BW, Wright-Patterson AFB, Oh
    (34th BS - B-52E)
  - 397th BW, Dow AFB, Me
    (596th BS - B-52G)
  - 416th BW, Griffiss AFB, NY
    (668th BS - B-52G)
- 45th Air Division (Loring)
  - 42nd BW, Loring AFB, Me
    (69th BS/70th BS - B-52G)
- 57th Air Division (Westover)
  - 99th BW, Westover AFB, Ma
    (346th BS/348th BS - B-52C)
- 822nd Air Division (Turner)
  - 39th BW, Eglin AFB, Fl
    (62nd BS - B-52G)
  - 68th BW, Seymour Johnson AFB, NC
    (51st BS - B-52G)

- 465th BW, Robins AFB, Ga
  (781st BS - B-52G)
- 484th BW, Turner AFB, Ga
  (824th BS - B-52D)
- 823rd Air Division (Homestead)
  - 19th BW, Homestead AFB, Fl
    (28th BS - B-52H)
  - 72nd BW, Ramey AFB, PR
    (60th BS - B-52G)
  - 306th BW, McCoy AFB, Fl
    (367th BS - B-52D)

Fifteenth Air Force, March AFB, Ca

- 14th Strategic Aerospace Division (Beale)
  - 5th BW, Travis AFB, Ca
    (23rd BS - B-52G)
  - 320th BW, Mather AFB, Ca
    (441st BS - B-52F)
  - 456th SAW, Beale AFB, Ca
    (744th BS - B-52G)
- 18th Strategic Aerospace Division (Fairchild)
  - 91st BW, Glasgow AFB, Mt
    (322nd BS - B-52D)
  - 92nd SAW, Fairchild AFB, Wa
    (325th BS - B-52D)
  - 462nd SAW, Larson AFB, Wa
    (768th BS - B-52D)
- 22nd Strategic Aerospace Division (Schilling)
  - 6th SAW, Walker AFB, NM
    (24th BS/40th BS - B-52E)
  - 461st BW, Amarillo AFB, Tx
    (764th BS - B-52D)
- 47th Strategic Aerospace Division (Castle)
  - 22nd BW, March AFB, Ca
    (2nd BS - B-52B)
  - 93rd BW, Castle AFB, Ca
    (328th BS/329th BS - B-52B/F)
- 819th Strategic Aerospace Division (Dyess)
  - 95th BW, Biggs AFB, Tx
    (334th BS - B-52B)
  - 96th SAW, Dyess AFB, Tx
    (337th BS - B-52E)
- 821st Strategic Aerospace Division (Ellsworth)
  - 28th BW, Ellsworth AFB, SD
    (77th BS - B-52D)

DISTRIBUTION OF B-52 FLEET - 1964

2nd Bomb Wing, Barksdale AFB, La (20th BS)

B-52F: 70044, 70046, 70051, 70053, 70063, 70139, 70140, 70141, 70143, 70153, 70156, 70162, 70164, 70165, 70168, 70169, 70176

5th Bomb Wing, Travis AFB, Ca (23rd BS)

B-52G: 76487, 76493, 76500, 76507, 76517, 80158, 80164, 80169, 80171, 80181, 80190, 80199, 80236, 92575, 92591, 92595, 92602

6th Strategic Aerospace Wing, Walker AFB, NM (24th/40th BS)

B-52E: 60634, 60635, 60638, 60644, 60645, 60648, 60649, 60651, 60652, 60653, 60656, 60701, 60705, 60706, 60707, 70020, 70023, 70097, 70098, 70099, 70105, 70107, 70112, 70117, 70127, 70128, 70132, 70133, 70136

7th Bomb Wing, Carswell AFB, Tx (9th BS)

B-52F: 70048, 70049, 70056, 70057, 70058, 70061, 70069, 70071, 70117, 70110, 70151, 70161, 70163, 70170, 70179, 70181

11th Strategic Aerospace Wing, Altus AFB, Ok (26th BS)

B-52E: 60641, 60704, 60709, 70014, 70029, 70101, 70103, 70104, 70106, 70110, 70111, 70113, 70114, 70125, 70129, 70137

17th Bomb Wing, Wright-Patterson AFB, Oh (34th BS)

B-52E: 60636, 60643, 60647, 60654, 60708, 60710, 60711, 70017, 70021, 70026, 70027, 70028, 70096, 70102, 70116, 70135, 70138

19th Bomb Wing, Homestead AFB, Fl (28th BS)

B-52H: 00008, 00023, 00026, 00029, 00036, 00043, 00051, 10002, 10003, 10008, 10009, 10011, 10012, 10014, 10027, 10039, 10040

22nd Bomb Wing, March AFB, Ca (2nd BS)

B-52B: 28710, 28711, 28713, 28714, 28715, 30366, 30367, 30368, 30369, 30370, 30372, 30373, 30374, 30375, 30376

28th Bomb Wing, Ellsworth AFB, SD (77th BS)

B-52D: 50066, 50107, 50675, 60615, 60657, 60658, 60660, 60674, 60676, 60680, 60682, 60683, 60691, 60693, 60694, 60697

39th Bomb Wing, Eglin AFB, Fl (62nd BS)

B-52G: 76485, 76489, 76497, 76499, 76509, 76510, 76520, 80167, 80175, 80189, 80228, 80235, 80238, 92566, 92583, 92589, 92593

42nd Bomb Wing, Loring AFB, Me (69th/70th BS)

B-52G: 76479, 76492, 76498, 76502, 76511, 80159, 80160, 80162, 80163, 80166, 80177, 80183, 80188, 80194, 80197, 80202, 80203, 80205, 80206, 80207, 80208, 80215, 80219, 80224, 80225, 80239, 80240, 80241, 80243, 80245, 92572, 92573, 92582, 92592

68th Bomb Wing, Seymour Johnson AFB, NC (51st BS)

B-52G: 80161, 80174, 80179, 80185, 80214, 80217, 80218, 80234, 80251, 80254, 80255, 80256, 80258, 92571, 92581, 92587, 92601

70th Bomb Wing, Clinton-Sherman AFB, Ok (6th BS)

B-52E: 60631, 60639, 60642, 60650, 60699, 60700, 60702, 60703, 60712, 70019, 70022, 70119, 70122, 70124, 70130, 70131

72nd Bomb Wing, Ramey AFB, PR (60th BS)

B-52G: 76468, 76469, 76470, 76471, 76472, 76473, 76474, 76475, 76516, 80178, 80184, 80211, 80221, 80232, 80253, 92578, 92580, 92590

91st Bomb Wing, Glasgow AFB, Mt (322nd BS)

B-52D: 50078, 50086, 50104, 50677, 60592, 60603, 60611, 60619, 60624, 60625, 60629, 60662, 60668, 60671, 60672, 60673, 60690, 60695

92nd Strategic Aerospace Wing, Fairchild AFB, Wa (325th BS)

B-52D: 50062, 50067, 50091, 50673, 50674, 50676, 50678, 50680, 60589, 60594, 60617, 60663, 60666, 60667, 60687, 60698

93rd Bomb Wing, Castle AFB, Ca (328th/329th BS)

B-52B: 20004, 20005, 20006, 20007, 20009, 20010, 20011, 20012, 28712 (note:- 20009 written off 7/2/64)

B-52F: 70030, 70031, 70032, 70033, 70034, 70035, 70037, 70039, 70042, 70060, 70064, 70065, 70145, 70149, 70152, 70154, 70159, 70160, 70173, 70180

95th Bomb Wing, Biggs AFB, Tx (334th BS)

B-52B: 30377, 30378, 30379, 30381, 30383, 30385, 30386, 30387, 30388, 30389, 30391, 30392, 30394, 30395, 30396, 30397, 30398

96th Strategic Aerospace Wing, Dyess AFB, Tx (337th BS)

B-52E: 60637, 60646, 70015, 70016, 70024, 70025, 70095, 70100, 70108, 70109, 70115, 70118, 70120, 70121, 70123, 70126, 70134

97th Bomb Wing, Blytheville AFB, Ar (340th BS)

B-52G: 76476, 76480, 76481, 76482, 76484, 76488, 76513, 76514, 80168, 80170, 80209, 80210, 80222, 80227, 80233, 80244, 80246, 92599

99th Bomb Wing, Westover AFB, Ma (346th/348th BS)

B-52C: 30400, 30401, 30402, 30403, 30404, 30405, 30407, 30408, 42664, 42665, 42666, 42667, 42668, 42670, 42671, 42672, 42673, 42674, 42675, 42678, 42679, 42680, 42681, 42683, 42684, 42685, 42686, 42687, 42688

B-52D: 50111, 60599, 60600

306th Bomb Wing, McCoy AFB, Fl (367th BS)

B-52D: 50049, 50050, 50051, 50052, 50053, 50054, 50055, 50056, 50072, 50074, 50077, 50084, 50085, 50105, 50106, 60582

319th Bomb Wing, Grand Forks AFB, ND (46th BS)

B-52H: 00030, 00040, 00059, 10016, 10020, 10022, 10024, 10025, 10028, 10029, 10030, 10031, 10032, 10033, 10034, 10035

320th Bomb Wing, Mather AFB, Ca (441st BS)

B-52F: 70040, 70041, 70045, 70047, 70050, 70052, 70055, 70059, 70062, 70066, 70068, 70072, 70171, 70172, 70177, 70182, 70183

340th Bomb Wing, Bergstrom AFB, Tx (486th BS)

B-52D: 50059, 50063, 50070, 50073, 50075, 50080, 50087, 50089, 50090, 50099, 50115, 50117, 60580, 60584, 60586, 60587, 60593

379th Bomb Wing, Wurtsmith AFB, Mi (524th BS)

B-52H: 00001, 00003, 00007, 00009, 00011, 00015, 00019, 00022, 00025, 00037, 00061, 10017, 10018, 10019, 10036, 10037, 10038

397th Bomb Wing, Dow AFB, Me (596th BS)

B-52G: 76483, 76486, 76494, 76503, 76506, 80172, 80176, 80204, 80212, 80230, 80248, 80257, 92564, 92565, 92570, 92579, 92598

410th Bomb Wing, K I Sawyer AFB, Mi (644th BS)

B-52H: 00005, 00014, 00018, 00024, 00031, 00033, 00035, 00039, 00042, 00045, 00046, 00047, 00055, 00057, 10004, 10005, 10015

416th Bomb Wing, Griffiss AFB, NY (668th BS)

B-52G: 76495, 76501, 76512, 76518, 80186, 80195, 80213, 80216, 80220, 80231, 80237, 80250, 92569, 92574, 92577, 92588, 92600

449th Bomb Wing, Kincheloe AFB, Mi (716th BS)

B-52H: 00002, 00013, 00028, 00032, 00034, 00041, 00044, 00048, 00049, 00052, 00053, 00054, 00056, 00062, 10001, 10010, 10013

450th Bomb Wing, Minot AFB, ND (720th BS)

B-52H: 00006, 00010, 00012, 00016, 00017, 00020, 00021, 00027, 00038, 00050, 00058, 00060, 10006, 10007, 10021, 10026

454th Bomb Wing, Columbus AFB, Ms (736th BS)

B-52F: 70054, 70067, 70070, 70142, 70144, 70146, 70150, 70155, 70157, 70158, 70167, 70174, 70175, 70178

456th Strategic Aerospace Wing, Beale AFB, Ca (744th BS)

B-52G: 76477, 76478, 76491, 76496, 76504, 76508, 76515, 80165, 80191, 80198, 80223, 92567, 92568, 92594, 92596, 92597

461st Bomb Wing, Amarillo AFB, Tx (764th BS)

B-52D: 60581, 60601, 60602, 60604, 60605, 60606, 60609, 60611, 60613, 60616, 60618, 60622, 60627, 60628, 60659, 60685, 60686, 60688, 60692

462nd Strategic Aerospace Wing, Larson AFB, Wa (768th BS)

B-52D: 50081, 50083, 50088, 50100, 50101, 50103, 50108, 50109, 50110, 50112, 50116, 60583, 60585, 60588, 60595, 60598 (note:- 50108 written off 10/11/64)

465th Bomb Wing, Robins AFB, Ga (781st BS)

B-52G: 76490, 76505, 76519, 80173, 80192, 80193, 80200, 80201, 80226, 80229, 80242, 80247, 80249, 80252, 92584, 92585, 92586

484th Bomb Wing, Turner AFB, Ga (824th BS)

B-52D: 50057, 50058, 50060, 50061, 50064, 50068, 50069, 50071, 50076, 50079, 50092, 50095, 50096, 50097, 50113, 60590, 60596 (note:- 50060 written off 13/1/64)

494th Bomb Wing, Sheppard AFB, Tx (864th BS)

B-52D: 50094, 50679, 60608, 60612, 60621, 60623, 60626, 60630, 60664, 60665, 60669, 60670, 60675, 60677, 60678, 60679, 60684, 60689, 60696

Test-dedicated aircraft

20003	NB-52A	AFFTC, Edwards AFB, Ca
20008	NB-52B	AFFTC, Edwards AFB, Ca
20013	NB-52B	AFSWC, Kirtland AFB, NM
30399	NB-52C	ASD, Wright-Patterson AFB, Oh
60620	NB-52D	AFSWC, Kirtland AFB, NM
60632	NB-52E	AFFDL/Boeing
70038	JB-52F	AFSC Armament Division, Eglin AFB, Fl
70073	B-52F	AFSC (Bailed to Boeing)

| 80182 | JB-52G | AFSC Armament Division, Eglin AFB, Fl |
| 00004 | B-52H | AFSC (Bailed to Boeing Wichita?) |

Ground instructional airframe

B-52A: 20001 With Chanute Technical Training Center, Il

Scrapped or retired airframes

BELOW NB-52B 52-0008 probably served at Edwards AFB longer than any other aeroplane, and 'dropped' just about every shape it could carry into the air. In this 22 May 1970 shot, the jet is carrying a Martin X-24A MK-F2 lifting body research vehicle which simulated earth landings like those later made by the shuttle. The NB-52 also carried research aircraft, rockets and even the Pegasus SSTO missile *(USAF)*

XB-52: 90230
YB-52: 90231
B-52A: 20002

ATTRITION LOSSES 1956-63

B-52B:	28716, 30371, 30380, 30382, 30384, 30390, 30393
B-52C:	30406, 42676, 42682
B-52D:	50065, 50082, 50093, 50098, 50102, 50114, 60591, 60597, 60607, 60610, 60661, 60681
B-52E:	60633, 60655, 70018
B-52F:	70036, 70043, 70166
B-52G:	80180, 80187, 80196, 92576

Unaccounted for:

B-52C:	42669, 42677
B-52E:	60640
B-52H:	10023

BELOW NB-52E 57-0119 was employed by the USAF to evaluate the 41,000-lb thrust GE TF39-1 turbofan engine employed on the C-5A Galaxy transport, which made its first flight on 30 June 1968. The C-5 suffered teething troubles when it first entered service, but none were attributed to the powerplant, perhaps due to the preliminary work done by this flying testbed *(via Roger F Besecker)*

RIGHT Wearing an unusual all-white paint scheme adorned with the badge of the USAF's Air Research and Development Command, this unmodified B-52G (58-0182) is thought to have been employed as a test-ship in weapons development
(via M J Kasiuba)

B-52 UNIT DISPOSITION AS AT DECEMBER 1970

Second Air Force, Barksdale AFB, La

─19th Air Division (Carswell)

   ├─2nd BW, Barksdale AFB, La
     (62nd BS/596th BS - B-52G)

   ├─7th BW, Carswell AFB, Tx
     (20th BS - B-52D)

   └─96th SAW, Dyess AFB, Tx
     (337th BS - B-52D)

─40th Air Division (Wurtsmith)

   ├─379th BW, Wurtsmith AFB, Mi
     (524th BS - B-52H)

   ├─410th BW, K I Sawyer AFB, Mi
     (644th BS - B-52H)

   └─449th BW, Kincheloe AFB, Mi
     (716th BS - B-52H)

─42nd Air Division (Blytheville)

   └─97th BW, Blytheville AFB, Ar
     (340th BS - B-52G)

─45th Air Division (Loring)

   ├─17th BW, Wright-Patterson AFB, Oh
     (34th BS - B-52H)

   ├─42nd BW, Loring AFB, Me
     (69th BS - B-52G)

   └─416th BW, Griffiss AFB, NY
     (668th BS - B-52G)

─47th Air Division (Castle)

   └─93rd BW, Castle AFB, Ca
     (328th BS/329th BS - B-52D/F)

─817th Air Division (Pease)

   ├─99th BW, Westover AFB, Ma
     (346th BS/348th BS - B-52D)

   └─380th SAW, Plattsburgh AFB, NY
     (528th BS - B-52G)

└─823rd Air Division (McCoy)

   ├─19th BW, Robins AFB, Ga
     (28th BS - B-52G)

   ├─68th BW, Seymour Johnson AFB, NC
     (51st BS - B-52G)

   ├─72nd BW, Ramey AFB, PR
     (60th BS - B-52G)

   └─306th BW, McCoy AFB, Fl
     (367th BS - B-52D)

Eighth Air Force, Andersen AFB, Guam

─43rd SW, Andersen AFB, Guam
  (B-52D)

└─307th SW, U-Tapao AB, Thailand
  (B-52D)

Fifteenth Air Force, March AFB, Ca

─4th Strategic Aerospace Division (Grand Forks)

   ├─92nd SAW, Fairchild AFB, Wa
     (325th BS - B-52D)

   └─319th BW, Grand Forks AFB, ND
     (46th BS - B-52H)

─14th Strategic Aerospace Division (Beale)

   ├─22nd BW, March AFB, Ca
     (2nd BS/486th BS - B-52D)

   ├─320th BW, Mather AFB, Ca
     (441st BS - B-52G)

   └─456th SAW, Beale AFB, Ca
     (744th BS - B-52G)

─810th Strategic Aerospace Division (Minot)

   └─5th BW, Minot AFB, ND
     (23rd BS - B-52H)

└─821st Strategic Aerospace Division (Ellsworth)

   └─28th BW, Ellsworth AFB, SD
     (77th BS - B-52D)

Note - Most B-52D Wings also possessed a few
B-52Cs for training purposes at this time

B-52 UNIT DISPOSITION AS AT DECEMBER 1976

Eighth Air Force, Barksdale AFB, La

─19th Air Division (Carswell)

   ├─2nd BW, Barksdale AFB, La
     (62nd BS/596th BS - B-52G)

   └─7th BW, Carswell AFB, Tx
     (9th BS/20th BS - B-52D)

─40th Air Division (Wurtsmith)

   ├─379th BW, Wurtsmith AFB, Mi
     (524th BS - B-52H)

   ├─410th BW, K I Sawyer AFB, Mi
     (644th BS - B-52H)

   └─449th BW, Kincheloe AFB, Mi
     (716th BS - B-52H)

─42nd Air Division (Blytheville)

   ├─19th BW, Robins AFB, Ga
     (28th BS - B-52G)

   ├─68th BW, Seymour Johnson AFB, NC
     (51st BS - B-52G)

   └─97th BW, Blytheville AFB, Ar
     (340th BS - B-52G)

─45th Air Division (Pease)

   ├─42nd BW, Loring AFB, Me
     (69th BS - B-52G)

   └─416th BW, Griffiss AFB, NY
     (668th BS - B-52G)

Fifteenth Air Force, March AFB, Ca

─4th Air Division (F E Warren)

   └─28th BW, Ellsworth AFB, SD
     (77th BS - B-52G)

─12th Air Division (Dyess)

   ├─22nd BW, March AFB, Ca
     (2nd BS - B-52D)

   └─96th BW, Dyess AFB, Tx
     (337th BS - B-52D)

─14th Air Division (Beale)

   ├─93rd BW, Castle AFB, Ca
     (328th BS - B-52G/H)

   └─320th BW, Mather AFB, Ca
     (441st BS - B-52G)

─47th Air Division (Fairchild)

   └─92nd BW, Fairchild AFB, Wa
     (325th BS - B-52G)

└─57th Air Division (Minot)

   ├─5th BW, Minot AFB, ND
     (23rd BS - B-52H)

   └─319th BW, Grand Forks AFB, ND
     (46th BS - B-52H)

3rd Air Division, Andersen AFB, Guam

└─43r SW, Andersen AFB, Guam
  (60th BS - B-52D)

B-52 UNIT DISPOSITION AS AT DECEMBER 1981

Eighth Air Force, Barksdale AFB, La

├ 19th Air Division (Carswell)

  ├ 2nd BW, Barksdale AFB, La
    (62nd BS/596th BS - B-52G)

  └ 7th BW, Carswell AFB, Tx
    (9th BS/20th BS - B-52D)

├ 40th Air Division (Wurtsmith)

  ├ 379th BW, Wurtsmith AFB, Mi
    (524th BS - B-52G)

  └ 410th BW, K I Sawyer AFB, Mi
    (644th BS - B-52H)

├ 42nd Air Division (Blytheville)

  ├ 19th BW, Robins AFB, Ga
    (28th BS - B-52G)

  ├ 68th BW, Seymour Johnson AFB, NC
    (51st BS - B-52G)

  └ 97th BW, Blytheville AFB, Ar
    (340th BS - B-52G)

└ 45th Air Division (Pease)

  ├ 42nd BW, Loring AFB, Me
    (69th BS - B-52G)

  └ 416th BW, Griffiss AFB, NY
    (668th BS - B-52G)

Fifteenth Air Force, March AFB, Ca

├ 4th Air Division (F E Warren)

  └ 28th BW, Ellsworth AFB, SD
    (37th BS/77th BS - B-52H)

├ 12th Air Division (Dyess)

  ├ 22nd BW, March AFB, Ca
    (2nd BS - B-52D)

  └ 96th BW, Dyess AFB, Tx
    (337th BS - B-52D)

├ 14th Air Division (Beale)

  ├ 93rd BW, Castle AFB, Ca
    (328th BS - B-52G/H)

  └ 320th BW, Mather AFB, Ca
    (441st BS - B-52G)

├ 47th Air Division (Fairchild)

  └ 92nd BW, Fairchild AFB, Wa
    (325th BS - B-52G)

└ 57th Air Division (Minot)

  ├ 5th BW, Minot AFB, ND
    (23rd BS - B-52H)

  └ 319th BW, Grand Forks AFB, ND
    (46th BS - B-52H)

3rd Air Division, Andersen AFB, Guam

  └ 43rd SW, Andersen AFB, Guam
    (60th BS - B-52D)

B-52 UNIT DISPOSITION AS AT DECEMBER 1989

Eighth Air Force, Barksdale AFB, La

├ 19th Air Division (Carswell)

  └ 7th BW, Carswell AFB, Tx
    (9th BS/20th BS - B-52H)

├ 40th Air Division (Wurtsmith)

  ├ 379th BW, Wurtsmith AFB, Mi
    (524th BS - B-52G)

  ├ 410th BW, K I Sawyer AFB, Mi
    (644th BS - B-52H)

  └ 416th BW, Griffiss AFB, NY
    (668th BS - B-52G)

├ 42nd Air Division (Blytheville)

  ├ 2nd BW, Barksdale AFB, La
    (62nd BS/596th BS - B-52G)

  └ 97th BW, Blytheville AFB, Ar
    (340th BS - B-52G)

└ 45th Air Division (Pease)

  └ 42nd BW, Loring AFB, Me
    (69th BS - B-52G)

Fifteenth Air Force, March AFB, Ca.

├ 3rd Air Division (Andersen)

  └ 43rd BW, Andersen AFB, Guam
    (60th BS - B-52G)

├ 12th Air Division (Dyess)

  └ 93rd BW, Castle AFB, Ca
    (328th BS - B-52G)

└ 57th Air Division (Minot)

  ├ 5th BW, Minot AFB, ND
    (23rd BS - B-52H)

  └ 92nd BW, Fairchild AFB, Wa
    (325th BS - B-52H)

B-52 UNIT DISPOSITION AS AT MAY 1993

Eighth Air Force, Barksdale AFB, La

├ 2nd Wg, Barksdale AFB, La
  (20th BS/596th BS - B-52H, tail-code 'LA')

├ 5th BW, Minot AFB, N.D.
  (23rd BS - B-52H, tail-code 'MT')

└ 410th BW, K I Sawyer AFB, Mi
  (644th BS - B-52H, tail-code 'KI')

Ninth Air Force, Shaw AFB, SC

├ 42nd BW, Loring AFB, Me
  (69th BS - B-52G, tail-code 'LZ')

└ 416th BW, Griffiss AFB, NY
  (668th BS - B-52G, tail-code 'GR')

Twelfth Air Force, Davis-Monthan AFB, Az

├ 92nd BW, Fairchild AFB, Wa
  (325th BS - B-52H, tail-code 'FC')

├ 93rd BW, Castle AFB, Ca
  (328th BS - B-52G, tail-code 'CA')

└ 366th Wg, Mountain Home AFB, Id
  (34th BS - B-52G, tail-code 'MO' - at Castle AFB, Ca)

B-52 UNIT DISPOSITION AS AT MARCH 1995

Eighth Air Force, Barksdale AFB, La

├ 2nd BW, Barksdale AFB, La
  (11th BS/20th BS/96th BS - B-52H, tail-code 'LA')

└ 5th BW, Minot AFB, ND
  (23rd BS/72nd BS - B-52H, tail-code 'MT')

Tenth Air Force (AFRes,) Bergstron AFB, Tx

└ 917th Wg, Barksdale AFB, La
  (93rd BS - B-52H, tail-code 'BD')

APPENDIX 8

STRATOFORTRESS ATTRITION

Serial	Model	Unit	Date	Location and Circumstances (where known)
53-0384	B	93 BW	16/2/56	Near Sacramento, Ca. Starboard forward alternator failed in flight, culminating in an uncontrollable fire which caused aircraft to break up.
53-0393	B	93 BW	16/9/56	Location unknown. In flight fire. Also reported as having occurred on 17/9/56.
52-8716	B	93 BW	30/11/56	Near Castle AFB, Ca. Crashed soon after take-off on night mission.
55-0082	D	42 BW	10/1/57	Crashed ten miles from Loring AFB, Me.
54-2676	C	Boeing	29/3/57	Destroyed during Boeing test flight from Wichita, Ks. Aircraft experienced complete loss of AC electrical power due to defective constant speed drive during negative G conditions. Aircraft then broke up and crashed. JB-52C.
53-0382	B	93 BW	6/11/57	Crashed on landing at Castle AFB, Ca. Landing gear lever latch failed during touch and-go landing, resulting in gear retracting while still on runway.
56-0597	D	92 BW	12/12/57	Crashed at Fairchild AFB, Wa. Incorrect wiring of stabiliser trim switch resulted in loss of control and caused aircraft to crash at end of runway.
56-0610	D	28 BW	11/2/58	Crashed short of runway at Ellsworth AFB, SD. Fuel pump screens iced over, leading to total power loss on final approach.
55-0102	D	42 BW	26/6/58	Destroyed by ground fire at Loring AFB, Me.
55-0093	D	42 BW	29/7/58	Crashed three miles south of Loring AFB, Me. Flew into ground in bad weather.
56-0661	D	92 BW	9/9/58	Crashed three miles north-east of Fairchild AFB, Wa. Mid-air collision with B-52D 56-0681. Also reported as having occurred on 8/9/58.
56-0681	D	92 BW	9/9/58	Crashed three miles north-east of Fairchild AFB, Wa. Mid-air collision with B-52D 56-0661. Also reported as having occurred on 8/9/58.
55-0065	D	42 BW	16/9/58	Crashed ten miles south of St Paul, Wi. Details unknown.
56-0633	E	11 BW	9/12/58	Crashed at Altus AFB, Ok. Improper use of stabiliser trim during overshoot.
53-0371	B	93 BW	29/1/59	Crashed at Castle AFB, Ca. Flapless take-off aborted at high speed.
56-0591	D	Boeing	23/6/59	Burns, Or. Horizontal stabiliser suffered turbulence-induced failure at low-level. One report states lost in accident at Larson AFB, Wa (aircraft was probably flying from there).
54-2682	C	99 BW	10/8/59	Crashed 20 miles east of New Hampton, NH. Nose radome failed in flight.
57-0036	F	4228 SW	15/10/59	Hardinsberg, Ky. Mid-air collision with KC-135A during airborne alert duty.
58-0180	G	72 BW	2/2/60	Ramey AFB, PR. Incorrect trim setting during touch-and-go approach. Also reported as having occurred on 1/2/60.
56-0607	D	92 BW	1/4/60	Burned out on runway at Fairchild AFB, Wa. Upper wing structure failed.
55-0114	D	99 BW	9/12/60	Crashed at unknown location after navigator ejected while aircraft descending to low-level route. Pilot then concluded that aircraft was breaking up and ordered all remaining crew members to eject or bail out.
55-0098	D	4170 SW	15/12/60	Crashed at Larson AFB, Wa. Aircraft had earlier collided with tanker during air-to-air refuelling. Starboard wing failed and aircraft caught fire during landing roll.
53-0390	B	95 BW	19/1/61	Monticello, Ut. Turbulence-induced structural failure at high level.
58-0187	G	4241 SW	24/1/61	Goldsboro, NC. Fatigue failure of starboard wing after fuel leak at high altitude. Loss of control resulted when flaps selected during ensuing emergency approach to Seymour Johnson AFB.

Serial	Model	Unit	Date	Location and Circumstances (where known)
57-0166	F	4134 SW	14/3/61	Near Yuba City, Ca. Cabin pressurisation failed, causing descent, with increased fuel consumption leading to fuel exhaustion before rendezvous with tanker. Aircraft was then abandoned by crew. Was engaged on airborne alert duty.
59-2576	G	4038 SW	30/3/61	Near Lexington, NC. Loss of control for unknown reason. Aircraft had logged 233 hours when accident occurred.
53-0380	B	95 BW	7/4/61	Shot down by NM ANG F-100 with AIM-9 Sidewinder. Wreckage fell to earth on Mount Taylor, NM. Firing circuit electrical fault caused inadvertent launch of missile.
58-0196	G	4241 SW	14/10/61	Off Newfoundland coast. Cause of loss not determined. Also reported as having occurred on 15/10/61.
53-0406	C	99 BW	24/1/63	Greenville, Me. Turbulence-induced structural failure at low-level.
57-0018	E	6 BW	30/1/63	Mora, NM. Turbulence-induced structural failure at high-level.
56-0655	E	6 BW	19/11/63	Destroyed by fire during maintenance at Walker AFB, NM. Also reported as having occurred on 21/11/63.
57-0043	F	454 BW	23/12/63	Crashed - details and location unknown.
55-0060	D	484 BW	13/1/64	Cumberland, Md. Excessive turbulence resulted in structural failure.
52-0009	B	93 BW	7/2/64	Crashed at unknown location due to fire in hydraulic system. Also reported as having occurred on 8/2/64.
55-0108	D	462 SAW	10/11/64	Crashed 60 miles south of Glasgow AFB, Mt. Engaged on night low level mission.
57-0047	F	320 BW	18/6/65	Pacific Ocean. Mid-air collision with B-52F 57-0179.
57-0179	F	7 BW	18/6/65	Pacific Ocean. Mid-air collision with B-52F 57-0047.
58-0256	G	68 BW	17/1/66	Near Palomares, Spain. Collided with KC-135A during air-to-air refuelling. A total of four nuclear weapons fell from wreckage. Also reported as having occurred on 19/1/66.
58-0228	G	2 BW	18/11/66	Location unknown. Flew into ground.
57-6494	G	72 BW	5/7/67	Crashed on take-off from Ramey AFB, PR. Life-raft inflated, causing control loss.
56-0595	D	4133 BW(P)	7/7/67	Pacific Ocean. Mid-air collision with B-52D 56-0627. A/c from 22 BW.
56-0627	D	4133 BW(P)	7/7/67	Pacific Ocean. Mid-air collision with B-52D 56-0595. A/c from 454 BW.
56-0601	D	4133 BW(P)	8/7/67	Vietnam. Destroyed in emergency landing at Da Nang. A/c from 22 BW.
61-0030	H	319 BW	2/11/67	Griffiss AFB, NY. Control lost during instrument approach when power loss occurred on number five and six engines. Asymmetric overshoot attempted with tragic results.
58-0188	G	380 SAW	21/1/68	Seven miles south-west of Thule AB, Greenland. Cabin fire caused crash on sea ice. Aircraft engaged on airborne alert duty. Also reported as having occurred on 22/1/68 and 24/1/68.
57-0173	F	7 BW	28/2/68	Crashed off Matagorda Island, Tx. Details unknown. Also reported as having occurred on 29/2/68.
54-2667	C	306 BW	30/8/68	Crashed near Cape Kennedy, Fl. Flap malfunction experienced, followed by total electrical failure and subsequent fuel starvation. Aircraft then abandoned by crew. Also reported as having occurred on 29/8/68.
60-0027	H	5 BW	4/10/68	Crashed eight miles short of runway at Minot AFB, ND. Fuel mismanagement during a landing approach resulted in multiple flame-out of Nos1-4 engines.
55-0103	D	306 BW	18/11/68	Aborted take-off and was destroyed by fire at Kadena AB, Okinawa.
55-0115	D	306 BW	3/12/68	Destroyed by fire at Kadena AB, Okinawa. Remnants salvaged on 2/1/69.
61-0037	H	5 BW	21/1/69	Minot AFB, ND. Incorrect trim selection caused stall on take-off.

Serial	Model	Unit	Date	Location and Circumstances (where known)
57-0149	F	93 BW	8/5/69	Crashed short of runway at Castle AFB, Ca. Aircraft wreckage consumed by fire.
56-0593	D	509 BW	10/5/69	Crashed into Pacific Ocean after take-off from Andersen AFB, Guam.
55-0676	D	70 BW	19/7/69	U-Tapao AB, Thailand. Take-off accident. A/c from 70 BW.
56-0630	D	70 BW	27/7/69	Crashed into Pacific Ocean following failure of starboard wing after take-off from Andersen AFB, Guam.
58-0215	G	42 BW	4/9/69	Crashed at Loring AFB, Me. Multiple engine failure on take-off.
57-0172	F	93 BW	8/10/69	Crashed at Castle AFB, Ca. Pitch-up during overshoot resulted in loss of control.
57-0041	F	93 BW	21/10/69	Crashed at Castle AFB, Ca. Landing accident of unspecified nature.
55-0089	D	28 BW	3/4/70	Crashed at Ellsworth AFB, SD. Landing accident of unspecified nature.
58-0208	G	42 BW	19/7/70	Loring AFB, Me. Destroyed by ground fire. Also reported as occurring on 20/7/70.
54-2666	C	99 BW	7/1/71	Crashed into Lake Michigan at night. Wing failure suspected as causative factor.
56-0625	D	306 BW	31/3/72	Crashed short of runway at McCoy AFB, Fl. Multiple engine failure caused attempted overshoot with dire consequences.
59-2574	G	416 BW	8/5/72	Griffiss AFB, NY. Aquaplaned on landing.
59-2600	G	72 SW(P)	8/7/72	Pacific Ocean. Mechanical failure after take-off from Andersen AFB, Guam. Also reported as having occurred on 7/7/72.
56-0677	D	307 SW	30/7/72	Thailand. Crashed after lightning strike and fire knocked out aircraft instruments.
55-0110	D	307 SW	22/11/72	Crashed in Thailand after being hit by SAM near Vinh, North Vietnam. 96 BW crew. Call-sign 'Olive 2'. This was the first B-52 to be lost as a direct result of enemy action.
58-0201	G	72 SW(P)	18/12/72	Crashed near Yen Vien, North Vietnam after being hit by SAM. 97 BW crew. Call-sign 'Charcoal 1'.
58-0246	G	72 SW(P)	19/12/72	Crashed in Thailand after being hit by SAM near Kinh No, North Vietnam. 2 BW crew. Call-sign 'Peach 2
56-0608	D	307 SW	19/12/72	Crashed in vicinity of Hanoi, North Vietnam after being hit by SAM. Aircraft from 99 BW. Call-sign 'Rose 1'.
57-6496	G	72 SW(P)	20/12/72	Crashed Yen Vien, North Vietnam after hit by SAM. 456 BW crew. Call-sign 'Quilt 3'.
57-6481	G	72 SW(P)	20/12/72	Crashed in Thailand after being hit by SAM near Yen Vien, North Vietnam. 42 BW crew. Call-sign 'Brass 2'.
56-0622	D	307 SW	20/12/72	Crashed near Yen Vien, North Vietnam after being hit by SAM. 99 BW crew. Aircraft from 7 BW. Call-sign 'Orange 3'.
58-0169	G	72 SW(P)	21/12/72	Crashed at Kinh No, North Vietnam after hit by SAM. 97 BW crew. Call-sign 'Tan 3'.
56-0669	D	43 SW	21/12/72	Crashed in Laos after being hit by SAM over Hanoi, North Vietnam. Aircraft from 306 BW. Call-sign 'Straw 2'.
58-0198	G	72 SW(P)	21/12/72	Crashed near Kinh No, North Vietnam after being hit by SAM. 92 BW crew. Call-sign 'Olive 1'.
55-0061	D	307 SW	22/12/72	Crashed near Bach Mai, North Vietnam after being hit by SAM. 22 BW crew. Aircraft from 96 BW. Call-sign 'Scarlet 1'.
55-0050	D	307 SW	22/12/72	Crashed near Bach Mai, North Vietnam after being hit by SAM. 7 BW crew. Aircraft from 43 SW. Call-sign 'Blue 1'.

Serial	Model	Unit	Date	Location and Circumstances (where known)
56-0674	D	307 SW	26/12/72	Crashed near Giap Nhi, North Vietnam after being hit by SAM. 449 BW crew. Aircraft from 96 BW. Call-sign 'Ebony 2'.
56-0584	D	307 SW	26/12/72	Crashed at U-Tapao AB, Thailand after being hit by SAM at Kinh No, North Vietnam. Aircraft from 22 BW. Call-sign 'Ash 1'.
56-0599	D	307 SW	27/12/72	Crashed in Thailand after being hit by SAM near Hanoi, North Vietnam. 28 BW crew. Aircraft from 7 BW. Call-sign 'Ash 2'.
56-0605	D	43 SW	27/12/72	Crashed near Trung Quan, North Vietnam after hit by SAM. 320 BW crew. Aircraft from 7 BW. Call-sign 'Cobalt 1'.
55-0056	D	307 SW	4/1/73	Crashed in South China Sea after being hit by SAM at Vinh, North Vietnam.
55-0097	D	43 SW	??/2/73	Salvaged at U-Tapao AB, Thailand after sustaining crash damage there on 15/10/72.
55-0116	D	307 SW	29/3/73	Scrapped at Da Nang AB, South Vietnam after making an emergency landing there with battle damage on 13/1/73. Date of salvage also reported as 28/3/73.
58-0174	G	456 BW	8/2/74	Beale AFB, Ca. Multiple engine failure and fire on take-off.
60-0006	H	17 BW	30/5/74	Near Wright-Patterson AFB, Oh. Rudder and elevator failure caused loss of control.
55-0058	D	43 SW	11/12/74	Crashed while flying from Andersen AFB, Guam. Experienced instrument malfunction, followed by loss of control and structural failure. Also reported as having occurred on 12/12/74.
57-6493	G	68 BW	3/9/75	Crashed near Williston, SC. Fuel leak experienced in starboard outer wing, with aircraft subsequently rolling inverted due loss of control.
61-0033	H	5 BW	14/11/75	Minot AFB, ND. Burnt out on ground caused when boost pump in tank ignited fuel.
60-0039	H	410 BW	1/4/77	K I Sawyer AFB, Mi. Flew into ground on approach for landing.
56-0594	D	22 BW	19/10/78	March AFB, Ca. Crashed about two miles south-east of base after 0730 take-off.
58-0209	G	19 BW	19/8/80	Robins AFB, Ga. Ground fire. Also reported as having occurred on 20/8/80.
55-0078	D	22 BW?	30/10/81	La Junta, Co. Crashed on low-level route during night mission.
59-2597	G	93 BW	29/11/82	Castle AFB, Ca. Post-landing fire in hydraulic system. Burnt-out on ground.
57-6482	G	93 BW	23/12/82	Mather AFB, Ca. Power loss on take-off. Also reported as occurring on 16/12/82.
57-6507	G	319 BW	27/1/83	Grand Forks AFB, ND. Ground fire during fuel cell maintenance. Also reported as having occurred on 26/1/83.
58-0161	G	19 BW	11/4/83	Crashed 20 miles north of St George, Ut. Flew into ground on *Red Flag* mission.
57-6479	G	92 BW	17/10/84	Crashed at Kayenta, Az. Flew into ground during night low-level mission. Was also reported as having occurred on 16/10/84.
58-0219	G	93 BW	11/2/88	Castle AFB, Ca. Overran runway and destroyed after aborted take-off.
60-0040	H	410 BW	6/12/88	K I Sawyer AFB, Mi. Exploded during touch-and-go approach.
58-0190	G	2 BW	20/7/89	Destroyed at Kelly AFB, Tx. Ground explosion and fire during depot maintenance work. Also reported as having occurred on 24/7/89.
59-2593	G	4300 BW(P)	3/2/91	Crashed into Indian Ocean 15 miles north of Diego Garcia Island. Mechanical failure after *Desert Storm* mission.
61-0026	H	92 BW	24/6/94	Crashed at Fairchild AFB, Wa. Experienced control loss and hit ground during touch-and-go approach while practising for air display to mark disbandment of unit.

APPENDIX 9

AIRCRAFT CONSIGNED TO MASDC/AMARC - IN ORDER OF ARRIVAL

Serial Number	Model	Inventory Number	Date to store
53-0381	B-52B		12/5/65
53-0372	B-52B		28/9/65
(RTS Castle circa 11/10/65 - see entry for 18/2/67)			
52-8710	B-52B		30/9/65
53-0386	B-52B		1/10/65
53-0398	B-52B		20/11/65
53-0375	B-52B		4/1/66
53-0367	B-52B		6/1/66
53-0374	B-52B		8/1/66
52-0004	B-52B		12/1/66
53-0376	B-52B		14/1/66
53-0368	B-52B		17/1/66
53-0366	B-52B		20/1/66
53-0373	B-52B		22/1/66
53-0370	B-52B		26/1/66
52-8715	B-52B	BC015	28/1/66
52-8712	B-52B		1/2/66
52-8713	B-52B		3/2/66
53-0385	B-52B		4/2/66
52-0006	B-52B		5/2/66
53-0389	B-52B		8/2/66
53-0369	B-52B		9/2/66
53-0391	B-52B		10/2/66
52-0005	B-52B		11/2/66
(To Lowry circa 28/4/66)			
52-0007	B-52B		12/2/66
(To Holloman circa 5/5/66)			
52-0010	B-52B		15/2/66
(To Holloman circa 5/5/66)			
52-0012	B-52B		16/2/66
(RTS Plattsburgh circa 17/3/66; see entry for 1/7/66)			
52-0011	B-52B		8/6/66
53-0395	B-52B		25/6/66
53-0397	B-52B		25/6/66
53-0383	B-52B		28/6/66
53-0392	B-52B		28/6/66
53-0387	B-52B		29/6/66
53-0396	B-52B		29/6/66
53-0378	B-52B		30/6/66
53-0388	B-52B		30/6/66
52-0012	B-52B		1/7/66
(See entry for 16/2/66)			
57-0114	B-52E		?/?/67
57-0141	B-52F		4/1/67
57-0167	B-52F		7/1/67
57-0117	B-52E		11/1/67
57-0029	B-52E		17/1/67
57-0113	B-52E		18/1/67
57-0014	B-52E		20/1/67
57-0156	B-52F		27/1/67
57-0044	B-52F	BC046	28/1/67
57-0070	B-52F		31/1/67
57-0157	B-52F		2/2/67
53-0372	B-52B		18/2/67
(See entry for 28/9/65)			

Serial Number	Model	Inventory Number	Date to store
57-0111	B-52E		18/4/67
57-0164	B-52F		19/4/67
57-0137	B-52E		21/4/67
57-0028	B-52E		28/6/67
57-0181	B-52F		29/6/67
(To Boeing-Wichita circa 10/10/67: tested to destruction)			
57-0144	B-52F		2/11/67 or 28/11/67
57-0068	B-52F		21/11/67
57-0030	B-52F		14/12/67
57-0040	B-52F		10/1/68
57-0146	B-52F		16/1/68
57-0049	B-52F	BC059	8/7/68
57-0158	B-52F		7/8/68
56-0642	B-52E	BC061	12/5/69
57-0133	B-52E	BC062	13/5/69
57-0135	B-52E	BC063	14/5/69
56-0703	B-52E	BC064	15/5/69
56-0712	B-52E	BC065	16/5/69
57-0109	B-52E	BC066	19/5/69
57-0101	B-52E	BC067	20/5/69
57-0110	B-52E	BC068	21/5/69
56-0699	B-52E	BC069	22/5/69
57-0102	B-52E	BC070	23/5/69
56-0641	B-52E	BC071	26/5/69
56-0701	B-52E	BC072	27/5/69
57-0122	B-52E	BC073	28/5/69
57-0125	B-52E	BC074	29/5/69
56-0643	B-52E	BC075	2/6/69
57-0138	B-52E	BC076	3/6/69
56-0709	B-52E	BC077	4/6/69
56-0700	B-52E	BC078	5/6/69
56-0654	B-52E	BC079	6/6/69
56-0710	B-52E	BC080	9/6/69
56-0702	B-52E	BC081	10/6/69
57-0124	B-52E	BC082	11/6/69
57-0066	B-52F	BC083	11/6/69
57-0104	B-52E	BC084	12/6/69
56-0631	B-52E	BC085	13/6/69
57-0107	B-52E	BC086	16/6/69
56-0647	B-52E	BC087	17/6/69
57-0116	B-52E	BC088	18/6/69
57-0025	B-52E	BC089	19/6/69
57-0022	B-52E	BC090	20/6/69
56-0711	B-52E	BC091	23/6/69
57-0127	B-52E	BC092	24/6/69
57-0023	B-52E	BC093	25/6/69
57-0026	B-52E	BC094	26/6/69
57-0053	B-52F	BC095	27/6/69
57-0180	B-52F	BC096	30/6/69
57-0160	B-52F	BC097	1/7/69
57-0163	B-52F	BC098	2/7/69
57-0067	B-52F	BC099	7/7/69
57-0054	B-52F	BC100	9/7/69
57-0176	B-52F	BC101	9/7/69
57-0037	B-52F	BC102	10/7/69
57-0155	B-52F	BC103	11/7/69
57-0175	B-52F	BC104	14/7/69
57-0046	B-52F	BC105	25/7/69
57-0016	B-52E	BC106	12/8/69
57-0120	B-52E	BC107	14/8/69
52-0003	NB-52A	BC108	15/10/69
57-0015	B-52E	BC109	13/11/69

Serial Number	Model	Inventory Number	Date to store	Serial Number	Model	Inventory Number	Date to store
57-0095	B-52E	BC110	14/11/69	54-2685	B-52C	BC172	29/7/71
56-0649	B-52E	BC111	17/11/69	57-0064	B-52F	BC173	2/8/71
57-0024	B-52E	BC112	18/11/69	54-2677	B-52C	BC174	3/8/71
56-0646	B-52E	BC113	19/11/69	57-0062	B-52F	BC175	4/8/71
56-0705	B-52E	BC114	24/11/69	53-0407	B-52C	BC176	5/8/71
56-0645	B-52E	BC115	25/11/69	57-0065	B-52F	BC177	9/8/71
56-0634	B-52E	BC116	8/12/69	53-0408	B-52C	BC178	10/8/71
57-0132	B-52E	BC117	10/12/69	57-0059	B-52F	BC179	11/8/71
56-0653	B-52E	BC118	12/12/69	53-0405	B-52C	BC180	12/8/71
57-0103	B-52E	BC119	5/1/70	57-0159	B-52F	BC181	16/8/71
57-0121	B-52E	BC120	6/1/70	54-2688	B-52C	BC182	17/8/71
57-0100	B-52E	BC121	7/1/70	57-0152	B-52F	BC183	18/8/71
57-0118	B-52E	BC122	8/1/70	54-2678	B-52C	BC184	19/8/71
56-0706	B-52E	BC123	9/1/70	54-2672	B-52C	BC185	24/8/71
57-0128	B-52E	BC124	12/1/70	57-0057	B-52F	BC186	25/8/71
57-0115	B-52E	BC125	12/1/70	54-2664	B-52C	BC187	26/8/71
56-0652	B-52E	BC126	12/1/70	57-0174	B-52F	BC188	30/8/71
56-0651	B-52E	BC127	19/1/70	53-0403	B-52C	BC189	31/8/71
57-0136	B-52E	BC128	20/1/70	57-0177	B-52F	BC190	1/9/71
56-0650	B-52E	BC129	21/1/70	54-2668	B-52C	BC191	2/9/71
57-0098	B-52E	BC130	22/1/70	54-2686	B-52C	BC192	7/9/71
56-0644	B-52E	BC131	23/1/70	57-0151	B-52F	BC193	8/9/71
57-0027	B-52E	BC132	26/1/70	54-2671	B-52C	BC194	9/9/71
57-0097	B-52E	BC133	27/1/70	57-0055	B-52F	BC195	13/9/71
57-0020	B-52E	BC134	28/1/70	54-2683	B-52C	BC196	14/9/71
57-0096	B-52E	BC135	29/1/70	57-0162	B-52F	BC197	15/9/71
57-0099	B-52E	BC136	30/1/70	54-2684	B-52C	BC198	16/9/71
57-0021	B-52E	BC137	2/2/70	57-0182	B-52F	BC199	20/9/71
57-0130	B-52E	BC138	3/2/70	54-2681	B-52C	BC200	21/9/71
56-0635	B-52E	BC139	4/2/70	57-0153	B-52F	BC201	22/9/71
56-0640	B-52E	BC140	5/2/70	54-2670	B-52C	BC202	23/9/71
57-0126	B-52E	BC141	6/2/70	57-0161	B-52F	BC203	24/9/71
57-0112	B-52E	BC142	9/2/70	54-2673	B-52C	BC204	27/9/71
57-0108	B-52E	BC143	10/2/70	53-0400	B-52C	BC205	28/9/71
56-0656	B-52E	BC144	11/2/70	53-0402	B-52C	BC206	29/9/71
56-0704	B-52E	BC145	12/2/70	56-0620	NB-52D	BC207	29/11/71
57-0123	B-52E	BC146	2/3/70	57-0183	B-52F	BC208	27/6/72
57-0129	B-52E	BC147	3/3/70	57-0168	B-52F	BC209	29/6/72
57-0017	B-52E	BC148	4/3/70	57-0139	B-52F	BC210	30/5/73
56-0639	B-52E	BC149	5/3/70	56-0632	NB-52E	BC211	26/6/74
57-0131	B-52E	BC150	6/3/70	53-0399	B-52C	BC212	28/7/75
57-0105	B-52E	BC151	9/3/70	56-0598	B-52D	BC213	29/1/76
56-0707	B-52E	BC152	10/3/70	55-0076	B-52D	BC214	23/6/77
57-0106	B-52E	BC153	11/3/70	57-0148	B-52F	BC215	15/8/78
56-0648	B-52E	BC154	12/3/70	55-0081	B-52D	BC216	15/8/78
56-0638	B-52E	BC155	13/3/70	57-0150	B-52F	BC217	17/8/78
53-0401	B-52C	BC156	23/3/71	56-0581	B-52D	BC218	17/8/78
57-0056	B-52F	BC157	7/4/71	55-0053	B-52D	BC219	22/8/78
54-2669	B-52C	BC158	6/7/71	55-0072	B-52D	BC220	22/8/78
54-2665	B-52C	BC159	7/7/71	56-0611	B-52D	BC221	24/8/78
54-2674	B-52C	BC160	8/7/71	56-0619	B-52D	BC222	24/8/78
54-2680	B-52C	BC161	8/7/71	56-0583	B-52D	BC223	30/8/78
57-0031	B-52F	BC162	12/7/71	57-0147	B-52F	BC224	30/8/78
54-2679	B-52C	BC163	13/7/71	57-0048	B-52F	BC225	31/8/78
57-0143	B-52F	BC164	14/7/71	56-0624	B-52D	BC226	1/9/78
57-0039	B-52F	BC165	19/7/71	57-0034	B-52F	BC227	5/9/78
54-2687	B-52C	BC166	20/7/71	56-0613	B-52D	BC228	5/9/78
57-0061	B-52F	BC167	21/7/71	57-0052	B-52F	BC229	7/9/78
54-2675	B-52C	BC168	22/7/71	56-0693	B-52D	BC230	7/9/78
57-0060	B-52F	BC169	26/7/71	56-0603	B-52D	BC231	12/9/78
53-0404	B-52C	BC170	27/7/71	55-0064	B-52D	BC232	12/9/78
57-0178	B-52F	BC171	28/7/71	56-0673	B-52D	BC233	14/9/78

Serial Number	Model	Inventory Number	Date to store	Serial Number	Model	Inventory Number	Date to store
55-0680	B-52D	BC234	14/9/78	55-0075	B-52D	BC296	14/10/82
56-0582	B-52D	BC235	19/9/78	55-0088	B-52D	BC297	15/10/82
57-0140	B-52F	BC236	21/9/78	55-0073	B-52D	BC298	18/10/82
57-0165	B-52F	BC237	21/9/78	56-0580	B-52D	BC299	19/10/82
55-0052	B-52D	BC238	21/9/78	55-0066	B-52D	BC300	20/10/82
57-0033	B-52F	BC239	26/9/78	55-0090	B-52D	BC301	21/10/82
56-0604	B-52D	BC240	27/9/78	55-0675	B-52D	BC302	22/10/82
57-0045	B-52F	BC241	28/9/78	55-0080	B-52D	BC303	26/10/82
57-0063	B-52F	BC242	28/9/78	56-0690	B-52D	BC304	28/10/82
57-0069	B-52F	BC243	2/10/78	55-0087	B-52D	BC305	1/11/82
55-0117	B-52D	BC244	3/10/78	56-0668	B-52D	BC306	2/11/82
55-0049	B-52D	BC245	4/10/78	56-0587	B-52D	BC307	3/11/82
56-0615	B-52D	BC246	5/10/78	55-0673	B-52D	BC308	4/11/82
56-0675	B-52D	BC247	5/10/78	55-0067	B-52D	BC309	?/11/82
57-0142	B-52F	BC248	10/10/78	56-0600	B-52D	BC310	8/11/82
56-0691	B-52D	BC249	10/10/78	56-0698	B-52D	BC311	9/11/82
57-0145	B-52F	BC250	11/10/78	55-0070	B-52D	BC312	10/11/82
55-0109	B-52D	BC251	12/10/78	56-0672	B-52D	BC313	3/5/83
56-0678	B-52D	BC252	12/10/78	55-0113	B-52D	BC314	4/5/83
56-0626	B-52D	BC253	16/10/78	56-0684	B-52D	BC315	5/5/83
55-0678	B-52D	BC254	17/10/78	55-0092	B-52D	BC316	25/7/83
57-0058	B-52F	BC255	17/10/78	55-0077	B-52D	BC317	25/7/83
56-0682	B-52D	BC256	19/10/78	56-0686	B-52D	BC318	22/8/83
57-0169	B-52F	BC257	20/10/78	56-0694	B-52D	BC319	22/8/83
57-0154	B-52F	BC258	7/11/78	56-0660	B-52D	BC320	23/8/83
55-0096	B-52D	BC259	8/11/78	56-0666	B-52D	BC321	24/8/83
56-0623	B-52D	BC260	9/11/78	55-0071	B-52D	BC322	?/?/83
56-0590	B-52D	BC261	9/11/78	56-0667	B-52D	BC323	12/9/83
57-0170	B-52F	BC262	14/11/78	56-0614	B-52D	BC324	12/9/83
55-0051	B-52D	BC263	15/11/78	56-0602	B-52D	BC325	12/9/83
57-0032	B-52F	BC264	17/11/78	56-0617	B-52D	BC326	20/9/83
57-0072	B-52F	BC265	21/11/78	55-0084	B-52D	BC327	20/9/83
55-0055	B-52D	BC266	21/11/78	56-0697	B-52D	BC328	20/9/83
56-0609	B-52D	BC267	27/11/78	55-0105	B-52D	BC329	?/?/83
55-0054	B-52D	BC268	28/11/78	55-0674	B-52D	BC330	4/10/83
55-0106	B-52D	BC269	28/11/78	57-6500	B-52G	BC331	11/5/89
56-0618	B-52D	BC270	30/11/78	58-0172	B-52G	BC332	30/6/89
57-0035	B-52F	BC271	30/11/78	57-6484	B-52G	BC333	6/7/89
57-0051	B-52F	BC272	5/12/78	57-6478	B-52G	BC334	27/7/89
56-0592	B-52D	BC273	7/12/78	57-6513	B-52G	BC335	7/8/89
57-0171	B-52F	BC274	7/12/78	59-2587	B-52G	BC336	?/1/90
56-0636	B-52E	BC275	30/7/81	58-0189	B-52G	BC337	1/2/90
56-0658	B-52D	BC276	29/4/82	59-2592	B-52G	BC338	7/2/90
55-0074	B-52D	BC277	29/4/82	58-0224	B-52G	BC339	12/2/90
55-0059	B-52D	BC278	3/5/82	57-6502	B-52G	BC340	15/2/90
56-0670	B-52D	BC279	3/5/82	58-0251	B-52G	BC341	27/2/90
56-0588	B-52D	BC280	5/5/82	57-6506	B-52G	BC342	8/3/90
56-0606	B-52D	BC281	5/5/82	57-6489	B-52G	BC343	20/3/90
56-0663	B-52D	BC282	25/5/82	58-0186	B-52G	BC344	29/3/90
56-0659	B-52D	BC283	25/5/82	58-0232	B-52G	BC345	3/4/90
55-0104	B-52D	BC284	27/5/82	58-0220	B-52G	BC346	5/7/90
56-0596	B-52D	BC285	28/5/82	57-6517	B-52G	BC347	13/7/90
56-0621	B-52D	BC286	1/10/82	58-0223	B-52G	BC348	31/7/90
56-0671	B-52D	BC287	1/10/82	57-6499	B-52G	BC349	7/8/90
55-0086	B-52D	BC288	4/10/82	57-6491	B-52G	BC350	9/8/90
55-0111	B-52D	BC289	5/10/82	58-0171	B-52G	BC351	16/8/90
55-0101	B-52D	BC290	6/10/82	57-6505	B-52G	BC352	27/8/90
55-0069	B-52D	BC291	8/10/82	57-6477	B-52G	BC353	21/9/90
55-0091	B-52D	BC292	8/10/82	57-6510	B-52G	BC354	11/10/90
56-0679	B-52D	BC293	11/10/82	57-6514	B-52G	BC355	18/10/90
55-0079	B-52D	BC294	12/10/82	57-6470	B-52G	BC356	23/10/90
55-0107	B-52D	BC295	13/10/82	58-0205	B-52G	BC357	15/11/90

Serial Number	Model	Inventory Number	Date to store	Serial Number	Model	Inventory Number	Date to store
58-0254	B-52G	BC358	4/12/90	58-0236	B-52G	BC420	13/10/92
57-6519	B-52G	BC359	11/12/90	59-2594	B-52G	BC421	15/10/92
58-0178	B-52G	BC360	18/12/90	58-0245	B-52G	BC422	20/10/92
57-6485	B-52G	BC361	20/12/90	59-2567	B-52G	BC423	22/10/92
58-0162	B-52G	BC362	16/4/91	59-2602	B-52G	BC424	27/10/92
58-0252	B-52G	BC363	18/4/91	58-0244	B-52G	BC425	29/10/92
57-6518	B-52G	BC364	23/4/91	57-6498	B-52G	BC426	3/11/92
57-6512	B-52G	BC365	25/4/91	58-0164	B-52G	BC427	5/11/92
59-2571	B-52G	BC366	30/4/91	58-0170	B-52G	BC428	10/11/92
58-0241	B-52G	BC367	2/5/91	58-0229	B-52G	BC429	12/11/92
57-6487	B-52G	BC368	9/5/91	58-0176	B-52G	BC430	17/11/92
58-0167	B-52G	BC369	28/5/91	58-0160	B-52G	BC431	19/11/92
58-0199	B-52G	BC370	4/6/91	59-2568	B-52G	BC432	24/11/92
58-0243	B-52G	BC371	11/6/91	57-6490	B-52G	BC433	1/12/92
57-6504	B-52G	BC372	2/7/91	58-0231	B-52G	BC434	3/12/92
58-0183	B-52G	BC373	?/7/91	58-0193	B-52G	BC435	8/12/92
58-0207	B-52G	BC374	25/7/91	58-0179	B-52G	BC436	10/12/92
59-2575	B-52G	BC375	6/8/91	57-6492	B-52G	BC437	15/12/92
59-2564	B-52G	BC376	8/8/91	58-0166	B-52G	BC438	21/12/92
57-6486	B-52G	BC377	15/8/91	57-6473	B-52G	BC439	25/2/93
57-6475	B-52G	BC378	20/8/91	58-0210	B-52G	BC440	10/3/93
58-0238	B-52G	BC379	22/8/91	59-2585	B-52G	BC441	15/4/93
59-2582	B-52G	BC380	27/8/91	58-0230	B-52G	BC442	6/5/93
58-0177	B-52G	BC381	5/9/91	57-6488	B-52G	BC443	29/7/93
50-0219	B-52G	BC382	10/9/91	58-0250	B-52G	BC444	7/10/93
57-6483	B-52G	BC383	19/9/91	59-2565	B-52G	BC445	12/10/93
58-0204	B-52G	BC384	24/9/91	58-0257	B-52G	BC446	14/10/93
58-0184	B-52G	BC385	26/9/91	58-0226	B-52G	BC447	19/10/93
57-6501	B-52G	BC386	3/10/91	58-0221	B-52G	BC448	21/10/93
57-6516	B-52G	BC387	8/10/91	59-2573	B-52G	BC449	26/10/93
58-0159	B-52G	BC388	10/10/91	58-0255	B-52G	BC450	28/10/93
57-6474	B-52G	BC389	15/10/91	57-6476	B-52G	BC451	2/11/93
58-0175	B-52G	BC390	16/10/91	58-0253	B-52G	BC452	4/11/93
58-0168	B-52G	BC391	22/10/91	58-0258	B-52G	BC453	9/11/93
58-0194	B-52G	BC392	24/10/91	58-0197	B-52G	BC454	16/11/93
58-0237	B-52G	BC393	29/10/91	58-0195	B-52G	BC455	18/11/93
58-0247	B-52G	BC394	5/11/91	58-0213	B-52G	BC456	23/11/93
59-2579	B-52G	BC395	12/11/91	59-2572	B-52G	BC457	11/1/94
58-0217	B-52G	BC396	15/11/91	59-2598	B-52G	BC458	13/1/94
58-0182	B-52G	BC397	10/6/92	58-0218	B-52G	BC459	18/1/94
59-2589	B-52G	BC398	17/6/92	57-6497	B-52G	BC460	20/1/94
59-2591	B-52G	BC399	19/6/92	59-2570	B-52G	BC461	24/1/94
59-2580	B-52G	BC400	6/7/92	58-0248	B-52G	BC462	25/1/94
57-6472	B-52G	BC401	8/7/92	57-6520	B-52G	BC463	27/1/94
59-2590	B-52G	BC402	13/7/92	58-0206	B-52G	BC464	1/2/94
58-0227	B-52G	BC403	15/7/92	58-0212	B-52G	BC465	8/2/94
57-6508	B-52G	BC404	22/7/92	58-0192	B-52G	BC466	10/2/94
57-6471	B-52G	BC405	29/7/92	59-2569	B-52G	BC467	15/2/94
57-6480	B-52G	BC406	5/8/92	58-0233	B-52G	BC468	17/2/94
58-0173	B-52G	BC407	5/8/92	58-0242	B-52G	BC469	22/2/94
58-0165	B-52G	BC408	10/8/92	59-2595	B-52G	BC470	24/2/94
58-0222	B-52G	BC409	12/8/92	58-0203	B-52G	BC471	3/3/94
57-6503	B-52G	BC410	19/8/92	58-0216	B-52G	BC472	8/3/94
57-6495	B-52G	BC411	26/8/92	58-0202	B-52G	BC473	10/3/94
58-0211	B-52G	BC412	2/9/92	59-2599	B-52G	BC474	15/3/94
58-0239	B-52G	BC413	9/9/92	58-0235	B-52G	BC475	29/3/94
59-2566	B-52G	BC414	16/9/92	59-2588	B-52G	BC476	5/4/94
58-0181	B-52G	BC415	23/9/92	58-0214	B-52G	BC477	12/4/94
57-6515	B-52G	BC416	30/9/92	58-0163	B-52G	BC478	14/4/94
59-2583	B-52G	BC417	1/10/92	59-2586	B-52G	BC479	22/4/94
57-6511	B-52G	BC418	6/10/92	58-0240	B-52G	BC480	3/5/94
59-2581	B-52G	BC419	8/10/92				

INDEX